CATALGUE

of the

WORLD'S

most popular

COINS

NINTH EDITION

By
FRED REINFELD
and
BURTON HOBSON

Henry VII (1485–1509) Silver groat circa 1500
(enlarged)

 STERLING PUBLISHING CO., Inc., New York

Oak Tree Press Co., Ltd.
London & Sydney

CJ63
.R4
1976ex

ACKNOWLEDGMENTS

The authors' thanks are due to Robert Friedberg of Gimbels Coin Department, who supplied valuable advice and information in the development of this book; to Sawyer McA. Mosser, Superior Stamp and Coin Company, the American Numismatic Society, who were most helpful in supplying pictures; to William A. Pettit, Robert Obojski, Rudolf Pospisil, Robert Weber, Fred Bertram, Mike Scott, Flight Lt. Peter Thornton-Pett, Jacques Beghin, T. A. Karlovich, Saburo Nobuki, Joel R. Anderson, Tom Hanley and Bill James for their knowledgeable suggestions and assistance.

Edited by Steven Morgenstern

Ninth Edition
Copyright © 1976, 1971, 1969, 1967, 1965, 1964, 1963, 1960, 1956
by Sterling Publishing Co., Inc.
419 Park Avenue South, New York, N.Y. 10016
Distributed in Australia and New Zealand by Oak Tree Press Co., Ltd.,
P.O. Box J34, Brickfield Hill, Sydney 2000, N.S.W.
Distributed in the United Kingdom and elsewhere in the British Commonwealth
by Ward Lock Ltd., 116 Baker Street, London W 1
Manufactured in the United States of America
All rights reserved
Library of Congress Catalog Card No.: 76–1168
Sterling ISBN 0-8069-6062–0 Trade   Oak Tree 7061-2205–4
6063 –9 Library
6064–7 Paper

CONTENTS

Names in parentheses are the general headings under which an area is listed.

Countries in Alphabetical Order

HOW TO USE THIS BOOK

Bear in mind that *the prices quoted in this book are for the coins in the condition in which the particular issue is usually encountered.* That is to say, prices are quoted for "Fine" (F) for coins issued before 1800 (including ancient coins, except where otherwise stated). From 1800 to the early 1900's, "Very Fine" (VF) is the condition. For modern foreign, the condition is "Extra Fine" (EF) or "Uncirculated" (Unc.).

These dates for determining condition are only approximate and vary with different countries. Coins in superior condition (especially those that are uncirculated) may be worth considerably more than the prices quoted here. Similarly, coins in inferior condition (especially those mutilated or damaged in any way) may be worth very much less.

When inclusive listings such as "1925-50" are used, it does not necessarily mean that the coin exists with every intervening date. But such a listing does mean that the first and last dates are known.

When descriptions of coins are omitted, they may be assumed to belong to the same type as the last previously described coin of a higher denomination. Coins pictured are described directly below unless otherwise stated.

In all cases where coins are not silver, their composition is given by means of the following abbreviations:

A or Al (aluminum)	I (iron)
Ac (acmonital)	Mg (magnesium)
Bi (billon)	N or Ni (nickel)
Bra (brass)	St (steel)
Br or Bro (bronze)	T (tin)
C (copper)	Z (zinc)
G (gold)	

F.A.O. COIN PLAN

Although the United Nations has issued no money in its own right, a number of member governments have released special coins in co-operation with the U.N. Food and Agricultural Organization's "Freedom-from-Hunger" campaign launched in 1968. The coins are sold at a premium over their face value with the extra revenue going toward agricultural development.

The designs show foods or include inscriptions that call attention to the F.A.O. project.

Total mintage of F.A.O. coins has already surpassed two and a half million, and plans call for participation by 80 countries with 240 issues by the end of 1976.

The countries that have issued coins so far are:

Algeria
Bahrain
Bangladesh
Bhutan
Bolivia
Botswana
Brazil
Burma
Burundi
China (Taiwan)
Cyprus
Dominican Republic
East Caribbean Territories:
  Antigua
  Barbados
  Dominica
  Grenada
  Montserrat
  St. Kitts-Nevis-Anguilla
  Saint Lucia
  Saint Vincent
Egypt
Gambia
Ghana
Guyana
Haiti
Honduras
India
Indonesia

Iran
Iraq
Jamaica
Jordan
Khmer
Korea, South
Lebanon
Liberia
Madagascar
Maldives
Mali
Malta
Mauritius
Morocco
Nepal
Nicaragua
Oman
Order of Malta
Pakistan
Panama
Poland
Rwanda
San Marino
Saudi Arabia
Seychelles
Singapore
Somalia
Sri Lanka
Sudan

Swaziland
Syria
Tanzania
Thailand
Tonga
Trinidad & Tobago
Tunisia
Turkey
Uganda
United Arab Emirates
Uruguay
Vatican
Vietnam
West African States
Western Samoa
Yemen Arab Republic
Yugoslavia
Zambia

DATING SYSTEMS

The system of dating used on coins often reflects a nation's culture. In the Western world, the familiar A.D. (*anno Domini* = in the year of our Lord) system refers to the birth of Christ. In the Moslem nations, the calendars are based on the year 622 A.D., the year of Mohammed's flight from Mecca to Medina.

Two important dating systems are based on the year 622. The A.H. system employs a lunar calendar with 354 days per year. To find the equivalent A.D. date, you must take 3% of the A.H. date (there are about 3% fewer days in a lunar year than a solar year), subtract the nearest whole number, then add 622. For instance, 1396 A.H. equals 1976 A.D., since $1396 - 42 + 622 = 1976$. You will find examples of A.H. dating on the coins of Saudi Arabia and the early coinage of Afghanistan.

Some Moslem nations employ a solar year, making the conversion between systems simpler. To convert S.H. dates to A.D., just add 621 to the S.H. date. For instance, 1355 S.H. equals 1976 A.D., since $1355 + 621 = 1976$. Examples of S.H. dating are found on the modern coinage of Afghanistan and Iran.

Several dating systems are confined to the coinage of a particular nation. The dates on Israeli coins refer to the Hebrew calendar, which is based on a lunar year and begins about 3760 B.C., the traditional time of Adam. Ethiopia has its own distinctive system, called the Ethiopian Era, which commenced at 7 years 8 months A.D. Many nations, particularly in the Orient, date their coins according to the year of the current ruler's reign.

For convenience, the catalogue listings give the A.D. equivalents for the dates actually shown on the coins described. For the purpose of identification, you should be aware that the A.D. date given does not necessarily appear in that form on the coins themselves.

AFARS AND ISSAS

Formerly known as French Somaliland, this French overseas territory changed its name in 1967.

1. 100 Francs (C-N) 1970. Bust of Republic.
   Rev. Camels   2.50
2. 50 Francs (C-N) 1970   1.75

3. 20 Francs (A-Br) 1968. Bust of Republic.
   Rev. Arabian dhow and ocean liner   1.25
4. 10 Francs (A-Br) 1969, 70   .75

5. 5 Francs (A) 1968. Bust of Republic. Rev.
   Antelope head   .50
6. 2 Francs (A) 1968   .35
7. 1 Franc (A) 1969, 71   .25

AFGHANISTAN

A constitutional monarchy in Asia, bordered by the USSR, Pakistan, India, and Iran.

100 Puls = 1 Afghani

1. 2½ Afghani. Throne room. Rev. Toughra
   and Arabic inscription   45.00

2. 1 Afghani.   6.00
3. ½ Afghani   3.50

5.

4. 25 Puls (C)   2.50
5. 10 Puls (C)   3.00

٠	١	٢	٣	٤	٥
0	1	2	3	4	5
٦	٧	٨	٩	١٠	
6	7	8	9	10	

MOHAMMED ZAHIR SHAH 1933-
(A.H. 1351-   )
Solar year dating begins 1313 = 1935

6.	5 Afghani (Al) Type of #1	4.00
7.	2 Afghani (Al)	2.00
8.	50 Puls (N-St or Br)	1.00
9.	25 Puls (A, Br or C-N)	.85
10.	10 Puls (C-N)	.60
11.	5 Puls (Bro)	.45
12.	3 Puls (Bro)	.40
13.	2 Puls (Bro)	.35

14. 5 Afghani (N-St) 1961- . Bust of King.
Rev. Value   1.00

15. 2 Afghani (N-St) 1961- . Winged sun.
Rev. Value   .75

16. 1 Afghani (N-St) 1962- . Three wheat
stalks. Rev. Value   .50

17. 5 Afghani (C-N-St) 1973. Arms. Rev.
Value, grain
18. 50 Puli (C-St) 1973. Rev. Value, stars
19. 25 Puli (Bra-St) 1973

ALBANIA

Albania is in southeastern Europe on the Adriatic Sea. It was a republic from 1925 to 1928, a kingdom under Zog I from 1928 to 1939, under Italian domination during World War II, and has been a People's Republic since 1946.

100 Qindar = 1 Lek
5 Lek = 1 Franka Ari
1 Lek = 1 Lira

1. 20 Franka Ari (G) 1926-27. Head of Zog. Rev. Double-headed eagle — 200.00
2. 10 Franka Ari (G) 1927 — 175.00

3. 20 Franka Ari (G) 1926-27. Bust of Skanderbeg. Rev. Winged lion — 175.00

4. 5 Franka Ari 1925-27. Head of Zog. Rev. Plowing scene — 200.00

5. 2 Franka Ari 1926-28. Sower. Rev. Eagle — 150.00

6. 1 Franka Ari 1927-28. Helmeted head. Rev. Prow of galley — 100.00

7. 1 Lek (N) 1926-27, 30-31. Classical head. Rev. Horseman — 8.00

8. ½ Lek (N) 1926. Double-headed eagle. Rev. Hercules and lion — 7.50
8a. ½ Lek (N) 1930-31. Arms on shield. Rev. Type of #8 — 6.00
9. ¼ Lek (N) 1926-27. Lion. Rev. Oak spray and value — 7.50
10. 10 Qinder Lek (Bro) 1926. Eagle head. Rev. Value between sprays — 25.00
11. 5 Qindar Lek (Bro) 1926. Lion head. Rev. Value over oak spray — 6.00
12. 2 Qindar Ari (Bro) 1935. Double-headed eagle. Rev. Value and spray — 5.00
13. 1 Qindar Ari (Bro) 1935 — 5.00

14. 2 Franka Ari 1935. Head of Zog. Rev. Arms — 20.00
15. 1 Franka Ari 1935, 37 — 15.00
16. 20 Franka Ari (G) 1937. Head of Zog. Rev. Arms (Commemorating 25th anniversary of independence) — 250.00
17. 2 Franka Ari 1937 — 30.00
18. 1 Franka Ari 1937 — 20.00

UNDER ITALIAN DOMINATION
(Victor Emmanuel III as king and emperor)

19. 10 Lek. 1939. Head of Victor Emmanuel III. Rev. Albanian arms and fasces — 50.00
20. 5 Lek 1939 — 20.00

21. 2 Lek (Ac) 1939-41 Helmeted bust — 6.00
22. 1 Lek (Ac) 1939-41. Bust facing right — 3.00
23. 0.50 Lek (Ac) 1939-41. Bust left — 2.50
24. 0.20 Lek (Ac) 1939-41. Bust right — 2.50

ALBANIA (continued)

25. 0.10 Lek (A-Br) 1940-41. Head of Victor
    Emmanuel III. Rev. Branch and value   5.00
26. 0.05 Lek (A-Br) 1940-41   3.00

37. 50 Qindarka (Al) 1969. Rev. Worker and
    soldier holding torch   1.50

PEOPLE'S REPUBLIC 1946-
27. 5 Lekë (Z) 1947, 57. Arms and stars. Rev.
    Value and stars   3.00

38. 20 Qindarka (Al) 1969. Rev. Value   1.00
39. 10 Qindarka (Al) 1969   .75
40. 5 Qindarka (Al) 1969   .50

28. 2 Lekë (Z) 1947, 57   2.00
29. 1 Lek (Z) 1947, 57   1.50
30. ½ Leku (Z) 1947, 57   1.00

31. 1 Lek (Al) 1964. Arms. Rev. Value   3.00
32. 50 Qindarka (Al) 1964   1.50
33. 20 Qindarka (Al) 1964   1.00
34. 10 Qindarka (Al) 1964   .85
35. 5 Qindarka (Al) 1964   .75

36. 1 Lek (Al) 1969. Arms. Rev. Soldier sub-
    duing enemy (Commemorates the 25th
    anniversary of liberation)   3.00

ALGERIA

Formerly a semi-autonomous department of France, this North African country became an independent republic in July 1962.

100 Centimes = 1 Franc = 1 Dinar

1. 100 Francs (C-N) 1950-53. Head of the Republic. Rev. Value ... 3.50
2. 50 Francs (C-N) 1949-50 ... 2.50
3. 20 Francs (C-N) 1949-56 ... 2.00

4. 1 Dinar (C-N) 1964- . Arms. Rev. Value ... 1.00
5. 50 Centimes (Al-Br) 1964- ... .65
6. 20 Centimes (Al-Br) 1964- ... .50
7. 10 Centimes (Al-Br) 1964- ... .35
8. 5 Centimes (Al) 1964- ... .30
9. 2 Centimes (Al) 1964- ... .25
10. 1 Centime (Al) 1964- ... .15

11. 5 Centimes (A) 1970. Dates of four-year plan in half-cogwheel, wreath. Rev. Value (F.A.O. coin plan) ... .35

12. 50 Centimes (C-N-Z) 1971. Compass, flask and open book. Rev. Value ... .50

13. 5 Dinar 1972. Wheat and oil derrick. Rev. Value (Commemorates 10th anniversary of independence) ... 3.50

14. 1 Dinar (C-N) 1972. Tractor and clasped hands. Rev. Value (F.A.O. coin plan) ... 1.50

15. 20 Centimes (Bra) 1972. Cornucopia with fruit. Rev. Value (F.A.O. coin plan) ... .75

16. 5 Dinar (N) 1974. Soldier. Rev. Value (Commemorates 20th anniversary of revolution) ... 2.50

17. 5 Centimes (A) 1974. Dates of second four-year plan in half-cogwheel, half-wreath. Rev. Value ... .25

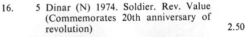

18. 50 Centimes (Bra) 1975. Kufic inscription. Rev. Value (Commemorates 30th anniversary of Revolt of May 8, 1945)

ANGOLA

This former Portuguese colony on the west coast of Africa became an independent nation in 1976, after months of bitter and bloody fighting.

100 Centavos = 1 Escudo
5 Centavos = 1 Macuta

1. 50 Centavos (N) 1922-23. Liberty head. Rev. Arms — 6.00

2. 20 Centavos (C-N) 1921-22. Rev. Value — 3.00
3. 10 Centavos (C-N) 1921-23 — 3.50

4. 5 Centavos (Br) 1921-23. Arms. Rev. Value — 5.00
5. 2 Centavos (Br) 1921 — 12.00
6. 1 Centavo (Br) 1921 — 7.00

NEW STATE 1926

7. 50 Centavos (N-Bro) 1927-28. Bust of the Republic. Rev. Arms and value — 6.50

8. 20 Centavos (N-Bro) 1927-28 — 2.50
9. 10 Centavos (N-Bro) 1927-28 — 2.00
10. 5 Centavos (N-Bro) 1927 — 1.75

11. 20 Escudos 1952-55. Crowned arms and value. Rev. Arms in cross — 6.00
12. 10 Escudos 1952-55 — 4.50

13. 2½ Escudos (C-N) 1953-69 — 1.00
14. 1 Escudo (Br) 1953-65. Crowned arms. Rev. Value — .80
15. 50 Centavos (N-Br) 1948-50 — 1.00

15a. 50 Centavos (Br) 1953-61. "Colonia de" dropped from legend — .30
16. 20 Centavos (Br) 1948-49 — 1.75

16a. 20 Centavos (Br) 1962 — .75
17. 10 Centavos (Br) 1948-49 — .50

18. 10 Escudos (C-N) 1969-70 — 1.50

19. 20 Escudos (N) 1971-72 — 1.50

20. 5 Escudos (C-N) 1972 — .75

12 • CATALOGUE of the WORLD'S MOST POPULAR COINS

ANTIGUA

An island in the Leeward group, it was discovered by Columbus on his 1493 voyage and settled by the British in 1632. (Now a member of the East Caribbean Territories.)

1. 1 Farthing (C) 1836. Palm tree. Rev. Value 80.00

2. 4 Dollars (C-N) 1970. Arms with ibexes. Rev. Bananas, sugar cane and value 5.00

ARGENTINA

Discovered 1515-16 by Spanish explorers and remained a Spanish colony until the provinces, in a successful revolution (May 25,1810), established an independent republic. For many years thereafter the provinces issued their own coinage.

PROVINCIAS DEL RIO DE LA PLATA
1 Real = 1 Sueldo

1. 8 Reales 1813, 15, 26-37. Arms.
    Rev. Sunburst 100.00
2. 4 Reales 1813, 15 .... 60.00
3. 2 Reales 1813, 15 .... 25.00

4. 1 Real 1813, 15, 24, 25 .... 15.00
5. ½ Real 1813, 15 .... 15.00

6. 8 Sueldos 1815. Type of preceding, with "S" for Sueldo instead of "R" for Real 110.00
7. 4 Sueldos 1815, 28, 32 .... 50.00

8. 2 Sueldos 1815, 1824-26 .... 20.00
9. 1 Sueldo 1815 .... 25.00
10. ½ Sueldo 1815 .... 25.00

LA RIOJA PROVINCE

11. 8 Reales 1838-40. The mountain Fama-
    tina, with flags and cannon crossed.
    Rev. Arms   75.00
12. 4 Reales 1846, 49, 50   20.00
13. 2 Reales 1843, 44   20.00

14. 2 Reales 1842. Bust of Gen. Rosas. Rev.
    Arms   60.00
15. 2 Reales 1859, 60. Arms. Rev. Prov de
    la Rioja   25.00
16. ½ Real 1854   12.00

CONFEDERACION ARGENTINA
100 Centavos = 1 Real

17. 4 Centavos (C) 1854. Sun. Rev. Value   4.00
18. 2 Centavos (C) 1854   5.00
19. 1 Centavo (C) 1854   6.00

REPUBLICA ARGENTINA
100 Centavos = 1 Peso

20. 1 Peso 1881-83. Liberty head. Rev. Arms   90.00
21. 50 Centavos 1881-83   10.00
22. 20 Centavos 1881-83   5.00
23. 10 Centavos 1881-83   2.50

24. 50 Centavos (N) 1941. Liberty head. Rev.
    Value   3.25
25. 20 Centavos (C-N) 1896-1942   .50
26. 10 Centavos (C-N) 1896-1942   .40
27. 5 Centavos (C-N) 1896-1942   .30
28. 2 Centavos (Br) 1882-96. Liberty head.
    Rev. Arms   1.50
29. 1 Centavo (Br) 1882-96   1.00

30. 2 Centavos (Br) 1939-50. Arms. Rev.
    Value   .40
31. 1 Centavo (Bro) 1939-48   .25

32. 20 Centavos (A-Br) 1942-50. Liberty head.
    Rev. Value   .75
33. 10 Centavos (A-Br) 1942-50   .25
34. 5 Centavos (A-Br) 1942-50   .25

35. 50 Centavos (N-St) 1952-56. Gen. San
    Martin. Rev. Value .... .75
36. 20 Centavos (C-N) 1950. Gen. Jose de San
    Martin. Rev. Value (Commemorates
    the 100th anniversary of his death) 1.00
36a. 20 Centavos (C-N) 1951, 52; (N-St) 1952-56.
    "Centenario" legend dropped .... .25

45. 10 Pesos (St) 1962-68. Gaucho. Rev.
    Value (12-sided) .... .50

37. 10 Centavos (C-N) 1950 .... 1.00
37a. 10 Centavos (C-N) 1951-52; (N-St)
    1952-56 .... .35
38. 5 Centavos (C-N) 1950 .... 1.00

46. 5 Pesos (St) 1961-68. Sailing ship. Rev.
    Value (12 sided) .... .50

38a. 5 Centavos (C-N) 1951-53; (N-St) 1953-56 .20

47. 25 Pesos (St) 1964-68. Replica of obverse
    of 1813 8 reales coin. Rev. Reverse of
    same (Commemorates first coin of in-
    dependent Argentina—12-sided planchet) 1.50

39. 1 Peso (N-St) 1957-62. Liberty Head. Rev.
    Value .... .50
40. 50 Centavos (N-St) 1957-61 .... .40

48. 10 Pesos (St) 1966. Museum. Rev. Value
    (Commemorates the 150th anniversary
    of declaration of independence) .... .75

41. 20 Centavos (N-St) 1957-61 .... .25
42. 10 Centavos (N-St) 1957-59 .... .20
43. 5 Centavos (N-St) 1957-59 .... .15

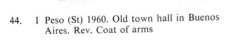

44. 1 Peso (St) 1960. Old town hall in Buenos
    Aires. Rev. Coat of arms 1.25

49. 25 Pesos (N-St) 1968. Head of Sarmiento
    (President, 1868-74). Rev. Value 1.25

CURRENCY REVALUATION

1 New Peso = 100 Old Pesos

50. 50 Centavos (Bra) 1970- . Liberty head.
Rev. Value ..... .75
51. 20 Centavos (Bra) 1970- ..... .50
52. 10 Centavos (Bra) 1970- ..... .20
53. 5 Centavos (Al) 1970- ..... .15
54. 1 Centavo (Al) 1970 ..... .15

55. 1 Peso (A-Br) 1974. Sun. Rev. Value,
laurel branch ..... .50

AUSTRALIA

Settlement of Australia began January 26, 1788 and six separate colonies developed—New South Wales, Tasmania, Western Australia, South Australia, Victoria and Queensland. The colonies became a federation of states in 1901 as the Commonwealth of Australia which is today a self-governing member of the British Commonwealth of Nations.

COLONIAL ISSUES

NEW SOUTH WALES

Name originally applied to much of continent, by 1840 area reduced to eastern third. During the early years of settlement, practically any coin that came to the colony was used in trade. In 1800, Governor Philip Gidley King proclaimed that certain British and foreign coins were to circulate at fixed rates. By about 1830 sufficient numbers of gold and silver coins had arrived from England to replace the foreign pieces in use. Small denomination coins were still scarce, however, and bronze penny and halfpenny tokens issued by various merchants came into circulation. These tokens did relieve the shortage of small change and they provided a means of advertising for the issuers as well. The tokens passed out of use during the 1860's, replaced by regular issue British bronze coins from London.

Proclamation Coins of 1800

1. An English Guinea (type of #186, p. 204)
2. A Johanna (type of #1, p. 367)
3. A Half Johanna (type of #2, p. 367)
4. A Ducat (type of #13, p. 331)
5. A Gold Mohur (type of #5, p. 243)
6. A Pagoda (type of #36, p. 245)
7. A Spanish Dollar (type of #36, p. 315)
8. A Rupee (type of #34, p. 244)
9. A Dutch Guilder (type of #3, p. 330)
10. An English Shilling (type of #188, p. 204)
11. A Copper coin of 1 oz. (type of #199, p. 205)

12.   5 Shillings 1813, called "ring" or "holey dollars." NEW SOUTH WALES 1813 counterstamped around hole. Rev. FIVE SHILLINGS counterstamp (an emergency issue made by cutting the centers out of Spanish milled dollars   850.00

13.   15 Pence 1813, called "dumps" (centers, restamped, of #12)   75.00

VICTORIA 1837-1901

14.   1 Sovereign (G) 1855, 1856. Young head with ribbon hair band. Rev. Inscription   250.00
15.   ½ Sovereign (G) 1855, 1856   200.00
16.   1 Sovereign (G) 1857-70. Young head with wreath of native Australian leaves. Rev. Inscription   100.00

17.   ½ Sovereign (G) 1857-66   100.00

19.

18.   1 Sovereign (G) 1871-87. Young head with ribbon hair band. Rev. St. George and dragon (same design as regular English issue but with Sydney mintmark, "S," below head)   75.00
19.   1 Sovereign (G) 1871-87. Rev. Shield ("S" mintmark below head or shield)   75.00
20.   ½ Sovereign (G) 1871-87   50.00

23.

21.   1 Sovereign (G) 1887-93. Jubilee head. Rev. St. George and dragon ("S" mintmark below horse)   75.00
22.   ½ Sovereign (G) 1887, 89, 91. Rev. Shield ("S" mintmark below)   60.00
23.   1 Sovereign (G) 1893-1901. Veiled head. Rev. St. George and dragon ("S" mintmark below horse)   50.00
24.   ½ Sovereign (G) 1893, 97, 1900   40.00

AUSTRALIA (continued)

25. 1 Penny token (C) 1852-68, also un-
    dated. Various types issued by mer-
    chants and tradesmen (mostly Sydney) 4.00
26. ½ Penny token (C) 4.00

VICTORIA

Originally part of New South Wales, Victoria
became a separate colony in 1851.

VICTORIA 1837–1901

27. 1 Sovereign (G) 1872-87. Young head.
    Rev. St. George and dragon (type of
    #18 with Melbourne mintmark "M"
    below head) 75.00
28. 1 Sovereign (G) 1872-87. Rev. Shield
    (type of #19 with "M" mintmark
    below head or shield) 75.00
29. ½ Sovereign (G) 1873-87 50.00
30. 1 Sovereign (G) 1887-93. Jubilee head.
    Rev. St. George and dragon (type of
    #21 with "M" mintmark below
    horse) 75.00
31. ½ Sovereign (G) 1887, 93. Rev. Shield
    ("M" mintmark below) 60.00
32. 1 Sovereign (G) 1893-1901. Veiled
    head. Rev. St. George and dragon
    (type of #23 with "M" mintmark
    below horse) 50.00
33. ½ Sovereign (G) 1896-1900 45.00

34. 1 Penny token (C) 1849-63, also un-
    dated. Various types issued by
    merchants and tradesmen (mostly
    Melbourne) 3.00
35. ½ Penny token (C) 3.50

QUEENSLAND

Originally part of New South Wales, Queensland became a separate colony in 1859.

36. 1 Penny token (C) 1863-65, also un-
    dated. Various types issued by mer-
    chants and tradesmen 6.00
37. ½ Penny token (C) 6.50

SOUTH AUSTRALIA

Settlement of this area began about 1836 and
South Australia was made a separate colony in
1842.

38. 1 Pound (G) 1852. Crown. Rev. Value 600.00

39. 1 Penny token (C) 1858, also undated.
    Various types issued by merchants
    and tradesmen 7.00
40. ½ Penny token (C) 1857 8.00

WESTERN AUSTRALIA.

Declared a separate colony in 1829.

41. 1 Sovereign (G) 1899-1901. Veiled
    head. Rev. St. George and dragon
    (type of #23 with Perth mintmark,
    "P," below horse) 50.00
42. ½ Sovereign (G) 1899, 1900 40.00

48. 1 Florin (2 shillings) 1910. Crowned
   bust. Rev. Arms   50.00
49. 1 Shilling 1910   15.00
50. 6 Pence 1910   8.00
51. 3 Pence 1910   5.00

43. 1 Penny token (C or Br) 1865-74, also
   undated. Various types issued by
   merchants and tradesmen   8.00

GEORGE V 1910-36

52. 1 Sovereign (G) 1911-31. Bare head.
   Rev. St. George and dragon (same
   design as regular English issue but
   with "S," "M" or "P" mintmark
   below horse)   80.00
53. ½ Sovereign (G) 1911-16   35.00
54. 1 Florin 1911-36. Crowned bust. Rev.
   Arms   3.50
55. 1 Shilling 1911-36   2.00
56. 6 Pence 1911-36   1.00
57. 3 Pence 1911-36   1.00

TASMANIA

Discovered in 1642 by Abel Tasman, the island
was named Van Dieman's Land. At first a depend-
ency of New South Wales, Van Dieman's Land
was declared a separate colony in 1825. The name
was changed to Tasmania in 1856.

44. 1 Penny token (C) 1850-74, also undated. Various types issued by merchants and tradesmen   5.00
45. ½ Penny token (C) 1855, also undated   5.50

58. 1 Penny (Br) 1911-36. Rev. Value   .50
59. ½ Penny (Br) 1911-36   .50

COMMONWEALTH ISSUES

EDWARD VII 1901-10

12 Pence = 1 Shilling
2 Shillings = 1 Florin

60. 1 Florin 1927. Rev. Parliament buildings (commemorates the first meeting
   of Parliament at Canberra)   4.50

46. 1 Sovereign (G) 1902-10. Bare head.
   Rev. St. George and dragon (same
   design as regular English issue but
   with distinctive Australian mintmark,
   "S," "M," or "P," below horse)   80.00
47. ½ Sovereign (G) 1902-10   40.00

61. 1 Florin 1935. Rev. Rider on horseback (commemorates the 100th anniversary of settlement at Melbourne)   75.00

GEORGE VI 1936-52

Coins issued after 1948 are without "IND IMP" (Emperor of India) in legend.

| 67. | 1 Penny (Br) 1938-48. Rev. Kangaroo | .75 |
| 67a. | 1 Penny (Br) 1949-52 (without "IND IMP") | .75 |

| 68. | ½ Penny (Br) 1938, 39. Rev. Value | 1.00 |

| 62. | 1 Crown 1937, 38. Bare head. Rev. Crown | 8.50 |

| 69. | ½ Penny (Br) 1939-48. Rev. Kangaroo | .60 |
| 69a. | ½ Penny (Br) 1949-52 (without "IND IMP") | .75 |

63.	1 Florin 1938-47. Rev. Modified arms	3.00
63a.	1 Florin 1951, 52 (without "IND IMP")	4.00
64.	1 Shilling 1938-48. Rev. Head of Merino Ram	1.50
64a.	1 Shilling 1950, 52 (without "IND IMP")	2.00

| 70. | 1 Florin 1951. Rev. Sword, mace, crown and stars in form of Southern Cross constellation (Commemorates the 50th year jubilee of the Commonwealth) | 5.50 |

65.	6 Pence 1938-48. Rev. Arms (type of #48)	1.00
65a.	6 Pence 1950-52 (without "IND IMP")	1.00
66.	3 Pence 1938-48. Rev. Wheat stalks	1.00
66a.	3 Pence 1949-52 (without "IND IMP")	.75

(Australian silver coins were struck at the U.S. mints in Denver and San Francisco 1942-44. "D" and "S" mint marks appear on the reverse of these issues.)

AUSTRALIA (continued)

ELIZABETH II 1952-

Coins issued 1955-64 have "F.D." in legend.

79.	20 Cents 1966- . Rev. Platypus	.50
80.	10 Cents 1966- . Rev. Lyre bird	.35

71.	1 Florin 1953, 54. Laureate head. Rev. Arms (type of #63)	6.00
71a.	1 Florin 1956-63 (with "F.D.")	3.00
72.	1 Shilling 1953, 54. Rev. Head of Merino Ram (type of #64)	5.00
72a.	1 Shilling 1955-63 (with "F.D.")	1.00
73.	6 Pence 1953-54. Rev. Arms (type of #48)	2.75
73a.	6 Pence 1955-63 (with "F.D.")	1.00
74.	3 Pence 1953-54. Rev. Wheat stalks (type of #66)	4.00
74a.	3 Pence 1955-64 (with "F.D.")	.75
75.	1 Penny (Br) 1953. Rev. Kangaroo (type of #67)	3.00
75a.	1 Penny (Br) 1955-64 (with "F.D.")	1.00
76.	½ Penny (Br) 1953-55. Rev. Kangaroo (type of #69)	2.00
76a.	½ Penny (Br) 1959-64 (with "F.D.")	1.00

81.	5 Cents 1966- . Rev. Spiny anteater	.25
82.	2 Cents (Br) 1966- . Rev. Frilled lizard	.15

83.	1 Cent (Br) 1966- . Rev. Flying mouse	.15

77.	1 Florin 1954. Rev. Lion and kangaroo (commemorates the royal visit of Queen Elizabeth and Prince Philip)	6.00

Decimal Coinage

100 Cents = 1 Dollar

84.	50 Cents (CN) 1970. Rev. Captain Cook and map (12-sided planchet, commemorates 200th anniversary of Cook's discovery)	3.00

78.	50 Cents (S) 1966. Draped bust with coronet. Rev. Arms	4.00
78a.	50 Cents (CN)1969- . (12-sided planchet)	1.75

AUSTRIA

For centuries the Hapsburgs of Austria were among the most powerful reigning families of Europe. The Austrian Hapsburgs extended their rule to include the duchies of Styria and Carinthia, the kingdoms of Hungary and Bohemia, and the countries of Tyrol and Schlick. From 1438 to 1806 the head of the Holy Roman Empire was always a Hapsburg. Besides the Imperial and Austrian Archducal coinages the numerous Hapsburg lands produced several local issues struck by members of the family. Coins from the various Hapsburg lands are of similar designs with some variation in mint symbols, armorial devices or legends. In 1867 the Dual Monarchy was established under the title of Austria-Hungary. After World War I, Austria was cut down to a tiny fraction of its previous size, and became a republic.

AUSTRIAN EMPIRE (REGIONAL ISSUES)
TYROL
SIGISMUND 1439-96

1. ½ Guldengroschen 1484. Half length bust. Rev. Mounted knight in armor   400.00

2. 1 Guldengroschen 1486. Duke standing 475.00 (These two coins are the first full dated coins ever struck)

SCHLICK
COUNT STEPHEN 1487-1526

3. Joachimstaler 1516-26. St. Joachim. Rev. Standing lion (Large silver pieces from Joachim's valley or "thal" were called "thalers" at first, changing to "taler," to "daler," finally to "dollar.")   275.00

TEUTONIC ORDER
ARCHDUKE MAXIMILIAN 1588-1618

4. Double Taler 1614. Archduke as Grand Master. Rev. Knight on horseback   275.00

HOLY ROMAN EMPIRE
(COINS OF THE EMPERORS)
FERDINAND I 1556-64

5. Taler. Bust.   200.00

AUSTRIA (continued)

MAXIMILIAN II 1564-76

6. Taler. Bust.   250.00

RUDOLF II 1576-1612

7. Taler. Bust.   125.00

MATTHIAS II 1612-19

8. Taler. Bust.   175.00

FERDINAND II 1619-37

9. Double Taler 1626 (Issued by Archduke Leopold to commemorate his marriage). Conjoined busts of Leopold and Claudia de' Medici. Rev. Eagle   175.00

FERDINAND III 1637-57

10.. Taler. Bust.   90.00

LEOPOLD I 1658-1705

11. Double Taler undated. Bewigged bust in armor.   250.00
12. Taler. Bust.   75.00

JOSEPH I 1705-11

13. Taler. Bust.   100.00

CHARLES VI 1711-40

14. Taler. Bust.   75.00

MARIA THERESA 1740-80

15. Taler 1741-80. Head. Rev. Imperial eagle 30.00

16. Trade Taler dated 1780. Older bust   4.50

JOSEPH II 1765-90

From the time of his father's death in 1765, Joseph II ruled jointly with his mother Maria Theresa until her death in 1780.

17. Taler 1765-90. Bust. Rev. Arms   35.00

LEOPOLD II 1790-92
18. Taler 1790-92. Head. Rev. Imperial eagle   30.00

FRANCIS II 1792-1806
FRANCIS I 1806-35

Joseph's successor, Francis, ruled as Holy Roman Emperor Francis II from 1792 to 1806, when the Empire was abolished. Thereafter he ruled as Francis I of Austria.

19.

19. Taler 1804-06. Head. Rev. Imperial eagle   65.00

FERDINAND I 1835-48

20. Taler 1835-48. Laureated Head. Rev. Imperial eagle   30.00
21. ½ Taler 1839-49   40.00
22. 20 Kreuzer 1837-48   10.00
23. 10 Kreuzer 1836-42   8.00
24. 5 Kreuzer 1836-48   6.00
25. 3 Kreuzer 1839-48   6.00

FRANZ JOSEPH 1848-1916

26. Double Taler 1854 (Marriage issue). Conjoined heads of Franz Joseph and Elizabeth. Rev. Marriage scene   125.00

27. Double Taler 1857 (Opening of South Austrian Railways). Laureated head. Rev. Lighthouse, engine, boat, and shields   1,200.00
28. Double Taler 1865-68. Laureated head. Rev. Imperial eagle   400.00

29. 2 Florins 1858-92. Laureated head. Rev. Imperial eagle (varieties)   40.00

34.	¼ Florin 1857-75	6.00
35.	20 Kreuzer 1868-72	3.00
36.	10 Kreuzer 1858-72	1.00
37.	5 Kreuzer 1858-67. Rev. Value	2.00
38.	4 Kreuzer (C) 1860-64. Double-headed eagle. Rev. Value	8.00
39.	3 Kreuzer (C) 1851	10.00
40.	1 Kreuzer (C) 1858-91	.50
41.	⁵⁄₁₀ Kreuzer (C) 1858-91	1.50

30. 2 Florins 1879 (Silver wedding anniversary). Accolated heads of Franz Joseph and Elizabeth. Rev. Seated female figure   30.00

42. 5 Corona 1900, 07, 09. Laureated old head. Rev. Imperial eagle in laurel and crown wreath   10.00

31. 2 Florins 1887 (Reopening of Kutten-berg silver mines). Laureated head. Rev. Cathedral   1,200.00
32. Taler 1852-56. Laureated head. Rev. Imperial eagle   50.00
32a. Taler 1857-67 (Size reduced)   25.00

43. 5 Corona 1908 (60th year of reign). Rev. Running figure of Fame   15.00
44. 2 Corona 1912-13. Head. Rev. Imperial eagle   3.00
45. 1 Corona 1892-1907. Laureated head   2.00
46. 1 Corona 1908 (60th year of reign). Old head. Rev. Crown over monogram   3.50
47. 1 Corona 1912-16   1.00

33. 1 Florin 1857-92   4.00

48. 20 Heller (N) 1892-1914. Eagle   1.00
49. 10 Heller (N) 1892-1916   .60
50. 2 Heller (Bro) 1892-1915   .25
51. 1 Heller (Bro) 1892-1916   .25

REPUBLIC
100 Heller = 1 Corona
10,000 Kronen = 1 Schilling
100 Groschen = 1 Schilling

52. 20 Kronen (G) 1923-24. Arms. Rev. Value in wreath 600.00

53. 100 Schillings (G) 1926-31, 33-34. Rev. Value in sprays 250.00
54. 25 Schillings (G) 1926-31, 33-34 .... 100.00

55. 100 Schillings (G) 1935-38. Double-headed eagle. Rev. Madonna of Mariazell 500.00
56. 25 Schillings (G) 1935-37. Rev. St. Leopold 100.00

57. 1 Schilling 1924. Parliament. Rev. Shield and value 3.00
58. 1 Schilling 1925-26, 32. Reduced size 2.00

59. 1000 Kronen (C-N) 1924. Tirolese woman. Rev. Value in wreath 4.00

60. 200 Kronen (Bro) 1924. Teutonic cross. Rev. Value 1.50

61. 100 Kronen (Bro) 1923-24. Eagle's head. Rev. Value 1.25
62. 5 Schillings 1934-36. Type of #55 .... 15.00

63. 1 Schilling (C-N) 1934-35. Eagle. Rev. Value 2.00

64. ½ Schilling 1925-26. Arms. Rev. Value 3.50

65. 50 Groschen (C-N) 1934-36. Eagle. Rev. Value 2.00
66. 10 Groschen (C-N) 1925, 28-29. Type of #59 .... .50
67. 5 Groschen (C-N) 1931-38. Type of ♯60 .... .50
68. 2 Groschen (Bro) 1925-30, 34-38. Cross. Rev. Value .... .40

69. 1 Groschen (Bro) 1925-38. Head of eagle. Rev. Value .... .25

AUSTRIA (continued)

COMMEMORATIVE SERIES

70. 2 Schillings 1928. Value within circle of 11 shields. Rev. Head of Schubert   12.50

78. 2 Schillings 1936. Rev. Head of Prince Eugene of Savoy   12.00
79. 2 Schillings 1937. Rev. Karlskirche in Vienna   15.00

POSTWAR ISSUES

71. 2 Schillings 1929. Rev. Head of Dr. Billroth   12.00
72. 2 Schillings 1930. Rev. Seated figure of Walther von der Vogelweide   15.00

80. 5 Schillings (A) 1952, 57   3.00

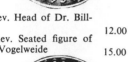

73. 2 Schillings 1931. Rev. Bust of Mozart   20.00
74. 2 Schillings 1932. Rev. Bust of Haydn   60.00

81. 2 Schillings (A) 1946-52.   1.50

82. 1 Schilling (A) 1946-57. Rev. Standing figure   .50

75. 2 Schillings 1933. Rev. Bust of Dr. Seipel   20.00
76. 2 Schillings 1935. Rev. Bust of Dr. Lueger   15.00

77. 2 Schillings 1934. Arms with double-headed eagle. Rev. Head of Dr. Dollfuss   15.00

83. 50 Groschen (A) 1946-55. Eagle. Rev. Value   .35
84. 20 Groschen (A-Bro) 1950-54   .50

AUSTRIA (continued)

85. 10 Schillings 1957-73. Female head   2.50

93. 25 Schillings 1955 (Commemorating re-opening of Bundestheater). Muse with mask, two girls drawing curtains. Rev. Value in circle of 9 shields   35.00

94. 25 Schillings 1956. Statue of Mozart. Rev. Value in circle of 9 shields   7.50

86. 5 Schillings 1960-68. Lipizaner stallion and rider   2.50
86a. 5 Shillings (C-N) 1968-   .75

95. 25 Schillings 1957. Mariazell Abbey. Rev. Circle of 9 shields around value   7.50

96. 25 Schillings 1958. Head of Von Welsbach (100th anniversary of famous scientist's birth)   7.50

87. 1 Schilling (A-Bro) 1959- . Edelweiss   .50

88. 50 Groschen (A-Bro) 1959- . Shield   .25

97. 50 Schillings 1959. Head of Andreas Hofer (leader of revolt against Napoleon's occupation of Tyrol). Rev. Eagle in circle of shields   12.00

89. 10 Groschen (Z) 1947-49. Eagle. Rev. Value   1.00

89a. 10 Groschen (A) 1951-   .25
90. 5 Groschen (Z) 1948-   .25
91. 2 Groschen (A) 1950-   .25
92. 1 Groschen (Z) 1947   1.00

98. 25 Schillings 1959. Head of Archduke Johann (army commander during Napoleonic War). Rev. Lion of Styria in circle of shields   16.00

99. 25 Schillings 1960. Corinthian Plebiscite 17.50

100. 25 Schillings 1961. Hayden church (40th anniversary of Burgenland's incorporation into Austrian Republic) 40.00

101. 25 Schillings 1962. Head of Anton Bruckner, famous composer 8.00

102. 50 Schillings 1963. Shields of Austria and Tyrol (600th anniversary of the union of Tyrol with Austria) 12.00

103. 25 Schillings 1963. Prince Eugen (300th anniversary of birth of this famous field marshal) 17.00

104. 50 Schillings 1964. Olympic Winter Games 12.00
105. 25 Schillings 1964. Franz Grillparzer, poet 10.00

106. 50 Schillings 1965. Rudolph of Hapsburg. Rev. Circle of shields (Commemorates founding of Vienna University in 1365) 15.00
107. 25 Schillings 1965. J. J. R. von Prechtl. Rev. Circle of Shields. (150th year of Vienna Technical High School) 10.00

108. 50 Schillings 1966. Bank Building. Rev. Circle of shields (150th anniversary of Austrian National Bank) 20.00
109. 25 Schillings 1966. Portrait of Ferdinand Raimund (1790-1836). Rev. Circle of Shields (honors famous Viennese poet) 17.50

110. 50 Schillings 1967. Half-length figure of
      Johann Strauss. Rev. Circle of shields
      (100th anniversary of Blue Danube
      Waltz)   10.00

111. 25 Schillings 1967. Portrait of Empress
      Maria Theresa (1717-1780). Rev. Circle
      of shields (250th anniversary of birth)   8.00

112. 50 Schillings 1968. Parliament building.
      Rev. Circle of shields (Commemorates
      50th anniversary of the Austrian Re-
      public)   17.50

113. 25 Schillings 1968. Belvedere Palace. Rev.
      Circle of shields (Honors 300th anni-
      versary of architect Lukas Von Hilde-
      brandt)   20.00

114. 50 Schillings 1969. Bust of Holy Roman
      Emperor Maximilian I. Rev. Circle of
      shields (Commemorates 450th anni-
      versary of his death)   10.00
115. 25 Schillings 1969. Portrait of Peter
      Roseger. Rev. Circle of shields (Com-
      memorates 125th anniversary of writer's
      birth)   15.00

116. 50 Schillings 1970. University of Innsbruck
      seal. Rev. Circle of shields (Com-
      memorates 300th anniversary of
      founding)   6.00
117. 50 Schillings 1970. Portrait of Dr. Karl
      Renner (1870-1950) Federal President
      1945-1950. Rev. Circle of shields   6.00

118. 25 Schillings 1970. Head of Franz Lehar.
      Rev. Circle of shields (Commemorates
      100th anniversary of composer's birth)   3.50

119. 50 Schillings 1971. Portrait of Julius Raab
      (1891-1964) Federal Chancellor 1953-
      1961. Rev. Circle of shields   6.00

120. 25 Schillings 1971. Stock exchange building.
      Rev. Circle of shields (Commemorates
      200th anniversary of Vienna Bourse)   3.50

AUSTRIA (continued)

120.   121.   126.   127.

121. 50 Schillings 1972. University seal. Rev. Circle of shields (Commemorates 350th anniversary of Salzburg University)   6.50

127. 50 Schillings 1974. Stylized radio transmitter. Rev. Circle of shields (Commemorates 50 years of Austrian radio)   5.00

122. 50 Schillings 1972. School building. Rev. Circle of shields (Commemorates 100th anniversary of Agricultural University)   6.50

123. 25 Schillings 1972. Portrait of Carl Michael Ziehrer (1843-1922). Rev. Circle of shields (Commemorates 50th anniversary of composer's death)   3.50

128. 50 Schillings 1974. Bishops Rupert and Virgil holding model of Salzburg Cathedral. Rev. Circle of shields (Commemorates 1200th anniversary of cathedral)   5.00

129. 50 Schillings 1974. Arms and Federal Police insignia. Rev. Circle of shields (Commemorates 125th anniversary of Federal Police)   5.00

124. 50 Schillings 1973. Inn. Rev. Circle of shields (Commemorates 500th anniversary of Bummerlhaus in Steyr)   6.50

125. 50 Schillings 1973. Bust of Theodor Körner (1873-1957). Rev. Circle of shields (Commemorates 100th anniversary of birth of former Federal President)   5.50

126. 50 Schillings 1973. Portrait of Max Reinhardt (1873-1943). Rev. Circle of shields (Commemorates 100th anniversary of theatrical director's birth)   3.50

130. 50 Schillings 1974. Floral design. Rev. Circle of shields (Commemorates International Garden Exhibition)   5.00

131. 10 Schillings (C-N) 1974- .   1.50

132. 100 Schillings 1975. Johann Strauss monument in Vienna City Park. Rev. Circle of shields (Commemorates 150th anniversary of composer's birth) 15.00

133. 100 Schillings 1975. Modern eagle over value. Rev. Sower in field (Commemorates 50th anniversary of schilling coinage) 15.00

134. 100 Schillings 1975. Eagle. Rev. Design symbolizing occupation (Commemorates 20th anniversary of State Treaty) 15.00

135. 100 Schillings 1976. Emblem of Winter Olympics. Rev. Circle of shields (Commemorates 1976 Games in Innsbruck) 10.00

136. 100 Schillings 1976. Eagle. Rev. Hasegg Mint, Olympic rings in background (Olympic commemorative) 10.00

137. 100 Schillings 1976. Rev. Modernistic skiier (Olympic commemorative) 10.00

138. 100 Schillings 1976. Rev. Bergisel ski jump (Olympic commemorative) 10.00

AZORES

The Azores comprise three groups of islands in the Atlantic Ocean just west of Portugal, which were known as far back as the fourteenth century. For centuries the islands were Portuguese colonies and were finally made part of Portugal for administrative purposes.

1000 Reis = 1 Crown

MARY II 1828-53

1. 80 Reis (C) 1829. Crowned shield. Rev.
   Value in wreath   20.00
2. 20 Reis (C) 1843   8.00

3. 10 Reis (C) 1843   7.50
4. 5 Reis (C) 1843   10.00

LOUIS I 1861-89

5. 20 Reis (C) 1865, 66   7.25
6. 10 Reis (C) 1865, 66   6.00
7. 5 Reis (C) 1865-80   4.75

CHARLES I 1889-1908

8. 10 Reis (C) 1901   8.00
9. 5 Reis (C) 1901   6.00

(Similar coins with values given in Roman numerals were issued for Portugal proper.)

BAHAMAS

The first landing of Columbus on October 12, 1492 took place on one of the 700 Bahamas islands. Originally Spanish, the islands were taken over by the British in 1783.

1. 1 Penny (C) 1806. Bust of George III.
   Rev. Three-masted man-o'-war   45.00

2. 5 Dollars 1966-70. Portrait of Queen
   Elizabeth with coronet. Rev. Coat of
   arms   24.00

3. 2 Dollars 1966-70. Rev. Two flamingos   15.00

4. 1 Dollar 1966-70. Rev. Conch shell   5.00

5. 50 Cents 1966-70. Rev. Blue marlin   2.50
6. 25 Cents (N) 1966. Rev. Native sloop   1.25

7. 15 Cents (C-N) 1966-70. Rev. Hibiscus
     blossom (square planchet)   .75
8. 10 Cents (C-N) 1966-70. Rev. Two bone-
     fish (scalloped edge planchet)   .60

9. 5 Cents (C-N) 1966-70. Rev. Pineapple   .50
10. 1 Cent (Bra) 1966-70. Rev. Starfish   .25

11. 100 Dollars (G) 1967. Elizabeth II. Rev.
     Columbus with flag   550.00

12. 50 Dollars (G) 1967, 71, 72. Rev. "Santa
     Maria," flagship of Columbus   175.00

13. 20 Dollars (G) 1967, 71, 72. Rev. Light-
     house   75.00
14. 10 Dollars (G) 1967, 71, 72. Rev. Fort   40.00
15. 100 Dollars (G) 1971, 72. Type of #2   375.00

16. 5 Dollars 1971. Elizabeth II. Rev. Arms   20.00
17. 2 Dollars 1971-73. Rev. Type of #3   15.00
18. 1 Dollar 1971-73. Rev. Type of #4   4.00
19. 50 Cents 1971-73. Rev. Type of #5   2.50
20. 25 Cents (N) 1971-73. Rev. Type of #6   1.00
21. 15 Cents (C-N) 1971-73. Rev. Type of #7   .75
22. 10 Cents (C-N) 1971-73. Rev. Type of #8   .50
23. 5 Cents (C-N) 1971-73. Rev. Type of #9   .25
24. 1 Cent (N-Bra) 1971-73. Rev. Type of
     #10   .20

25.   5 Dollars 1972, 73. Rev. Newly designed
      arms   20.00

32.   200 Dollars (G) 1974-75. Elizabeth II,
      date of independence. Rev. Type of
      #26   275.00
33.   150 Dollars (G) 1974-75. Rev. Type of #27   200.00
34.   100 Dollars (G) 1974-75. Rev. Type of #28   135.00
35.   50 Dollars (G) 1974-75. Rev. Type of #29   60.00

26.   100 Dollars (G) 1973. Rev. Arms   150.00

36.   100 Dollars (G) 1974. Two flamingoes,
      inscription. Rev. Arms (Commemor-
      ates Independence Day)   125.00

27.   50 Dollars (G) 1973. Rev. Crawfish   75.00
28.   20 Dollars (G) 1973. Rev. Four flamingoes   30.00
29.   10 Dollars (G) 1973. Rev. Tobacco dove   20.00

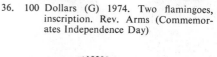

30.   50 Dollars (G) 1973. Rev. Two flamin-
      goes, inscription (Commemorates In-
      dependence Day)   125.00
31.   10 Dollars 1973. Rev. "Santa Maria,"
      inscription (Commemorates Indepen-
      dence Day)   25.00

37.   10 Dollars 1974. Head of Sir Milo B.
      Butler, governor general. Rev. Arms   35.00

38.	5 Dollars 1974- . Arms. Rev. Flag	12.50
39.	2 Dollars 1974- . Rev. Type of #3	15.00
40.	1 Dollar 1974- . Rev. Type of #4	1.50
41.	50 Cents 1974- . Rev. Type of #5	1.25
42.	25 Cents (N) 1974- . Rev. Type of #6	.75
43.	15 Cents (N) 1974- . Rev. Type of #7 (square planchet)	.60
44.	10 Cents (C-N) 1974- . Rev. Type of #8 (scalloped planchet)	.40
45.	5 Cents (C-N) 1974- . Rev. Type of #9	.25
46.	1 Cent (N-Bra) 1974- . Rev. Type of #10	.15

47.	100 Dollars (G) 1975. Parrot. Rev. Arms (Commemorates second anniversary of independence)	125.00

48.	10 Dollars 1975. Yellow elder, national flower. Rev. Arms (Commemorates Independence Day)	35.00
48a.	10 Dollars (C-N) 1975	

BAHRAIN

An independent Arab state made up of the island of Bahrain and several smaller islands in the Gulf of Persia near the east coast of Arabia. It was under the protection of Great Britain from 1861 until 1971, when Bahrain became an independent nation.

1. 100 Fils (C-N) 1965. Tree in circle. Rev.
   Value 1.75
2. 50 Fils (C-N) 1965 .... 1.00
3. 25 Fils (C-N) 1965 .... .60
4. 10 Fils (Br) 1965 .... .30
5. 5 Fils (Br) 1965 .... .20
6. 1 Fil (Br) 1965 .... .15

7. 10 Dinars (G) 1968. Bust of Sheik Isa bin Sulman Al Khalifah. Rev. Arms (Commemorates the opening of Isa Town) 150.00
8. 500 Fils 1968 .... 5.00

9. 250 Fils (C-N) 1969. Dhow and date palm (F.A.O. coin plan) 3.00

BANGLADESH

Formerly East Pakistan; became independent in 1971.

1. 50 Poisha (C-N) 1973. Arms. Rev. Bird ..... .50

2. 25 Poisha (St) 1973. Rev. Fish .... .35

3. 10 Poisha (St) 1973. Rev. Leaf .... .25

4. 5 Poisha (A) 1973. Rev. Cogwheel, plow .... .20

5. 25 Poisha (St) 1974-75. Rev. Carp, bananas and gourd (F.A.O. coin plan) .... .35

6. 10 Poisha (A) 1974-75. Rev. Tractor, seedlings and rice (F.A.O. coin plan) ..... .30

BANGLADESH (continued)

7. 5 Poisha (A) 1974-75. Rev. Cogwheel,
    plow (F.A.O. coin plan)   .25

8. 1 Poisha (A) 1974. Rev. Value   .15

9. 1 Taka (C-N) 1975. Rev. Family of four
    (F.A.O. coin plan)

BARBADOS

The most easterly of the West Indian islands,
Barbados is a British crown colony. Originally
explored by the Portuguese, it was claimed by the
British in 1605. (Now one of the British Caribbean
Territories.)

1. 1 Penny (C) 1788. Negro head with
    crown and plume of three ostrich
    feathers. Rev. pineapple   35.00

2. 1 Penny (C) 1792. Type of #1. Rev.
    Neptune   20.00
3. 1 Halfpenny (C) 1792. Type of #2   17.50

4. 4 Dollars (C-N) 1970. Arms. Rev. Bananas
    and sugar cane (F.A.O. coin plan,
    East Caribbean Territories)   5.00

5. 10 Dollars 1973- . Arms. Rev. Seated
figures of Neptune   20.00
5a. 10 Dollars (C-N) 1974   12.50

9. 25 Cents (C-N) 1973. Rev. Morgan Lewis
Sugar Mill   1.25
10. 10 Cents (C-N) 1973- . Rev. Tern   1.00

11. 5 Cents (Bra) 1973- . Rev. Lighthouse   .75
12. 1 Cent (Br) 1973- . Rev. Trident   .50

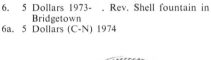

6. 5 Dollars 1973- . Rev. Shell fountain in
Bridgetown   12.50
6a. 5 Dollars (C-N) 1974   6.50

13. 100 Dollars (G) 1975. Arms. Rev. Sailing
ship (Commemorates 350th anniver-
sary of English landing at Barbados)   65.00

7. 2 Dollars 1973- . Rev. Two fish, coral   5.00

8. 1 Dollar (C-N) 1973- . Rev. Flying fish
(7-sided planchet)   2.50

Almost 100 times larger than Belgium, this huge territory in central Africa was originally the private property of Leopold II of Belgium. In 1909 it became a Belgian colony, and in 1960 it became the Republic of the Congo.

100 Centimes = 1 Congo Franc

LEOPOLD II 1865-1909

1.	5 Francs 1887-96. Head. Rev. Crowned arms supported by lions	100.00
2.	2 Francs 1887-96. Rev. Crowned arms in wreath	20.00
3.	1 Franc 1887-96	10.00
4.	50 Centimes 1887-96	7.50

5.	10 Centimes (C) 1888-94 (Center hole). Crowned initials. Rev. Star	5.00
6.	5 Centimes (C) 1887-94	3.50
7.	2 Centimes (C) 1887-88	3.00
8.	1 Centime (C) 1887-88	4.50
9.	20 Centimes (C-N) 1906-09	2.00
10.	10 Centimes (C-N) 1906-09	2.00
11.	5 Centimes (C-N) 1906-09	1.50

ALBERT I 1909-34

12.	1 Franc (C-N) 1920-30. Laureate head. Rev. Palm tree	2.75

13.	50 Centimes (C-N) 1921-29	2.00

14.	20 Centimes (C-N) 1910-11	1.50
15.	10 Centimes (C-N) 1910-28	1.00
16.	5 Centimes (C-N) 1910-28	.75
17.	2 Centimes (C) 1910, 19	3.50
18.	1 Centime (C) 1910, 19	3.25

LEOPOLD III 1934-51
(under authority of Banque du Congo Belge)

19.	5 Francs (N-Bro) 1936-37. Head of Leopold III. Rev. Lion	25.00
20.	50 Francs 1944. Elephant. Rev. Value	30.00

21.	2 Francs (Bra) 1943 (Hexagonal). Elephant. Rev. Value	16.00
22.	2 Francs (Bra) 1946, 47 (Round)	2.00
23.	1 Franc (Bra) 1944-49	1.50

COINAGE FOR BELGIAN CONGO AND RUANDA-URUNDI TRUST TERRITORY.

24.	5 Francs (Bra) 1952. Palm tree. Rev. Star	2.50

25.	5 Francs (A) 1956-59. Crowned arms. Rev. Palm tree	1.25
26.	1 Franc (A) 1957-60	.75
27.	50 Centimes (A) 1954, 55	.60

BELGIUM

Part of the Low Countries (Netherlands) after the readjustment of Europe in 1815 following Napoleon's downfall. Proclaimed its independence October 16, 1830 and elected Prince Leopold (of Saxe-Coburg) King of the Belgians.

As two languages are spoken in Belgium, coins issued from 1886 have both French and Flemish inscriptions.

100 Centimes = 1 Franc

LEOPOLD I 1831-65

1. 5 Francs 1832-49. Laureate head. Rev. Value 17.00

2.	5 Francs 1849-65. Bare head. Rev. Arms	13.00
3.	2½ Francs 1848-50	20.00
4.	2 Francs 1834-44	30.00
5.	1 Franc 1833-44, 49, 50	20.00
6.	½ Franc 1833-44, 49, 50	15.00
7.	¼ Franc 1834-44, 49, 50	25.00

8. 20 Centimes (S) 1852-58, (C-N) 60, 61 .... 3.50

9.	10 Centimes (C) 1832-56, (C-N) 61-64. Lion. Rev. Monogram	2.75
10.	5 Centimes (C) 1832-60, (C-N) 61-64	2.00
11.	2 Centimes (C) 1833-65	6.50
12.	1 Centime (C) 1832-62	8.00

LEOPOLD II 1865-1909

13. 20 Francs (G) 1867-82. Bearded head. Rev. Crowned arms 35.00

14.	5 Francs 1865-76. Rev. Crowned arms in wreath	10.00
15.	2 Francs 1866-87. Rev. Crowned arms	6.00
15a.	2 Francs 1904, 09. Rev. Value in wreath	4.00
16.	1 Franc 1866-69, 87	7.50
16a.	1 Franc 1904, 09. Rev. Value in wreath	7.00
17.	50 Centimes 1866-1899	7.00
17a.	50 Centimes 1907, 09. Rev. Value in wreath	2.50

18.	25 Centimes (C-N) 1908, 09. (Center hole). Crowned "L"s. Rev. Value and spray	.30
19.	10 Centimes (C-N) 1894-1906	1.00
20.	5 Centimes (C-N) 1894-1907	.25
21.	2 Centimes (C) 1869-76, 1902-09. Lion and shield. Rev. Crowned script	.50
22.	1 Centime (C) 1869-1902, 1907	1.25

BELGIUM (continued)

23. 5 Francs 1880. Conjoined heads (Commemorates 50th anniversary of independence)   125.00
24. 2 Francs 1880. Rev. Crowned arms   30.00
25. 1 Franc 1880   10.00

ALBERT I 1909-34

26. 20 Francs (G) 1914. Uniformed bust. Rev. Shield on crowned mantle   50.00
27. 2 Francs 1910-12. Head. Rev. Value in wreath   3.00
28. 1 Franc 1910-14   1.50
29. 50 Centimes 1910-14   2.00
30. 25 Centimes (C-N) 1910-13, 1920-29. Center hole   .75
31. 10 Centimes (C-N) 1920-29; (N-Bra) 1930-32   .50
32. 5 Centimes (C-N) 1910-14, 1920-32; (N-Bra) 1930-32   .50
33. 20 Francs (N) 1931, 32. Head. Rev. Shield   15.00

38. 10 Francs (N) 1930 (Centenary of independence). Heads of three rulers of modern Belgium. Rev. Value   15.00
39. 5 Francs (N) 1930-34. Head. Rev. Value   2.00

40. 2 Francs (N) 1923, 24, 30. Allegory of Belgium wounded but victorious. Rev. Caduceus   .50

41. 1 Franc (N) 1922-35   .35
42. 50 Centimes (N) 1922-34   .35

LEOPOLD III 1934-51
(Regency 1944-51)

43. 50 Francs 1935. St. Michael and the Dragon (Railroad Centenary). Rev. Exhibition hall   50.00

44. 50 Francs 1939, 40. Head. Rev. Shields of nine provinces   11.00
45. 20 Francs 1934, 35. Rev. Crowned laurel, wheat and oak   6.00
46. 5 Francs (N) 1936, 37. Rev. Value   2.00

47. 5 Francs (N) 1938, 39. Lion. Rev. Shields   2.00
48. 1 Franc (N) 1939, 40   .75

49. 25 Centimes (N-Bra) 1938, 39; (Z) 1942-47. Crowned "L"s. Rev. Shields. Center hole   .75
50. 10 Centimes (N-Bra) 1938, 39; (Z) 1941-46   .50
51. 5 Centimes (N-Bra) 1938-40; (Z) 1941-43   .75

BELGIUM (continued)

POSTWAR

52. 100 Francs 1948-54. Heads of the four kings. Dedicated to the Belgian dynasty 6.00

53. 50 Francs 1948-54. Mercury head 5.00
54. 20 Francs 1949-55. ..... 2.50

55. 5 Francs (C-N) 1948-   Ceres head ..... .45
56. 1 Franc (C-N) 1950- ..... .25

BAUDOUIN I 1951-

57. 50 Centimes (Br) 1952-   Miner's head ..... .15
58. 20 Centimes (Br) 1953-63 ..... .50

59. 25 Centimes (C-N) 1964-   Crowned monogram. Rev. Value ..... .15

60. 50 Francs 1958 (Brussels Fair). Head of king. Rev. Building and value; symbol of Fair in field. French legend 12.50
60a.   as #60, Flemish legend 12.50

61. 50 Francs 1960. Conjoined heads of Baudouin and Fabiola (Marriage commemorative). Rev. Crowned arms of Belgium and Aragon 12.50

62. 10 Francs (N) 1969- . Head of King Baudouin. Rev. Arms ..... .75

BELIZE

Formerly known as British Honduras.

1. 5 Cents (N-Bra) 1973- . Queen Elizabeth
   II. Rev. Value   .25

2. 1 Cent (Br) 1973-   .15

3. 50 Cents (C-N) 1974-   2.50

4. 25 Cents (C-N) 1974-   1.00
5. 10 Cents (C-N) 1974-   .50

6. 10 Dollars (C-N) 1974- . Arms. Rev. Great
   Curassow   15.00

7. 5 Dollars (C-N) 1974- . Rev. Keelbilled
   toucan   7.50

8. 1 Dollar (C-N) 1974- . Rev. Scarlet
   macaws   3.50

9. 50 Cents (C-N) 1974. Rev. Birds in flight   1.50
9a. 50 Cents (C-N) 1975-   (value stated as
    numeral)   1.50

10. 25 Cents (C-N) 1974. Rev. Bird on branch   1.00
10a. 25 Cents (C-N) 1975- (value stated as
     numeral)   1.00

11. 10 Cents (C-N) 1974. Rev. Bird on branch   .50
11a. 10 Cents (C-N) 1975- (value stated as
     numeral)   .50

BELIZE (continued)

12. 5 Cents (N-Bra) 1974. Rev. Two birds on
     branch   .25
12a. 5 Cents (N-Bra) 1975- (value stated as
     numeral)   .25

13. 1 Cent (Br) 1974. Rev. Birds in flight   .15
13a. 1 Cent (Br) 1975- (value stated as
     numeral)   .15

14. 100 Dollars (G) 1975. Arms. Rev. National
    Assembly Building   75.00

BERMUDA

Off the Carolina coast of the United States,
Bermuda is made up of some 300 islands discovered about 1510 by Juan de Bermudez and settled
by the British a century later.

1. 1 Penny (Bro) 1793. Bust of George III.
    Rev. Three-masted fighting ship of the
    line   40.00

2. 1 Crown (C-N) 1959. Crowned head of
    Elizabeth II. Rev. Map and ships
    (350th anniversary of founding of
    colony)   20.00

3. 1 Crown 1964. Head of Elizabeth II.
    Rev. Lion supporting Bermuda arms   5.00

BERMUDA (continued)

DECIMAL COINAGE

10. 1 Dollar 1972. Commemorates English royalty silver wedding anniversary — 7.50

11. 20 Dollars (G) 1970. Rev. Seagull — 400.00

4. 1 Dollar 1970. New portrait of Queen with coronet. Rev. Map of Bermuda (struck in proof only) — 20.00

5. 50 Cents (CN) 1970- . Rev. Lion supporting arms — 1.25

12. 100 Dollars (G) 1975. Rev. Royal monograms and Parliamentary Mace (Commemorates royal visit) — 140.00

6. 25 Cents (CN) 1970- . Rev. Bird of Spring — .70
7. 10 Cents (CN) 1970- . Rev. Bermuda lilies — .35

8. 5 Cents (CN) 1970- . Rev. Angelfish — .25
9. 1 Cent (Br) 1970- . Rev. Wild hog — .15

13. 25 Dollars 1975 — 40.00

BHUTAN

Located in the eastern Himalayas, Bhutan was formerly a protectorate of British India, but now has complete control of both domestic and foreign affairs.

1. ½ Rupee 1928. Bust of Maharajah. Rev. Eight lucky Buddhist symbols with inscription in center   25.00
2. ½ Rupee (N) 1928, 50   6.00
3. 1 Paisa (Br) 1928   35.00

4. 1 Paisa (Bro) 1951. Eight Buddhist symbols. Rev. Symbols   2.00

DECIMAL COINAGE
100 Paisa (Chetrums) = 1 Rupee (Ngultrum)
100 Rupees = 1 Sertum

5. 5 Sertums (G) 1966. Bust of Maharajah. Rev. Arms (Commemorates 40th anniversary of reign)   350.00
6. 2 Sertums (G) 1966   200.00
7. 1 Sertum (G) 1966   125.00
8. 3 Rupees (C-N) 1966   6.00
8a. 3 Rupees 1966 (silver proof issue)   40.00
9. 1 Rupee (C-N) 1966   1.50
10. 50 Naya Paisa (C-N) 1966   1.00
11. 25 Naya Paisa (C-N) 1966   .50

12. 1 Sertum (G) 1970   75.00

13. 15 Ngultrum 1974. Farmer cultivating rice. Rev. Arms (F.A.O. coin plan)   6.00

14. 1 Ngultrum (C-N) 1974. Bust of Maharajah. Rev. Thunderbolt within cross, ribbons, value   .75

15. 25 Chetrums (C-N) 1974. Rev. Two fish with ribbons, value   .50
16. 20 Chetrums (A-Br) 1974. Type of #13 (F.A.O. coin plan)   .30

17. 10 Chetrums (A) 1974. Rev. Buddhist symbol with ribbons, value (scalloped planchet)   .25
18. 5 Chetrums (A) 1974. Rev. Buddhist wheel of life   .15

BIAFRA

In 1967 the eastern region of Nigeria proclaimed itself the independent nation of Biafra. This sparked a war which lasted nearly three years, ending with the surrender of the Biafran forces in 1971.

1. 2½ Shillings (A) 1969. Coconut palm. Rev. Lion   7.00

2. 1 Shilling (A) 1969. Rev. Eagle on elephant tusk   6.00

3. 3 Pence (A) 1969. Rev. Value   12.50

BOLIVIA

Once part of the Inca empire, Bolivia was a Spanish colony for three centuries. Gaining independence in 1825, the new colony was named for Simón Bolívar, the famed Liberator.

Early issues of the Spanish colony bear the name of the reigning Spanish monarch. The designs are similar to those of other Spanish-American mints. The Potosí mint mark appears in monogram or with the name spelled out in full. Early planchets are irregular in form and crudely engraved.

The famous and legendary gold doubloons, issued from 1772 to 1820, bear the head of the reigning Spanish monarch and are valued at $200.00. Many of them are from the Potosí mint.

8 Reales (Sueldos) = 1 Peso or Piece-of-Eight
100 Centavos = 1 Boliviano

1791 gold doubloon (8 escudos)

PHILIP IV 1621-65

1. 8 Reales 1651-61. Shield and Quartered arms. Rev. Pillars   85.00

2. 2 Reales 1652-64   35.00
3. 1 Real 1652-64   20.00

CHARLES II 1665-1700

4. 8 Reales 1676-94   70.00

5.	4 Reales 1692	45.00
6.	2 Reales 1665-94	20.00
7.	1 Real 1671-89	9.00

PHILIP V 1700-46

8.	8 Reales 1723-38	65.00
9.	2 Reales 1703-42	20.00

10.	1 Real 1733-41	9.00

FERDINAND VI 1746-59

11.	8 Reales 1746-59	50.00
12.	4 Reales 1749-54	28.00
13.	2 Reales 1750-58	11.00
14.	1 Real 1752-59	8.00

CHARLES III 1759-88

First coinage: same as preceding type (shield and arms.)

15.	8 Reales 1760-73	45.00
16.	4 Reales 1767-69	25.00
17.	2 Reales 1763-76	8.00
18.	1 Real 1763	6.00

Second coinage: Crowned arms. Rev. Globes between Pillars. Mint mark appears as monogram in legend.

19.	8 Reales 1767-70	125.00

20.	4 Reales 1767-70	100.00
21.	2 Reales 1768-70	20.00
22.	1 Real 1767-70	28.00

Third coinage: Laureate bust to right. Rev. Crowned arms between pillars.

23.	8 Reales 1774-89	26.00

24.	4 Reales 1773-89	24.00
25.	2 Reales 1773-89	7.25
26.	1 Real 1773-89	6.00
27.	½ Real 1773-89	6.00

CHARLES IV 1788-1808

28.	8 Reales 1789, 90. Bust of Charles III	40.00
29.	4 Reales 1789	55.00
30.	2 Reales 1789, 90	10.50
31.	1 Real 1789, 90	8.00
32.	½ Real 1790	8.00

33.	8 Reales 1791-1808. Bust of Charles IV	20.00
34.	4 Reales 1791-1808	20.00
35.	2 Reales 1791-1808	6.50
36.	1 Real 1791-1808	6.00
37.	½ Real 1791-1808	4.75
38.	¼ Real 1796-1808. Castle. Rev. Lion	10.00

FERDINAND VII 1808-25

39.	8 Reales 1808-25. Draped bust	18.00
40.	4 Reales 1808-25	24.00
41.	2 Reales 1808-25	7.25
42.	1 Real 1816-25	6.00

43.	½ Real 1816-25	4.75
44.	¼ Real 1809-25. Castle. Rev. Lion	10.00

REPUBLICA BOLIVIANA 1825-

45. 8 Sueldos 1827-40. Uniformed bust of
    Bolivar. Rev. Tree between two llamas   20.00
46. 4 Sueldos 1827-30   8.00
47. 2 Sueldos 1827-30   6.00

69. 50 Centavos (C-N) 1939; (Bro) 1942.
    Native scene. Rev. Caduceus   .50
70. 20 Centavos (Z) 1942   1.50
71. 10 Centavos (C-N) 1893-1919, 35, 37, 39;
    (Z) 1942   .75
72. 5 Centavos (C-N) 1893-1919, 35   .50

48. 1 Sueldo 1827-30   6.50
49. ½ Sueldo 1827-30   7.25

NEW STANDARD

50. 8 Sueldos 1848-51. Bare head of Bolivar   30.00
51. 8 Sueldos 1852-59. Laureated head of
    Bolivar   20.00
52. 4 Sueldos 1853-59   7.00
53. 2 Sueldos 1854-59   8.00
54. 1 Sueldo 1854-57   10.00
55. ½ Sueldo 1853-59   4.00
56. ¼ Sueldo 1852, 53. Llama. Rev. Mountain   15.00
57. 1 Peso 1859-63. Weight 400 grains   14.00
58. ½ Peso 1860. Weight 200 grains   45.00
59. ¼ Peso 1859-63. Weight 100 grains   6.00
60. ⅛ Peso 1859-63. Weight 50 grains   6.00
61. 1/16 Peso 1859-63. Weight 25 grains   4.75

73. 10 Bolivianos (Bro) 1951. Bolivar head   2.00

74. 5 Bolivianos (Bro) 1951. Arms   .75

DECIMAL COINAGE
100 Centavos = 1 Boliviano

75. 1 Boliviano (Bro) 1951. Native scene   .75

CURRENCY REVALUATION

1 Peso Boliviano = 1,000 Old Bolivianos

76.   1 Peso Boliviano (Ni-St) 1968- . Arms.
    Rev. Value   .75

62. 1 Boliviano 1864-79. Shield of arms.
    Rev. Value in wreath   15.00
63. 50 Centavos 1873-1909   8.00
64. 20 Centavos [⅕ Boliviano] (S) 1864-66,
    70, 1904, 09   3.00
65. 10 Centavos [1/10 Boliviano] (S) 1864-67,
    70-1900; (C-N) 1883, 1892   2.00
66. 5 Centavos [1/20 Boliviano] (S) 1864, 65,
    71-1900; (C-N) 1883, 1892   3.00
67. 2 Centavos (C) 1878, 83   4.50
68. 1 Centavo (C) 1878, 83   2.50

77. 50 Centavos (N-St) 1965-. Arms. Rev.
    Value   .50
78. 20 Centavos (N-St) 1965-   .25
79. 10 Centavos (C-St) 1965-   .20
80. 5 Centavos (C-St) 1965-   .15

BOLIVIA (continued)

81. 1 Peso Boliviano (Ni-St) 1968. Native
    scene. Rev. Value (F.A.O. coin plan) 10.00
82. 25 Centavos (C-N) 1971, 1972. Native
    scene. Rev. Value (12-sided planchet) .35

83. 500 Pesos Boliviano 1975. Conjoined heads
    of Bolivar and President Banzer. Rev.
    Arms
84. 250 Pesos Bolivianos 1975
85. 100 Pesos Bolivianos 1975

BOTSWANA

Formerly the British Protectorate called Bechuana-
land, landlocked within South Africa, Botswana
became an independent state on September 30, 1966.
It is a member of the British Commonwealth.

1. 50 cents 1966. Head of Seretse Khama.
   Rev. Arms   10.00
2. 10 Thebe (G) 1966   100.00

3. 25 Thebe (C-N) 1976. Brahma bull (F.A.O.
   coin plan)
4. 10 Thebe (C-N) 1976
5. 5 Thebe (Br) 1976
6. 1 Thebe (A) 1976

BRAZIL

The largest country in South America, with an area slightly greater than that of the U.S.A. Discovered in 1500 by Pedro Alvares Cabral, Brazil remained a Portuguese colony until 1822, when it declared its independence and became an empire. In 1889 the emperor was deposed and Brazil became a republic.

Issues of the colonial era bear the name of the reigning Portuguese monarch.

1000 Reis = 1 Milreis

COLONIAL COINAGE

1. 960 Reis 1809-18, 1818-22   16.00
2. 640 Reis 1695-1701, 1749-68, 1787-1805, 1809-22. Crowned arms of Portugal. Rev. Globe and cross   14.00

3. 320 Reis 1695-1701, 1749-68, 1783-1802, 1809-21   11.00
4. 160 Reis 1695-99, 1751-73, 1779-90, 1810-21   18.00
5. 80 Reis (S) 1696-99, 1751-71, 1787-96, (C) 1811-18   8.00
6. 40 Reis (C) 1694-99, 1715-99, 1802-18   6.00
7. 20 Reis (C) 1694-99, 1715-99, 1802-18   4.75
8. 10 Reis (C) 1695-97, 1715-99, 1802-18   4.00
9. 5 Reis (C) 1753-91   4.00

10. Counterstamped Dollar. Portuguese arms and value counterstamped on both sides of Spanish dollars from the various American mints   50.00

EMPIRE OF BRAZIL 1822-1889
PEDRO I 1822-1831

11. 80 Reis (C) 1823-31. Value in wreath. Rev. Crowned arms   6.00
12. 40 Reis (C) 1823-31   3.25
13. 20 Reis (C) 1823-30   3.25
14. 10 Reis (C) 1824-28   7.25

PEDRO II 1831-1889

15. 2000 Reis 1851-89   18.00
16. 1000 Reis 1849-89   6.50

17. 500 Reis 1849-89   4.00

BRAZIL (continued)

18. 200 Reis (S) 1854-69; (N) 1871-89   2.00
19. 100 Reis (N) 1871-89   1.50
20. 50 Reis (N) 1886-88   3.00

REPUBLIC OF BRAZIL 1889-

21. 2000 Reis 1906-34. Liberty head with cap. Rev. Value in wreath   5.00
22. 1000 Reis (S) 1889, 1906-13; (A-Bro) 1924-31   2.00

23. 500 Reis (S) 1889, 1906-13; (A-Bro) 1924-30   1.50
24. 400 Reis (C-N) 1901, 1918-35. Liberty Head type   1.25

25. 200 Reis (C-N) 1889-1901, 1918-35   .75
26. 100 Reis (C-N) 1889-1901, 1918-35   .75
27. 50 Reis (C-N) 1918-31   .75
28. 40 Reis (Bro) 1889-1912   1.00
29. 20 Reis (Bro) 1889-1912   1.00

FOURTH CENTENNIAL OF DISCOVERY
(an issue of outstanding interest)

30. 4000 Reis 1900. Pedro Alvarez Cabral, explorer   400.00

31. 2000 Reis 1900   85.00

32. 1000 Reis 1900   50.00

33. 400 Reis 1900   35.00

BRAZIL (continued)

CENTENNIAL OF INDEPENDENCE

41. 200 Reis (C-N) 1932. Globe. Rev. Ship   3.50

34. 2 Milreis 1922. Dom Pedro and Pres. Pessoa. Rev. Shields of the Empire and Republic   4.50
35. 1 Milreis (A-Br) 1922. Rev. Torch, crown and liberty cap   2.50
36. 500 Reis (A-Br) 1922   1.25

42. 100 Reis (C-N) 1932. Bust of Cazique Tiberica   3.00

FOURTH CENTENNIAL OF COLONIZATION

CELEBRATED MEN SERIES

37. 2000 Reis 1932. Bust of John III   6.00

43. 5000 Reis 1936-38. Santos Dumont   4.50

38. 1000 Reis (A-Bro) 1932. Da Sousa   4.50

44. 2000 Reis 1935. Caxias facing left   3.50
44a. 2000 Reis (A-Br) 1936-38. Caxias facing right   3.00

39. 500 Reis (A-Bro) 1932. Bust of Ramalho   10.00

45. 1000 Reis (A-Bro) 1935-38. Father Anchieta   1.50

40. 400 Reis (C-N) 1932. Map of South America   4.00

46. 500 Reis (A-Bro) 1935-38. Feijo   2.50

47. 400 Reis (C-N) 1936-38. Cruz   2.00

48. 300 Reis (C-N) 1936-38. Gomes   2.00

49. 200 Reis (C-N) 1936-38. Maua   2.00

50. 100 Reis (C-N) 1936-38. Tamandare   1.50

NEW GOVERNMENT

51. 2000 Reis (A-Bro) 1939. Marshal Peixoto   4.00

52. 1000 Reis (A-Bro) 1939. Tobias Barreto   4.00

53. 500 Reis (A-Bro) 1939. Machado de Assis   2.50

54. 400 Reis (C-N) 1938-42. Bust of President Vargas   1.00
55. 300 Reis (C-N) 1938-42   .50
56. 200 Reis (C-N) 1938-42   .60
57. 100 Reis (C-N) 1938-42   .50

NEW MONETARY STANDARD 1942

(100 Centavos = 1 Cruzeiro)

58. 5 Cruzeiros (A-Bro) 1942, 43. Map of Brazil   2.50

59. 2 Cruzeiros (A-Bro) 1942-56   1.25
60. 1 Cruzeiro (A-Bro) 1942-56   1.00

61. 50 Centavos (C-N) 1942-43; (A-Bro) 1943-47. Bust of President Vargas   .75
62. 20 Centavos (C-N) 1942-43; (A-Bro) 1943-48   .50
63. 10 Centavos (C-N) 1942-43; (A-Bro) 1943-47   .35

64. 50 Centavos (A-Bro) 1948-56. President Dutra. Rev. Value   .60

BRAZIL (continued)

65. 20 Centavos (A-Bro) 1948-56. Rui Barbosa   .50

66. 10 Centavos (A-Bro) 1947-55. Jose Bonifacio   .40

67. 2 Cruzeiros (A-Bro) 1956; (A) 1957-61 Star. Rev. Value   .75
68. 1 Cruzeiro (A-Bro) 1956; (A) 1957-61   .75
69. 50 Centavos (A-Bro) 1956; (A) 1957-61   .40
70. 20 Centavos (A) 1956-61   .40
71. 10 Centavos (A) 1956-61   .25

72. 50 Cruzeiros (C-N) 1965- . Liberty head. Rev. Value   .75

73. 20 Cruzeiros (Al) 1965- . Map   .40
74. 10 Cruzeiros (Al) 1965   .25

CURRENCY REVALUATION

1 New Cruzeiro = 1,000 Old Cruzeiros

75. 1 Cruzeiro (N) 1970; (C-N) 1975- . Head of Brazilia. Rev. Floral spray   2.00

76. 50 Centavos (N) 1967; (C-N) 1970- . Rev. Ship   1.50
77. 20 Centavos (CN) 1967, 70; (St) 1975. Rev. Oil derrick   .40
78. 10 Centavos (CN) 1967, 70; (St) 1974   .25
79. 5 Centavos (St) 1967, 69. Rev. Value   .25
80. 2 Centavos (St) 1967, 69   .15
81. 1 Centavo (St) 1967, 69   .10

82. 300 Cruzeiros (G) 1972. Faces of Pedro I, first ruler of Brazil, and General Emilio Garrastazu Medici, current president. Rev. Map (Commemorates 150th anniversary of independence)   200.00
83. 20 Cruzeiros 1972   10.00
84. 1 Cruzeiro (N) 1972   1.50

85. 5 Centavos (St) 1975. Head of Brazilia. Rev. Cow (F.A.O. coin plan)   .15
86. 2 Centavos (St) 1975. Rev. Soja tree (F.A.O. coin plan)   .10
87. 1 Centavo (St) 1975. Rev. Sugar plant (F.A.O. coin plan)   .10

BRITISH CARIBBEAN TERRITORIES

Made up of Windward and Leeward Islands, Trinidad and Tobago, Jamaica, and Barbados, this was strictly a monetary grouping, with no political significance. The unified currency ceased with the establishment of the Eastern Caribbean Territories in 1965.

ELIZABETH II 1952-

1. 50 Cents (C-N) 1955. Crowned head. Rev. Britannia above arms of territories   4.00

2. 25 Cents (C-N) 1955-65. Rev. "Golden Hind"   1.25
3. 10 Cents (C-N) 1955-65   .75
4.   5 Cents (N-Bra) 1955-65   1.50

5.   2 Cents (Bro) 1955-65. Rev. Value in wreath   .60
6.   1 Cent (Bro) 1955-65   .50

7. ½ Cent (Bro) 1955-58. Rev. Value   1.50

BRITISH GUIANA

British Crown Colony on the northeastern coast of South America since the seventeenth century; rich in diamond and aluminum deposits. Coins bear the image of the reigning British monarch. Since 1966 it has been an independent state (as GUYANA).

20 Stivers = 1 Guilder
2 Guilders = 1 Shilling
50 Pence = 1 British Guiana Dollar

GEORGE III 1760-1820

1. 3 Guilders 1809, 16. Laureate bust. Rev. Crowned value   350.00

2. 2 Guilders 1809, 16   200.00
3. 1 Guilder 1809, 16   55.00
4. ½ Guilder 1809, 16   50.00
5. ¼ Guilder 1809, 16   20.00

6. 1 Stiver (C) 1813   12.00
7. ½ Stiver (C) 1813   10.00

WILLIAM IV 1830-37

8. 3 Guilders 1832. Bust   450.00
9. 2 Guilders 1832   300.00
10. 1 Guilder 1832, 35, 36 (Coins minted in 1836 bear inscription BRITISH GUIANA on reverse)   45.00
11. ½ Guilder 1832, 35, 36   40.00
12. ¼ Guilder 1832, 35, 36   20.00
13. ⅛ Guilder 1832, 35, 36   15.00

VICTORIA 1837-1901

14. 4 Pence 1891 - 1901. Head. Rev. Value   4.75

EDWARD VII 1901-10

15. 4 Pence 1903, 1908-10. Crowned bust. Rev. Value   8.00

GEORGE V 1910-36

16. 4 Pence 1911, 13, 16-31, 36. Crowned bust. Rev. Value   5.00

GEORGE VI 1936-52

17. 4 Pence 1938-45. Crowned head. Rev. Value   2.00

BRITISH HONDURAS

A British Crown Colony in Central America, British Honduras changed its name to Belize in 1973.

100 Cents = 1 British Honduras Dollar

VICTORIA 1837-1901

1. 50 Cents 1894-1901. Diademed head. Rev.
    Value in double circle 20.00
2. 25 Cents 1894-1901 .... 10.00
3. 10 Cents 1894 .... 12.00
4. 5 Cents 1894 .... 10.00
5. 1 Cent (Br) 1885-94 .... 9.00

EDWARD VII 1901-10

6. 50 Cents 1906-07. Crowned bust. Rev.
    Type of #1 .... 40.00
7. 25 Cents 1906-07 .... 20.00

8. 5 Cents (C-N) 1907-09 .... 35.00
9. 1 Cent (Bro) 1904, 06, 09 .... 30.00

GEORGE V 1910-36

10. 50 Cents 1911-19. Crowned bust. Rev.
    Type of #1 .... 24.00
11. 25 Cents 1911-19 .... 13.00
12. 10 Cents 1918-19, 36 .... 8.00
13. 5 Cents (C-N) 1911-19, 36. Rev. Type of #8 .... 6.00
14. 1 Cent (Bro) 1911-13 .... 90.00
15. 1 Cent (Bro) 1914-36. Rev. Value in or-
    namental wreath, type of #19 .... 8.00

GEORGE VI 1936-52

(Coins after 1947 drop EMPEROR OF INDIA legend)

16. 10 Cents 1939-46. Crowned head. Rev.
    Type of #1 .... 4.00
17. 25 Cents (C-N) 1952 .... 4.00
18. 5 Cents (C-N) 1939; (N-Bra) 42-47 .... 5.00
18a. 5 Cents (N-Bra) 1949-52. Crowned head.
    Rev. Value 2.00

19. 1 Cent (Bro) 1937-51 .... 2.00

ELIZABETH II 1952-

20. 50 Cents (C-N) 1954-71. Head. Rev. Value 2.00
21. 25 Cents (C-N) 1955-73 .... 1.00
22. 10 Cents (C-N) 1956-70 .... .50
23. 5 Cents (N-Bra) 1956-73 .... .35

24. 1 Cent (Bro) 1954 (round edge). 2.00

24a. 1 Cent (Bro) 1956-73. (scalloped edge) .... .25

BRITISH VIRGIN ISLANDS

These 36 islands in the Caribbean Sea were formerly part of the Leeward Islands. In 1956 they became a separate crown colony.

5. 5 Cents (C-N) 1973- . Rev. Zenaida doves ..... .25
6. 1 Cent (Br) 1973- . Rev. Carib and hummingbird ..... .15

7. 100 Dollars (G) 1975. Queen Elizabeth II. Rev. Royal tern 135.00

1. 1 Dollar 1973-74. Queen Elizabeth II. Rev. Frigate birds 8.00
1a. 1 Dollar (C-N) 1974- 7.00

2. 50 Cents (C-N) 1973- . Rev. Pelicans 1.50

3. 25 Cents (C-N) 1973- . Rev. Mangrove cuckoos ..... .50
4. 10 Cents (C-N) 1973- . Rev. Ringed kingfisher ..... .35

BRITISH WEST AFRICA

Formerly made up of British Cameroons, British Togoland, Gambia, Gold Coast, Nigeria, and Sierra Leone, which have all become independent states. Part of the Cameroons joined the former French Cameroun in the Federal Republic of Cameroun; the Gold Coast and British Togoland became the Republic of Ghana. Nigeria absorbed the balance of Togoland.

12 Pence = 1 Shilling

EDWARD VII 1901-10

1.	1 Penny (C-N) 1907-10 (Center hole). Six-pointed star. Rev. Crowned value	4.00
2.	1/10 Penny (A) 1907-08	5.00
2a.	1/10 Penny (C-N) 1908-10	2.00

GEORGE V 1910-36

3.	2 Shillings 1913-20. Crowned bust. Rev. Palm tree	6.00
3a.	2 Shillings (Bra) 1920-28, 36.	4.50
4.	1 Shilling 1913-20	4.00
4a.	1 Shilling (Bra) 1920-28, 36	3.00
5.	6 Pence 1913-20. Rev. Value in wreath	4.75
5a.	6 Pence (Bra) 1920-36.	4.75
6.	3 Pence 1913-20	4.00
6a.	3 Pence (Bra) 1920-36	2.00

7.	1 Penny (C-N) 1911. Type of #1	45.00
7a.	1 Penny (C-N) 1912-36	4.00
8.	1/2 Penny (C-N) 1911	20.00
8a.	1/2 Penny (C-N) 1912-36	3.00

9.	1/10 Penny (C-N) 1911	5.00
9a.	1/10 Penny (N) 1912-36	1.50

EDWARD VIII 1936

10.	1 Penny (C-N)1936. Type of #1	2.00

11.	1/2 Penny (C-N)1936	1.50
12.	1/10 Penny (C-N)1936	1.00

GEORGE VI 1936-52
(Coins issued after 1948 drop "IND. IMP." from legend.)

13.	2 Shillings (N-Bra) 1938-48. Crowned head. Rev. Type of #3	3.50
13a.	2 Shillings (N-Bra) 1949-52	6.00
14.	1 Shilling (N-Bra) 1938-48	2.50
14.	1 Shilling (N-Bra) 1949-52	1.75

15.	6 Pence (Bra) 1938-47, 52	2.50
16.	3 Pence (C-N) 1938-48	1.50
17.	1 Penny (C-N) 1937-47. Type of #1	1.00
17a.	1 Penny (C-N) 1951	25.00
18.	1/2 Penny (C-N) 1937-47	1.00
18a.	1/2 Penny (C-N) 1949-51	7.50
19.	1/10 Penny (C-N) 1938-47	1.25
19a.	1/10 Penny (C-N) 1949-50	4.00
20.	1 Penny (Br) 1952. Type of #1	.75
21.	1/2 Penny (Br) 1952	1.00
22.	1/10 Penny (Br) 1952	2.50

ELIZABETH II 1952-

23.	3 Pence (C-N) 1957. Head. Rev. Value	35.00
24.	1 Penny (Bro) 1956-58.	3.00

25.	1/10 Penny (Bro) 1954-57. (Center hole).	1.25

BRUNEI

A self-governing sultanate situated in northwest Borneo, between Sabah and Sarawak, Brunei's external affairs and defense are the responsibility of the British Government. Brunei remained outside the Federation of Malaysia when Sabah and Sarawak joined in 1963, but used Malaysian coins.

1. 50 Sen (CN) 1967. Head of Sultan Omar Ali Saifuddin III. Rev. Ornamental design 1.25

2. 20 Sen (CN) 1967 ..... .85
3. 10 Sen (CN) 1967 ..... .50

4. 5 Sen (CN) 1967 ..... .25
5. 1 Sen (Br) 1967 ..... .20

6. 50 Sen (CN) 1968- . Head of Sultan Hassanal Bolkiah. Rev. Native ornament ..... .75
7. 20 Sen (CN) 1968- ..... .50
8. 10 Sen (CN) 1968- ..... .30
9. 5 Sen (CN) 1968- ..... .20
10. 1 Sen (Br) 1968- ..... .15

11. 1 Dollar (C-N) 1970. Rev. Cannon 20.00

BULGARIA

Bulgaria was a Turkish province up to the Russo-Turkish War, which resulted in Bulgaria's liberation in 1877. After World War II, this Balkan kingdom became a People's Republic.

100 Stotinki = 1 Lev

ALEXANDER II 1879-86

1.	5 Leva 1884-85. Crowned arms. Rev. Value in wreath	15.00
2.	2 Leva 1882	5.00
3.	1 Lev 1882	2.50
4.	50 Stotinki 1883	2.50
5.	10 Stotinki (C) 1881	3.00
6.	5 Stotinki (C) 1881	4.00
7.	2 Stotinki (C) 1881	5.00

FERDINAND I 1887-1918

8.	20 Leva (G) 1912 (25-year Jubilee). Head. Rev. Arms	125.00
9.	5 Leva 1892, 94. Head. Rev. Value in wreath	15.00

10.	2 Leva 1891-94, 1912-13	4.75

10a.	2 Leva 1910. Head right	3.75
11.	1 Lev 1891-94, 1912-13	4.50
11a.	1 Lev 1910. Head right	4.00

12.	50 Stotinki 1891, 1912-13	2.00
12a.	50 Stotinki 1910. Head right	3.50

13.	20 Stotinki (C-N) 1888, 1906-13. Crowned arms. Rev. Value in wreath	2.00
14.	10 Stotinki (C-N) 1888, 1906-13	1.50
15.	5 Stotinki (C-N) 1888, 1906-13	1.00
16.	2½ Stotinki (C-N) 1888	4.00
17.	2 Stotinki (Bro) 1901, 12	1.00
18.	1 Stotinki (Bro) 1901, 12	1.25

BORIS III 1918-43

19.	100 Leva 1930-37. Head. Rev. Value	8.50
20.	50 Leva (S) 1930-34; (C-N) 40	4.00
21.	20 Leva (S) 1930; (C-N) 40	2.50

22.	10 Leva (C-N) 1930. Cavalier of Madara. Rev. Value in wreath	2.00
23.	5 Leva (C-N) 1930	1.50

24.	2 Leva (A) 1923; (C-N)1925. Arms on mantle. Rev. Value in wreath	.75
25.	1 Leva (A) 1923; (C-N)1925	.60
26.	50 Stotinki (A-Bro) 1937	.50

SIMEON II 1943-46

27. 10 Leva (I) 1943. Arms. Rev. Value in wreath   1.50
28. 5 Leva (I) 1943   2.00

29. 2 Leva (I) 1943-   1.50

COMMUNIST ISSUES

30. 1 Lev (C-N) 1960. Arms. Rev. Value   1.50
31. 50 Stotinki (C-N) 1959. Arms. Rev. Value 1.00
32. 25 Stotinki (C-N) 1951-   .75
33. 20 Stotinki (C-N) 1952-   .50
34. 10 Stotinki (C-N) 1951-   .40
35. 5 Stotinki (Bra) 1951-   .30
36. 3 Stotinki (Bra) 1951-   .25
37. 1 Stotinka (Bra) 1951   .20
38. 1 Lev (Ni-Bra) 1962. Arms. Rev. Value   1.75
39. 50 Stotinki (Ni-Bra) 1962   1.00
40. 20 Stotinki (Ni-Bra) 1962   .50
41. 10 Stotinki (Ni-Bra) 1962   .40
42. 5 Stotinki (Bra) 1962   .25
43. 2 Stotinki (Bra) 1962   .20
44. 1 Stotinka (Bra) 1962   .15

45. 5 Leva 1963. Saint Cyril and Saint Methodius. Rev. Value (Commemorates 1,100th anniversary of Cyrillic script and Slavonic alphabet)   15.00

46.

46. 5 Leva 1964. Head of Georgi Dimitrov, former Premier. Rev. Flag above value (Commemorates 20th anniversary of republic)   12.50

47. 2 Leva (CN) 1966. Robed figure. Rev. Ancient pillars (Commemorates 1050th anniversary of death of scholar Kliment Ochridsky)   3.50

48. 2 Leva (CN) 1969. Liberty monument. Rev. Value (Commemorates 25th anniversary of Socialist Revolution)   3.00

49. 1 Lev (CN) 1969. Guerilla fighter's monument   1.50

50. 2 Leva (CN) 1969. Battle scene, defense of Shipka Pass. Rev. Value (Commemorates 90th anniversary of liberation from the Turks)   3.00

51. 1 Lev (CN) 1969. Czar Alexander II monument   1.50

55. 2 Leva (C-N) 1972. Head of Dobri Chintulov. Rev. Value (Commemorates 150th anniversary of scholar's birth)   3.00

52. 5 Leva 1970 Arms. Rev. Head of Ivan Vazov (Commemorates 120th anniversary of writer's death)   8.50

56. 5 Leva 1973. Head of Wassil Lewski. Rev. Arms, value (Commemorates 100th anniversary of patriot's death)   12.00

57. 5 Leva 1973. Figures with flag. Rev. Arms (Commemorates 30th anniversary of antifascist uprising)   12.00

53. 5 Leva 1971. Head of Georgi Rakowski. Rev. Value (Commemorates 150th anniversary of birth of patriot, revolutionary writer)   12.00

58. 5 Leva 1974. Head of Alexander Stambulijski. Rev. Arms (Commemorates 50th anniversary of politician's death   15.00

54. 5 Leva 1972. Paissii Chilendarski holding open book. Rev. Arms, value (Commemorates 250th anniversary of historian's birth)   12.00

59. 5 Leva 1974. Two soldiers. Rev. Arms (Commemorates 30th anniversary of Socialist Revolution)   12.50

The British administered Burma as a part of India up to 1937, when they gave Burma self-government as far as internal affairs were concerned. During World War II, Burma was overrun by the Japanese, and in 1948 became a completely independent republic.

16 Annas = 1 Rupee
100 Pyas = 1 Kyat or Tical

MINDON MIN 1852-78

1.	1 Rupee 1852. Peacock. Rev. Value in wreath	20.00
2.	½ Rupee 1852	15.00
3.	¼ Rupee 1852	17.50
4.	⅛ Rupee 1852	20.00
5.	1/16 Rupee 1852	25.00

REPUBLIC 1948-

6.	8 Annas (N) 1949-50. Lion. Rev. Value in wreath	7.00

7.	4 Annas (N) 1949-50	4.00
8.	2 Annas C-N) 1949-51 (Square-shaped)	2.00

9.	1 Anna (C-N) 1949-51 (Scalloped-edge)	1.50
10.	½ Anna (C-N) 1949 (Square-shaped)	.75

11.	1 Kyat (C-N) 1952- (Round)	4.00
12.	50 Pyas (C-N) 1952-66	2.00

13.	25 Pyas (C-N) 1952-65 (Scalloped planchet)	1.00
14.	10 Pyas (C-N) 1952-65 (Square-shaped)	.50
15.	5 Pyas (C-N)1952-66 (Scalloped edge)	.40
16.	1 Pya (Bro) 1952-66 (Round)	.35

17.	50 Pyas (Al) 1966. Head of Gen. Aung San. Rev. Value in wreath	1.50

18.	25 Pyas (Al) 1966 (Scalloped edge)	.75
19.	10 Pyas (Al) 1966 (Square-shaped)	.50
20.	5 Pyas (Al) 1966 (Scalloped edge)	.35
21.	1 Pya (Al) 1966 (Round planchet)	.25

BURUNDI

Formerly part of the Belgian U.N. Trusteeship of Ruanda-Urundi, it became an independent kingdom in July, 1962. The republic was established in 1966.

MWAMBUTSA IV 1962-66

1.   Franc (Bra) 1965   1.00

REPUBLIC 1966-

2. 10 Francs (C-N) 1968, 71. Inscription. Rev. Value within circle of grain stalks (F.A.O. coin plan)   1.50

3.   5 Francs (Al) 1968-71. Inscription. Rev. Value 1.00

4.   1 Franc (A) 1970. Sunrise. Rev. Value   .60

CAMBODIA

Cambodia became an independent constitutional monarchy in 1953 after nearly a century of French control. In 1970 the monarchy fell and the Khmer Republic was established.

100 Centimes = 1 Franc

3.

1.   1 Piastre 1860. Head of King Norodom I. Rev. Arms and value   400.00
2.   4 Francs 1860   120.00
3.   2 Francs 1860   30.00
4.   1 Franc 1860   25.00
5. 50 Centimes 1860   15.00
6. 25 Centimes 1860   12.50
7. 10 Centimes (Br) 1860   6.00
8.   5 Centimes (Br) 1860   5.00

9. 50 Centimes (A-Mg) 1953. Royal emblems. Rev. Value in wreath   .75

10. 20 Centimes (A-Mg) 1953. Urn   .50
11. 10 Centimes (A-Mg) 1953. Bird   .35

DECIMAL COINAGE
100 Sen = 1 Riel

12. 50 Sen (A-Mg) 1959. Type of #9, new currency values   .60
13. 20 Sen (A-Mg) 1959. Type of #10   .30
14. 10 Sen (A-Mg) 1959. Type of #11   .20

A French Associated Territory on the west coast of Africa; originally mandated to France after World War I. In 1960 it achieved independence and in 1961 became the Federal Republic of Cameroun after being joined by part of the British Cameroons. It is associated with the French Community, and a member of the Equatorial African States monetary union.

100 Centimes = 1 Franc

1. 2 Francs (A-Bro) 1924-25. Liberty head. Rev. Value between sprays   3.50
2. 1 Franc (A-Bro) 1924-26   2.00
3. 50 Centimes (A-Bro) 1924-26   1.50

4. 1 Franc (A-Bro) 1943. Rooster. Rev. Cross of Lorraine   4.00
5. 50 Centimes (A-Bro) 1943   3.00

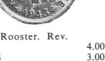

6. 2 Francs (A) 1948. Bust of the Republic. Rev. Antelope head   1.00
7. 1 Franc (A) 1948   .35

In 1958 the coinage was combined with that of French Equatorial Africa.

8. 25 Francs (A-Br) 1958. Three antelope heads. Rev. Value   1.00

9. 10 Francs (A-Br) 1958   .50
10. 5 Francs (A-Br) 1958   .35

INDEPENDENT STATE 1960

11. 50 Francs (A-Br) 1960. Three antelope heads. Rev. Value. ("1st Janvier" legend commemorates independence)   4.00

12. 100 Francs (N) 1966-68   2.75

13. 100 Francs (N) 1971, 72   2.50

14. 100 Francs (N) 1975

CANADA

After settling in Canada, the French waged a struggle of continental proportions with the British for control of the fur trade. Finally in 1763 Canada became a British colony. In 1867 it was made a Dominion of the British Empire with considerable powers of self-government. In 1926 Canada became a completely self-governing Dominion within the framework of the British Commonwealth of Nations.

Prior to the general Canadian issue of coinage in 1858 a number of private tokens were struck and some of the commoner types are shown below. Several provinces, New Brunswick, Newfoundland, Nova Scotia and Prince Edward Island, had their own coinages before they were incorporated into the Dominion of Canada (see separate listings for these coins).

As for issues of the Dominion, prices are given for the commonest date of each variety. Canadian coins are popularly collected by date. Consequently, many specific dates command prices higher than those quoted here. (See *Coin Collector's Handbook*.)

100 Cents = 1 Dollar

EARLY TOKENS

1. Penny token (Deux Sous) (C) 1837. Province du Bas Canada (Quebec)   4.00

2. Penny token (C) 1850-57. Bank of Upper Canada (Ontario)   2.50

3. Bouquet Sou (C) (undated) (issued 1835-37) 3.25

PROVINCE OF CANADA
VICTORIA 1837-1901

4.	20 Cents 1858. Head. Rev. Value	75.00
5.	10 Cents 1858	10.00
6.	5 Cents 1858	15.00
7.	1 Cent (Bro) 1858-59	2.50

DOMINION OF CANADA
VICTORIA 1837-1901

8.	50 Cents 1870-1901. Diademed head. Rev. Crowned value in wreath	50.00
9.	25 Cents 1870-1901	7.50
10.	10 Cents 1870-1901	10.00
11.	5 Cents 1870-1901	4.00

12.	1 Cent (Bro) 1876-1901. Rev. Value in dotted circle	1.50

EDWARD VII 1901-10

13.	50 Cents 1902-10. Crowned bust. Rev. Type of #8	25.00
14.	25 Cents 1902-10	10.00
15.	10 Cents 1902-10	8.00
16.	5 Cents 1902-10	1.50

17.	1 Cent (Bro) 1902-10. Rev. Type of #12	1.25

CANADA (continued)

GEORGE V 1910-36

18. 10 Dollars (G) 1912-14. Crowned bust.
Rev. Arms with maple leaves   325.00
19. 5 Dollars (G) 1912-14   200.00

20. 1 Dollar 1935 (Jubilee year). Rev. Voyageurs in canoe   30.00

21. 1 Dollar 1936 (Regular issue). Type of
#20 without commemorative inscription   25.00
22. 50 Cents 1911-36. Rev. Type of #8   7.50
23. 25 Cents 1911-36   4.00
24. 10 Cents 1911-36   2.00

25. 5 Cents 1911-21   1.25

26. 5 Cents (N) 1922-36   3.00
27. 1 Cent (Bro) 1911-20 (Large size). Rev.
Type of #12   1.00
28. 1 Cent (Bro) 1920-36 (Reduced size)   .75

GEORGE VI 1936-52

(Coins issued 1937-47 have the title "D.G. Rex
et Ind. Imp." Coins issued 1948-52 bear the title
"Dei Gratia Rex.")

29. 1 Dollar 1937-38, 45-52. Head of King
George. Rev. Voyageur and Indian in
canoe   7.50

30. 1 Dollar 1939. Head Rev. Parliament
buildings in Ottawa, legend FIDE
SVORVM REGNAT—"The King reigns
on the loyalty of his subjects." (Commemorates Royal visit of King George
VI and Queen Elizabeth)   12.50

31. 1 Dollar 1949. Head. Rev. Sailing ship
Matthew of discoverer John Cabot
(Commemorates Newfoundland's en-
trance into the Dominion)   20.00

32. 50 Cents 1937-52. Rev. Arms of Canada   2.50
33. 25 Cents 1937-52. Rev. Caribou head   2.00

34. 10 Cents 1937-52. Rev. Fishing schooner   1.00

35. 5 Cents (N) 1937-42, Rev. Beaver   1.25

36. 5 Cents (tombac-bra) 1942 (Twelve-sided). Type of #35   2.00
36a. 5 Cents (N) 1946-50; (St) 51-52.   .60

37. 5 Cents (Bra) 1943; (St) 44-45. Rev. Large "V" and torch with Morse Code motto: "We win when we work willingly"   1.00

38. 5 Cents (N) 1951 (Twelve-sided coin commemorating bicentennial of nickel industry). Rev. Refining plant over maple leaves   2.00

39. 1 Cent (Bro) 1937-52. Rev. Maple leaves   .35

ELIZABETH II 1952-

40. 1 Dollar 1953- . Head. Rev. Voyageurs   5.00

41. 50 Cents 1953-58. Rev. Arms of Canada   3.00
41a. 50 Cents 1959-64. New reverse   2.00
42. 25 Cents 1953-64. Rev. Caribou head   1.00
43. 10 Cents 1953-64. Rev. Fishing schooner   .50
44. 5 Cents (St) 1953-54. Rev. Beaver (twelve-sided)   1.50
44a. 5 Cents (N) 1955-62 (twelve-sided)   .30
44b. 5 Cents (N) 1963-64. (round planchet)   .15
45. 1 Cent (Br) 1953-64. Rev. Maple leaves   .10

46. 1 Dollar 1958. Head. Rev. Raven totem pole, Canadian Rockies in background (Commemorates 100th anniversary of British Columbia's entrance into the Dominion)   10.00

47. 1 Dollar 1964. Head. Rev. Floral emblems, fleur-de-lis, shamrock, thistle and rose—representing the four main nationality groups of Canada, French, Irish, Scotch and English (Commemorates 1864 conference of Fathers of the Confederation at Charlottetown, Prince Edward Island, which led to Confederation at Quebec Conference in 1867)   5.00

58. 10 Cents 1967. Rev. Mackerel .35
59. 5 Cents (N) 1967. Rev. Rabbit .15
60. 1 Cent (Br) 1967. Rev. Dove .10

48. 1 Dollar 1965, 66. New portrait of Queen
with coronet. Rev. Voyageurs 4.50
48a. 1 Dollar (N) 1968- (smaller planchet) 1.50
49. 50 Cents 1965, 66. Rev. Arms of Canada 2.00
49a. 50 Cents (N) 1968- (smaller planchet) .75
50. 25 Cents 1965-68. Rev. Caribou head 1.00
50a. 25 Cents (N) 1968- .40
51. 10 Cents 1965, 66; (50% S) 1968. Rev.
Fishing schooner .25
51a. 10 Cents (N) 1968 .20
51b. 10 Cents (N) 1969- . Rev. Redesigned,
smaller ship .20
52. 5 Cents (N) 1965- . Rev. Beaver .15
53. 1 Cent (Br) 1965- . Rev. Maple leaves .10

61. 1 Dollar (N) 1970. Rev. Crocus plant
(Commemorates Manitoba centennial) 1.75

54. 20 Dollars (G) 1967. Rev. Coat of arms
(Commemorates centennial of Confederation) 250.00

55. 1 Dollar 1967. Rev. Canada goose in
flight 6.00

62. 1 Dollar (N) 1971. Rev. Arms, dogwood
blossoms above. (Commemorates bicentennial of entry of British Columbia
into Confederation) 2.00
63. 1 Dollar 1971. Rev. Arms of British
Columbia (struck in size of pre-1968
silver dollars and sold as numismatic
item) 10.00

56. 50 Cents 1967. Rev. Howling wolf 3.00
57. 25 Cents 1967. Rev. Wildcat .75

64. 1 Dollar (N) 1973. Rev. Legislature building (Commemorates Prince Edward
Island bicentennial) 2.00

CANADA (continued)

65. 1 Dollar 1973. Rev. Officer of Royal Canadian Mounted Police on horseback (Commemorates 100th anniversary of R.C.M.P.) 7.50

66. 25 Cents (N) 1973. Rev. Royal Canadian Mounted Policeman in parade uniform, with banner 1.00

69. 5 Dollars 1973. Rev. Yachts, city of Kingston (Olympic commemorative) 8.50

70. 5 Dollars 1973. Rev. Map of North America, Canada highlighted (Olympic commemorative) 8.50

71. 10 Dollars 1974. Rev. Temple of Zeus (Olympic commemorative) 17.50

67. 10 Dollars 1973. Rev. Skyline of Montreal (Commemorates 1976 Olympic Games) 15.00

68. 10 Dollars 1973. Rev. World map, Canada highlighted (Olympic commemorative) 15.00

72. 10 Dollars 1974. Rev. Head of Zeus 17.50

73. 5 Dollars 1974. Rev. Laurel wreath and 5-ring Olympic symbol — 9.00
74. 5 Dollars 1974. Rev. Athlete holding Olympic torch — 9.00

78. 5 Dollars 1975. Rev. Oarsman — 8.00
79. 5 Dollars 1975. Rev. Indian paddling — 8.00

75. 1 Dollar 1974. Rev. Value, old and new city scenes (Commemorates 100th anniversary of founding of Winnipeg) — 7.25
75a. 1 Dollar (N) 1974 — 2.75

81. 10 Dollars 1975. Rev. Runner's head (men's hurdles, Olympic commemorative) — 17.50
82. 10 Dollars 1975. Rev. Female head (shotput) — 17.50

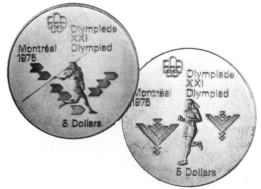

76. 10 Dollars 1975. Rev. Indians playing lacrosse (Olympic commemorative) — 17.50
77. 10 Dollars 1975. Rev. Cyclists — 17.50

83. 5 Dollars 1975. Rev. Female javelin thrower — 8.00
84. 5 Dollars 1975. Rev. Marathon runner — 8.00

90. 100 Dollars (G) 1976. Queen Elizabeth II.
    Rev. Athena with athlete   110.00

85. 10 Dollars 1975. Rev. Symbolic figure
    paddling (Olympic commemorative)   17.50
86. 10 Dollars 1975. Rev. Two abstract figures
    (sailing)   17.50

91. 10 Dollars 1976. Rev. Soccer scene (Olym-
    pic commemorative)   17.50
92. 10 Dollars 1976. Rev. Field hockey scene   17.50

87. 5 Dollars 1975. Rev. Abstract swimmer   8.00
88. 5 Dollars 1975. Rev. Abstract woman
    diver   8.00

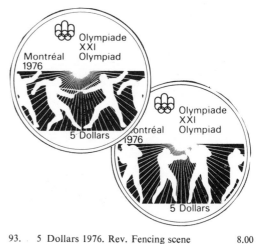

89. 1 Dollar 1975. Rev. Cowboy on bucking
    horse (Commemorates 100th anniver-
    sary of founding of Calgary)   5.00
89a. 1 Dollar (N) 1975   2.00

93. 5 Dollars 1976. Rev. Fencing scene   8.00
94. 5 Dollars 1976. Rev. Boxing scene   8.00

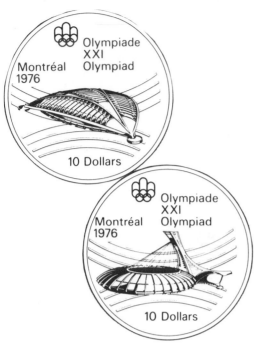

95. 10 Dollars 1976. Rev. Velodrome building
    (Olympic commemorative)   17.50
96. 10 Dollars 1976. Rev. Olympic stadium   17.50

97. 5 Dollars 1976. Rev. Olympic flame   8.00
98. 5 Dollars 1976. Rev. Olympic village   8.00

CAPE VERDE ISLANDS

A group of islands about 375 miles off the west coast of Africa. They have been Portuguese possessions since the end of the fifteenth century.

100 Centavos = 1 Escudo

1. 1 Escudo (N-Bro) 1930. Bust of Republic. Rev. Arms in wreath over value   8.00
2. 50 Centavos (N-Bro) 1930   3.00

3. 20 Centavos (Bro) 1930. Head of Republic.   3.00
4. 10 Centavos (Bro) 1930   2.00
5. 5 Centavos (Bro) 1930   1.50

6. 1 Escudo (N-Bro) 1949. Arms over date. Rev. Value   2.00
7. 50 Centavos (N-Bro) 1949   1.00

8. 10 Escudos 1953. Arms over value. Rev. Shield over date   6.00
9. 5 Escudos (CN) 1968   3.00
10. 2½ Escudos (N-Bro) 1953-68   2.00

A British colony comprised of three islands in the West Indies.

1. 25 Dollars 1972. Queen Elizabeth II. Rev. Conjoined heads of Queen and Prince Phillip (Commemorates royal wedding anniversary)   50.00
2. 25 Dollars (G) 1972   90.00

5. 1 Dollar 1972- . Rev. Flower   5.00
6. 50 Cents 1972- . Rev. Fish   3.00

7. 25 Cents (C-N) 1972- . Rev. Schooner   .75
8. 10 Cents (C-N) 1972- . Rev. Turtle   .50

9. 5 Cents (C-N) 1972- . Rev. Lobster   .25
10. 1 Cent (Br) 1972- . Rev. Thrush   .15

11. 100 Dollars (G) 1974. Bust of Winston Churchill. Rev. Arms (Commemorates 100th anniversary of statesman's birth)   120.00
12. 25 Dollars 1974   50.00

3. 5 Dollars 1972- . Rev. Arms, value (proof only)   15.00

13. 100 Dollars (G) 1975. Bust of Queen Elizabeth II. Rev. Portraits of five queens   125.00
14. 50 Dollars 1975   60.00

4. 2 Dollars 1972- . Rev. Silver heron (proof only)   8.75

CENTRAL AFRICAN REPUBLIC

Formerly part of French Equatorial Africa, became an independent republic in 1960.

1. 100 Francs (N) 1971. Antelopes. Rev. Value   2.50

CEYLON

A large island in the Indian Ocean, southeast of India. Ceylon was successively conquered by the Portuguese, the Dutch, and the English. In 1948 Ceylon became a dominion in the British Commonwealth of Nations. When Ceylon became an independent republic in 1972, the traditional name Sri Lanka was officially adopted.

20 Stivers = 1 Gulden
4 Farthings = 1 Penny
100 Cents = 1 Rupee

GEORGE III 1760-1820

1.	2 Stivers (C) 1815. Head. Rev. Elephant	6.00
2.	1 Stiver (C) 1815	4.00

3. ½ Stiver (C) 1815   5.00

GEORGE IV 1820-30

4. 1 Rix Dollar 1821. Head. Rev. Elephant   20.00

5. ½ Farthing (C) 1827-30. Rev. Seated Britannia   10.00

WILLIAM IV 1830-37

6. 1½ Pence 1834-37   4.00
7. ½ Farthing (C) 1837. Rev. Seated Britannia   25.00

VICTORIA 1837-1901

8. 1½ Pence 1838-62. Head. Rev. Value   2.50
9. ½ Farthing (C) 1839-56   2.00
10. ¼ Farthing (C) 1839-53   20.00

CEYLON (continued)

New coinage: Head. Rev. Value

11.	50 Cents 1892-1900. Rev. Plant and value	5.00
12.	25 Cents 1892	3.00
13.	10 Cents 1892-1900	2.50
14.	5 Cents (C) 1870-92	6.00

15.	1 Cent (C) 1870-1901. Head. Rev. Plant and value	1.50
16.	½ Cent (C) 1870-1901	1.50
17.	¼ Cent (C) 1870-1901	1.50

EDWARD VII 1901-10

18.	50 Cents 1902-10. Crowned bust. Rev. Plant and value	6.00
19.	25 Cents 1902-10	4.00
20.	10 Cents 1902-10	2.00

21.	5 Cents (C-N) 1909, 10. (Square shape with rounded corners.) Crowned bust. Rev. Value	1.00
22.	1 Cent (Bro) 1904-10. Rev. Plant and value	1.25
23.	½ Cent (Bro) 1904-09	5.00
24.	¼ Cent (Bro) 1904	1.25

GEORGE V 1910-36

25.	50 Cents 1913-29. Type of #18	3.50

(coin image)

26.	25 Cents 1911-26. Crowned bust. Rev. Plant and value	1.25
27.	10 Cents 1911-28	1.25
28.	5 Cents (C-N) 1912-26. Type of #21, bust left	1.00
29.	1 Cent (Br) 1912-29. Type of #22, bust left	.90
30.	½ Cent (Br) 1912-26	.70

GEORGE VI 1936-52

(Coins issued from 1937 to 1945 carry the title "King and Emperor of India." Coins issued in 1951 carry the title "King George the Sixth.")

31.	50 Cents 1942. Crowned head. Rev. Type of #11	5.00
32.	10 Cents 1941	1.50
33.	50 Cents (N-Bra) 1943, 51. Rev. Crowned value between leaves	1.25
34.	25 Cents (N-Bra) 1943-51	.50

35.	10 Cents (N-Bra) 1944, 51 (Scalloped-edge)	.40
36.	5 Cents (N-Bra) 1942-45. Rev. Type of #21 (Square-shaped)	.30
37.	2 Cents (N-Bra) 1944, 51 (Scalloped edge)	.15
38.	1 Cent (Bro) 1937-45. Rev. Type of #22 (Round)	.25
39.	½ Cent (Bro) 1937, 40	.75

ELIZABETH II 1952-

40.	5 Rupees 1957 (Commemorating 2500 years of Buddhism). Animals in circular pattern. Rev. Inscription	10.00

SRI LANKA

41. 1 Rupee (C-N) 1957. Buddhist wheel.
     Rev. Inscription   3.00

51. 1 Rupee (C-N) 1972. New arms of Re-
     public. Rev. Value   1.00

42. 2 Cents (N-Bra) 1955-57. Head of Eliza-
     beth. Rev. Value (scalloped edge)   .20

52.	50 Cents (C-N) 1972	.60
53.	25 Cents (C-N) 1973	.50
54.	10 Cents (N-Bra) 1973	.35
55.	5 Cents (N-Bra) 1973	.25
56.	2 Cents (A) 1973	.15
57.	1 Cent (A) 1973	.10

58.	1 Rupee (C-N) 1976. Type of #50	
	(F.A.O. coin plan)	.15
59.	50 Cents (C-N) 1976	.10
60.	25 Cents (C-N) 1976	.10
61.	10 Cents (Bra) 1976	.10
62.	5 Cents (Bra) 1976	.10
63.	2 Cents (A) 1976	.10
64.	1 Cent (A) 1976	.10

43. 1 Rupee (C-N) 1963-71   1.25
44. 50 Cents (C-N) 1963-71. Arms of Ceylon.
     Rev. Value   .75
45. 25 Cents (C-N) 1963-71   .40

46. 10 Cents (N-Bra) 1963-71. (scalloped edge)   .25
47. 5 Cents (N-Bra) 1963-71. (square planchet)   .20
48. 2 Cents (A) 1963-71. (scalloped edge)   .15
49. 1 Cent (A) 1963-71. (round planchet)   .15

50. 2 Rupees (CN) 1968. Statue of old
     Buddhist king. Rev. Value (F.A.O.
     issue)   2.50

CHAD

This former territory in French Equatorial Africa became a republic in 1960.

1. 100 Francs (N) 1971, 72. Antelope. Rev.
   Value   2.50

CHILE

The Spaniards began the conquest of Chile toward the middle of the sixteenth century, after which Chile remained a Spanish colony until 1818, when it became a republic thanks to the liberating efforts of San Martin and O'Higgins.

Early issues under Spanish rule bear the name of the reigning Spanish monarch. The designs are similar to those of other Spanish-American issues.

The Santiago mint mark appears as $\overset{o}{S}$ in the legend. Some of the famous gold doubloons (8 escudos) were issued at the Santiago mint. They are valued at $250.

8 Reales = 1 Peso or Piece-of-Eight
10 Centavos = 1 Decimo
100 Centavos = 1 Peso
100 Centesimos = 1 Escudo

1805 gold doubloon (8 escudos)

CHARLES III 1759-88

1. 8 Reales 1773-89. Bust. Rev. Spanish
    arms   400.00
2. 2 Reales 1773-89   50.00
3. ½ Real 1773-89   32.00

CHARLES IV 1788-1808

4. 8 Reales 1790, 91. Bust of Charles III.
    Rev. Arms   400.00

5.	4 Reales 1789-91	240.00
6.	2 Reales 1789-91	24.00
7.	1 Real 1789-91	24.00
8.	½ Real 1789-91	24.00
9.	¼ Real 1790-91	48.00

10.	8 Reales 1792-1808. Bust of Charles IV.	
	Rev. Arms	180.00
11.	4 Reales 1792-1808	105.00
12.	2 Reales 1792-1808	40.00
13.	1 Real 1792-1808	18.00
14.	½ Real 1792-1808	14.00
14a.	¼ Real 1792-95	10.00
15.	¼ Real 1796-1808. Castle. Rev. Lion	32.00

FERDINAND VII 1808-17

16.	4 Reales 1808-15. Bust of Charles IV.	140.00
	Rev. Arms	
17.	2 Reales 1808-09	32.00
18.	1 Real 1808-17	18.00
19.	½ Real 1808-17	14.00

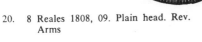

20.	8 Reales 1808, 09. Plain head. Rev. Arms	200.00

21.	8 Reales 1810, 11. Laureate head	120.00
21a.	2 Reales 1810, 11	20.00

22.	8 Reales 1812-17. Draped bust	150.00

22a.	2 Reales 1812-17	18.00
23.	¼ Real 1808-18. Castle. Rev. Lion	27.50

CHILE • 83

REPUBLIC OF CHILE 1817-

24.	1 Peso 1817-34. Volcano. Rev. Column	60.00
25.	2 Reales 1834	35.00
26.	1 Real 1834	30.00
27.	½ Real 1833, 34	25.00
28.	¼ Real 1832, 34. Value on both sides	30.00

38.	1 Centavo 1835, 51-53. Star. Rev. Value	6.00
39.	½ Centavo 1835, 51-53	4.50

40.	1 Peso 1895-97, 1902-05, 10. Condor on mountain peak. Rev. Value in wreath	6.50
41.	1 Peso 1915, 17, 21-32. Reduced size	3.00
42.	50 Centavos 1902-06	2.50
43.	20 Centavos 1895-1900, 1906-20	2.00
44.	10 Centavos 1896-1920	.75
45.	5 Centavos 1896-1919	.50

29.	8 Reales 1839-49. Arms. Rev. Condor breaking chain	100.00
30.	2 Reales 1843, 52	4.75
31.	1 Real 1836-50	6.00
32.	½ Real 1838-51	10.00

46.	2½ Centavos (C) 1886-1908. Republic head. Rev. Value	1.00
47.	2 Centavos (C) 1878-95, 1919	1.00
48.	1 Centavo (C) 1878-1904, 08, 19	2.00
49.	½ Centavo (C) 1883-94	1.00

(Assay and size of coins vary from year to year.)

50.	100 Pesos (G) 1926, 32, 46-63. Head of republic with coiled hair. Rev. Arms	180.00
51.	50 Pesos (G) 1926-62	110.00

33.	1 Peso 1853-62. Condor with shield	50.00
33a.	1 Peso 1867-91. New condor design	5.00

34.	50 Centavos 1853-72. Flying condor	10.00
35.	20 Centavos 1852-93	2.00
36.	1 Decimo 1852-94	1.00
37.	½ Decimo 1851-94	.85

52.	20 Pesos (G) 1896-1917, 26, 58-61	125.00
53.	10 Pesos (G) 1896, 1901	150.00
54.	5 Pesos (G) 1898, 1900	135.00
55.	5 Pesos 1927. Condor on mountain peak	20.00
56.	2 Pesos 1927	7.50

57.	1 Peso (S) 1932; (C-N) 1933, 40		1.25
58.	20 Centavos (C-N) 1920-41		1.00
59.	10 Centavos (C-N) 1920-41		.40
60.	5 Centavos (C-N) 1920-38.		.75

71. 5 Escudos (C-N) 1971, 72; (A) 1972- .
Lautaro, famous Indian, on horseback.
Rev. Arms and value .50

61. 1 Peso (C) 1942-54; (A) 1954-58. Bust of
Bernardo O'Higgins. Rev. Value .50
62. 50 Centavos (C) 1942 1.25
63. 20 Centavos (C) 1942-53 .40

72. 2 Escudos (C-N) 1971- . Caupolican, famous Indian. .50

73. 1 Escudo (C-N) 1971, 72. Jose Miguel
Carrera, military dictator 1811-13 .40

64. 10 Pesos (A) 1956-59. Flying condor. Rev.
Value 1.00
65. 5 Pesos (A) 1956 .75

74. 50 Centesimos (A-Br) 1971. Manuel Rod-
riguez, freedom fighter .25

75. 20 Centesimos (A-Br) 1971. Jose Manuel
Balmaceda, President of Republic 1886-
91 .20

CURRENCY REVALUATION
100 Centesimos = 1 Escudo

76. 10 Centesimos (A-Br) 1971. Bernardo
O'Higgins, first governor of independent
Chile, 1818-23 .10

66. 10 Centesimos (A-Br) 1960- 70. Flying condor. Rev. Value .50
67. 5 Centesimos (A-Br) 1961-70 .35
68. 2 Centesimos (A-Br) 1964-70 .25
69. 1 Centesimo (A) 1960-63 .50
70. ½ Centesimo (A) 1962-63 .50

77. 100 Escudos (N-Bra) 1974. Condor. Rev.
Value in wreath .75
78. 50 Escudos (N-Bra) 1974 (12-sided planchet) .50
79. 10 Escudos (A) 1974 .40

CHILE • 85

CHILE (continued)

MONETARY REFORM

80. 1 Peso (C-N) 1975. Portrait of Bernardo O'Higgins. Rev. Value

81. 50 Centavos (C-N) 1975. Type of #77
82. 10 Centavos (A-Br) 1975 (12-sided planchet)
83. 5 Centavos (A-Br) 1975 (12-sided planchet)
84. 1 Centavo (A) 1975

CHINA

After thousands of years of existence the Chinese Empire came to an end in 1911 and was succeeded by a republic. Years of war, unrest, and civil strife followed, until by 1949 the Chinese Communists had complete control of the mainland. All that was left to the Chinese Nationalists was the island of Formosa.

Prior to 1875 the coinage of China consisted of brass "cash" money, silver passing only by weight. Silver coins of the principal nations of the world were in circulation, each piece being verified by the "chop" or mark of the merchant passing them.

During the time of the Empire, coins were issued by the various provinces in the denominations shown on coins #1 to #10. The name of the issuing province and the denomination are identified in English on every legend. (Each province issued some—but not necessarily all—of the denominations.) The general design of these coins is a Chinese inscription on the obverse, with a dragon and an English legend on the reverse. Most of these coins were issued during the period 1896-1911.

In addition to issues under the Empire, there were some later issues by the individual provinces during the Republic. These are similar in design and value to the issues of the Chinese Republic.

10 Cash = 1 Cent
100 Cents = 1 Dollar
1 Dollar = 0.72 Tael, or 7 Mace
and 2 Candereens
10 Candereens = 1 Mace
10 Mace = 1 Tael

PROVINCIAL ISSUES UNDER THE EMPIRE

1. Dollar (7 Mace and 2 Candareens)   20.00
2. 50 Cents (3 Mace and 6 Candareens)   10.00

3. 20 Cents (1 Mace and 4.4 Candareens)   6.00
4. 10 Cents (7.2 Candareens)   4.00
5. 5 Cents (3.6 Candareens)   1.50
6. 20 Cash (C or Bra)   1.50

7. 10 Cash (C or Bra)   1.25
8. 5 Cash (C or Bra)   .75
9. 2 Cash (C or Bra)   .65

10.   1 Cash (C or Bra)   .40

REPUBLIC 1911-49

11. Dollar 1912 (To commemorate election as Provisional President of the republic). Bust of Sun Yat-sen. Rev. Inscription   35.00

12. Dollar 1912. Bust of Li Yuan-hung in uniform and military cap   100.00

13. Dollar 1912 (To commemorate election as Vice-President of the republic). Bust without cap   70.00

14. Dollar 1912. Bust of Yuan Shi-kai (President 1912-16) with plumed hat   120.00

15. Dollar 1914-21. Bust of Yuan Shi-kai in profile (a regular-issue coin struck in great numbers)   10.00

22. Dollar 1921 (Commemorating election as President). Bust of Hsu Shih-chang. Rev. Bamboo-covered Pavillion   200.00

16. 20 Cash (C or Bra) 1912. Crossed flags   2.75
17. 10 Cash (C or Bra) 1912   2.00
18. 5 Cash (C or Bra) 1912   1.75

23. Dollar 1923 (Commemorating election as President). Bust of Tsao Quan in military uniform   100.00
24. Dollar 1923. Bust of Tsao Quan in civil dress   100.00

19. 1 Cent [10 Cash] (Bra or Bro) 1917. Wreath of barley. Center hole   2.00
20. ½ Cent [5 Cash] (Bra or Bro)   1.25

21. Dollar 1916 (Commemorating Pres. Yuan's proclamation declaring himself Emperor of China). Type of #14. Rev. Dragon   150.00

25. Dollar 1923. Dragon and phoenix (entire issue rejected and not placed in circulation because of the imperial symbol of the dragon and phoenix)   225.00
26. 20 Cents 1926   4.75
27. 10 Cents 1926   3.25

CHINA (continued)

28. Dollar 1924 (Commemorating peaceful unification of the country and election as President). Bust of Tuan Chi-sui   85.00

29. Dollar 1928 (Kwei Chow Province). View of automobile   550.00

32. 20 Cents (N) 1936-39, (C-N) 1942. Bust of Sun Yat-sen. Ancient Pu (spade money) 1.50
33. 10 Cents (N) 1936-39, (C-N) 1940-41   .75
34. 5 Cents (N) 1936-39, (C-N) 1940-41   .75

35. 1 Cent (Bra or Bro) 1936-40. Spade. Rev. Sun   .75
36. ½ Cent (Bra or Bro) 1936-40   4.00

30. Dollar 1932. Bust of Sun Yat-sen in military uniform. Rev. Chinese junk, birds, sun, and value (withdrawn issue)   100.00

31. Dollar 1933, 34. Birds and sun omitted (national dollar regular issue)   10.50

PEOPLE'S REPUBLIC OF CHINA
(Communist China)

1.	5 Fen (Al) 1955-	. Arms. Rev. Value	2.00
2.	2 Fen (Al) 1956-		1.25
3.	1 Fen (Al) 1955-		1.00

COLOMBIA

Conquered by the Spanish Conquistadors during the first half of the sixteenth century, the colony, known as New Granada, gained its independence in 1819. Curiously enough, Colombia is the only country named for Christopher Columbus.

The early colonial issues bear the name of the reigning Spanish monarch. Designs are similar to those of other Spanish-American mints. The mint mark for Santa Fe de Bogota is NR in the legend on the reverse. The mint mark for Popayan is P or PN in the legend. On coins of the republic the mint mark is Ba. Gold doubloons of the colonial period are valued at $150.

8 Reales = 1 Peso or Piece-of-Eight
10 Centavos = 1 Decimo
100 Centavos = 1 Peso

1769 gold doubloon (8 escudos)

Spanish-American coins struck at Popayan mint. The mint mark is P or PN in the legend.

CHARLES IV 1788-1808

1.	2 Reales 1793-1800. Bust. Rev. Arms	75.00
2.	1 Real 1792-1804	45.00
3.	½ Real 1795-1801	80.00
4.	¼ Real 1796-1808. Castle. Rev. Lion	20.00

FERDINAND VII 1808-24

5.	8 Escudos (G) 1808–20. Bust of Charles IV. Rev. Arms	750.00
6.	4 Escudos (G) 1818, 19	1,000.00
7.	2 Escudos (G) 1808–19	250.00
8.	1 Escudo (G) 1808–20	150.00
9.	8 Reales 1810-20. Bust of Charles IV	400.00

10.	2 Reales 1810-23	35.00

COLOMBIA (continued)

11. 1 Real 1810-19   35.00
12. ½ Real 1810-19   25.00

13. ¼ Real 1810-17. Castle. Rev. Lion   25.00

NUEVA GRANADA 1815-19
REPUBLICA DE COLOMBIA 1820-36

14. 8 Reales 1819, 20. Indian head. Rev.
    Pomegranate   95.00
15. 2 Reales 1815, 16, 19-21   20.00
16. 1 Real 1813-16, 19, 21   25.00
17. ½ Real 1814, 21   35.00

18. ¼ Real 1814,15, 20, 21. Liberty cap. Rev.
    Pomegranate   35.00

19. 8 Reales 1834-36. Fasces between cornu-
    copiae. Rev. Value   65.00
20. 1 Real 1827-36   10.00
21. ½ Real 1834-36   18.00

22. ¼ Real 1826-36. Cornucopia   12.00

REPUBLICA DE LA NUEVA GRANADA 1837-58

23. 8 Reales 1837, 47. Shield of arms. Rev.
    Value   50.00
24. 8 Reales 1839-46. Condor flying above
    cornucopia   40.00

25. 2 Reales 1839-45, 47-53   10.00
26. 1 Real 1837-47, 51-53. Pomegranate 7.50
27. ½ Real 1838-47, 50-53   7.50
28. ¼ Real 1837-58   7.00

29. 10 Reales 1847-51. Condor. Rev. Value
    (several varieties)   50.00
30. 1 Peso 1855-58. Type of #29   35.00
31. 2 Decimos 1854-58. Shield   7.00

32. 1 Decimo (C) 1847, 48   4.75
32a. 1 Decimo 1853-58. Cornucopias 5.00
33. ½ Decimo (C) 1847, 48. Type of #32 7.50
33a. ½ Decimo 1853-58. Type of #32a 7.00

COLOMBIA • 91

COLOMBIA (continued)

CONFEDERACION GRANADINA 1859-61

34.   1 Peso 1859 - 62. Condor. Rev. Value   35.00

35.	2 Reales 1862. Pointed shield	8.75
36.	1 Decimo 1859, 60. Pomegranate	10.00
37.	½ Decimo 1860, 61	20.00
38.	¼ Decimo 1860, 61	15.00

ESTADOS UNIDOS DE COLOMBIA 1862-86

39.   1 Peso 1862-67. Condor above arms   30.00

40.	1 Peso 1871. Liberty head. Rev. Value	60.00
41.	5 Decimos (50 Centavos) 1868-86	7.50
42.	2 Decimos (20 Centavos) 1866, 67, 70-85	5.50
43.	1 Decimo (10 Centavos) 1863-86	3.00
44.	½ Decimo (5 Centavos) 1863-85	2.00
45.	¼ Decimo (2½ Centavos) 1863-81. Pomegranate	4.00

46.	2½ Centavos (C-N) 1881, 86; (C) 1885	.35
47.	1¼ Centavos (C-N) 1874	5.00

REPUBLICA DE COLOMBIA 1887-

48.	50 Centavos (5 Decimos). Liberty head 1887-1908	10.00
48a.	50 Centavos 1887. Head of Soledad Roman (wife of President Rafael Nunez)	35.00

49.	20 Centavos 1897	2.00
50.	10 Centavos 1897	3.00
51.	5 Centavos (C-N) 1886-1902. Head facing left. Rev. Value	.60
51a.	5 Centavos 1902. Rev. Cornucopias	2.00

52.   50 Centavos 1892. Bust of Columbus   7.25

53.	5 Pesos (G) 1913-19. Workman cutting stone	50.00
53a.	2½ Pesos (G) 1913	50.00
54.	10 Pesos (G) 1919-24. Bolivar head. Rev. Arms	85.00
55.	5 Pesos (G) 1919-30	55.00
56.	2½ Pesos (G) 1919-28	40.00

57.	50 Centavos 1912-33. Bolivar head. Rev. Arms	4.00
58.	20 Centavos 1911-42	2.00
59.	10 Centavos 1911-42	1.00

60.	5 Centavos (CN) 1917-50. Liberty head. Rev. Value	.50
61.	2 Centavos (CN) 1918-47	.50
62.	1 Centavo (CN) 1918-48; (Ni-St) 1952-58	.15

COLOMBIA (continued)

63. 50 Centavos 1947, 48. Bolivar   8.00

68. 50 Centavos (C-N) 1958-66. Head of Bolivar to right. Rev. Arms   1.00
69. 20 Centavos (C-N) 1956-66.   .50

70.   73.

64. 20 Centavos 1945-51. Santander   2.50
65. 10 Centavos 1945-52. Santander   1.25

70. 10 Centavos (C-N) 1952-66. Indian head   .50
71. 5 Centavos (Br) 1942-66. Liberty cap in wreath. Rev. Value   .35
72. 2 Centavos (Br) 1948-50   .75
73. 2 Centavos (Al-Br) 1952-65. Liberty head   .35
74. 1 Centavo (Br) 1942-66. Liberty cap in wreath. Rev. Value   .25

66. 20 Centavos 1953. Bolivar   .75

75. 50 Centavos (CN) 1960. Same as #68 but "1810-1960" below head (Commemorates 1810 uprising)   4.00
76. 20 Centavos (CN) 1960. Same as #69 but "1810-1960" dates   3.50
77. 10 Centavos (CN) 1960. Same as #70 but "1810-1960" dates   3.50
78. 5 Centavos (Br) 1960. Same as #71 but "1810-1960" dates   5.00
79. 2 Centavos (Al-Br) 1960. Same as #73 but "1810-1960" dates   3.50
80. 1 Centavo (Br) 1960. Same as #74 but "1810-1960" dates   2.75

81. 50 Centavos (C-N) 1965. Head of Jorge Eliecer Gaitan. Rev. Arms (honors political leader assassinated in 1948)   1.50
82. 20 Centavos (C-N) 1965   .75

67. 1 Peso 1956. (Commemorating 200th anniversary of the Popayan mint). Building. Rev. Wreath   15.00

COLOMBIA • 93

83. 1 Peso (CN) 1967. Head of Bolivar. Rev. Value (10-sided planchet)   1.00

90. 50 Centavos (Ni-St) 1970- . Head of Santander. Rev. Value (12-sided planchet)   .50
91. 20 Centavos (Ni-St) 1969- (round planchet)   .25
92. 10 Centavos (Ni-St) 1969-   .20

84. 50 Centavos (N-St) 1967-69. Head of Santander. Rev. Value   .50
85. 20 Centavos (N-St) 1967-69   .50
86. 10 Centavos (N-St) 1967-69   .25

93. 5 Pesos (Ni-St) 1971. Emblem. Rev. Value (Commemorates the sixth Pan-American Games in Cali)   4.00

87. 5 Centavos (C-St) 1967- . Type of #71   .25
88. 1 Centavo (C-St) 1967   .15

94. 1 Peso (C-N-Z) 1974. Bust of Bolivar. Rev. Value   .40

89. 5 Pesos (CN) 1968. Cross of fish representing four corners of the earth. Rev. Value (Commemorates the 39th Eucharistic Congress held in Bogota)   3.00

COMORO ISLANDS

An archipelago in the Indian Ocean located between Madagascar and Mozambique. Acquired by France in 1886, the islands which were formerly attached to the government of Madagascar are now an autonomous overseas territory in the French Community.

100 Centimes = 1 Franc

1. 5 Francs 1890 (Mohammedan Era 1308).
    Weapons. Star, crescent, flags   350.00
2. 10 Centimes (Bro) 1890, 1901. Inscriptions   15.00
3. 5 Centimes (Bro) 1890, 1901   11.00

4. 20 Francs (Ni-Bra) 1964. Liberty head.
   Rev. Value, conch shells and fish   1.25
5. 10 Francs (Ni-Bra) 1964   .75

6. 5 Francs (Al) 1964. Rev. Value and
    palm trees   .75
7. 2 Francs (Al) 1964   .40
8. 1 Franc (Al) 1964   .35

CONGO (Kinshasa)

Originally the private property of Leopold II of Belgium, this territory became a Belgian colony in of the Congo. In 1971 the name was officially changed to Zaire.

KATANGA PROVINCE

1. 5 Francs (Br) 1961. Bananas. Rev. Baluba cross   3.00
1a. 5 Francs (G) 1961   100.00
2. 1 Franc (Br) 1961   2.00

REPUBLIC

3. 10 Francs (Al) 1965. Lion. Rev. Inscription   **2.00**

NEW CURRENCY SYSTEM
1 Likuta = 10 Francs

4. 5 Makuta (CN) 1967-69. Portrait of Joseph Mobuto. Rev. Value   2.50

5. 1 Likuta (Al) 1967. Arms. Rev. Value   1.50
6. 10 Sengi (Al) 1967. Leopard. Rev. Value   .75

CONGO, PEOPLE'S REPUBLIC

An independent republic since 1960, formerly a territory in French Equatorial Africa.

1. 100 Francs (N) 1971. Antelopes. Rev. Value   2.50

COOK ISLANDS

A self-governing group of 15 islands in South Pacific Ocean under New Zealand administration. They were discovered by Captain James Cook on his second voyage in 1773.

1. 1 Dollar (CN) 1970. Queen Elizabeth II. Rev. Capt. James Cook and sailing ship (Commemorates the 200th anniversary of Cook's first voyage)   18.00

COOK ISLANDS (continued)

2. 1 Dollar (C-N) 1972- . Rev. Tangaroa, Polynesian god   6.00

3. 50 Cents (C-N) 1972- . Rev. Bonito   1.25
4. 20 Cents (C-N) 1972- . Rev. Tern   .75

5. 10 Cents (C-N) 1972- . Rev. Oranges   .40
6. 5 Cents (C-N) 1972- . Rev. Hibiscus   .25

7. 2 Cents (Br) 1972- . Rev. Pineapples   .20
8. 1 Cent (Br) 1972- . Rev. Taro leaf   .15

COOK ISLANDS (continued)

9. 7½ Dollars 1973, 74. Rev. Portrait of Captain James Cook, with map and ship (Commemorates 200th anniversary of discovery of Hervey Islands)   35.00

10. 2½ Dollars 1973, 74. Rev. Two ships, map of globe (Commemorates Cook's second Pacific voyage)   17.50

11. 2 Dollars 1973. Rev. Queen seated holding scepter (Commemorates 20th anniversary of coronation)   15.00

12. 100 Dollars (G) 1974, 75. Rev. Sir Winston Churchill, flag and House of Parliament in background   150.00

13. 50 Dollars (G) 1974

14. 100 Dollars (G) 1975. Rev. Sailing ship, portraits of King George III and James Cook (Commemorates 200th anniversary of Cook's second Pacific voyage)   135.00

COSTA RICA

After Costa Rica gained its independence from Spain, it was a part of Mexico for a short time and then joined the Central American Federation, eventually becoming an independent republic.

8 Reales = 1 Peso or Piece-of-Eight
100 Centimos = 1 Colon
100 Centavos = 1 Peso

AS A STATE OF THE CENTRAL AMERICAN FEDERATION

(Early issues carry the mint mark CR.)

1. 8 Reales 1831. Mountains and sun. Rev. Tree   600.00
2. 2 Reales 1848-49   20.00
3. 1 Real 1831-50   18.00

4. 1 Real 1846-47, 49-50. Female bust. Rev. Coffee plant   12.00
5. ½ Real 1831-49. Type of #1   17.50
6. ¼ Real 1845. Three mountains. Rev. Tree   60.00

(During the period circa 1850 small coins of England, the United States, and some other countries were counterstamped with a lion surrounded by "Habilitada por el Gobierno" in a small circle.)

6a. 2 Reales (British coin, 1 Shilling; head of Victoria. Rev. Value in wreath. Lion counterstamp)   12.50

COSTA RICA • 97

COSTA RICA (continued)

REPUBLICA DE COSTA RICA

7.	¼ Peso 1850-55. Arms. Rev. Tree	10.00
8.	⅛ Peso 1850-55	12.00
9.	1/16 Peso 1850-55	16.00
10.	50 Centavos 1865-75, 80-90	7.50
11.	25 Centavos 1864-75, 86-93	4.75
12.	10 Centavos 1865-75, 86-92	4.50
13.	5 Centavos 1865-75, 85-92	3.00
14.	1 Centavo (C-N) 1865-68, 74	6.00
15.	20 Colones (G) 1897-1900. Head of Columbus. Rev. Arms	200.00
16.	10 Colones (G) 1897-1900	75.00

17.	5 Colones (G) 1899-1900	50.00
18.	2 Colones (G) 1900, 01, 15-28	40.00
19.	50 Centimos 1902-03. Arms. Rev. Value	10.00
20.	10 Centimos 1905-14	1.00
21.	5 Centimos 1905-14	1.50
22.	10 Centimos (Bra or Bro) 1917-47. Rev. Value in wreath	.35
23.	5 Centimos (Bra or Bro) 1917-47	.25
24.	2 Centimos (C-N) 1903	3.00

BANK ISSUES

25.	2 Colones (C-N) 1948; (St) 1954; (C-N) 1961-	1.00
26.	1 Colon (C-N) 1935-48; (St) 1954; (C-N) 1961-	.65
27.	50 Centimos (C-N) 1935-48, 65-	.35
28.	25 Centimos (C-N) 1935-48 (Bra) 1944-46; (Br) 1945; (C-N) 1967-	.25
29.	10 Centimos (C-N) 1951; (St) 1953-	.20
30.	5 Centimos (Bra) 1942-47 (C-N) 1951 (St) 1953-	.15

1935 coins were issued by the Banco Internacional de Costa Rica (B.I.C.R. at bottom of reverse); 1937-48 coins by the Banco Nacional de Costa Rica (B.N.C.R.); 1951- coins by the Banco Central de Costa Rica (B.C.C.R.).

CRETE

This Mediterranean island off the coast of Greece had one of the most remarkable civilizations of ancient times. It became a department of Greece in 1898 and was united with Greece ten years later.

100 Lepta = 1 Drachma

PRINCE GEORGE OF GREECE
(High Commissioner 1898-1906)

1.	5 Drachmas 1901. Head. Rev. Crowned arms on mantle	65.00

2.	2 Drachmas 1901	20.00
3.	1 Drachma 1901	12.00
4.	50 Lepta 1901	10.00

5.	20 Lepta (C-N) 1900. Crown. Rev. Value in wreath	7.25
6.	10 Lepta (C-N) 1900	5.00
7.	5 Lepta (C-N) 1900	6.00

8.	2 Lepta (Bro) 1900-01	6.00
9.	1 Lepton (Bro) 1900-01	7.00

CUBA

The largest island in the West Indies. After centuries of Spanish rule, Cuba became an independent republic under the terms of the treaty that ended the Spanish-American War.

100 Centavos = 1 Peso

PROVISIONAL GOVERNMENT

1. Souvenir Peso 1897   50.00

REPUBLIC

2. 20 Pesos (G) 1915-16. Head of Jose Marti. Rev. Arms of Cuba in wreath   200.00
3. 10 Pesos (G) 1915-16   110.00
4. 5 Pesos (G) 1915-16   60.00
5. 4 Pesos (G) 1915-16   170.00
6. 2 Pesos (G) 1915-16   45.00
7. 1 Peso (G) 1915-16   125.00

8. 1 Peso 1915-16, 32-34. Star and rays. Rev. Arms in wreath   25.00
9. 40 Centavos 1915-20   10.00
10. 20 Centavos 1915-32, 48-49   2.00
11. 10 Centavos 1915-20, 48-49   1.50
12. 5 Centavos (C-N) 1915-20, 46, 60, 61; (Bra) 43. Value in star. Rev. Type of #8   .50
13. 2 Centavos (C-N) 1915-16   .50
14. 1 Centavo (C-N) 1915-38, 46, 61; (Bra) 43   .40

15. 1 Peso 1934-39. Liberty head. Rev. Arms   50.00

FIFTIETH ANNIVERSARY OF THE REPUBLIC

16. 40 Centavos 1952. Morro Castle. Rev. Star, tree, and wheel   7.50
17. 20 Centavos 1952   3.50
18. 10 Centavos 1952   2.00

MARTI CENTENARY

19. 1 Peso 1953. Head of Marti. Rev. Rising sun   12.00

20. 50 Centavos 1953. Rev. Scroll with inscription   4.00

CUBA (continued)

21. 25 Centavos 1953. Rev. Liberty cap   3.50

22. 1 Centavo (Bra) 1953. Rev. Star in triangle   1.00

23. 1 Centavo (C-N) 1958. Rev. Star in triangle   .40

24. 40 Centavos (C-N) 1962- . Bust of Camilio Cienfuegos (peasant leader). Rev. Arms   7.50

25. 20 Centavos (C-N) 1962-68. Bust of Marti. Rev. Arms. Legend "PATRIA O MUERTE" (Fatherland or death)   5.00

26. 5 Centavos (A) 1963- . Arms. Rev. Value in star   1.00

27. 1 Centavo (A) 1963-   .75
28. 20 Centavos (A) 1969-   2.50

CURACAO

Curacao was discovered by the Spaniards and became a Dutch colony in 1634. This island in the West Indies is part of the Netherland Antilles today. It is made up of two groups of islands in the Caribbean off the northern coast of Venezuela. Two of the islands, Aruba and Curacao, have large oil refineries.

100 Cents = 1 Guilder (Gulden)

WILHELMINA 1890-1948

1. ¼ Guilder 1900. Head. Rev. Crowned arms   6.00
2. ⅒ Guilder 1901   10.00

3. 1 Rixdollar (New coinage 2½ Guilder) 1944. Crowned arms   10.00
4. 1 Guilder 1944. Arms   4.00

5. ¼ Guilder 1944, 47. Head. Rev. Value   1.50
6. ⅒ Guilder 1944, 47, 48   1.50

7. 5 Cents (C-N) 1948. (Diamond shape, rounded corners.) Plant. Rev. Value   1.00

8. 2½ Cents (Br) 1944-48. Lion. Rev. Value   1.25
9. 1 Cent (Br) 1944, 47   .25

CYPRUS

Cyprus, a Mediterranean island off the coast of Turkey, became British in 1878 and made a Crown Colony in 1925. It became an independent republic within the British Commonwealth in 1960.

9 Piastres = 1 Shilling
100 Mils = 1 Pound Sterling

VICTORIA 1837-1901

1.	18 Piastres 1901. Crowned "old" bust. Rev. Crowned shield and value	25.00
2.	9 Piastres 1901	12.00
3.	4½ Piastres 1901	11.00
4.	3 Piastres 1901	11.00
5.	1 Piastre (Bro) 1879-1900. Coroneted "young" head. Rev. Value	9.00
6.	½ Piastre (Bro) 1879-1900	8.00
7.	¼ Piastre (Bro) 1879-1901	8.00

EDWARD VII 1901-10

8.	18 Piastres 1907. Crowned bust. Rev. Type of #1	25.00
9.	9 Piastres 1907	17.50
10.	1 Piastre (Bro) 1908	25.00
11.	½ Piastre (Bro) 1908	20.00
12.	¼ Piastre (Bro) 1902-08	6.00

GEORGE V 1910-36

13.	45 Piastres 1928. Crowned bust. Rev. Lions	30.00

14.	18 Piastres 1913, 21. Rev. Type of #1	12.50
15.	9 Piastres 1913, 19, 21	7.25
16.	4½ Piastres 1921	5.00
17.	1 Piastre (Br) 1922, 27, 30, 31. Crowned bust. Rev. Value	10.00

17a.	1 Piastre (C-N) 1934. Scalloped edge. Crowned bust. Rev. Value	1.50
18.	½ Piastre (Bro) 1922, 27, 30-31 (Round)	7.50
18a.	½ Piastre (C-N) 1934 (Scalloped)	1.00
19.	¼ Piastre (Bro) 1922, 26	4.00

GEORGE VI 1936-52

20.	18 Piastres 1938, 40. Crowned head. Rev. Type of #13	10.00
21.	9 Piastres 1938, 40	7.00
22.	4½ Piastres 1938	6.00

23.	1 Piastre (C-N) 1938; (Bro) 1942-46, 49. Crowned head. Rev. Type of #17a	.75
24.	½ Piastre (C-N) 1938; (Bro) 1942-45, 49	.60

25.	2 Shillings (C-N) 1947, 49. Type of #20	3.25
26.	1 Shilling (C-N) 1947, 49	2.50

ELIZABETH II 1952-

27.	100 Mils (C-N) 1955-57. Crowned bust. Rev. Brig	2.00

28.   50 Mils (C-N) 1955. Rev. Fern leaves   1.00

29.   25 Mils (C-N) 1955. Rev. Bull's head   .50

30.   5 Mils (C-N) 1955, 56. Rev. Figure of an-
      cient inhabitant   .40

31.   3 Mils (Bro) 1955. Rev. Fish   .15

REPUBLIC 1963-

32. 100 Mils   (C-N) 1963- . Emblem.   Rev.
      Moufflon (wild sheep)   1.25

33. 50 Mils (C-N) 1963- . Rev. Bunch of grapes .75
34. 25 Mils (C-N) 1963- . Rev. Cedar branch   .40

35.   5 Mils (Br) 1963- . Rev. Ancient galley .20
36.   1 Mil (A) 1963. Rev. Numeral in wreath   .10

37. 500 Mils (CN) 1970. Double cornucopia. Rev.
      Youth holding basket of fruit (F.A.O.
      coin plan)   3.50
37a. 500 Mils (S) 1970 (proof issue)   85.00

CZECHOSLOVAKIA

A republic formed from parts of the old Austro-Hungarian empire after World War I. In 1938 the country was occupied by the Germans. The republic was reestablished in 1945. It has been a Communist republic since February, 1948.

100 Haleru = 1 Koruna
1 Ducat = 77-3/10 Koruny

1. 2 Ducats (G) 1923, 29-38 (Commemorating fifth anniversary of the republic). Lion on shield. Rev. St. Wenceslaus   100.00
2. 1 Ducat (G) 1923-39   40.00
3. 20 Koruny 1933-34. Arms. Rev. Three standing figures   6.00

4. 10 Koruny 1928 (Commemorating tenth anniversary). Bust of Pres. Masaryk. Rev. Arms   4.00

5. 10 Koruny 1930-33. Arms. Rev. Seated female figure and branch   4.00

6. 5 Koruny (C-N) 1925-27; smaller planchet (S) 1928-32; (N) 1937-38. Lion. Rev. Large "5" and smelting furnace   3.00

7. 20 Koruny 1937 (Commemorating the death of Masaryk). Bust of Masaryk. Rev. Arms   7.50

8. 1 Koruna (C-N) 1922-38. Lion. Rev. Kneeling female figure with sheaf of wheat   .75
9. 50 Haleru (C-N) 1921-22, 24-27, 31. Lion. Rev. Value above wreath   .50
10. 25 Haleru (C-N) 1933. Lion. Rev. Value   1.50
11. 20 Haleru (C-N) 1921-38. Lion. Rev. Sheaf of wheat   .50
12. 10 Haleru (Bro) 1922-38. Lion. Rev. Bridge   .75
13. 5 Haleru (Bro) 1923-38   .50
14. 2 Haleru (Z) 1923-25   5.00

SLOVAKIA
(German puppet state set up in March, 1939)

15. 50 Koruny 1944. Bust of Tiso. Rev. Arms   8.00
16. 20 Koruny 1939 ("Election" commemorative)   15.00

17. 20 Koruny 1941. Sts. Cyril and Methodius. Rev. Arms   6.00
18. 10 Koruny 1944. Three figures   5.00

CZECHOSLOVAKIA (continued)

19. 5 Koruny (N) 1939. Head of Father
    Hlinka. Rev. Arms   3.50
20. 1 Koruna (C-N) 1940-42, 44, 45. Arms.   2.50

21. 50 Halierov (C-N) 1940-41; (A) 43, 44;
    Rev. Value and plow   2.50

22. 20 Halierov (Br) 1940-42; (A) 42, 43.
    Nitra Castle   3.00
23. 10 Halierov (Br) 1939-42. Bratislava
    Castle   3.00
24. 5 Halierov (Z) 1942. Value   8.00

REPUBLIC 1945-

25. 50 Koruny 1947. Lion. Rev. Female figure   4.00

26. 100 Koruny 1948 (Commemorating six
    hundredth anniversary of Charles Uni-
    versity in Prague). Lion. Rev. Kneel-
    ing figure and standing figure   6.00

27. 50 Koruny 1948 (Commemorating third
    anniversary of liberation from the
    Germans). Rev. Standing figure   4.00

28. 100 Koruny 1948 (Commemorating thir-
    tieth anniversary of liberation from
    Austria). Rev. Figure with wreath   8.00

29. 100 Koruny 1949 (Commemorating seven
    hundredth anniversary of granting of
    mining privileges of Jihlava). Lion.
    Rev. Miner   6.00

30. 100 Koruny 1949 (Commemorating Sta-
    lin's 70th birthday). Bust of Stalin.
    Rev. Arms   7.50
31. 50 Koruny 1949   5.00

32. 100 Koruny 1951 (Commemorating 30th anniversary of Communist Party). Bust of Klement Gottwald. Rev. Arms   7.50

45. 100 Koruny 1955 (Tenth anniversary of liberation from Nazis). Four figures   25.00

33.	2 Koruny (C-N) 1947-48. Janosik, Czech national hero		1.00
34.	1 Koruna (C-N) 1946-47; (A) 50-53. Type of #8		.85
35.	50 Haleru (Br) 1947-50; (A) 51-53. Type of #9		.70
36.	20 Haleru (Br) 1947-50; (A) 51-52. Type of #11		.25
37.	1 Koruna (A-Bro) 1957-60. Rev. Kneeling figure		.75
38.	25 Haleru (A) 1953-54 Arms. Rev. Value		.45
39.	10 Haleru (A) 1953-58		.35
40.	5 Haleru (A) 1953-55		.50
41.	3 Haleru (A) 1953-54		.20
42.	1 Haler (A) 1953-60		.15

46. 50 Koruny 1955. Soldier   15.00

COMMEMORATIVE SERIES

47. 25 Koruny 1955. Soldier   8.00
48. 10 Koruny 1955. Kneeling soldier   6.00

43. 25 Koruny 1954 (Tenth anniversary of Slovak uprising). Soldier. Rev. Arms   10.00
44. 10 Koruny 1954   8.00

49. 10 Koruny 1957. Willenberg commemorative. Head. Rev. Lion   8.75
50. 10 Koruny 1957. Komensky commemorative   7.25

51. 1 Korun (A-Br) 1961- . Lion on shield. Rev. Woman planting linden tree .60

63. 10 Korun 1966. Arms. Rev. Horseman with falcon (Commemorates the founding of Moravia) 6.00

64. 10 Korun 1967. Arms above landscape. Rev. University building (Commemorates 500th anniversary of University of Bratislava) 12.00

52. 50 Haleru (Br) 1963- . Rev. Value .40
53. 25 Haleru (A) 1962-65 .30
54. 10 Haleru (A) 1961-74 .25
55. 5 Haleru (A) 1962- .20
56. 3 Haleru (A) 1963 .15
57. 1 Haleru (A) 1962-63 .10

65. 50 Korun 1968. Arms. Rev. Female head (Commemorates 50th anniversary of republic) 25.00
66. 25 Korun 1968. Arms. Rev. National Museum in Prague (150th anniversary) 10.00

58. 10 Korun 1964. Workers' hands. Rev. Lion (Commemorates 20th anniversary of Slovak uprising in 1944) 6.00

67. 10 Korun 1968. Triga. Rev. Arms. (100th anniversary of National Theater in Prague) 12.00

59. 25 Korun 1965. Lion on shield. Rev. Girl's head and dove (Commemorates 20th anniversary end of World War II) 8.00
60. 10 Korun 1965. Rev. Portrait of Jan Huss (Honors 550th anniversary of religious martyr) 12.00
61. 5 Koruny (CN) 1966. Arms. Rev. Value over building equipment, star 1.50
62. 3 Koruny (CN) 1965-69. Arms. Rev. Flower, value 1.00

68. 25 Korun 1969. Arms. Rev. Head of Jan E. Purkyne (Commemorates 100th anniversary of scientist's death) 12.50
69. 25 Korun 1969. Arms. Rev. Flame (Commemorates 25th anniversary of 1944 Slovak uprising) 15.00

CZECHOSLOVAKIA (continued)

70. 50 Korun 1970. Arms. Rev. Lenin (Commemorates 100th anniversary of birth)   10.00

74. 50 Korun 1971. Arms. Rev. Head of Pavel Orszagh (pen name, Hviezdoslaw). Commemorates 50th anniversary of poet's death   10.00

74a. 50 Korun 1971. Arms. Rev. Five figures with hammer and sickle (Commemorates 50th anniversary of national communist party)   10.00

71. 25 Korun 1970. Arms. Rev. Stylized face (Commemorates 50th anniversary of Slovak National Theatre)   10.00

75. 50 Korun 1972. Arms. Rev. J. V. Myslbek (Commemorates 50th anniversary of sculptor's death)   10.00

72. 25 Korun 1970. Arms. Rev. Stylized star over mountains (Commemorates 25th anniversary of liberation)   8.00

76. 20 Korun 1972. Arms. Rev. Andrej Sladkovic (Commemorates 100th anniversary of poet's death)   5.00

77. 2 Korun (C-N) 1972- . Arms. Rev. Value   .60

73. 100 Korun 1971. Arms. Rev. Bust of Josef Manes (Commemorates 100th anniversary of painter's death)   16.00

78. 20 Haleru (Bra) 1972- . Arms. Rev. Value   .40

CZECHOSLOVAKIA (continued)

79. 50 Korun 1973. Armed revolutionary worker, hammer and sickle. Rev. Arms (Commemorates 25th anniversary of republic) — 9.00

80. 50 Korun 1973. Josef Jungmann. Rev. Arms (Commemorates 200th anniversary of writer's birth) — 9.00

81. 100 Korun 1974. Friedrich Smetana. Rev. Arms (Commemorates 150th anniversary of composer's birth) — 12.00
82. 50 Korun 1974. Janko Jesensky. Rev. Arms (Commemorates 100th birthday of writer) — 8.00
83. 10 Haleru (A) 1974. Type of #78 — .15

84. 50 Korun 1975. Stanislav Kostka Neumann. Rev. Arms (Commemorates 100th anniversary of poet's birth) — 8.00

DANISH WEST INDIES

A group of 68 islands, also known as the Virgin Islands. They became Danish territory late in the seventeenth century, and were sold to the United States in 1917 for $25,000,000.

500 Bits or 100 Cents = 5 Francs or 1 Daler

CHRISTIAN IX 1863-1906

1. 20 Francs or 4 Dalers (G) 1904, 05. Head. Rev. Seated female figure — 400.00

2. 2 Francs or 40 Cents 1905. Bust. Rev. Three female figures — 60.00
3. 20 Cents 1878, 79. Head. Rev. Ship — 50.00
4. 1 Franc or 20 Cents 1905. Type of #2 — 30.00
5. 10 Cents 1878, 79. Head. Rev. Sugar cane — 50.00
6. 50 Bits or 10 Cents 1905. Head. Rev. Olive branch — 17.00
7. 5 Cents 1878, 79. Type of #3 — 40.00

8. 25 Bits or 5 Cents (N) 1905. Crowned monogram of "C9." Rev. Sickle, caduceus, and trident — 10.00
9. 10 Bits or 2 Cents (Bro) 1905 — 20.00
10. 5 Bits or 1 Cent (Bro) 1905 — 10.00
11. 2½ Bits or ½ Cent (Bro) 1905 — 10.00

FREDERICK VIII 1906-12

12. 2 Francs or 40 Cents 1907. Head. Rev. Type of #2 — 85.00
13. 1 Franc or 20 Cents 1907 — 30.00

CHRISTIAN X 1912-17

14. 5 Bits or 1 Cent (Bro) 1913. Crowned monogram of "C10." Rev. Type of #8 — 25.00

DANZIG

Danzig, a port on the Baltic, was a Free City during the Middle Ages. It was then of great commercial importance and enjoyed considerable prosperity. It was Polish from 1455-1772 and later was part of the German Empire. After World War I, Danzig issued its own coins and stamps when it again became a Free City at the head of the Polish Corridor. In 1939 it was proclaimed part of Germany again. Today it is once more under Polish administration.

100 Pfennigs = 1 Gulden

1. 5 Gulden 1923-27; 32 (modified design). Church. Rev. Arms between lions ... 75.00

2. 2 Gulden 1923. Galley. Rev. Arms between lions ... 25.00
3. 1 Gulden 1923 ... 15.00

4. ½ Gulden 1923, 27. Sailing vessel. Rev. Crowned crosses and value ... 10.00

5. 10 Pfennigs (C-N) 1923. Arms. Rev .Value ... 4.50
6. 5 Pfennigs (C-N) 1923, 28 ... 3.50

7. 2 Pfennigs (Bro) 1923, 26, 37. Crowned crosses. Rev. Value ... 2.50
8. 1 Pfennig (Bro) 1923-37 ... 3.00

9. 5 Gulden 1932. Grain Elevator. Rev. Arms between lions ... 275.00
10. 2 Gulden 1932. Galley. Rev. Type of #9 ... 75.00
11. 1 Gulden (N) 1932. Large "1." Rev. Crowned crosses ... 12.50
12. ½ Gulden (N) 1932 ... 10.00

13. 10 Pfennigs (A-Bro) 1932. Cod fish. Rev. Value ... 3.00

14. 5 Pfennigs (A-Bro) 1932. Flounder. Rev. Value ... 2.50

15. 10 Gulden (N) 1935. City hall. Rev. Arms between lions ... 200.00

16. 5 Gulden (N) 1935. Galley. Rev. Type of #15 ... 100.00

DENMARK

The Kingdom of Denmark was once much more important than it is today. Toward the end of the fourteenth century the Danes obtained control of both Sweden and Norway. Sweden obtained its freedom in 1521, but Danish domination of Norway continued until 1814.

$$120 \; Skilling = 1 \; Speciedaler$$
$$96 \; Skilling = 1 \; Rigsbankdaler$$
$$16 \; Skilling = 1 \; Mark$$
$$6 \; Marks = 1 \; Daler$$
$$4 \; Marks = 1 \; Krone$$
$$100 \; Ore = 1 \; Krone$$

CHRISTIAN IV 1588-1648

1.	1 Krone 1618-24. King standing. Rev. Crown	150.00
2.	½ Krone 1618-24	50.00
3.	¼ Krone 1618	25.00
4.	Taler 1624-47. Bust. Rev. 13 shields	175.00
5.	½ Taler 1624-46	70.00

6.	8 Skilling 1606-25. Bust. Rev. Arms and value	20.00
7.	4 Skilling 1596-1645	15.00
8.	2 Skilling 1594-1621	12.50
9.	1 Skilling 1595-1621	10.00

FREDERICK III 1648-70

10.	Taler 1649-62. Bust. Rev. Shields	200.00

11.	1 Krone 1651. Armored bust. Rev. Crown	140.00
12.	½ Krone 1651	40.00

13.	4 Marks 1659. Crowned Monogram. Rev. Hand and Sword	175.00
13a.	4 Marks 1652-70. Rev. Arms	40.00
14.	2 Marks 1652-69	35.00
15.	Taler 1664-69. Bust. Rev. Arms	120.00
16.	4 Skilling 1667-69. Arms. Rev. Value	17.50
17.	2 Skilling 1648-70	14.00
18.	1 Skilling 1648-67	12.00

CHRISTIAN V 1670-99

19.	4 Marks 1671-94. Monogram. Rev. Arms	50.00
20.	2 Marks 1671-96	25.00
21.	1 Mark 1672-92	12.00

22.	Taler 1687-93. Draped bust. Rev. Arms	200.00
23.	½ Taler 1693. Bust. Rev. Arms in circle of shields	60.00
24.	8 Skilling 1672-97. Monogram. Rev. Value	25.00
25.	2 Skilling 1676-94	20.00
26.	1 Skilling 1676-96	15.00

DENMARK (continued)

FREDERICK IV 1699-1730

27. 4 Marks 1711-23. King mounted on horse-
    back   125.00
28. 1 Krone 1725-26. Monogram. Rev.
    Arms   85.00

CHRISTIAN VI 1730-46

29. 4 Marks 1731, 32. Armored bust. Rev.
    Crown   120.00
30. 24 Skilling 1732-43. Monogram. Rev. Arms   50.00
31. 1 Skilling 1735-46   40.00

FREDERICK V 1746-66

32. Taler 1747. King standing under canopy   145.00
33. Taler 1764-65. Laureate bust. Rev. Oval
    shield   80.00
34. 24 Skilling 1750-64. Monogram. Rev. Arms   20.00
35. 8 Skilling 1763. Rev. Value   17.00
35a. 4 Skilling 1764   12.00
36. 2 Skilling 1756-61   12.00
37. 1 Skilling 1751-65   10.00

CHRISTIAN VII 1766-1808

38. Taler 1769. Bust. Rev. Arms in ribbon   250.00
39. Taler 1769-85. Monogram. Rev. Shield   75.00

40. ½ Taler 1769-86   35.00
41. ¼ Taler 1769   24.00
42. 1 Taler 1791-1801. Head. Rev. Crowned
    arms   60.00
43. ⅔ Taler 1795, 96   40.00
44. ⅓ Taler 1795-1803   40.00
45. 24 Skilling 1767, 78-83. Monogram. Rev.
    Arms   15.00
46. 8 Skilling 1778-95   7.00
47. 4 Skilling 1778, 83, 88, 1807   6.00
48. 2 Skilling 1778-88, 1800-07   8.00
49. 1 Skilling 1779-82   5.00

During the reign of Christian VII a series of
speciedalers was issued for the provinces of
Schleswig and Holstein.

50. Speciedaler 1788-1808   100.00

DENMARK (continued)

FREDERICK VI 1808-39

60. Rigsbankdaler 1842-48. Head. Rev. Coat
    of arms 100.00
61. 32 Rigsbankskilling 1842-43 .... 50.00
62. 16 Rigsbankskilling 1842-44 .... 50.00
63. 8 Rigsbankskilling 1843 .... 40.00
64. 4 Rigsbankskilling 1841-42. Head. Rev.
    Crown 15.00
65. 3 Rigsbankskilling 1842 .... 10.00
66. 2 Rigsbankskilling (C) 1842 .... 35.00
67. 1 Rigsbankskilling (C) 1842 .... 20.00
68. ½ Rigsbankskilling (C) 1842 .... 12.50
69. ⅕ Rigsbankskilling (C) 1842 .... 10.00

51. Speciedaler 1813-39. Head. Rev. Shield 60.00
52. 12 Skilling (C) 1812 .... 20.00
53. 8 Skilling 1809. Monogram. Rev. Value 6.00
54. 6 Skilling (C) 1813. Arms. Rev. Value 20.00
55. 4 Skilling (C) 1815 .... 15.00
56. 3 Skilling (C) 1815 .... 10.00
56a. 2 Skilling (C) 1809-11. Head. Rev. Arms ... 7.50

FREDERICK VII 1848-63

57. 2 Skilling (C) 1818 .... 20.00
58. 1 Skilling 1808-09. Monogram. Rev. Value ... 10.00
58a. 1 Skilling (C) 1813. Head. Rev. Value 10.00

CHRISTIAN VIII 1839-48

70. Speciedaler 1848. Head of Frederick VII.
    Rev. Head of Christian VIII. Com-
    memorates accession to throne 250.00

59. 1 Speciedaler 1840-48. Head. Rev. Two
    wild men supporting arms 200.00

71. Speciedaler 1849-54. Head. Rev. Arms 200.00

81. 2 Rigsdaler 1863. Head of Christian IX.
Rev. Head of Frederick VII (Accession to throne)   300.00

72. 2 Rigsdaler 1854-63. Head. Rev. Value   200.00
73. 1 Rigsdaler 1854, 55   75.00

74. ½ Rigsdaler 1854, 55   40.00
75. 16 Skilling 1854-58   15.00
76. 4 Skilling 1854-56   10.00
77. 1 Skilling (Br) 1856-63   3.25
78. ½ Skilling (Br) 1857   6.00

82. 2 Rigsdaler 1864-72. Head. Rev. Value   400.00

CHRISTIAN IX 1863-1906

83. 2 Kroner 1875-99. Head. Rev. Arms   25.00

79. 20 Kroner (G) 1873-1900. Head. Rev.
Female seated   150.00
80. 10 Kroner (G) 1873-1900   150.00

84. 2 Kroner 1888. Commemorating 25th
year of reign   50.00

DENMARK (continued)

85. 2 Kroner 1892. Commemorating golden
    wedding   30.00

101. 20 Kroner (G) 1913-31. Head. Rev. Arms   100.00
102. 10 Kroner (G) 1913-17   75.00

86. 2 Kroner 1903. Bust. Rev. Seated figure.
    Commemorating 40th year of reign   45.00
87. 1 Krone 1875-98. Head. Rev. Arms   8.00
88. 25 Ore 1874-1905. Head. Rev. Value, dol-
    phin   7.50
89. 10 Ore 1874-1905   3.50
90. 5 Ore (Bro) 1874-1906. Initial.
    Rev. Value, dolphin   7.50
91. 2 Ore (Bro) 1874-1906   3.00
92. 1 Ore (Bro) 1874-1904   2.00

103. 2 Kroner 1912. Bust of Christian X.
    Rev. Head of Frederik VIII (Acces-
    sion to throne)   25.00

FREDERICK VIII 1906-12
93. 20 Kroner (G) 1908-12. Head. Rev. Arms   125.00
94. 10 Kroner (G) 1908-09   100.00

104. 2 Kroner 1915-16. Regular issue   7.50

105. 2 Kroner 1923. Silver wedding. Con-
    joined busts   10.00

95. 2 Kroner 1906. Bust of Frederick VIII.
    Rev. Bust of Christian IX (Accession
    to throne)   35.00
96. 25 Ore 1907, 11. Head. Rev. Value   10.00
97. 10 Ore 1907-12   5.00
98. 5 Ore (Bro) 1907-12. Monogram. Rev.
    Value   7.25
99. 2 Ore (Bro) 1907-12   2.00
100. 1 Ore (Bro) 1907-12   1.50

106. 2 Kroner 1930. Sixtieth birthday   8.00

DENMARK (continued)

107.   2 Kroner 1937. Twenty-fifth year of rule   15.00

117.   5 Kroner (C-N) 1960-72. Head of
       King. Rev. Arms   2.50

108.   2 Kroner (A-Bro) 1924-41   4.00

118.   2 Kroner (A-Br) 1947-59   3.50
119.   1 Krone (A-Br) 1947-59; (C-N) 1960-72   1.00
120.   25 Ore (C-N) 1948-60. Monogram. Rev.
       Value   .75

109.   2 Kroner 1945. Seventy-fifth birthday   20.00

120a. 25 Ore (C-N) 1960-67. Rev. Value in
       wreath   .60
121.   10 Ore (C-N) 1948-60. Rev. Value   .50
121a. 10 Ore (C-N) 1960-72. Rev. Value in
       wreath   .20

110.   1 Krone 1915-16. Head. Rev. Dolphins   3.50
110a. 1 Krone (A-Br) 1924-41. Crowned "CX."
       Rev. Crown   2.50
111.   ½ Krone (A-Bro) 1924-40. Crowned
       "CX." Rev. Crown   10.00

122.   5 Ore (Z) 1950-64; (Br) 1960-72   .50
123.   2 Ore (Z) 1948-72   .15
124.   1 Ore (Z) 1948-72   .15

112.   25 Ore (S) 1913-19; (C-N) 1920-47; (Z)
       1941-45. Rev. Value, with and without
       center hole   2.00
113.   10 Ore (S) 1914-19; (C-N) 1920-47; (Z)
       1941-45   1.00
114.   5 Ore (Bro) 1913-23; (Iron) 1918-19;
       (Bro) 1927-41; (A) 1941; (Z) 1942-45   .50
115.   2 Ore (Bro) 1913-23, 1926-41; (Iron)
       1918-19; (A) 1941; (Z) 1942-47   .30
116.   1 Ore (Bro) 1913-23, 1926-41; (Iron)
       1918-19; (Z) 1941-46   .20

125.   2 Kroner 1953. Conjoined busts. Rev.
       Map of Greenland   50.00

DENMARK (continued)

126. 2 Kroner 1958. Head of King. Rev. Head of Princess Margrethe. (For her 18th birthday)   20.00

130. 10 Kroner 1968. Head of King. Rev. Head of Princess Benedikte (Wedding commemorative)   18.00

127. 5 Kroner 1960. Conjoined heads of **King Frederick and Queen Ingrid (Silver Wedding commemorative)**   16.75

131. 25 Ore (CN) 1966-72. Monogram. Rev. Value (center hole)   .30

MARGRETHE II 1972-

128. 5 Kroner 1964. Wedding commemorative   16.00

132. 10 Kroner 1972. Head of Margrethe II. Rev. Head of Frederik IX (Accession to throne)   12.00

129. 10 Kroner 1967. Head of King. Rev. Conjoined heads of Princess Margrethe and Prince Henrik (Wedding commemorative)   12.00

133. 5 Krone (C-N) 1973- . Head. Rev. Crowned shield between oak leaves   2.50

DENMARK (continued)

134. 1 Krone (C-N) 1973- . Head. Rev. Crowned shield	.50

135. 25 Ore (C-N) 1973- . Crowned monogram, oak-branch. Rev. Value (center hole)	.25

136. 10 Ore (C-N) 1973- . Crowned monogram. Rev. Value between oak leaves	.20

137. 5 Ore (C-St) 1973- . Rev. Value	.15

DOMINICAN REPUBLIC

With Haiti, the Dominican Republic shares Hispaniola, a West Indies island discovered by Columbus on his 1492 voyage. After many revolts against French, Spanish and Haitian rule, the Dominican Republic successfully revolted against Haiti in 1844.

$$100 \, Centesimos = 1 \, Franc$$
$$100 \, Centavos = 1 \, Peso$$

1.	5 Francs 1891. Liberty head. Rev. Arms	100.00
2.	1 Franc 1891	14.00
3.	50 Centesimos 1891	7.50
4.	10 Centesimos 1891. Arms. Rev. Value	5.00
5.	5 Centesimos 1891	3.00
6.	1 Peso (base silver) 1897	25.00
7.	½ Peso 1897	15.00
8.	20 Centavos 1897	8.00
9.	10 Centavos 1897	4.00

10.	5 Centavos (C-N) 1877. Open book. Rev. Value	8.00
11.	2½ Centavos (C-N) 1877. Cross. Rev. Value	7.50
11a.	2½ Centavos (C-N) 1882, 88. Book and cross. Rev. Value in wreath	1.50
12.	1¼ Centavos (C-N) 1882, 88	5.00
13.	1 Centavo (Bra) 1877. Date. Rev. Value	2.00

14.	1 Peso 1939-52. Indian in feather headdress. Rev. Arms	32.00
15.	½ Peso 1937-61	5.00
15a.	½ Peso (CN) 1967-	2.00
16.	25 Centavos 1937-61	2.75
16a.	25 Centavos (CN) 1967-	2.00
17.	10 Centavos 1937-61	1.75

17a. 10 Centavos (CN) 1967- .40
18. 5 Centavos (CN) 1937- .25
18a. 5 Centavos (Bi) 1944 6.00

19. 1 Centavo (Br) 1937- 61. Palm tree. Rev. Arms .75

20. 30 Pesos (G) 1955 (Twenty-fifth year of Trujillo regime) 300.00

21. 1 Peso 1955. Military bust of President Trujillo. Rev. Arms (Commemorates 25th year of regime) 30.00

22. 1 Peso 1963. Indian in feather head-dress. Rev. Arms and commemorative legend. (100th anniversary of restoration of Republic) 25.00
23. ½ Peso 1963 7.50

24. 25 Centavos 1963. Indian in feather head-dress. Rev. Arms and commemorative legend. (100th anniversary of restoration of Republic) 2.00
25. 10 Centavos 1963 1.00
26. 5 Centavos (C-N) 1963 .50
27. 1 Centavo (Br) 1963 .40

28. ½ Peso (C-N) 1967- . Indian in feather headdress. Rev. Arms 2.00
29. 25 Centavos (C-N) 1967- 1.75
30. 10 Centavos (C-N) 1967- .50
31. 1 Centavo (Br) 1968- .15

32. 1 Centavo (Br) 1969. Indian in feather headdress. Rev. Arms (F.A.O. coin plan) .60

33. 1 Peso (CN) 1969. Arms. Rev. Fortress (Commemorates 125th anniversary of independence) 9.00

34. 1 Peso 1972. Door of mint building. Rev. Arms (Commemorates 25th anniversary, founding of Banco Central) 15.00

DOMINICAN REPUBLIC (continued)

35. 30 Pesos (G) 1974. Emblem of Central American and Caribbean Games. Rev. Arms (Commemorates 12th Games)   125.00

36. 1 Peso 1974. Arms of Santo Domingo on map of Dominican Republic. Rev. Arms (Commemorates 12th Central American and Caribbean Games)   16.00
37. 100 Pesos (G) 1975. Arms. Rev. Indian idol (Commemorates mining in Pueblo Viejo)
38. 10 Pesos 1975

39. 10 Pesos 1975. Arms and value with commemorative inscription. Rev. Replica of 16th century coin (Commemorates 16th assembly, governors of the Interamerican Bank of Development)   20.00

EAST AFRICA

This area was made up of three former British protectorates, Kenya, Uganda, Tanganyika, which have become independent countries within the British Commonwealth. Nyasaland, also formerly part of East Africa, was a protectorate within the Federation of Rhodesia and Nyasaland until 1963, when it withdrew. In July 1964 it achieved independence as Malawi.

1 Florin = 1 Rupee
100 Cents = 1 Shilling

EAST AFRICA PROTECTORATE
VICTORIA 1837-1901

1. 1 Pice (¼ Anna) (C) 1897-99. Coroneted head. Rev. Value in scrolled circle   4.00

EAST AFRICA AND UGANDA PROTECTORATE
EDWARD VII 1901-10

2. 50 Cents 1906, 09-10. Crowned bust. Rev. Lion and mountains   8.00
3. 25 Cents 1906-10   5.00
4. 10 Cents (C-N) 1907, 10 (Center hole). Crown and ornaments. Rev. Elephant tusks   3.00
5. 1 Cent (Al) 1907-08   3.00
5a. 1 Cent (C-N) 1909-10   1.50
6. ½ Cent (Al) 1908   15.00
6a. ½ Cent (C-N) 1909   8.00

GEORGE V 1910-36

7. 50 Cents 1911-19. Crowned bust. Rev. Type of #2   7.50
8. 25 Cents 1911-18   8.00
9. 10 Cents (C-N) 1911-13, 18. Type of #4   4.00
10. 5 Cents (C-N) 1913-19   2.50
11. 1 Cent (C-N) 1911-18   2.00

EAST AFRICA 1920-

12. 1 Florin 1920-21. Type of #7, larger size   25.00
13. 1 Shilling - 50 Cents 1920-21   175.00
14. 25 Cents 1920-21   25.00

EAST AFRICA (continued)

15.	1 Shilling 1921-25. Smaller size	3.00
16.	50 Cents—½ Shilling 1921-24	2.25
17.	10 Cents (Br) 1921-36. Type of #4	2.00
18.	5 Cents (Br) 1921-36	1.50
19.	1 Cent (Br) 1922-35	1.00

EDWARD VIII 1936

20.	10 Cents (C) 1936. Crown above center hole. Rev. Elephant tusks	2.50
21.	5 Cents (C) 1936	1.50

GEORGE VI 1936-52

22.	1 Shilling , 1937-46. Crowned head. Rev. Type of #7	2.50
22a.	1 Shilling (C-N) 1948-52. ET INDIA IMPERATOR dropped from obverse	2.00

23.	50 Cents 1937-44	1.50
23a.	50 Cents (C-N) 1948-52. Type of #22a	1.25

ELIZABETH II 1952-

24.	50 Cents (C-N) 1954-63. Crowned head. Rev. Lion	1.00
25.	10 Cents (Bro) 1956. Type of #4	1.50
26.	5 Cents (Bro) 1955-63.	.25
27.	1 Cent (Bro) 1954-62	.75

INDEPENDENT ISSUES

28.	10 Cents (Br) 1964 . Value above center hole. Rev. Elephant tusks	.50
29.	5 Cents (Br) 1964	.30

EAST CARIBBEAN TERRITORIES

When the British Caribbean Territories currency grouping disbanded in 1965, the East Caribbean Territories, comprised of Barbados, the Leeward Islands and the Windward Islands, was founded to provide a common currency.

1. 4 Dollars (C-N) 1970. Arms. Rev. Bananas and sugar cane. Issued with common reverse design for Antigua, Barbados, St. Kitts-Nevis-Anguilla, Dominica, Grenada, Montserrat, St. Lucia, and St. Vincent (Commemorates inauguration of Caribbean Development Bank, F.A.O. coin plan)   Each 5.00

ECUADOR

After three centuries of Spanish rule, Ecuador was united to Colombia upon its liberation in 1819. Ecuador obtained its independence in 1836 and became a republic.

8 Reales = 5 Francs = 1 Dollar or Piece-of-Eight
10 Centavos = 1 Decimo
100 Centavos = 1 Sucre
25 Sucres = 1 Condor

EL ECUADOR EN COLOMBIA

1. 2 Reales 1833-35. Fasces. Rev. Sun above mountains   16.75

2. 1 Real 1833 - 35   16.00
3. ½ Real 1833, 35   20.00

REPUBLICA DEL ECUADOR

4. 4 Reales 1841-43. Fasces. Rev. Sun above mountains   16.00

5. 2 Reales 1836-41   10.00
6. 1 Real 1836-40   8.00
7. ½ Real 1838, 40   17.50
8. 8 Reales 1846. Bust of Liberty. Rev. Arms   500.00
9. 4 Reales 1855-57, 62   16.75

10. 2 Reales 1847-57, 62   12.50
11. ½ Real 1848, 49   15.00
12. ¼ Real 1849-55   30.00

13. 5 Francs 1858   150.00

NEW COINAGE

14. 1 Sucre 1884-97. Head of General Sucre   10.00
15. ½ Sucre 1884   20.00

16. 2 Decimos 1884-96, 1912-16   1.50
17. 1 Decimo 1884-1916   1.25
18. ½ Decimo 1893-1915   1.00
19. 10 Centavos (C-N) 1918-19. Arms. Rev. Value   1.50
19a. 10 Centavos (C-N) 1924. Head of Bolivar. Rev. Arms   1.50
20. 5 Centavos (C-N) 1884-86, 1909-19. Type of #19   1.50
20a. 5 Centavos (C-N) 1924. Head of Bolivar. Rev. Arms   1.50
21. 2½ Centavos (C-N) 1917   16.00

22. 2 Centavos (C) 1872; (C-N) 1909   5.00
23. 1 Centavo (C) 1872, 90; (C-N) 1884-86, 1909   4.00
24. ½ Centavo (C-N) 1884-86; (C) 1890; (C-N) 1909   3.00

25.   1 Condor (G) 1928. Bust of Bolivar   200.00

26.   2 Sucres 1928, 30. Head of Sucre. Rev.
       Arms   **2.00**
27.   1 Sucre 1928, 30, 34   **1.00**
28.   5 Decimos (50 Centavos) 1928, 30   1.00

29.   10 Centavos (N) 1928. Bust of Bolivar   1.25
30.   5 Centavos (N) 1928. Arms. Rev. Value   1.25

31. 2½ Centavos (N) 1928   2.50
32.   1 Centavo (Bro) 1928   1.50

LAWS OF 1937-42

33.   5 Sucres 1943-44. Head of Gen. Sucre.
       Rev. Arms   5.00

34.   2 Sucres 1944   3.00
35.   1 Sucre (N) 1937, 1946   .60
36.   1 Sucre (CN) 1959   .65
37.   1 Sucre (Ni-St) 1964-   .50

38. 50 Centavos (N-St) 1963- . Arms. Rev.
       Value   .50
39. 20 Centavos (N) 1937; (Bra) 1942-44;
       (C-N) 1946; (N-St) 1959-   .25
40. 10 Centavos (N) 1937; (Bra) 1942; (C-N)
       1946; (N-St) 1964-   .25
41.   5 Centavos (N) 1937; (Bra) 1942-44;
       (C-N) 1946; (N-St) 1970   .20

EGYPT (Modern)

In ancient times a center of civilization, Egypt was conquered by the Ottoman Turks as far back as 1517, and remained part of the Turkish Empire for four centuries. In 1915 Egypt was detached from Turkish rule and declared a British protectorate. In 1922 Egypt became an independent kingdom and in 1953 a republic. Egypt and Syria formed the United Arab Republic in 1958. Although Syria withdrew in 1961, Egypt retained the name until 1971.

During the years of Turkish rule, all Egyptian coins carried the *Toughra*—the Sultan's calligraphic emblem, as explained in the section on Turkish coins. In the case of all Egyptian coins issued during the reign of Abdul Hamid II from 1876 to 1909, the opening date of the reign appears together with the year of issue on the reverse. The opening year (1876) appears as 1293 in the Mohammedan dating system and is inscribed in Turkish figures.

In the case of Mohammed V, who ruled from 1909 to 1915, the opening date is A.H. 1327. (See the explanation of Mohammedan dates in the section devoted to the coins of Iran.)

1 Ochr-el-Guerche = 1/10 Guerche or Piastre
10 Milliemes = 1 Guerche or Piastre
100 Piastres = 1 Pound Egyptian

UNDER TURKISH RULE
ABDUL HAMID II 1876-1909

1.	20 Piastres 1876-1909. Toughra in wreath. Rev. Inscription in wreath	12.00
2.	10 Piastres 1876-1909	6.00
3.	5 Piastres 1876-1909	4.00

4.	2 Piastres 1876-1909	2.00
5.	1 Piastre 1876-1909	1.50

6.	10 Ochr-el-Guerche [1 Piastre](C-N)1876-1909. Toughra in wreath. Rev. Inscription in circle of stars	1.75
7.	5 Ochr-el-Guerche(C-N)1876-1909. Toughra in closed wreath. Rev. Inscription	1.00
8.	2 Ochr-el-Guerche (C-N)1876-1911	.75
9.	1 Ochr-el-Guerche (N) 1876-1911	.50

MOHAMMED V 1909-15

10.	20 Piastres 1910-12, 14. Toughra in wreath. Rev. Inscription in wreath	12.00
11.	10 Piastres 1910-12, 14	4.75
12.	5 Piastres 1910-14	3.00
13.	2 Piastres 1910-11	2.00
14.	1 Piastre 1910-11	2.50

BRITISH PROTECTORATE 1915-22
SULTAN FUAD I 1917-22

15.	10 Piastres 1920. Inscription. Rev. Inscription and value	25.00
16.	5 Piastres 1920	40.00
17.	2 Piastres 1920	60.00

EGYPT (continued)

INDEPENDENT KINGDOM
KING FUAD I 1922-36

18.	100 Piastres (G) 1922-30. Bust. Rev. Inscription in circle	75.00
19.	50 Piastres (G) 1923-30	60.00
20.	20 Piastres (G) 1923-30	40.00

21.	20 Piastres 1923. Civilian bust. Rev. Inscription	17.50

2.	20 Piastres 1929, 33. Military bust. Rev. Inscription	17.50
23.	10 Piastres 1923-33. Bust. Rev. Inscription	7.00
24.	5 Piastres 1923-33	5.00
25.	2 Piastres 1923-29	2.00
26.	10 Milliemes (C-N) 1924-35	1.00
27.	5 Milliemes (C-N) 1924-35	.60

28.	2½ Milliemes (C-N) 1933 (Octagonal shape)	1.25
29.	2 Milliemes (C-N) 1924, 29	.60
30.	1 Millieme (Bro) 1924-35	.60

31.	½ Millieme (Bro) 1924-32	2.00

FAROUK I 1936-52

32.	50 Piastres (G) 1938. Bust. Rev. Value and dates	70.00
33.	20 Piastres (G) 1938	40.00

34.	20 Piastres 1937, 39	12.00
35.	10 Piastres 1937, 39	3.50
36.	5 Piastres 1937, 39	2.00
37.	2 Piastres 1937-42	1.00

38.	2 Piastres 1944. (Hexagonal shape)	1.00

39.	10 Milliemes (C-N) 1938, 41. Bust. Rev. Inscription	.50
40.	5 Milliemes (C-N) 1938, 41	.45
41.	2 Milliemes (C-N) 1938	.75
42.	1 Millieme (Br) 1938-50	.50

EGYPT (continued)

43. 1 Millieme (C-N) 1938 (Center hole)   1.00
44. ½ Millieme (Bro) 1938. Type of #42   1.50

45. 10 Milliemes (Bro) 1938, 43 (Scalloped
     edge). Type of #39   .75
46. 5 Milliemes (Bro) 1938, 43   .65

REPUBLIC 1952-

47. 5 Pounds (G) 1955, 57. Pharaoh in chariot.
     Rev. Winged sun (Commemorates 3rd
     and 5th anniversaries of Revolution)   450.00
48. 1 Pound (G) 1955, 57   75.00

49. 50 Piastres 1956. Pharaoh with broken
     chain and Liberty torch. Rev.
     Winged sun (Commemorates the Bri-
     tish Evacuation of Egypt)   10.00

50. 25 Piastres 1956 (Nationalization of Suez
     Canal). Suez Canal Co. building at
     Port Said.   12.00

51. 25 Piastres 1957 (Inauguration of the Na-
     tional Assembly)   10.00

52. 20 Piastres 1956-59. Sphinx. Rev. Value   10.00
53. 10 Piastres 1955-57   3.00

54. 5 Piastres 1955-59   3.00
55. 10 Milliemes (Al-Br) 1954-59   1.00

56. 5 Milliemes (Al-Br) 1954-59   .90
57. 1 Millieme (Al-Br) 1954-59   .75

EGYPT (continued)

UNITED ARAB REPUBLIC 1958-71

58. 20 Milliemes (Al-Br) 1958. Tractor wheel.
Rev. Value (Commemorates the Agricultural and Industrial Fair) 2.00

59. ½ Pound (G) 1958. Pharaoh in chariot.
Rev. Winged sun (Commemorates founding of the U.A.R.) 70.00

60. 20 Piastres 1960. Saladin type eagle. Rev.
Value 10.00
61. 10 Piastres 1959, 60 .... 2.50
62. 10 Piastres (CN) 1967 .... 1.75
63. 5 Piastres 1960 .... 1.00
63a. 5 Piastres (CN) 1967 .... 1.00
64. 10 Milliemes (A-Br) 1960 .... .50
64a. 10 Milliemes (A) 1967 .... .35
65. 5 Milliemes (A-Br) 1960 .... .25
65a. 5 Milliemes (A) 1967 .... .25
66. 2 Milliemes (A-Br) 1962- .... .20
67. 1 Milliemes (A-Br) 1960- .... .15

68. 25 Piastres 1960. National Assembly commemorative 8.00

70.

69. 5 Pounds (G) 1960. Aswan Dam commemorative 450.00
70. 1 Pound (G) 1960 .... 75.00

71. 10 Pounds (G) 1964. View of Aswan High
Dam. Rev. Inscription (Commemorates dedication of the Dam) 300.00
72. 5 Pounds (G) 1964 .... 175.00
73. 50 Piastres 1964 .... 8.50
74. 25 Piastres 1964 .... 3.50
75. 10 Piastres 1964 .... 2.50
76. 5 Piastres 1964 .... 1.50

77. 5 Piastres (CN) 1968. Globe encircled by
gear. Rev. Value (Commemorates the International Industrial Fair) 1.00
78. 5 Pounds (G) 1968. Open Koran above
globe (Commemorates 1,400th anniversary of the Koran) 125.00
79. 1 Pound 1968. Aswan High Dam. Rev.
Value (Commemorates start of power generation) 7.50

80. 10 Piastres (CN) 1969. Emblem (Commemorates the Cairo International Fair) 1.50

81. 5 Piastres (C-N) 1969. Two arms holding
     wrenches. Rev. Value (Commemorates
     Handcraft Fair)   1.50

90. 10 Piastres (C-N) 1970-71. Abstract ship
     design within cogwheel. Rev. Value
     (1970 date commemorates Workers'
     Congress)   1.50

ARAB REPUBLIC OF EGYPT 1971-

82. 5 Pounds (G) 1970. Gamal Abdul Nasser.
     Rev. Value (Commemorates death of
     President)   200.00
83. 1 Pound (G) 1970   100.00
84. 1 Pound (S) 1970   8.00
85. 50 Piastres 1970   5.00
86. 25 Piastres 1970   3.50
87. 1 Pound 1970. Buildings (Commemor-
     ates 1000th anniversary of Al-Azhar
     University)   11.25

90a. 10 Piastres (C-N) 1972 (Commemorates
     Cairo State Fair)   .75

93.

91. 5 Pounds (G) 1973. Bank building. Rev.
     Value (Commemorates 75th anniversary
     of National Bank)   250.00
92. 1 Pound (G) 1973   100.00
93. 25 Piastres 1973   1.25
94. 5 Piastres (C-N) 1973   .25

88. 10 Piastres (C-N) 1970. Farming scene.
     Rev. Value (F.A.O. coin plan)   2.75

89. 10 Piastres (C-N) 1970. Bank building at
     sunrise. Rev. Value (Commemorates
     50th anniversary of Egypt Bank)   1.50

95. 1 Pound 1973. Aswan Dam. Rev. Value
     (F.A.O. coin plan)   7.50
96. 5 Milliemes (A) 1973   .25

EGYPT (continued)

97. 5 Piastres (C-N) 1973. Mother and child. Rev. Value (Commemorates 25th anniversary of UNICEF) .50

98. 10 Milliemes (A-Br) 1973. Eagle. Rev. Value .25
99. 5 Milliemes (A-Br) 1973 .20

100. 5 Piastres (C-N) 1974. Soldier. Rev. Value (Commemorates Yom Kippur War)

101. 5 Piastres (C-N) 1975. Bust of Nefertiti (F.A.O. coin plan, commemorates International Women's Year)

102. 10 Milliemes (Bra) 1975. Wheat gatherer and fisherman, goddess Isis seated (F.A.O. coin plan)

103. 5 Milliemes (Bra) 1975

EQUATORIAL AFRICAN STATES

All the territories of French Equatorial Africa (known as French Congo until 1910) became independent states within the French Community in August, 1960. They are Gabon, Republic of the Congo (formerly Middle Congo), Chad, Central African Republic (formerly Ubangi-Shari) and Cameroon.

100 Centimes = 1 Franc

1. 50 Francs (C-N) 1961, 63. Three antelope heads. Rev. Value 4.00
2. 25 Francs (A-Br) 1962- . New legend 1.00
3. 10 Francs (A-Br) 1961- .60
4. 5 Francs (A-Br) 1961- .50
5. 1 Franc (Al) 1969 - .40

6. 100 Francs (N) 1966, 67. Three antelope heads. Rev. Value 2.50

EQUATORIAL GUINEA

A new African republic made up from two former Spanish provinces, the island of Fernando Poo, the mainland area of Rio Muni, and several smaller islands.

1. 50 Pesetas (CN) 1969. President Macias. Rev. Value   7.50

2. 25 Pesetas (CN) 1969. Crossed elephant tusks. Rev. Arms and value   5.00
3. 5 Pesetas (CN) 1969   3.00
4. 1 Peseta (A-Br) 1969   1.50

MONETARY REFORM

5. 10 Ekuele (C-N) 1975. Bust of President Nguema. Rev. Rooster

6. 5 Ekuele (C-N) 1975. Rev. Field workers

7. 1 Ekuele (Bra) 1975. Rev. Group of tools

ERITREA

Located on the northeast coast of Africa, Eritrea was an Italian colony up to World War II. Since 1950 it has been a self-governing unit of Ethiopia.

100 Centesimi = 1 Lira
100 Cents = 1 Tallero

UMBERTO I 1878-1900

1. 5 Lire 1891, 96. Head of Humbert I of Italy   175.00
2. 2 Lire 1890-96   60.00
3. 1 Lira 1890-96   50.00
4. 50 Centesimi 1890   35.00

VICTOR EMMANUEL III 1900-44

5. 1 Tallero 1918. Female bust. Rev. Crowned eagle over Italian arms (struck in the style of the Maria Theresa dollar, with which it was meant to compete)   30.00

ESTONIA

After years of Danish, Polish, and Swedish rule, Estonia was annexed by the Russians early in the eighteenth century. Estonia became a free country in 1918, but was reabsorbed by the U.S.S.R. in 1940.

100 Penni = 1 Mark
100 Marka = 1 Kroon
100 Senti = 1 Kroon

1. 10 Marka (N-Bro) 1925-26. Three lions.
   Rev. Value 6.00
2. 5 Marka (C-N) 1922; (N-Bro) 1924-26 ... 5.00
3. 3 Marka (C-N) 1922; (N-Bro) 1925-26 ... 3.75
4. 1 Marka (C-N) 1922; (N-Bro) 1924-26 ... 3.25

5. 2 Krooni 1930. Tallinn castle. Rev. Arms
   in wreath 20.00

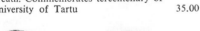

6. 2 Krooni 1932. Facade. Rev. Arms in
   wreath. Commemorates tercentenary of
   University of Tartu 35.00

7. 1 Kroon 1933. Lyre. Rev. Arms in
   wreath (Commemorates 10th Singing
   Festival) 30.00

8. 1 Kroon 1934. Viking ship. Rev. Arms ... 15.00

9. 50 Senti (N-Bro) 1936. Three lions.
   Rev. Value 12.00

10. 25 Senti (N-Bro) 1928 .... 12.00
11. 20 Senti (N-Bro) 1935 .... 5.00
12. 10 Senti (N-Bro) 1931 .... 4.75
13. 5 Senti (Bro) 1931 .... 4.00
14. 2 Senti (Bro) 1934 .... 4.00

15. 1 Sent (Bro) 1929 .... 3.00
15a. 1 Sent (Bro) 1939. New legend 17.50

ETHIOPIA

An independent kingdom in northeast Africa. An Italian invasion of Ethiopia in 1895 resulted in disastrous defeat for the Europeans. A second Italian invasion in 1936, however, was successful and caused Emperor Haile Selassie to flee. He was restored to power in 1941.

16 Guerche = 1 Menelik Talari
100 Cents or Matoñas = 1 Talari

MENELIK II 1889-1913

1.	1 Talari 1894-1903. Crowned head. Rev. Lion	45.00
2.	½ Talari 1894-97	20.00
3.	¼ Talari 1894-1903	8.00
4.	⅛ Talari 1894	50.00
5.	¹⁄₁₆ Talari 1897-1903	3.00

HAILE SELASSIE 1930-36, 1941-74

6.	50 Matoña or Cents (N) 1931. Crowned head. Rev. Lion	8.00
7.	25 Matoña or Cents (N) 1931	4.50
8.	10 Matoña or Cents (N) 1931	4.75
9.	5 Matoña or Cents (C) 1931	7.25
10.	1 Matoña or Cents (C) 1931	5.00

11.	50 Cents 1944. Bust of Emperor. Rev. Lion	4.00
12.	25 Cents (Br) 1944	30.00
12a.	25 Cents (Br) 1944 (scalloped edge)	1.00
13.	10 Cents (Br) 1944	.40
14.	5 Cents (Br) 1944	.25
15.	1 Cent (Br) 1944	.20

FALKLAND ISLANDS

A British colony located in the south Atlantic.

1.	10 Pence (C-N) 1974. Queen Elizabeth II. Rev. Two Seals	.75

2.	5 Pence (C-N) 1974. Rev. Bird in flight	.40
3.	2 Pence (Br) 1974. Rev. Gull in flight	.25

4.	1 Penny (Br) 1974. Rev. Two penguins	.20
5.	½ Penny (Br) 1974. Rev. Fish	.15

FIJI

Made up of some 250 islands lying northeast of Australia, Fiji was annexed by Great Britain in 1874 and remained a British Crown Colony until 1970, when it became an independent nation within the Commonwealth.

12 Pence = 1 Shilling
2 Shillings = 1 Florin

GEORGE V 1910-36

1. 1 Florin 1934-36. Crowned bust. Rev.
   Shield   8.00

2. 1 Shilling 1934-36. Rev. Native boat   6.00
3. 6 Pence 1934-36. Rev. Turtle   5.00

4. 1 Penny (C-N) 1934-36 (Center hole).
   Crown. Rev. Value   2.00
5. ½ Penny (C-N) 1934   5.00

EDWARD VIII 1936

6. 1 Penny (C-N) 1936. Type of #4   4.00

GEORGE VI 1936-1952

7. 1 Florin 1937-45. Crowned head. Rev.
   Type of #1   5.00
8. 1 Shilling 1937-43. Rev. Type of #2   2.50
9. 6 Pence 1937-43. Rev. Type of #3   2.00
10. 1 Penny (C-N) 1937-41, 45, 49-52; (Bra)
    1942-43. Type of #4   1.50
11. ½ Penny (C-N) 1940-41, 49-52; (Bra)
    1942-43. Type of #4, smaller size   .75

12. 3 Pence (N-Br) 1947, 1950-52. Rev.
    Native hut (twelve-sided planchet)   1.50

ELIZABETH II 1952-

13. 1 Florin (C-N) 1957-65. Crowned head.
    Rev. Arms   2.50
14. 1 Shilling (C-N) 1957-65. Rev. Native
    boat   1.25
15. 6 Pence (C-N) 1953-67. Rev. Turtle   .75
16. 3 Pence (N-Br) 1955-67. Rev. Native
    hut (twelve-sided planchet)   .50
17. 1 Penny (C-N) 1954-68. Center hole   .40

18. ½ Penny (C-N) 1954   1.00

FIJI (continued)

DECIMAL COINAGE

100 Cents = 1 Dollar

19. 1 Dollar (CN) 1969. Draped bust with
     coronet. Rev. Arms   6.50

20. 20 Cents (CN) 1969- . Rev. Tabua (native
     ceremonial object)   .75
21. 10 Cents (CN) 1969. Rev. Ula tavatava
     (throwing club)   .40

22. 5 Cents (CN) 1969- . Rev. Lali (drum)   .25
23. 2 Cents (Br) 1969- . Rev. Fan   .15
24. 1 Cent (Br) 1969- . Rev. Tanoa (wooden
     bowl)   .10

26. 100 Dollars (G) 1974. Rev. Cakoban, king of
     Fiji Islands until 1874 (Commemorates
     100th anniversary of cession to Great
     Britain)   150.00
27. 25 Dollars 1974   35.00

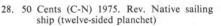

28. 50 Cents (C-N) 1975. Rev. Native sailing
     ship (twelve-sided planchet)   1.50

25. 1 Dollar (CN) 1970. Rev. Great Seal of
     Fijian Kingdom (Commemorates in-
     dependence)   12.50
25a. 1 Dollar 1970 (silver proof issue)   100.00

FINLAND

Finland was part of the kingdom of Sweden until 1809 when it became an autonomous Grand Duchy of the Russian Empire. Finland declared its independence in 1917 and became a republic in 1919.

100 Pennia = 1 Markka

UNDER RUSSIAN RULE

1. 20 Markkaa (G) 1878-1913. Crowned double-headed eagle. Rev. Value in wreath — 150.00
2. 10 Markkaa (G) 1878-1913 — 100.00

3. 2 Markkaa 1865-74, 1905-08 — 12.50
4. 1 Markka 1864-74, 90-93, 1907-08, 15 — 4.00
5. 50 Pennia 1864-74, 89-93, 1907-08, 11, 15-17 — 2.00

6. 25 Pennia 1865-76, 89-99, 1901-17 — 2.00

7. 10 Pennia (C) 1865-76, 89-91, 95-99, 1900-17. Crowned monogram. Rev. Value in wreath — 3.00
8. 5 Pennia (C) 1865-75, 88-92, 96-99, 1901-17 — 2.50
9. 1 Penni (C) 1864-76, 81-99, 1901-16 — .75

REVOLUTIONARY PERIOD 1917-18

10. 50 Pennia 1917. Double-headed eagle without crown above. Rev. Value in wreath — 4.50
11. 25 Pennia 1917 — 3.00
12. 10 Pennia (C) 1917 — 8.00
13. 5 Pennia (C) 1917 — 4.00
14. 1 Penni (C) 1917 — 3.00

15. 5 Pennia (C) 1918. Three trumpets. Rev. Value (Communist issue) — 80.00

REPUBLIC 1919-

16. 200 Markkaa (G) 1926. Lion on sword. Rev. Value and sprays — 500.00
17. 100 Markkaa (G) 1926 — 450.00

18. 20 Markkaa (A-Bro) 1931-39. Arms in wreath. Rev. Value in wreath — 5.00
19. 10 Markkaa (A-Bro) 1928-39 — 4.00
20. 5 Markkaa (A-Bro) 1928-42; (Bra) 46-49; (St) 51-52 — 2.50
21. 1 Markka (C-N) 1921-24, 28-40; (Bro) 40-43, 49-51; (I) 43-52. Lion on sword. Rev. Value — 1.50
22. 50 Pennia (C-N) 1921-40; (Bro) 40-43; (I) 43-48 — 1.50
23. 25 Pennia (C-N) 1921-40; (Bro) 40-43; (I) 43-45 — .50

24. 10 Pennia (Br) 1919-40 — 1.00

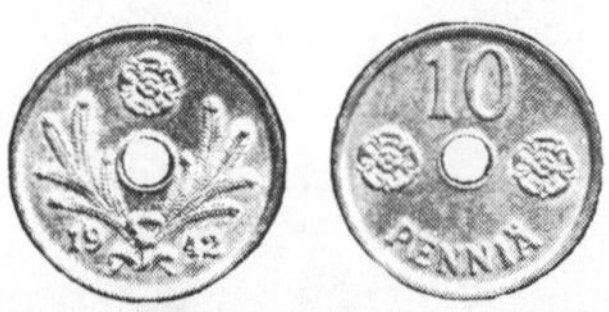

25. **10 Pennia (Bro) 1941-43; (I) 43-45 (Center hole). Two pine branches. Rev. Value** — 1.00
26. **5 Pennia (Br) 1918-40. Lion on sword. Rev. Value** — .50
27. **5 Pennia (Bro) 1941-43. Type of #25** — .40
28. 1 Penni (Br) 1919-24. Type of #26 — 1.00

FINLAND (continued)

POST WAR COINAGE

29. 200 Markkaa 1956-59. Arms. Rev. Value   5.50
30. 100 Markkaa 1956-60   4.00

38. 1 Markka 1964-68. Lion on sword. Rev.
    Value, background of trees   2.00
38a. 1 Markka (C-N) 1969-   .75

31. 50 Markkaa (A-Bro) 1952-62. Lion on
    sword. Fir tree and value   4.00
32. 20 Markkaa (A-Bro) 1952-62   1.50
33. 10 Markkaa (A-Bro) 1952-62   3.00

39. 50 Pennia (A-Br)   1963-   Rev. Value
    and tree   .85
40. 20 Pennia (A-Br)   1963-   1.00
41. 10 Pennia (A-Br)   1963-   .25
42. 5 Pennia (Br) 1963-   Arms of St.
    Hans. Rev. Value   .25
43. 1 Penni (Br) 1963-69; (Al) 1969-   .10

34. 5 Markkaa (I) 1952, 53; (N-I) 1953-62.
    Arms of St. Hans. Rev. Value   .50
35. 1 Markka (I) 1952, 53; (N-I) 1953-62   .40

44. 10 Markkaa 1967. Five flying ospreys. Rev.
    Construction scene (Commemorates 50th
    anniversary of independence)   10.00

36. 500 Markkaa 1951-52 (Commemorating
    15th Olympiad). Chain links. Rev.
    Value in wreath   40.00

37. 1000 Markkaa 1960. Bust of J. V. Snellman
    (Minister of Finance in 1860). Rev.
    Value in wreath (Commemorates the
    change from ruble currency to the
    present markkaa system)   25.00

45. 10 Markkaa 1970. Portrait of Juho Kusti
    Paaskivi. Rev. Value on stone slabs
    (Commemorates 100th anniversary of
    statesman's birth)   10.00

46. 10 Markkaa 1971. Six runners. Rev. View of
    Helsinki (Commemorates 10th European
    Athletic Championships)   7.25

47. 5 Markkaa (A-Br) 1972- . Icebreaker
    within seven-sided field. Rev. Value,
    birds   2.50

48. 10 Markkaa 1975. Portrait of Urho Kek-
    konen. Rev. Trees (Commemorates 75th
    birthday of president)

FRANCE

Few countries have had as stormy a history as France. Since the abolition of the monarchy in 1792, this country has had three revolutions, five republics, two empires, one restoration of the monarchy, one provisional government, and several disastrous wars.

The constitution of the Fifth Republic adopted in 1958 created a French Community made up of the French Republic (Metropolitan Departments, Overseas Departments and Territories), Member States, and former possessions which retain only special relations with the Community.

The ecu was a small coin using a shield (*ecu*) as a device. The gold ecu was replaced by the louis d'or in 1640. The denier was a minor coin, deriving from the Roman denarius.

100 Centimes = 1 Franc
12 Deniers = 1 Sol
3 Deniers = 1 Liard

LOUIS XIII 1610-43

1. 1 Ecu 1641-43. Bust. Rev. Crowned arms 225.00

2. ½ Ecu 1642-43   80.00
3. ¼ Ecu 1642-43   35.00
4. ¹⁄₁₂ Ecu 1642-43   15.00

5. 1 Denier (C). Bust. Rev. Fleur de lis   6.00

LOUIS XIV 1643-1715

6. 1 Louis d'or (G) 1644-49, 1694-1701.
    Bust. Rev. Fleur de lis   rare

7. ½ Louis d'or (G) 1644-1709. Bust. Rev.
    Eight "L"s in form of cross   175.00

8. 1 Ecu 1643-1715. Bust. Rev. Fleur de lis 60.00

9. ½ Ecu 1643-1715   16.00

FRANCE (continued)

18. 1 Ecu 1716-18. Boy head. Rev. Arms   45.00

10.	¼ Ecu 1643-1715	10.00
11.	1/12 Ecu 1643-1715	6.50
12.	1 Liard (C) 1648-58, 1693-1713	4.75
13.	6 Deniers (C) 1710-13. Bust. Rev. Fleur de lis	8.00

14. 4 Deniers (C) 1692-1708   4.75

19. 1 Ecu 1720-40. Young bust. Rev. Arms   28.00

15. 2 Deniers (C) 1696-1700   3.25

LOUIS XV 1715-74

20.	1 Ecu 1740-74. Old head. Rev. Arms	25.00
21.	½ Ecu 1716-70	15.00
22.	¼ Ecu 1715-25	8.75

16.	1 Louis d'or (G) 1716-35, 47-73. Bust. Rev. Arms	400.00
17.	½ Louis d'or (G) 1716-43	225.00

23. 24 Sols 1726   12.00

24.	12 Sols 1743-71	10.00
25.	6 Sols 1743-79	10.00

26.	1 Sol (C) 1719-23, 66-74. Bust. Rev. Arms	6.00
27.	½ Sol (C) 1720-23, 67-74	6.00

LOUIS XVI 1774-93

28.	Double Louis d'or (G) 1775-92	450.00

29.	1 Louis d'or (G) 1768-92. Bust. Rev. Oval shield	250.00

30.	1 Ecu 1774-92. Bust. Rev. Shield	25.00

31.	½ Ecu 1780-92	16.00
32.	⅙ Ecu 1777-90	7.25
33.	⅒ Ecu 1786-90	4.75

CONSTITUTIONAL PERIOD 1789-93

34.	12 Deniers (C or Bra) 1791-93	7.25
35.	6 Deniers (C or Bra) 1791-93	8.00
36.	3 Deniers (C or Bra) 1791-93	8.75

37.	1 Ecu 1792-93. Bust of Louis XVI. Rev. Angel	35.00

FIRST REPUBLIC 1793-1804

One of the most startling reforms ushered in by the French Revolution was a new calendar starting on September 22, 1792, the formal opening date of the new republic. There were twelve months of thirty days each (Vendémaire, Brumaire, Frimaire, Nivôse, Ventôse, Germinal, Floréal, Prairial, Messidor, Thermidor, and Fructidor) plus five feast days to fill out the year. The new era was numbered from the Year 1.

38.	1 Ecu 1793-94. Angel. Rev. Value	200.00

FRANCE (continued)

39. 2 Sols (Br) 1793. Tablet. Rev. Scales   10.00
40. 1 Sol (Br) 1793   12.00
40a. ½ Sol (Br) 1793   60.00

DIRECTORY 1795-1799

41. 5 Francs Year 4 to 7 (1795-98). Hercules group. Rev. Value   50.00

42. 2 Decimes [20 Centimes] (C) Year 4-5. Head of republic. Rev. Value in wreath   20.00
43. 1 Decime (C) Year 4-7   4.00
44. 5 Centimes (C) Year 4-7   2.00

45. 1 Centime (C) Year 6-7   1.00

CONSULATE 1799-1804

46. 5 Francs Year 8-11. Hercules group, type of #41   11.00

47. 5 Francs Year 11-12. Bare head of Bonaparte, First Consul. Rev. Value   80.00
48. 2 Francs Year 12   60.00
49. 1 Franc Year 11-12   25.00
50. ½ Franc Year 11-12   15.00
51. ¼ Franc Year 12   10.00
52. 1 Decime [10 Centimes] (C) Year 8-9   5.00
53. 5 Centimes (C) Year 8-9   4.00
54. 1 Centime (C) Year 8   5.00

FIRST EMPIRE — NAPOLEON 1804-14, 1815

55. 40 Francs (G) 1807-13. Laureate head   160.00
56. 20 Francs (G) 1807-15   75.00

57. 5 Francs Year 12-14. 1806-07 bare head; 1807-08 laureate head. Rev. Value in wreath, "Republique Francaise"   50.00

FRANCE (continued)

58. 5 Francs 1809-14. Laureate head. Rev.
     Value, "Empire Francais"   40.00
59. 5 Francs 1815. Type of #58. The famous
     "Hundred Days" coin struck after
     Napoleon's escape from Elba   100.00
60. 2 Francs Year 12-14, 1806-14   30.00
61. 1 Franc Year 12-14, 1806-14   15.00
62. ½ Franc Year 12-14, 1806-14   8.00
63. ¼ Franc Year 12-14, 1806-09   15.00

64. 10 Centimes (Billon) 1808-10. Value. Rev.
     Large "N"   2.00
65. 5 Centimes (C) 1808   60.00

LOUIS XVIII 1814-15, 1815-24

66. 20 Francs (G) 1814-24   60.00

67. 5 Francs 1814-15 (First restoration). Head.
     Rev. Shield, "Piece de 5 Francs"   25.00

68. 5 Francs 1816-24 (Second restoration).
     Bust. Rev. Shield   15.00
69. 2 Francs 1816-24   20.00
70. 1 Franc 1816-24   18.00
71. ½ Franc 1816-24   15.00
72. ¼ Franc 1817-24   10.00

CHARLES X 1824-30

73. 20 Francs (G) 1825-30. Bust, head right   60.00

74. 5 Francs 1824-30. Head. Rev. Arms   10.00

FRANCE (continued)

75. 2 Francs 1825-30   20.00
76. 1 Franc 1825-30   15.00
77. ½ Franc 1825-30   10.00
78. ¼ Franc 1825-30   5.00

LOUIS PHILIPPE 1830-48

79. 20 Francs (G) 1830-48. Bust, head left   50.00

90. 5 Francs 1848-49. Hercules group   7.50

80. 5 Francs 1830-31. Bare head. Rev. Value   5.00

81. 5 Francs 1831-48. Laureated head   4.00
82. 2 Francs 1831-48   15.00
83. 1 Franc 1831-48   8.00
84. ½ Franc 1831-45   7.25
85. ¼ Franc 1831-45   2.00
86. 50 Centimes 1845-48   3.00
87. 25 Centimes 1845-48   2.00

91. 5 Francs 1849-51. Ceres head   10.00

SECOND REPUBLIC 1848-52

92. 2 Francs 1849-51   100.00
93. 1 Franc 1849-51   15.00
94. 50 Centimes 1849-51   12.00
95. 20 Centimes 1849-51   8.00

88. 20 Francs (G) 1848-49. Angel   60.00
88a. 20 Francs (G) 1849-51. Ceres   50.00

89. 10 Francs (G) 1850-51. Ceres   50.00

96. 1 Centime (C) 1848-51   2.00

FRANCE (continued)

97. 5 Francs 1852. Head of Louis Bonaparte
    as President. Rev. Value in wreath ... 15.00
98. 1 Franc 1852 ... 25.00
99. 50 Centimes 1852 ... 15.00

SECOND EMPIRE — NAPOLEON III 1852-70

100. 20 Francs (G) 1853-70 ... 60.00
101. 10 Francs (G) 1855-69 ... 20.00
102. 5 Francs (G) 1854-69 ... 40.00

103. 5 Francs 1854-59. Bare head ... 15.00

104. 5 Francs 1861-70. Laureate head ... 6.50

105. 2 Francs 1853-59. Bust. Rev. Value in
     wreath ... 150.00
105a. 2 Francs 1866-70. Type of #104 ... 4.00
106. 1 Franc 1853-64. Type of #105 ... 10.00
106a. 1 Franc 1866-70. Type of #104 ... 2.00
107. 50 Centimes 1853-63. Type of #105 ... 5.00
107a. 50 Centimes 1864-69. Laureated bust.
      Rev. Crown ... 1.50
108. 20 Centimes 1853-63. Type of #105 ... 3.00
108a. 20 Centimes 1864-66. Type of #107a ... 1.50

109. 10 Centimes (C) 1852-65 ... .75
110. 5 Centimes (C) 1853-65 ... .50
111. 2 Centimes (C) 1853-63 ... .50
112. 1 Centime (C) 1853-70 ... 1.00

THIRD REPUBLIC 1870-1940

113. 20 Francs (G) 1871-98. Angel ... 60.00

113a. 10 Francs (G) 1889-99. Ceres ... 40.00

114. 5 Francs 1870-78. Hercules group ... 5.00

FRANCE (continued)

126. 1 Franc 1898-1920   1.25
127. 50 Centimes 1897-1920   1.00

128. 25 Centimes (N) 1903   .60
128a. 25 Centimes (N) 1904-05. Rev. Fasces   .60

115. 5 Francs 1870-71. Ceres head   10.00
116. 2 Francs 1870-95. Ceres head   5.00
117. 1 Franc 1871-95   2.00
118. 50 Centimes 1871-95   2.00

129. 10 Centimes (C) 1898-1921. Head of
    republic   .35
130. 5 Centimes (C) 1898-1921   .30
131. 2 Centimes (C) 1898-1920. Rev. Value   1.00
132. 1 Centime (C) 1898-1920   .75

133. 100 Francs (G) 1935-36. Head of repub-
    lic   250.00

119. 10 Centimes (C) 1870-98. Ceres   1.00
120. 5 Centimes (C) 1871-98   .60
121. 2 Centimes (C) 1877-97   1.00
122. 1 Centime (C) 1872-97   .50

123. 20 Francs (G) 1899-1914. Head of
    republic. Rev. Rooster   70.00
124. 10 Francs (G) 1899-1914   50.00

134. 20 Francs 1929-38. Head of republic   4.00
135. 10 Francs (S) 1929-39; (C-N) 1945-50   1.00

125. 2 Francs 1898-1920. Sower walking   1.75

136. 5 Francs (N) 1933. Liberty head. Rev.
    Value   2.50

FRANCE (continued)

136a. 5 Francs (N) 1933-38; (A-Bro) 1938-46;
     (A) 1945-52. Head of Marianne   1.00

145. 2 Francs (A) 1943-44. Fasces, "ETAT
     FRANCAIS" legend. Rev. Value   .45
146. 1 Franc (A) 1942-44   .25
147. 50 Centimes (A) 1942-44   .20
148. 20 Centimes (Z) 1941-44 (center hole)   1.00
148a. 20 Centimes (I) 1944   20.00
149. 10 Centimes (Z) 1941-44   .25

137. 2 Francs (A-Br) 1931-41; (A) 1941-59   .25
137a. 2 Francs (Bra) 1944. FRANCE in
     wreath. Rev. Value (Allied occupation
     issue)   2.50
138. 1 Franc (A-Br) 1931-41; (A) 1941-59   .20
139. 50 Centimes (A-Br) 1931-41; (A) 1941-47   .15

FOURTH REPUBLIC 1946-58

150. 100 Francs (C-N) 1954-58. Liberty head.
     Rev. Value   1.50

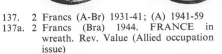

140. 25 Centimes (N) 1914-17; (C-N) 1917-38;
     (N-Bro) 1938-40 (center hole)   .20
141. 20 Centimes (Z) 1945-46   5.00
142. 10 Centimes (N) 1914; (C-N) 1917-38;
     (N-Br) 1938-39; (Z) 1941-46   .25
143. 5 Centimes (C-N) 1917-38; (N-Br) 1938-
     39   .40

WARTIME VICHY ISSUES

151. 50 Francs (A-Br) 1950-58   .75

144. 5 Francs (Ni-Br) 1941. Marshal Petain.
     Rev. Fasces and value   25.00

152. 20 Francs (A-Br) 1950-54   .75

153. 10 Francs (A-Br) 1950-58 .25

**FIFTH REPUBLIC 1958-
NEW STANDARD (Heavy Franc)**
100 Old Francs = 1 New Franc

154. 10 Francs 1964-73. Hercules group. Rev.
Value in wreath (Type of #41, 90,
114) 7.50

155. 5 Francs 1960-69. Sower. Rev. Laurel
branch and value 3.00
156. 1 Franc (N) 1960- .60
157. ½ Franc (N) 1965- .30

158. 50 Centimes (A-Br) 1962-64. Liberty
head. Rev. Value 1.00
159. 20 Centimes (A-Br) 1962- .25
160. 10 Centimes (A-Br) 1962- .20
161. 5 Centimes (A-Br) 1966- .15

162. 5 Centimes (St) 1961-64. Wheat stalk.
Rev. Value .15
163. 1 Centime (St) 1962- .10
164. 5 Francs (C-N) 1970- . Type of #155 1.50
165. 50 Francs 1974- . Type of #154 20.00

166. 10 Francs (C-N-A) 1974- . Modernistic
map of France. Rev. Construction
scene 4.00

**FRENCH COCHIN CHINA
(see INDO-CHINA)**

FRENCH EQUATORIAL AFRICA

Up to 1910 this overseas territory was known as French Congo. French Equatorial Africa was made up of Gabon and Middle Congo (on the Atlantic coast) and Ubangi-Shari and Chad (further inland). In 1960 these areas became independent member states of the French Community (Middle Congo taking the name of Republic of the Congo, Ubangi-Shari becoming the Central African Republic).

100 Centimes = 1 Franc

1. 1 Franc (Bra) 1942; (Br) 1943. Rooster. Rev. Cross of Lorraine 4.00

2. 50 Centimes (Bra) 1942; (Br) 1943 .... 3.25

3. 2 Francs (A) 1948. Bust of Republic. Rev. Antelope head .... .75
4. 1 Franc (A) 1948 .... .40

COINAGE UNIFIED WITH CAMEROONS

FRENCH GUIANA

Formerly a French colony on the northeast coast of South America it is now an overseas department in the French Community. Used as a penal colony (including the famous Devil's Island) from about 1795 on. In 1945 this policy was discontinued and the French government removed all the prisoners.

100 Centimes = 1 Franc

1. 10 Centimes (base metal, silvered) 1818, 1846. Crowned monogram. Rev. Value 6.00

FRENCH INDO-CHINA
(see INDO-CHINA)

FRENCH POLYNESIA

This colony, also known as French Establishments in Oceania, is made up of 105 islands in the South Pacific. The chief ones are the Society Islands (including Tahiti), Marquesas Islands, Tubuai Islands, Tuamotu Islands, and the Gambier Islands. It is now the overseas territory of French Polynesia.

100 Centimes = 1 Franc

1. 5 Francs (A) 1952. Seated female figure. Rev. Island scene 1.00
2. 2 Francs (A) 1949 .... .50
3. 1 Franc (A) 1949 .... .25
4. 50 Centimes (A) 1949 .... .15

5. 5 Francs (A) 1965. Seated figure. Rev. Island scene, new legend .... .75
6. 2 Francs (A) 1965, 73 .... .35
7. 1 Franc (A) 1965 .... .25
8. 50 Centimes (A) 1965 .... .15

9. 50 Francs (N) 1967. Head of Republic. Rev. Native harbor scene 2.50

10. 20 Francs (N) 1967- . Head of Republic. Rev. Native plants and flowers 1.50
11. 10 Francs (N) 1967- . Head of Republic. Rev. Native mask 1.00

FRENCH SOMALILAND

A French overseas territory located on the Gulf of Aden in eastern Africa. In 1967 the name was changed to the French Territory of Afars and Issas.

100 Centimes = 1 Franc

1. 5 Francs (A) 1948, 59, 65. Bust of Republic. Rev. Antelope head .75
2. 2 Francs (A) 1948, 59, 65 .60
3. 1 Franc (A) 1948, 59, 65 .50

(Coins dated 1959 drop "UNION FRANCAISE" from inscription)

4. 20 Francs (A-Bro) 1952, 1965. Republic. Rev. Arabian dhow in foreground 2.50
5. 10 Francs (A-Bro) 1965 1.25

FRENCH WEST AFRICA

A former French overseas territory made up of Dahomey, French Guinea, French Sudan, Ivory Coast, Mauritania, Niger, Senegal, and Upper Volta. During 1958-60 it was broken up into independent nations within the French Community. French Sudan is now known as Mali.

100 Centimes = 1 Franc

1. 1 Franc (A-Bro) 1944. Head of Republic. Rev. Value 5.00
2. 50 Centimes (A-Bro) 1944 6.00

3. 2 Francs (A) 1948-55. Bust of Republic. Rev. Antelope head .50
4. 1 Franc (A) 1948-55 .30
5. 25 Francs (A-Bro) 1956 1.50
6. 10 Francs (A-Bro) 1956 1.00
7. 5 Francs (A-Bro) 1956 .75

UNIFIED COINAGE WITH TOGO

8. 25 Francs (A-Br) 1957 1.50
9. 10 Francs (A-Br) 1957 .75

GABON

An independent republic in western Africa.

1. 100 Francs (N) 1971, 72. Antelope. Rev. Value 2.50

THE GAMBIA

Formerly a British Colony and Protectorate in western Africa, the Gambia gained independence in 1965, and proclaimed a republic in 1970.

1. 4 Shillings (CN) 1966. Draped bust of Queen Elizabeth with coronet. Rev. Crocodile 2.50

2. 2 Shillings (CN) 1966. Rev. Head of Wildebeest 1.25

3. 1 Shilling (CN) 1966. Rev. Palm tree .... .75

4. 6 Pence (CN) 1966. Rev. Groundnuts .... .40

5. 3 Pence (N-Bra) 1966. Rev. Bushfowl .... .25
6. 1 Penny (Br) 1966. Rev. Native sailboat .... .25

7. 8 Shillings (CN) 1970. Rev. Hippopotamus 4.00
7a. 8 Shillings (S) 1970 .... 20.00

DECIMAL COINAGE
100 Bututs = 1 Dalasi

8. 1 Dalasi (C-N) 1971. Portrait of Sir Dawda Kairaba Jawara. Rev. Type of #1 .... 2.00
9. 50 Bututs (C-N) 1971. Rev. Type of #2 .... 1.00
10. 25 Bututs (C-N) 1971. Rev. Type of #3 .... .50
11. 10 Bututs (N-Bra) 1971. Rev. Type of #5 .... .25
12. 5 Bututs (Br) 1971. Rev. Type of #6 .... .15
13. 1 Butut (Br) 1971. Rev. Type of #4 .... .15

14. 1 Butut (Br) 1974. Type of #13 with FOOD FOR MANKIND inscription added to reverse .... .15

15. 10 Dalasi 1975. Rev. Arms (Commemorates 10th anniversary of independence) 15.00

After World War I Germany lost this colony. It was divided up into three parts and mandated to other countries.

100 Heller = 1 Rupee

GERMAN EAST AFRICA COMPANY

1. 2 Rupees 1893-94. Helmeted Kaiser Wilhelm II. Rev. Arms — 150.00
2. 1 Rupee 1890-1902 — 8.50
3. ½ Rupee 1891-1901 — 10.00
4. ¼ Rupee 1891-1901 — 5.00

5. 1 Pesa (C) 1890-92. German eagle. Rev. Arabic inscription — 2.00

GERMAN EAST AFRICA

6. 15 Rupees (G) 1916. Elephant and mountains. Rev. German eagle — 350.00

7. 1 Rupee 1904-14. Helmeted Kaiser Wilhelm II. Rev. Value in wreath — 7.50
8. ½ Rupee 1904-14 — 8.00
9. ¼ Rupee 1904-14 — 5.00

10. 10 Heller (C-N) 1908-11, 14. Crown over center hole. Rev. Value and sprays — 3.00
11. 5 Heller (C-N) 1913-14 — 3.00

12. 5 Heller (Bro) 1908-09. Crown. Rev. Value in wreath — 9.00
13. 1 Heller (Bro) 1904-13 — 1.00
14. ½ Heller (Bro) 1904-06 — 2.00

15. 20 Heller (Bra) 1916. Crown and date. Rev. Value in wreath — 6.00
15a. 20 Heller (C) 1916 — 8.00
16. 5 Heller (Bra) 1916 — 4.50

GERMAN NEW GUINEA

A German colony from 1884 to 1914, this included the northeastern part of the island of New Guinea, as well as some smaller islands. The whole area was mandated to Australia in 1920.

100 Pfennigs = 1 Mark

1. 5 Marks 1894. Bird of paradise. Rev.
   Value   250.00
2. 2 Marks 1894   70.00
3. 1 Mark 1894   30.00
4. ½ Mark 1894   35.00

5. 10 Pfennigs (C) 1894   15.00

6. 2 Pfennigs (C) 1894. Plant. Rev. Value   25.00
7. 1 Pfennig (C) 1894   6.00

GERMANY

Until 1871 Germany was made up of independent states and cities which had separate rulers, laws, taxes, armies, and coinage. After these states and cities were welded into the German Empire, the issue of new coinage was divided into two categories.

Gold coins, as well as silver coins of 2, 3 and 5 Marks or more, continued to be issued by the states and cities. Coins of the states carry a portrait of the ruler on the obverse, and a crowned eagle on the reverse. (A "small" eagle is found on coins issued before 1889; a larger eagle appears on coins issued from 1891 on.) Coins issued by the Empire carry an eagle on the obverse, and the value in a wreath on the reverse.

This system was maintained until 1918, when the coinage of the states and cities came to an end.

100 Pfennigs = 1 Mark

GERMAN EMPIRE

1.	1 Mark 1873-87. Small eagle	1.00

2.	1 Mark 1891-1916. Large eagle	.85
3.	50 Pfennigs 1875-78, 96-1903	3.00
4.	½ Mark 1905-09, 11-19	.75
5.	25 Pfennigs (N) 1909-12	2.50

6.	20 Pfennigs (S) 1873-77; (C-N) 87-88, 90, 92	3.00
7.	10 Pfennigs (C-N) 1873-76, 88-1916; (I) 15-22; (Z) 17-22	.35
8.	5 Pfennigs (C-N) 1874-76, 88-1915; (I) 15-22	.25

9.	2 Pfennigs (C) 1873-77, 1904-16	.20
10.	1 Pfennig (C) 1873-1916	.50
11.	1 Pfennig (A) 1916-18	.60

GERMAN STATES:

The coinage of the German states and cities was large and varied. Many of the pre-1800 coins are strikingly colorful pieces.

ANHALT

A duchy of central Germany, made up of Bernburg, Dessau, and Cothen.

Bernburg line

12. Taler 1806, 09. Arms. Rev. Value in wreath   400.00

ALEXIUS FRIEDRICH CHRISTIAN 1796-1834

ALEXANDER CARL 1834-63

13.	Double Taler 1840-55. Head. Rev. Crowned arms in mantle	350.00
14.	Taler 1859. Head. Rev. Crowned and supported arms	50.00
15.	Mining Taler 1834. Crowned arms in mantle. Rev. Inscription	40.00

16. Mining Taler 1846-62. Crowned bear on
     wall. Rev. Inscription   35.00
(On the death of Alexander Carl the Bernburg territory united with Dessau.)

Cothen line
HEINRICH 1830-47

17. Double Taler 1840. Head. Rev. Helmeted
     and supported arms   650.00
(On the death of Heinrich the Cothen territory
united with Dessau.)

Dessau line
LEOPOLD FRIEDRICH 1817-71

18. Double Taler 1839-46. Head. Rev. Crowned
     arms in mantle   500.00
19. Taler 1858-69. Head. Rev. Crowned and
     supported arms   40.00
20. Taler 1863 (Commemorating the separa-
     tion of the duchies in 1603 and their
     reunion in 1863). Head. Rev. Shield in
     sprays   30.00

FRIEDRICH I 1871-1904

21. 20 Marks (G) 1875. Head. Rev. Eagle   200.00
22. 2 Marks 1876   100.00
23. 20 Marks (G) 1896 (25th anniversary of
     reign)   175.00
24. 10 Marks (G) 1896   200.00

25. 5 Marks 1896   350.00
26. 2 Marks 1896   75.00
27. 20 Marks (G) 1901. 70th birthday   175.00
28. 10 Marks (G) 1901. 70th birthday   200.00

FRIEDRICH II 1904-18
29. 20 Marks (G) 1904. Head. Rev. Eagle   150.00

30. 5 Marks 1914 (Silver wedding). Acco-
     lated heads of the Duke and Duchess   75.00
31. 3 Marks 1909-11. Head. Rev. Eagle   30.00
32. 3 Marks 1914 (Silver wedding). Type of
     #30   15.00
33. 2 Marks 1904. Type of #29   100.00

BADEN
A grand duchy located in the southwest corner
of Germany.

CARL FRIEDRICH 1738-1811

34. Taler 1803. Large head. Rev. Crowned
     shield in sprays   750.00
35. Taler 1809-11. Small head. Rev. Crowned
     shield over sprays   250.00

CARL LUDWIG FRIEDRICH 1811-18
36. Kronen Taler 1813-19. Crowned and man-
     tled shield. Rev. Value in wreath   100.00

LUDWIG 1818-30
37. Taler 1819-21. Head. Rev. Crowned arms
     in mantle   125.00
38. 2 Gulden 1821-25. Head. Rev. Crowned
     shield in sprays   100.00

39. Taler 1829-30 (reduced size). Head.
     Crowned arms in wreath   75.00

LEOPOLD 1830-52

40. Kronen Taler 1830-37. Head. Rev. Crowned and supported shield — 75.00
41. Kronen Taler 1832 (Commemorating the visit of their highnesses and their children to the mint). Head. Rev. Inscription. Rare — 500.00

42. Mining Taler 1834. Head. Rev. Crown above crossed hammers — 175.00

43. Mining Taler 1836. Head. Rev. Griffin with shield — 175.00

44. Kronen Taler 1836 (Commemorating a customs union of the German states). Head. Rev. Inscription within a circle of shields of ten German states — 100.00

45. Double Taler 1841-43. Head. Rev. Value in wreath — 125.00
46. Double Taler 1844 (Commemorating erection of statue to his father). Head. Rev. Statue — 175.00

47. Double Taler 1845-52. Head. Rev. Crowned, mantled, and supported arms — 200.00

48. 2 Gulden 1846-52. Head. Rev. Crowned and supported arms — 45.00

FRIEDRICH (regent) 1852-56

49. Double Taler 1852-55. Head. Rev. Crowned, mantled, and supported arms — 600.00

50. 2 Gulden 1856. Head. Rev. Crowned arms
    supported by griffons   250.00

FRIEDRICH I 1856-1907

51. Taler 1857-65. Head. Rev. Crowned, man-
    tled, supported arms   40.00
52. Taler 1865-71. Bearded head   35.00

53. 20 Marks (G) 1872-74. Head. Rev. Small
    eagle   150.00
54. 10 Marks (G) 1872-88   100.00
55. 5 Marks (G) 1877   125.00

56. 5 Marks 1875-88. Rev. Small eagle   30.00
57. 2 Marks 1876-88   40.00
58. 20 Marks (G) 1894-95. Head. Rev. Large
    eagle   150.00

59. 10 Marks (G) 1890-1901   100.00
60. 5 Marks 1891-1902   20.00
61. 2 Marks 1892-1902   15.00

62. 5 Marks 1902 (50th year of reign)   35.00
63. 2 Marks 1902   10.00
64. 10 Marks (G) 1902-07. Head with long
    beard. Rev. Eagle   100.00
65. 5 Marks 1902-07   15.00
66. 2 Marks 1902-07   10.00

67. 5 Marks 1906 (Golden wedding). Heads
    of Friedrich and Louise   40.00
68. 2 Marks 1906   10.00
69. 5 Marks 1907 (Death of the grand duke)   42.50
70. 2 Marks 1907   12.50

FRIEDRICH II 1907-18

71. 20 Marks (G) 1911-14. Head. Rev. Eagle   100.00
72. 10 Marks (G) 1909-13   150.00

73. 5 Marks 1908, 13   20.00
74. 3 Marks 1908-15   6.00
75. 2 Marks 1911-13   50.00

BAVARIA

A kingdom in southernmost Germany.

MAXIMILIAN JOSEPH 1806-25

79. Double Taler 1839-41. Bare head. Rev.
    Value in wreath   120.00
80. Double Taler 1842-48. Bare head. Rev.
    Crowned and supported arms   115.00

76. Taler 1806-25. Bust. Rev. Arms and sup-
    porters (varieties)   120.00

81. 2 Gulden 1845-48   45.00

During this reign a series of beautiful commemorative Talers (1825-37) and Double Talers (1837-48)
was issued in addition to the regular coinage. Values
average $200 for Talers and $275 for Double Talers.

MAXIMILIAN II 1848-64

82. Double Taler 1849-64. Head. Rev. Crowned
    and supported arms   160.00

77. Taler 1809-25. Bare head. Rev. Crown
    over crossed mace and sword   65.00

LUDWIG I 1825-48

83. Taler 1857-64   35.00
84. 2 Gulden 1848-56   40.00

(During this reign commemorative Double Talers
were struck 1848-56 in addition to regular coinage.)

78. Taler 1826-37. Bare head. Rev. Crown in
    wreath   100.00

GERMANY (continued)

LUDWIG II 1864-86

85. Double Taler 1865-69. Head. Rev. Crowned
    and supported arms   very rare
86. Taler 1864-71. Head. Rev. Arms (varieties)   50.00

91. 5 Marks (G) 1877-78   200.00

92. 5 Marks 1874-76   25.00
93. 2 Marks 1876-83   20.00

OTTO 1886-1913

94. 20 Marks (G) 1895-1913. Head. Rev.
     Eagle   100.00
95. 10 Marks (G) 1888-1912   100.00
96. 5 Marks 1888. Rev. Small eagle   150.00
97. 2 Marks 1888   125.00

87. Taler 1866-71. Head. Rev. Madonna and
    child   25.00

98. 5 Marks 1891-1913. Rev. Large eagle   7.50
99. 3 Marks 1908-13   5.00
100. 2 Marks 1891-1913   5.00

88. Taler 1871. (Victorious conclusion of
    Franco-Prussian War). Head. Rev.
    Seated female   25.00
89. 20 Marks (G) 1872-78. Head. Rev. Eagle 150.00
90. 10 Marks (G) 1872-81   125.00

101. 5 Marks 1911 (90th birthday of the
     Prince regent). Head of Luitpold   35.00
102. 3 Marks 1911   10.00
103. 2 Marks 1911   7.50

GERMANY (continued)

104. 20 Marks (G) 1914. Head. Rev. Eagle   1000.00
105.   5 Marks 1914   50.00
106.   3 Marks 1914   20.00
106a 2 Marks 1914   17.50

110. Taler 1865 (Second German shooting
       festival). Type of #108   35.00
111. Taler 1871 (Victory in Franco-Prussian
       War). Type of #108   37.50
112. 20 Marks (G) 1906. Crowned and sup-
       ported arms of Bremen. Rev. Eagle   200.00
113. 10 Marks (G) 1907   200.00

107.   3 Marks 1918 (Golden Wedding)   very rare

114.   5 Marks 1906   75.00
115.   2 Marks 1904   25.00

BREMEN (Free City)

This important commercial city on the North Sea became a "free city" in 1646.

108. Taler 1863 (50th anniversary of War of
       Liberation). Inscription. Rev. Crowned
       and supported arms   67.50

BRUNSWICK (Braunschweig)

A duchy in north central Germany, famous for its remarkable coinage in the sixteenth, seventeenth, and eighteenth centuries.

HEINRICH JULIUS 1589-1613

109. Taler 1864 (Opening of the new Bremen
       Bourse). Rev. Building   100.00

116.   Taler. Wild man. Rev. Arms   165.00

FRIEDRICH ULRICH 1613-34

AUGUST II 1634-66

118. Taler. Bell over city. Rev. Arms   200.00

117.   Triple taler. Duke on horseback. Rev.
        Arms   rare

119. 1¼ Taler. Four fields with Neptune on
      dolphin, heron baiting, mine, al-
      chemy. Rev. Fortuna on globe, sail-
      ing ship in background   400.00

120. Taler 1636. Duke August holding helmet. Rev. His brothers Frederick and George — 175.00

RUDOLPH AUGUST 1666-84

121. Taler. Wild man. Rev. Arms — 140.00

RUDOLPH AUGUST AND ANTON ULRICH
(joint rulers) 1685-1704

122. Broad Taler. Conjoined heads. Rev. Insignia — 170.00

123. 24 Mariengroschen (½ Taler). Wild man. Rev. Value — 50.00

ANTON ULRICH 1704-14

124. Taler. Wild man. Rev. Arms — 90.00
125. 24 Mariengroschen — 35.00

AUGUST WILHELM 1714-31

126. Taler. Wild man. Rev. Arms — 90.00
127. 24 Mariengroschen — 40.00
128. 6 Mariengroschen — 15.00
129. 2 Mariengroschen — 10.00

LUDWIG RUDOLPH 1731-35

130. Taler. Bust. Rev. Arms — 100.00

CARL I 1735-80

131. Taler — 90.00
132. 24 Mariengroschen — 30.00

133. 4 Mariengroschen — 10.00

134. 2 Mariengroschen — 8.00

CARL WILHELM FERDINAND 1780-1806

135. 16 Groschen. Arms. Rev. Value — 15.00

CARL FRIEDRICH WILHELM 1815-23
(Under guardianship of George, Prince regent and later George IV of England.)

136. 24 Groschen 1815-23. Crowned arms. Rev. Value and legend — 40.00

137. 1/12 Taler 1816-23. Running horse. Rev. Value — 8.00
138. 1 Groschen 1819-21 — 8.00
139. 6 Pfennigs 1816-23 — 6.00
140. 4 Pfennigs 1823 — 6.00
141. 2 Pfennigs (C) 1820, 23 — 4.00
142. 1 Pfennig (C) 1816-23 — 3.00

WILHELM 1831-84

143. Double Taler 1842-55. Head. Rev. Crowned and mantled arms — 100.00

144. Double Taler 1856 (25th year of reign). Rev. Arms in wreath — 125.00

145. Taler 1837-71. Head. Rev. Crowned and mantled arms (varieties) — 50.00

146. 20 Marks (G) 1875. Head. Rev. Eagle — 250.00

(Brunswick was governed by Prussia from 1884 to 1913.)

GERMANY (continued)

ERNST AUGUST 1913-18

147. 5 Marks 1915 (Commemorating Ernst August's accession to the duchy). Accolated heads of Ernst August and Victoria Luise. Rev. Eagle ... 500.00
148. 3 Marks 1915 ... 300.00

DANZIG (see page 109)

FRANKFURT-ON-THE-MAIN (Free City)

Located in the Prussian province of Hesse-Nassau, Frankfurt became a free city as early as 1219.

149. Double Taler 1840-44. View of city and river. Rev. Value in wreath ... 150.00
150. Double Taler 1841-55. Arms (eagle). Rev. Value in wreath ... 100.00
151. Double Taler 1860-66. Bust of Franconia. Rev. Eagle ... 60.00

152. Taler 1857-58. Bust of Franconia with towers in background. Rev. Eagle ... 85.00
153. Taler 1859-65. Type of #152 (no towers) ... 20.00

154. 2 Gulden 1845-56. Arms of city (eagle). Rev. Value in wreath ... 60.00
155. 1 Gulden 59,61 ... 25.00
156. ½ Gulden 42-49 ... 30.00

(In addition to the regular coinage a series of beautiful commemorative coins was issued 1848-63. Value averages from $50 to $500.)

HAMBURG (Free City)

Located on the North Sea, Hamburg is Germany's leading port. It became a free city in the thirteenth century.

157. 48 Schillings 1761-63. Lion. Rev. Eagle ... 50.00
158. 32 Schillings 1795-96 ... 22.00
159. 16 Schillings 1727 ... 20.00
160. 8 Schillings 1726-97 ... 10.00
161. 4 Schillings 1725-38 ... 8.00
162. 2 Schillings 1727 ... 7.50

163. 32 Schillings 1808. City towers. Rev. Inscription ... 50.00

164. 20 Marks (G) 1875-89. Arms of city.
Rev. Small eagle 70.00
165. 10 Marks (G) 1873-88 . . . . 75.00

166. 5 Marks (G) 1877 . . . . 250.00

191.	⅙ Taler 1727-46	13.00
192.	Taler 1727-50. Wild man and tree	35.00
193.	⅔ Taler 1727-60	24.00
194.	⅓ Taler 1731-60	9.00
195.	⅙ Taler 1730-60	9.00
196.	Taler 1727-60. St. Andrew with cross	50.00
197.	⅓ Taler 1731-58	18.00
198.	⅙ Taler 1727-59	12.00
199.	Taler 1729-60. Running horse	45.00
200.	⅔ Taler 1727-60	27.00
201.	⅓ Taler 1734-54	16.00
202.	⅙ Taler 1727-32	9.00

GEORGE III 1760-1820

167. 5 Marks 1875-88. Arms of city. Rev.
Small eagle 15.00
168. 20 Marks (G) 1893-1913. Rev. Large
eagle 60.00
169. 10 Marks (G) 1890-1913 . . . . . 85.00
170. 5 Marks 1891-1913 . . . . 10.00
171. 3 Marks 1908-14 . . . . 6.00
172. 2 Marks 1892-1914 . . . . 6.00

HANNOVER

A kingdom located in northwest Germany. From
1714 to 1837 the kings of Hannover were also
kings of England.

GEORGE I 1714-27

173. Taler 1716-27. Bust of King 200.00
174. ⅔ Taler 1715-27 . . . . 40.00
175. ⅓ Taler 1716-26 . . . . 18.00
176. ⅙ Taler 1726-36 . . . . 15.00
177. Taler 1717-27. Wild man and tree . 65.00
178. ⅔ Taler 1717-27 . . . . 25.00
179. ⅓ Taler 1718-27 . . . . 12.00
180. ⅙ Taler 1720-25 . . . . 8.00
181. Taler 1718-26. St. Andrew with cross 35.00
182. ⅓ Taler 1719-24 . . . . 13.00
183. ⅙ Taler 1719-24 . . . . 8.00
184. Taler 1717-27. Running horse . . . 45.00
185. ⅔ Taler 1722-27 . . . . 25.00
186. ⅓ Taler 1720-23 . . . . 15.00
187. ⅙ Taler 1719-27 . . . . 9.00

GEORGE II 1727-60

188. Taler 1729-51. Bust of King 100.00
189. ⅔ Taler 1727-54 . . . . 30.00
190. ⅓ Taler 1729-36 . . . . 16.00

203.	Taler 1773-1801. Bust of King	65.00
204.	⅔ Taler 1772-1814	28.00
205.	⅓ Taler 1774-1804	17.00
206.	⅙ Taler 1773-1807	10.00
207.	Taler 1764-76. Wild man and tree	40.00
208.	⅔ Taler 1762-89	14.00
209.	⅓ Taler 1764-89	10.00
210.	⅙ Taler 1762-1804	6.00
211.	Taler 1764-76. St. Andrew with cross	55.00
212.	⅓ Taler 1764-1804	18.00
213.	⅙ Taler 1761-1804	10.00
214.	⅔ Taler 1761-1805. Crowned arms. Rev. Value	30.00
215.	½ Taler 1820. Running horse	15.00
216.	1/12 Taler 1801-16	8.00
217.	1/24 Taler 1817-18	7.00

GEORGE IV 1820-30

218. ⅔ Taler 1822-29. Bust of King . . . 40.00

GERMANY (continued)

219. 16 Groschen 1820-30. Running horse ... 20.00
220. ⅙ Taler 1821 ... 25.00
221. 3 Groschen 1820-24 ... 6.50
222. ½₄ Taler 1826-28. Monogram ... 5.00
223. 4 Pfennigs 1822-30 ... 4.00

WILLIAM IV 1830-37

233. Double Taler 1854-66. Head. Rev. Crowned
    and supported arms ... 100.00
234. Taler 1857-66. Head. Rev. Arms ... 30.00

(Hannover sympathized with Austria in the Austro-Prussian War. In revenge, the victorious Prussians formally annexed Hannover as a province of the Prussian kingdom.)

224. Taler 1834-37. Bust of King ... 40.00
225. ⅔ Taler 1834 ... 125.00
226. ⅙ Taler 1834 ... 15.00
227. ½₂ Taler 1834-37 ... 8.00
228. ⅔ Taler 1832-33. Arms. Rev. Value ... 50.00
229. 16 Groschen 1830-34. Running horse ... 30.00
230. ½₄ Taler 1834-37 ... 5.00
231. 4 Pfennigs 1835-37 ... 5.00

HESSE

Divided into a number of smaller duchies, chiefly Hesse-Cassel and Hesse-Darmstadt. Hesse-Cassel is famous as the source of mercenary soldiers, many of whom fought on the British side during the American Revolution.

HESSE-CASSEL

FRIEDRICH II 1760-85

ERNST AUGUST 1837-51

232. Taler 1838-49. Head. Rev. Arms (varieties) ... 45.00

235.   Taler 1776-79. Head. Rev. Arms ... 25.00

WILLIAM IX 1785-1803
236. Taler 1787-1802. Head. Rev. Arms   30.00

WILLIAM I 1803-21
237. Taler 1819-20. Head. Rev. Value   150.00

WILLIAM II 1821-47
238. Double Taler 1840-47. Arms. Rev. Value 125.00

239. Taler 1821-22. Head. Rev. Value in wreath 150.00
240. Taler 1832-42. Arms. Rev. Value   25.00

FRIEDRICH WILHELM 1847-66

241. Double Taler 1851-55. Head. Rev. Arms 150.00
242. Taler 1851-65. Head. Rev. Arms   40.00

HESSE-DARMSTADT

LUDWIG I 1790-1830
243. Taler 1809. Head. Rev. Crowned shield   200.00

244. Taler 1819. Uniformed bust. Rev. Crowned
      and mantled arms   200.00

245. Taler 1825. Head. Rev. Crowned and
      mantled arms   175.00

LUDWIG II 1830-48
246. Double Taler 1839-42. Head. Rev. Value
      in wreath   150.00
247. Double Taler 1844. Head. Rev. Crowned,
      supported, and mantled arms   175.00
248. Kronen Taler 1833-37. Head. Rev. Crowned
      and mantled arms   150.00

249. 2 Gulden 1845-47. Head. Rev. Shield sup-
      ported by lions   50.00

LUDWIG III 1848-77

250. Double Taler 1854. Head. Rev. Crowned,
      mantled, and supported arms   200.00

GERMANY (continued)

251. 2 Gulden 1848-56. Head. Rev. Arms supported by lions   60.00
252. Taler 1857-71   35.00
253. 20 Marks (G) 1872-74. Head. Rev. Eagle   200.00

254. 10 Marks (G) 1872-77   120.00
255. 5 Marks (G) 1877   250.00

256. 5 Marks 1875-76   60.00
257. 2 Marks 1876-77   150.00

LUDWIG IV 1877-92

258. 10 Marks (G) 1878-88. Head. Rev. Small eagle   200.00
259. 5 Marks (G) 1878-88   275.00
260. 5 Marks 1888   750.00
261. 2 Marks 1888   400.00
262. 20 Marks (G) 1892. Head. Rev. Large eagle   900.00
263. 10 Marks (G) 1890   450.00
264. 5 Marks 1891   450.00
265. 2 Marks 1891   200.00

ERNST LUDWIG 1892-1918

266. 20 Marks (G) 1893-1911. Head. Rev. Eagle   175.00
267. 10 Marks (G) 1893-98   400.00
268. 5 Marks 1895-1900   100.00
269. 3 Marks 1910   40.00
270. 2 Marks 1895-1900   180.00

271. 5 Marks 1904 (400th anniversary of Philip the Magnanimous). Accolated heads of Philip and Ernst Ludwig   75.00
271a. 2 Marks 1904   20.00

272.   3 Marks 1917 (25th anniversary of reign) 1200.00

LUBECK (Free City)

This Baltic port was one of the most important cities of the old Hanseatic League. From about 1500 Lubeck's commerce declined.

273. 10 Marks (G) 1901-10. Double-headed eagle. Rev. Eagle   400.00

274. 5 Marks 1904-13   150.00
275. 3 Marks 1908-14   40.00
276. 2 Marks 1901-12   60.00

MECKLENBURG

Located in northeast Germany on the Baltic and made up of two duchies — Mecklenburg-Schwerin and Mecklenburg-Strelitz.

MECKLENBURG-SCHWERIN

ADOLF FRIEDRICH 1592-1658
277. Double taler. Head. Rev. Fortuna   1000.00

277.

286.   2 Marks 1904   40.00

287.   5 Marks 1915 (Centenary as grand
       duchy). Busts of Friedrich Franz I
       and Friedrich Franz IV   220.00
288.   3 Marks 1915   80.00

MECKLENBURG-STRELITZ

FRIEDRICH WILHELM 1860-1904

FRIEDRICH FRANZ II 1842-83
278. Taler 1848, 64, 67. Head. Rev. Crowned
       shield in wreath   40.00
279. 20 Marks (G) 1872. Rev. Eagle   300.00
279a. 10 Marks (G) 1872-78   450.00
280.   2 Marks 1876   100.00

FRIEDRICH FRANZ III 1883-97
281. 10 Marks (G) 1890. Head. Rev. Eagle 200.00

FRIEDRICH FRANZ IV 1897-1918
282. 20 Marks (G) 1901. Head. Rev. Eagle 1200.00
283. 10 Marks (G) 1901   550.00
284.   2 Marks 1901   125.00

289. Taler 1870. Head. Rev. Crowned arms   40.00
290. 20 Marks (G) 1873-74. Head. Rev. Eagle 850.00
291. 10 Marks (G) 1873-74, 80   2000.00
292.   2 Marks 1877   150.00

ADOLF FRIEDRICH 1904-14
293. 20 Marks (G) 1905. Head. Rev. Eagle very rare
294. 10 Marks (G) 1905   very rare

285.   5 Marks 1904 (Grand duke's marriage).
       Conjoined busts. Rev. Eagle   90.00

295.   3 Marks 1913   200.00
296.   2 Marks 1905   175.00

NASSAU

A duchy in west central Germany. Because Duke Adolph sided with Austria in the Austro-Prussian War of 1866, Prussia annexed the duchy.

WILHELM 1816-39

297. Taler 1816-25. Head. Rev. Crowned and
mantled arms 200.00

298. Taler 1817. Arms. Rev. Value in wreath 150.00
299. Taler 1831-37. Head. Rev. Supported arms 130.00

ADOLPH 1839-66

300. Double Taler 1840. Head. Rev. Value in
wreath 160.00

301. Double Taler 1844-54. Head. Rev. Crowned
and mantled arms 160.00

302. Double Taler 1860. Head. Rev. Crowned
and mantled arms 175.00

303. Taler 1859-63. Head. Rev. Crowned and
supported arms 45.00
304. Taler 1864 (25th anniversary of reign).
Head. Rev. Inscription 60.00

305. 2 Gulden 1846-47. Head. Rev. Crowned
arms supported by lions 75.00

OLDENBURG

A duchy on the North Sea.

PAUL FRIEDRICH AUGUST 1829-53

306. Double Taler 1840. Head. Rev. Value in
wreath 800.00
307. Taler 1846. Head. Rev. Crowned shield 50.00

NICOLAUS FRIEDRICH PETER 1853-1900

PRUSSIA

In the eighteenth century this kingdom became the leading military power in Germany and eventually took the initiative in uniting the German states in the German Empire.

FRIEDRICH II (the Great) 1740-86

308. Taler 1858-66. Head. Rev. Crowned shield   40.00

309. 10 Marks (G) 1874. Head. Rev. Eagle   rare

313. Taler 1764-86. Head. Rev. Eagle   60.00

310.   2 Marks 1891   100.00

FRIEDRICH WILHELM II 1786-97

314.   Taler 1786-91. Armored bust. Rev. Eagle   110.00
315.   Taler 1790-97. Bust. Rev. Supported arms   60.00

FRIEDRICH AUGUST 1900-18

FRIEDRICH WILHELM III 1797-1840

311.   5 Marks 1900-01. Head. Rev. Eagle   200.00
312.   2 Marks 1900-01   100.00

316.   Taler 1797-1809. Bust. Rev. Shield and supporters (wild men)   60.00

317. Taler 1809-16. Head. Rev. Value in wreath   60.00

318. Taler 1816-22. Military bust. Rev. Eagle,
    flags, cannon   30.00
319. Taler 1823-40. Head. Rev. Crowned arms   40.00
320. Mining Taler 1826-28. Head. Rev. In-
    scription   40.00
321. Double Taler 1839-41. Head. Rev. Crowned
    and mantled arms   100.00

FRIEDRICH WILHELM IV 1840-61

326. Mining Taler 1841-60. Head. Rev. In-
    scription (varieties)   30.00

322. Double Taler 1841-56. Head. Rev. Crowned
    and mantled arms   80.00
323. Taler 1841-56   25.00
324. Double Taler 1858-59. Head. Rev. Eagle   150.00

WILHELM I 1861-88

325. Taler 1857-61   25.00

327. Taler 1861 (Coronation issue). Accolated
    crowned busts. Rev. Monograms   20.00

GERMANY (continued)

336.	5 Marks 1874-76. Head. Rev. Eagle	20.00
337.	2 Marks 1876-84	30.00

FRIEDRICH III 1888

338.	20 Marks (G) 1888. Head. Rev. Eagle	80.00
339.	10 Marks (G) 1888	60.00

340.	5 Marks 1888. Head. Rev. Eagle	75.00
341.	2 Marks 1888	20.00

WILHELM II 1888-1918

342.	20 Marks (G) 1888-89. Head. Rev. Small eagle	80.00
343.	10 Marks (G) 1889	1500.00

328.	Double Taler 1861-71. Head. Rev. Eagle	150.00
329.	Taler 1861-71. Head. Rev. Eagle	20.00
330.	Mining Taler 1861-62. Head. Rev. Inscription	40.00
331.	Taler 1866 (Commemorating victory in the Austro-Prussian War). Laureate head. Rev. Eagle	25.00

332.	Taler 1871 (Commemorating victory in the Franco-Prussian War). Rev. Seated female figure	15.00

344.	5 Marks 1888	250.00
345.	2 Marks 1888	150.00
346.	20 Marks (G) 1890-1913. Head. Rev. Large eagle	75.00
347.	10 Marks (G) 1890-1912	65.00
348.	5 Marks 1891-1908	15.00
349.	3 Marks 1908-12	9.00
350.	2 Marks 1891-1912	8.00

333.	20 Marks (G) 1871-88. Head. Rev. Eagle	100.00
334.	10 Marks (G) 1872-88	100.00

335.	5 Marks (G) 1877-78	175.00

351.	5 Marks 1901 (200th anniversary of the kingdom). Busts of Wilhelm II and Friedrich I	30.00
352.	2 Marks 1901	6.00

353. 3 Marks 1910 (Centenary of University of Berlin). Heads of Friedrich Wilhelm III and Wilhelm II. Rev. Eagle   35.00

360. 20 Marks (G) 1913-15. Uniformed bust. Rev. Eagle   75.00

354. 3 Marks 1911 (Centenary of University of Breslau)   20.00

361. 5 Marks 1913-14   15.00

356.

355. 3 Marks 1913 (Centenary of the War of Liberation). King on horseback. Rev. Eagle on snake   8.00
356. 2 Marks 1913   6.00
357. 3 Marks 1913 (25th year of reign). Uniformed bust, laurel branch and dates 1888-1913 below. Rev. Eagle   8.00
358. 2 Marks 1913   6.00

362. 3 Marks 1914   10.00

REUSS

A small state lying between Bavaria and Saxony.

Elder line

HEINRICH XXII 1859-1902

363. 20 Marks (G) 1875. Head. Rev. Eagle   rare

359. 3 Marks 1915 (Centenary of anniversary of uniting of Mansfeld with Prussia). St. George and dragon   150.00

364. 2 Marks 1877. Head. Rev. Small eagle   200.00

365. 2 Marks 1892, 99, 1901. Head. Rev.
Large eagle   160.00

HEINRICH XXIV 1902-18.

366. 3 Marks 1909. Head. Rev. Eagle   180.00

Younger line

HEINRICH XIV 1867-86

367. 20 Marks (G) 1881. Head. Rev. Eagle 1200.00
368. 10 Marks (G) 1882   very rare
369. 2 Marks 1884   250.00

SAXON DUCHIES

A number of duchies located west of Saxony.
These include: Saxe-Altenburg, Saxe-Coburg-
Gotha, Saxe-Meiningen, and Saxe-Weimar.

SAXE-ALTENBURG

ERNST 1853-1908

370. Taler 1858-69. Head. Rev. Crowned and
mantled arms   60.00
371. 20 Marks (G) 1887. Head. Rev. Eagle 500.00
372. 5 Marks 1901. Head. Rev. Eagle (75th
birthday)   300.00
373. 2 Marks 1901   200.00

374. 5 Marks 1903 (50th year of reign)   130.00

SAXE-COBURG-GOTHA

ERNST II 1893-1900

375. Double Taler 1847-54. Head. Rev. Arms 200.00
376. Taler 1846-70. Head. Rev. Arms   55.00
377. 20 Marks (G) 1872, 86. Head. Rev. Eagle 600.00

ALFRED 1893-1900

378. 20 Marks (G) 1895. Head. Rev. Eagle   900.00

379. 5 Marks 1895   800.00

380. 2 Marks 1895   200.00

CARL EDWARD 1900-18

381. 20 Marks (G) 1905. Head. Rev. Eagle   600.00
382. 10 Marks (G) 1905   500.00
383. 5 Marks 1907   400.00
384. 2 Marks 1905   200.00

SAXE-MEININGEN

GEORGE II 1866-1914

385. Taler 1867. Head. Rev. Arms   90.00
386. 20 Marks (G) 1872, 82, 89. Head. Rev.
     Small eagle   700.00
387. 20 Marks (G) 1900, 05, 10, 14. Head.
     Rev. Large eagle   rare
388. 10 Marks (G) 1890, 98, 1902, 09, 14 1,500.00

389. 5 Marks 1901-02, 08. Head. Rev. Eagle 90.00
390. 3 Marks 1908, 13   40.00
391. 2 Marks 1901-02, 13   120.00

393.

392. 3 Marks 1915 (Death of duke)   45.00
393. 2 Marks 1915   40.00

SAXE-WEIMAR

CARL ALEXANDER 1853-1901

394. Double Taler 1855. Head. Rev. Arms   300.00

395. Taler 1858-70   45.00
396. 20 Marks (G) 1892, 96. Head. Rev.
     Eagle   500.00
397. 2 Marks 1892 (Golden wedding)   75.00
398. 2 Marks 1898 (80th birthday)   75.00

WILHELM ERNST 1901-18

399. 20 Marks (G) 1901. Head. Rev. Eagle 1200.00
400. 2 Marks 1901   100.00

401. 5 Marks 1903 (Marriage of grand duke).
      Heads of Wilhelm Ernst and Caroline   180.00
402. 2 Marks 1903   30.00

403. 5 Marks 1908 (350th anniversary of
      University of Jena). Facing bust of
      Johann Friedrich   80.00
404. 2 Marks 1908   35.00

405. 3 Marks 1910 (Second marriage of duke)   30.00

406. 3 Marks 1915 (Centenary of grand duchy). Busts of Wilhelm Ernst and Carl August   60.00

SAXONY

Formerly a kingdom in eastern Germany. Notable for picturesque pre-1800 coinage.

407. Frederick III ("the Wise"). Taler 1500-07 Bust with cap   275.00

408. Christian I. Taler 1586-91. Bust in armor. Rev. Arms   75.00

409. Albert, John, Ernst, Frederick, Wilhelm, Bernard, John Frederick, Frederick Wilhelm. Taler 1610-15. Four facing busts. Rev. Four facing busts   100.00

410. John George I. Taler 1630 (Jubilee of Augsburg Confession)   200.00

414. Taler 1816-23. Military bust. Rev. Arms   40.00
415. Mining Taler 1817-23. Military bust. Rev.
      Arms   60.00
416. Taler 1824-27. New bust and arms   35.00
417. Mining Taler 1824-27. New bust and arms   70.00

418. Taler 1827 (Death of king). Head. Rev.
      Inscription   75.00
419. Mining Taler 1827. Head. Rev. Inscrip-
      tion   120.00

ANTON 1827-36

411. John George I. Triple Taler 1650 (Peace
      of Westphalia)   1200.00

FRIEDRICH AUGUST 1806-27

412. Taler 1806-16. Head. Rev. Shield   50.00

413. Mining Taler 1807-16. Head. Rev. Arms   100.00

420. Taler 1827-36. Head. Rev. Shield   40.00

421. Mining Taler 1828-36   90.00
422. Taler 1836 (Death of king). Head. Rev. Shield and torches   75.00
423. Mining Taler 1836   175.00

FRIEDRICH AUGUST II 1836-54

424. Double Taler 1839-54. Head. Rev. Crowned and mantled arms   80.00

JOHANN 1854-73

431. Double Taler 1855-59. Head. Rev. Crowned and mantled arms   75.00
432. Taler 1854-59   25.00
433. Mining Taler 1854-58   40.00
434. Double Taler 1861. Head. Rev. Arms supported by lions   100.00
435. Taler 1860-71   25.00

425. Taler 1836-38. Head. Rev. Crowned shield   70.00
426. Mining Taler 1836-38   120.00
427. Taler 1839-54. Head. Rev. Crowned and mantled arms   25.00
428. Mining Taler 1841-54   45.00

436. Mining Taler 1858-71. Head. Rev. Supported arms   30.00

437. Taler 1871 (Victorious conclusion of Franco-Prussian War). Head. Rev. Victory on horseback   40.00

429. Double Taler 1854 (Death of king). Head. Rev. Two seated female figures   175.00
430. Taler 1854   45.00

Obverse of #438

438. Double Taler 1872 (Golden wedding anniversary). Accolated busts of king
and queen. Rev. Crown and inscription in wreath. (*See page* 176) 75.00
439. 20 Marks (G) 1872-73. Head. Rev. Eagle 80.00
440. 10 Marks (G) 1872-73 80.00

ALBERT 1873-1902

441. 20 Marks (G) 1874-78. Head. Rev. Small
eagle 150.00
442. 10 Marks (G) 1874-88 100.00
443. 5 Marks (G) 1877 250.00

444. 5 Marks 1875-89. Head. Rev. Small eagle 80.00
445. 2 Marks 1876-88 70.00
446. 20 Marks (G) 1894-95. Head. Rev. Large
eagle 120.00
447. 10 Marks (G) 1891-1902 100.00
448. 5 Marks 1891-1902 30.00
449. 2 Marks 1891-1902 10.00
450. 5 Marks 1902 (Death of king) 50.00
451. 2 Marks 1902 15.00

GEORGE 1902-04

452. 20 Marks (G) 1903. Head. Rev. Eagle 125.00
453. 10 Marks (G) 1903-04 90.00

454. 5 Marks 1903-04 45.00
455. 2 Marks 1903-04 20.00
456. 5 Marks 1904 (Death of king) 60.00
457. 2 Marks 1904 20.00

FRIEDRICH AUGUST III 1904-18

458. 20 Marks (G) 1905-14. Head. Rev. Eagle 120.00

459. 10 Marks (G) 1905-12 125.00

460. 5 Marks 1907-14 17.50
461. 3 Marks 1908-13 6.00
462. 2 Marks 1905-14 15.00

463. 5 Marks 1909 (500th anniversary of the
University of Leipzig). Busts of Fried-
rich the Pugnacious and Friedrich
August III 75.00

464. 3 Marks 1913 (Dedication of the National Battle Monument at Leipzig).
View of the monument 8.50

464a. 3 Marks 1917 (400th anniversary of
Reformation) very rare

SCHAUMBURG-LIPPE

A principality in north-central Germany.

ADOLF GEORGE 1860-93

465. Taler 1865. Head. Rev. Arms supported
by angels 60.00

GERMANY (continued)

466. 20 Marks (G) 1874. Head. Rev. Eagle   rare

GEORGE 1893-1911
467. 20 Marks (G) 1898, 1904. Head. Rev.
    Eagle   600.00
468. 5 Marks 1898, 1904   400.00
469. 2 Marks 1898, 1904   200.00
470. 3 Marks 1911 (Death of prince)   50.00

478. 5 Marks 1903   750.00

WURTTEMBERG

A kingdom in south Germany lying between Baden and Bavaria.

WILHELM I 1816-64

SCHWARZBURG-RUDOLSTADT

The principalities of Schwarzburg-Rudolstadt and Schwarzburg-Sondershausen are located between Saxony and Bavaria.

GUNTHER VICTOR 1890-1918
471. 10 Marks (G) 1893. Head. Rev. Eagle   800.00

479. Taler 1825-37. Head. Rev. Crowned arms
    in sprays   70.00

472. 2 Marks 1898   125.00

SCHWARZBURG-SONDERSHAUSEN

CARL GUNTHER 1880-1909

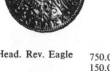

473. 20 Marks (G) 1898. Head. Rev. Eagle   750.00
474. 2 Marks 1896   150.00
475. 2 Marks 1905 (25th year of reign)   40.00
476. 3 Marks 1909 (Death of prince)   40.00

WALDECK-PYRMONT

A principality in west-central Germany.

FRIEDRICH 1893-1918
477. 20 Marks (G) 1903. Head. Rev. Eagle 1,000.00

480. Double Taler 1840-55. Head. Rev. Value
    in wreath   125.00
481. 2 Gulden 1845-56. Head. Rev. Helmeted
    and supported arms   50.00
482. Taler 1857-64   30.00

KARL 1864-91

483. Taler 1865-70. Head. Rev. Helmeted and supported arms — 30.00

484. Taler 1871 (Victorious conclusion of Franco-Prussian War). Head. Rev. Angel standing on cannon and flags — 30.00
485. 20 Marks (G) 1872-76. Head. Rev. Small eagle — 100.00
486. 10 Marks (G) 1872-88 — 100.00
487. 10 Marks (G) 1890-91. Head. Rev. Large eagle — 120.00
488. 5 Marks (G) 1877-78. Rev. Small eagle — 200.00
489. 5 Marks 1874-88. Head. Rev. Eagle — 25.00
490. 2 Marks 1876-88 — 20.00

WILHELM II 1891-1918

491. 20 Marks (G) 1894-1914. Head. Rev. Eagle — 65.00
492. 10 Marks (G) 1893-1913 — 75.00
493. 5 Marks 1892-1913 — 7.50
494. 3 Marks 1908-14 — 8.00
495. 2 Marks 1892-1914 — 10.00

496. 3 Marks 1911 (Silver wedding). Heads of king and queen. Rev. Eagle — 12.50

496a. 3 Marks 1916 (25th year of reign) — 1,500.00

GERMAN REPUBLIC

1924 COINAGE REFORM

497. 5 Marks 1927-33. Oak tree. Rev. Eagle — 35.00
498. 3 Marks 1924, 25. Eagle. Rev. Value — 12.50
499. 3 Marks 1931-33. Eagle and inscription. Rev. Value in oak wreath — 100.00
500. 2 Marks 1925-31 — 8.75
501. 1 Mark 1925-27. No inscription — 7.50

502. 50 Pfennigs (A-Bro) 1924, 25; (N) 27-38. Eagle in circle. Rev. Large "50" — 3.50
503. 10 Reichspfennigs (A-Bro) 1924-36. Wheat stalks. Rev. Value — .75
504. 5 Reichspfennigs (A-Bro) 1924-26, 30-36. — .50

505. 4 Pfennigs (Bro) 1932. Eagle. Rev. Large "4" — 4.00
506. 2 Pfennigs (Bro) 1924-36 — .75
507. 1 Pfennig (Bro) 1924-36 — .50

COMMEMORATIVE ISSUES

508. 5 Marks 1925 (1000th year of the Rhineland). Knight in armor with shield. Rev. Value — 30.00
509. 3 Marks 1925 — 17.50

510. 3 Marks 1926 (700th year of Lubeck as
      a free city). Arms. Rev. Value   42.50

516. 3 Marks 1927 (400th anniversary of the
      University of Marburg). Arms. Rev.
      Eagle   65.00

511. 5 Marks 1927 (Centenary of Bremer-
      haven). Ship. Rev. Eagle on shield   100.00
512. 3 Marks 1927   50.00

517. 3 Marks 1928 (400th anniversary of
      death of Albrecht Durer). Bust of
      Durer. Rev. Eagle   100.00

514.

513. 5 Marks 1927 (450th anniversary of the
      University of Tuebingen). Bust of
      Eberhard. Rev. Eagle   125.00
514. 3 Marks 1927   95.00

518. 3 Marks 1928 (900th anniversary of
      founding of Naumburg). Man with
      shield   55.00

515. 3 Marks 1927 (1000th anniversary of
      founding of Nordhausen). Two seated
      crowned figures facing each other.
      Rev. Value   50.00

519. 3 Marks 1928. (1000th anniversary of
      Dinkelsbuhl). Medieval statue. Rev.
      Eagle   175.00

520. 5 Marks 1929 (200th anniversary of birth of Lessing). Head of Lessing. Rev. Eagle 37.50

521. 3 Marks 1929 .... 18.75

527. 5 Marks 1930 (Graf Zeppelin's world flight). Zeppelin encircling world. Rev. Eagle 70.00

528. 3 Marks 1930 .... 27.50

530.

522. 5 Marks 1929 (1000th anniversary of founding of Meissen). Man with two shields. Rev. Eagle 112.50

523. 3 Marks 1929 .... 30.00

529. 5 Marks 1930 (Evacuation of the Rhineland). Eagle on bridge. Rev. Eagle on shield 60.00

530. 3 Marks 1930 .... 17.50

524. 5 Marks 1929 (10th anniversary of Weimar Constitution). Head of Hindenburg. Rev. Hand 40.00

525. 3 Marks 1929 .... 16.00

531. 3 Marks 1930 (700th anniversary of Walther von der Vogelweide). Bust of Von der Vogelweide. Rev. Eagle on shield 42.50

526. 3 Marks 1929 (Union of Waldeck with Prussia). Eagle. Rev. Eagle 45.00

532. 3 Marks 1931 (300th anniversary of the rebuilding of Magdeburg). View of city 60.00

GERMANY (continued)

533. 3 Marks 1931 (Centenary of death of
Freiherr von Stein). Head of Stein.
Rev. Eagle   50.00

541. 5 Marks 1935, 36. Bust of Hindenburg   3.00

542. 1 Mark (N) 1933-39. Eagle. Rev. Value
in wreath   1.00
543. 50 Pfennigs (A) 1935. Eagle. Rev. Value   .70

534. 5 Marks 1932 (Centenary of death of
Goethe). Head of Goethe. Rev. Eagle   500.00
535. 3 Marks 1932   37.50

LAW OF MARCH 18, 1933

544. 5 Marks 1934 (175th anniversary of
birth of Friedrich Schiller). Head of
Schiller   60.00
545. 2 Marks 1934.   30.00

NAZI REGIME

536. 5 Marks 1933 (450th anniversary of
birth of Martin Luther). Bust of
Luther. Rev. Eagle   37.50

537. 2 Marks 1933.   7.50

538. 5 Marks 1934, 35. Potsdam Garrison
Church. Rev. Eagle   3.00

546. 5 Marks 1936-39. Bust of Hindenburg.
Rev. Eagle and swastika   4.00
547. 2 Marks 1936-39   1.50

539. 5 Marks 1934 (Anniversary of Nazi
rule). Type of #538 with date: 21
Marz 1933   8.00

540. 2 Marks 1934.   6.25

548. 50 Pfennig (N) 1938,39. Eagle and
swastika. Rev. Value   20.00

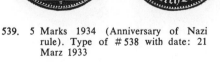

548a. 50 Pfennig (A) 1939-44. Eagle and
     swastika. Rev. Value   .75
549. 10 Pfennig (A-Br) 1936-39, (Z) 40-45 .60
550. 5 Pfennig (A-Br) 1936-39, (Z) 40-44 .50
551. 2 Pfennig (Br) 1936-40   .50
552. 1 Pfennig (Br) 1936-40, (Z) 40-45   .45

GERMAN FEDERAL REPUBLIC
(West Germany)

WESTERN OCCUPATION ZONE

560.   5 Marks 1951-74. Eagle. Rev. Value   2.25

561.   2 Marks (C-N) 1951   20.00

553. 10 Pfennig (Z) 1945-48. Type of #549
     without swastika   5.00
554. 5 Pfennig (Z) 1947-48. Type of #550
     without swastika   4.00
555. 1 Pfennig (Z) 1945-46. Type of #552
     without swastika   10.00

562.   2 Marks (C-N) 1957-71. Head of Max
      Planck. Rev. Eagle and value   1.75

556. 50 Pfennig (C-N) 1949, 50. Girl holding
     plant. Rev. Value   1.50

563.   1 Mark (C-N) 1950-   .75

557. 10 Pfennig (Bra-St) 1949. Plant. Rev.
     Value   .45
558. 5 Pfennig (Bra-St) 1949   .50
559. 1 Pfennig (Bro-St) 1948-49   .90

564. 50 Pfennigs (C-N) 1950-   Girl holding
     plant. Rev. Value   .45

565. 10 Pfennigs (Bra-St) 1950-   Cluster of
     leaves. Rev. Value   .15
566. 5 Pfennigs (Bra-St) 1950-   .10
567. 2 Pfennigs (Br) 1950-68; (Br-St) 1967- .10
568. 1 Pfennig (Br-St) 1950-   .10

569. 5 Marks 1952. Franconian eagle. Rev.
      Eagle and value   225.00

570. 5 Marks 1955. Bust of Friedrich Schiller.
      Rev. Eagle and value (Commemorates
      150th anniversary of poet's death)   225.00

571. 5 Marks 1955. Wigged bust of Ludwig
      Wilhelm, Margrave of Baden, 1655-
      1705. Rev. Eagle and value (Com-
      memorates 300th anniversary of birth) 175.00

572. 5 Marks 1957. Head of Baron Joseph
      Von Eichendorff. Rev. Eagle (Honors
      100th anniversary of writer's death)   175.00

573. 5 Marks 1964. Head of Johann Gott-
      lieb Fichte. Rev. Eagle (Honors
      150th anniversary of philosopher's
      death)   75.00

574. 5 Marks 1966. Portrait of Gottfried
      Wilhelm Leibnitz. Rev. Eagle (Honors
      250th anniversary of philosopher's
      death)   12.50
575. 5 Marks 1967. Conjoined heads of Wil-
      helm and Alexander Von Humboldt.
      Rev. Eagle   15.00

576. 5 Marks 1968. Bust of Friedrich Wilhelm
      Raiffeisen. Rev. Arms (Commemor-
      ates 150th anniversary of banker's
      birth)   5.00
577. 5 Marks 1968. Bust of Johannes Guten-
      berg. Rev. Arms (Commemorates
      400th anniversary of printer's death) 6.00

578. 5 Marks 1968. Head of Max von
      Pettenkoffer. Rev. Arms (Commemor-
      ates 150th anniversary of scientist's
      birth)   4.50

584.   2 Marks (C-N) 1970- . Head of Theodor Heuss. Rev. Arms   1.50

579.   10 Marks (issued 1969). Circle of banners. Rev. Arms (Commemorates the 1972 Olympic Games)   15.00

585.   5 Marks 1971. Parliament building in Berlin. Rev. Arms (Commemorates 100th anniversary of German unification)   3.50

580.   5 Marks 1969. Head of Theodor Fontane. Rev. Arms (Commemorates 150th anniversary of writer's birth)   4.00

581.   5 Marks 1969. Bust of Gerhard Mercator Rev. Arms (Commemorates 375th anniversary of cartographer's death)   4.00

586.   5 Marks 1971. Initials. Rev. Arms (Commemorates 500th anniversary of Albrecht Dürer's birth)   3.50

582.   2 Marks (C-N) 1969- . Head of Konrad Adenauer. Rev. Arms   1.50

587.   10 Marks 1972 (issued 1971). Two figures. Rev. Arms (Commemorates 1972 Olympic Games)   8.00

583.   5 Marks 1970. Head of Ludwig van Beethoven. Rev. Arms (Commemorates 200th anniversary of composer's birth)   3.50

588.   10 Marks 1972. Type as #579, obverse inscription reads MUNCHEN, instead of DEUTSCHLAND   8.00

589.   10 Marks 1972. Olympic grounds. Rev. Arms (Commemorates 1972 Olympic Games)   6.00

590.   10 Marks 1972. Olympic torch. Rev. Arms (Commemorates 1972 Olympic Games)   6.00

591.   10 Marks 1972. Symbol of Olympic unity. Rev. Arms   7.50

592.   5 Marks 1973. Map of solar system. Rev. Arms (Commemorates 500th anniversary of Copernicus' birth)   3.00

593.

593.   5 Marks 1973. Interior of St. Paul's Church in Frankfurt. Rev. Arms (Commemorates 125th anniversary of Parliament of 1848)   3.00

594.   5 Marks 1974. Shield design. Rev. Arms (Commemorates 25th anniversary of constitution)   3.00

595.   5 Marks 1974. Bust of Immanuel Kant. Rev. Arms (Commemorates 250th anniversary of philosopher's birth)   3.00

596.   5 Marks 1975. Friedrich Ebert. Rev. Arms (Commemorates 50th anniversary of President's death)   4.00

597.   5 Marks (C-N) 1975- . Modern arms. Rev. Value   2.50

GERMANY (continued)

598. 5 Marks 1975. Albert Schweitzer. Rev. Arms (Commemorates 100th anniversary of humanitarian's birth)   4.00

599. 5 Marks 1975. Building facades. Rev. Arms (Commemorates European Monument Protection Year)   3.75

GERMAN DEMOCRATIC REPUBLIC
(East Germany)

1. 50 Pfennig (A-Br) 1950. Factory and plow. Rev. Value   3.50

2. 10 Pfennig (A) 1948-50. Gear and wheat ear. Rev. Value   .50
3. 5 Pfennigs (A) 1948-50   .35
4. 1 Pfennig (A) 1948-50   .30

5. 10 Pfennig (A) 1952-53. Hammer and compass between wheat ears. Rev. Value   .40
6. 5 Pfennig (A) 1952-53   .35
7. 1 Pfennig (A) 1952-53   .25
8. 2 Marks (A) 1957. Hammer and compass within wreath of wheat. Rev. Value   2.00
9. 1 Mark (A) 1956-   1.50

10. 50 Pfennig (A) 1958-   .60
11. 10 Pfennig (A) 1963-   .25
11a. 5 Pfennig (A) 1968-   .25
12. 1 Pfennig (A) 1960-   .15

13. 20 Marks 1966. Bust of Gottfried Wilhelm Leibnitz. Rev. Hammer and compass (Commemorates 250th anniversary of scholar-philosopher's death)   30.00

20.

21.

14. 10 Marks 1966. Bust of Karl Friederick Schinkel. Rev. Hammer and compass (Commemorates 125th anniversary of architect's death)   35.00

15. 20 Marks 1967. Head of Wilhelm Von Humboldt. Rev. Hammer and compass (Commemorates 200th anniversary of author's birth)   25.00

21. 10 Marks 1969. Meissen pitcher (Commemorates 250th anniversary of death of inventor Johann Bottger)   10.00

22. 5 Marks (CN) 1969. Inscription (Commemorates 20th anniversary of People's Republic)   3.50

23. 5 Marks (CN) 1969. Head of Heinrich Hertz (Commemorates 75th anniversary of physicist's death)   10.00

16. 10 Marks 1967. Head of Kathe Kollwitz. Rev. Hammer and compass (Commemorates 100th anniversary of painter's birth)   15.00

17. 20 Marks 1968. Head of Karl Marx. Rev. Hammer and compass (Commemorates 150th anniversary of birth)   25.00

24. 20 Pfennig (Al-Br) 1969- . Hammer and compass. Rev. Value   .30

25. 20 Marks 1970. Head of Friedrich Engels. Rev. Arms (Commemorates 150th anniversary of socialist philosopher's birth)   20.00

18. 10 Marks 1968. Inscription (Commemorates the 500th anniversary of death of Johannes Gutenberg, famous inventor and printer)   12.50

19. 5 Marks (CNZ) 1968. Head of Robert Koch (Commemorates 125th anniversary of bacteriologist's birth)   20.00

20. 20 Marks 1969. Head of Goethe. Rev. Hammer and compass (Commemorates the 220th anniversary of writer's birth)   20.00

26. 10 Marks 1970. Bust of Ludwig van Beethoven. Rev. Arms (Commemorates 200th anniversary of composer's death)   10.00

27. 5 Marks (C-N-Z) 1970. X-ray tube. Rev. Arms (Commemorates 125th anniversary of Wilhelm Röntgen's birth)   7.50

28. 20 Marks 1971. Heads of Rosa Luxemburg and Karl Liebknecht, Communist leaders (Commemorates 100th anniversary of Liebknecht's birth)   20.00

29. 20 Marks (C-N-Z) 1971. Head of Ernst Thälmann. Rev. Arms (Commemorates 85th anniversary of politician's birth)   8.00

30. 20 Marks (C-N-Z) 1971. Head of Heinrich Mann. Rev. Arms (Commemorates 100th anniversary of author's birth)   12.00

31. 10 Marks 1971. Initials. Rev. Arms (Commemorates 500th anniversary of Albrecht Dürer's birth)   10.00

32. 5 Marks (C-N-Z) 1971. Brandenburg Gate. Rev. Arms   3.25

33. 5 Marks (C-N-Z) 1971. Earth's path around the sun. Rev. Arms (Commemorates 400th anniversary of Johannes Kepler's birth)   8.00

34.   35.

34. 20 Marks 1972. Winged snake. Rev. Arms (Commemorates 500th anniversary of birth of Lucas Cranach, artist)   20.00

35. 20 Marks (C-N-Z) 1972. Head of Wilhelm Pieck, first President of DDR. Rev. Arms   8.50

36. 20 Marks (C-N-Z) 1972. Bust of Friedrich Schiller, author. Rev. Arms   8.00

37. 10 Marks 1972. Portrait of Heinrich Heine. Rev. Arms (Commemorates 175th anniversary of poet's birth)   10.00

38. 10 Marks (C-N-Z) 1972. Five figures with flag. Rev. Arms (Buchenwald memorial)   5.00

39. 5 Marks (C-N-Z) 1972. Cathedral at Meissen. Rev. Arms   5.00

40. 5 Marks (C-N-Z) 1972. Musical notes. Rev. Arms (Commemorates 75th anniversary of death of Johannes Brahms, composer)   15.00

41. 20 Marks 1973. Portrait of August Bebel. Rev. Arms (Commemorates 60th anniversary of politician's death)   20.00

42. 20 Marks (C-N-Z) 1973. Head of Otto Grotewohl. Rev. Arms   6.00

46. 10 Marks 1974. Bust of Caspar David Friedrich. Rev. Arms (Commemorates 200th anniversary of artist's birth)   30.00

43. 10 Marks (C-N-Z) 1973. Emblem of 10th annual World Youth Game Festival. Rev. Arms   10.00

47. 10 Marks (C-N-Z) 1974. Arms and motto. Rev. Value (Commemorates 25th anniversary of DDR)   7.50

43a. 10 Marks 1973. Bust of Bertolt Brecht, playwright. Rev. Arms   7.50

48. 10 Marks 1974. Modern city. Rev. Arms (Commemorates 25th anniversary of DDR)   20.00

49. 5 Marks (C-N-Z) 1974. Early telephone. Rev. Arms (Commemorates 100th anniversary of death of Philipp Reis, physicist)   10.00

44. 5 Marks (C-N-Z) 1973. Glider. Rev. Arms (Commemorates 125th anniversary of birth of Otto Lilienthal, aeronautical engineer)   6.00

45. 20 Marks 1974. Portrait of Immanuel Kant. Rev. Arms (Commemorates 250th anniversary of philosopher's birth)   25.00

50. 20 Marks 1975. Musical score. Rev. Arms (Commemorates 250th anniversary of death of J. S. Bach)   25.00

51. 10 Marks 1975. Head of Albert Schweitzer.
Rev. Arms (Commemorates 100th anniversary of humanitarian's birth) 16.00

52. 10 Marks (C-N) 1975. National arms of
Warsaw Pact nations. Rev. Arms
(Commemorates 20th anniversary of
pact) 6.00

53. 5 Marks (C-N-Z) 1975. Head of Thomas
Mann. Rev. Arms (Commemorates
100th anniversary of author's birth) 7.50

54. 5 Marks (C-N-Z) 1975. Three conjoined
heads. Rev. Arms (Commemorates
International Women's Year) 5.00

55. 10 Marks (C-N) 1976. Portrait of soldier.
Rev. Arms. (Commemorates 20th anniversary of National People's Army)

56. 5 Marks (C-N-Z) 1976. Military hat,
sword. Rev. Arms (Commemorates
Ferdinand Von Schill, military hero) 7.50

GHANA

The former British Crown Colony of the Gold Coast in West Africa and Togoland united in 1957 as the State of Ghana with Dominion status in the British Commonwealth. Ghana became a republic within the Commonwealth in 1960.

NEW CURRENCY SYSTEM
100 Pesewas = 1 Cedi

8. 50 Pesewas (CN) 1965. Head of Nkrumah.
   Rev. Star   2.00
9. 25 Pesewas (CN) 1965   1.25
10. 10 Pesewas (CN) 1965   .60
11. 5 Pesewas (CN) 1965 (scalloped edge)   .40

1. 10 Shillings 1958. Head of Kwame
   Nkrumah. Rev. Star (proof issue)   15.00
2. 2 Shillings (C-N) 1958   1.50
3. 1 Shilling (C-N) 1958   .60
4. 6 Pence (C-N) 1958   .40

12. 20 Pesewas (CN) 1967. Cocoa plant. Rev.
    Value   1.25
13. 10 Pesewas (CN) 1967   .65
14. 5 Pesewas (CN) 1967, 73   .50

5. 3 Pence (C-N) 1958 (scalloped edge)   .30

15. 2½ Pesewas (CN) 1967 (scalloped edge)   .40

6. 1 Penny (Br) 1958   .25
7. ½ Penny (Br) 1958   .20

16. 1 Pesewas (Br) 1967. Drums. Rev. Star   .25
17. ½ Pesewas (Br) 1967   .20

GIBRALTAR

A British Crown Colony on the Rock of Gibraltar, a peninsula of southern Spain. This strategic fortress has been maintained by the British since 1704.

VICTORIA 1837-1901

1. 2 Quarts (C) 1842. Head. Rev. Castle, key below 12.00
2. 1 Quart (C) 1842 .... 7.50
3. ½ Quart (C) 1842 .... 5.50

4. 1 Crown (CN) 1967–70. Portrait of Queen Elizabeth with coronet. Rev. Castle 3.50
4a. 1 Crown (S) 1967 (proof issue) 50.00

DECIMAL COINAGE

5. 25 New Pence (C-N) 1971. Portrait of Queen Elizabeth II. Rev. Barbary ape 2.50
5a. 25 New Pence (S) 1971 (proof issue) 30.00

6. 25 New Pence (C-N) 1972. Rev. Conjoined arms (Commemorates Royal Silver Wedding Anniversary) 2.00
6a. 25 Pence (S) 1972. (proof issue) 30.00

7. 100 Pounds (G) 1975. Rev. Arms, value 200.00

8. 50 Pounds (G) 1975. Rev. Our Lady of Europa 100.00
9. 25 Pounds (G) 1975. Rev. Lion with key 50.00

Because of its many and varied issues, British coinage is one of the most interesting and popular fields of numismatics.

$$4 \; Farthings = 1 \; Penny$$
$$12 \; Pence = 1 \; Shilling \; (or \; Testoon)$$
$$4 \; Pence = 1 \; Groat$$
$$2 \; Shillings = 1 \; Florin$$
$$5 \; Shillings = 1 \; Crown$$
$$20 \; Shillings = 1 \; Pound \; Sterling$$
$$(or \; Sovereign)$$
$$21 \; Shillings = 1 \; Guinea$$

The spelling of the monarch's name as it actually appears on coins is given in brackets below each listing. English coins were all undated prior to 1548. Many of the coins struck between 1548 and 1661 are also without dates. Up to 1662 the coinage was hand-hammered by the same methods used in ancient times.

WILLIAM I (the Conqueror) 1066–1087
(crudely lettered PILLEMVS or variant)

Following his victory at the Battle of Hastings, Duke William of Normandy established himself on the throne of England as King William I. His coinage consisted of silver pennies in the pattern of the preceding Saxon issues.

1. 1 Penny (undated). Head. Rev. Cross   85.00

WILLIAM II 1087–1100
(PILLEMVS or variant)

The coins bear the same legends as the preceding reign but the issues of William II can be distinguished from those of William I by differences in the design and workmanship.

2. 1 Penny. Head. Rev. Cross   250.00

HENRY I 1100–1135
(hENRICVS or variant)

During this reign many coins were struck in base silver on short-weight planchets.

3. 1 Penny. Head. Rev. Cross   110.00

STEPHEN 1135–1154
(STIEFNE or variant)

Henry's daughter Matilda was away from England at the King's death, and Stephen, grandson of William the Conqueror, was confirmed as ruler. Not wishing to be ruled by a woman, the Norman nobles supported his claim. A few coins, all rare, were issued during this reign with Matilda's legends.

4. 1 Penny. Head. Rev. Cross   115.00

HENRY II 1154–1189
(hENRI or hENRICVS)

The legends are similar to those of the first Henry but the workmanship is quite different and the reverse shows a distinctive "short cross" design.

5. 1 Penny. Facing head. Rev. "Short cross type" (this type was continued through the reigns of Richard I and John with little change in design; all bear the name of Henricus)   35.00

RICHARD I 1189-99
(hENRICVS on coins)

Richard was crusading in the Holy Land or fighting in Normandy during most of his reign. The "short cross" pennies with Henry's legends were continued with slight variations in the design.

6. 1 Penny. Facing head. Rev. "Short cross"   25.00

JOHN 1199–1216
(hENRICVS on coins)

Henry's legend and the short cross design were continued under John. His later issues are distinguished by superior workmanship.

7. 1 Penny. Facing head. Rev. "Short cross"   20.00

HENRY III 1216–1272
(hENRICVS III or TERCI)

A new design type, the "long cross" penny, was introduced during this reign. Extending the cross to the edge of the coin was supposed to discourage clipping.

8. 1 Penny. Facing head. Rev. "Short cross type"   18.00

9. 1 Penny. Facing head. Rev. "Long cross type"   18.00

EDWARD I 1272–1307
(EDWARDVS or variant)

The "long cross" pennies continued into this reign which also saw the introduction of a new denomination, the groat or fourpenny piece.

10.	1 Groat. Facing head. Rev. Cross	400.00
11.	1 Penny	12.50
12.	1 Halfpenny	22.00
13.	1 Farthing	28.00

EDWARD II 1307–1327
(EDWARDVS or variant)

The inscriptions on Edwardian coins do not show whether they are of the first, second or third monarch of that name. The issues may be differentiated by minor variations in design. Silver halfpennies and farthings first issued under Edward I were continued in this reign.

14. 1 Penny. Facing head. Rev. Cross   10.00

15.	1 Halfpenny	35.00
16.	1 Farthing	22.00

EDWARD III 1327–1377
(EDWARDVS or variant)

The coinage of gold was permanently established under Edward III.

17.	1 Noble (G). King standing in ship	400.00
18.	½ Noble (G)	260.00
19.	¼ Noble (G)	220.00
20.	1 Groat. Facing head. Rev. Cross	50.00
21.	½ Groat	18.00
22.	1 Penny	10.00
23.	1 Halfpenny	12.50
24.	1 Farthing	22.00

RICHARD II 1377–1399
(RICARD)

The larger size coins that had come into use allowed space for longer titles.

25.	1 Groat. Facing bust. Rev. Cross	100.00
26.	½ Groat	110.00
27.	1 Penny	28.00
28.	1 Halfpenny	20.00
29.	1 Farthing	85.00

HENRY IV 1399–1413
(hENRICVS or variant)

Coins of Henry IV are the scarcest of any reign with the single exception of Edward V.

30.	1 Groat. Facing bust. Rev. Cross	275.00
31.	1 Penny. Facing bust. Rev. Cross	100.00

32.	1 Halfpenny	80.00
33.	1 Farthing	225.00

GREAT BRITAIN (continued)

HENRY V 1413–1422
(hENRICVS or variant)

As on the Edwardian issues, the inscriptions do not show whether coins are of the fourth, fifth or sixth Henry. Collectors can differentiate between the issues because of minor variations in the designs.

34.	1 Groat. Facing bust. Rev. Cross	65.00
35.	½ Groat	40.00

36.	1 Penny	30.00
37.	1 Halfpenny	25.00
38.	1 Farthing	75.00

HENRY VI 1422–1461 and 1470–1471
(hENRICVS or variant)

Henry was deposed and imprisoned in the Tower of London for nine years during the War of the Roses. The gold Angel was introduced during his imprisonment and specimens bearing Henry's inscription were struck during his short restoration.

39.	1 Angel (G). St. Michael slaying dragon. Rev. Cross and arms on ship	400.00
40.	1 Groat. Facing head. Rev. Cross	25.00
41.	1 Penny	15.00
42.	1 Halfpenny	15.00
43.	1 Farthing	90.00

EDWARD IV 1461–1470 and 1471–1483
(EDWARD)

Edward was forced to flee the country during the restoration of Henry VI but the House of York was soon re-established upon the throne.

44.	1 Groat. Facing head. Rev. Cross	25.00
45.	½ Groat	15.00
46.	1 Penny	12.50
47.	1 Halfpenny	30.00
48.	1 Farthing	240.00

EDWARD V 1483
(EDWARD)

A lad of 12, young Edward reigned only a few weeks before his uncle seized the crown and had him murdered. Small quantities of silver groats, gold angels and half angels were struck during this short period. They can be identified by a boar's head mint mark in the legend. All coins of this reign are quite rare.

49.	1 Angel (G). St. Michael slaying dragon. Rev. Cross and arms on ship	rare
50.	1 Groat. Facing head. Rev. Cross	1 000.00

RICHARD III 1483–1485
(RICARD)

The coins of this reign show the same legends as those of Richard II.

51.	1 Groat. Facing head. Rev. Cross	120.00
52.	1 Penny	80.00

HENRY VII 1485–1509
(hENRIC VII or SEPTIM)

The English coinage was reformed under Henry and the shilling first appeared (then called a testoon or teston from the Italian testa—head). The obverse and reverse designs are quite different from the preceding issues.

53.	1 Sovereign (G). King on throne. Rev. Arms	rare

54. 1 Groat. Facing bust. Rev. Cross   20.00
55. ½ Groat   15.00
56. 1 Penny   28.00
57. 1 Halfpenny   40.00

58. 1 Groat. Profile issue. Rev. Quartered arms (the first coin to display the royal arms)   40.00
59. ½ Groat   25.00

HENRY VIII 1509–1547
(hENRICVS VIII or variant)

Silver coins were steadily debased during this reign. The shilling finally reached a proportion of two-thirds copper to one-third silver and earned Henry the nickname "Old Coppernose".

60. 1 Groat. Profile bust. Rev. Quartered arms   30.00
61. ½ Groat   15.00
62. 1 Penny. King on throne with orb and sceptre   15.00

63. 1 Testoon or shilling. Facing bust. Rev. Arms   110.00
64. 1 Groat   55.00
65. ½ Groat   30.00
66. 1 Penny   30.00

EDWARD VI 1547–1553
(EDWARD)

The first dated English coins were struck during Edward's reign. The silver crown of 1551 was the first of this denomination.

67. 1 Crown 1551-53. King on horseback. Rev. Shield on cross   325.00
68. 1 Halfcrown 1551-53   160.00
69. 1 Shilling 1548-51. Crowned bust to right. Rev. Shield (dates in Roman numerals)   65.00

70. 1 Shilling (XII in field). Facing head   35.00
71. 6 Pence (VI in field)   45.00
72. 3 Pence (III in field)   55.00
73. 1 Penny. Double rose   25.00

GREAT BRITAIN (continued)

MARY 1553–1554
(MARIA)

Mary's coinage is divided into two parts—coins of her own reign and of the period when she shared the throne with Philip of Spain.

74.	1 Groat. Profile portrait	50.00

PHILIP AND MARY 1554–1558
(PHILIP Z MARIA)

The marriage was accomplished by proxy and Philip spent only a few months in England during the entire joint reign.

79.	1 Shilling, hammered coinage	30.00

75.	1 Shilling. Busts face to face	85.00
76.	6 Pence	80.00

ELIZABETH I 1558–1603
(ELIZABETH or ELIZAB)

Machinery was introduced into the mint for a short time during Elizabeth's reign but opposition from the workers forced a return to hand-hammering methods.

79a.	1 Shilling, milled coinage	45.00

80.	6 Pence, hammered		20.00
80a.	6 Pence, milled		28.00
81.	1 Groat, hammered		15.00
82.	1 Groat, milled		30.00
83.	3 Pence, hammered		15.00
84.	3 Pence, milled		35.00
85.	½ Groat, hammered		15.00
86.	½ Groat, milled		28.00
87.	1 Penny, hammered		14.00

77.	1 Crown. Crowned profile portrait, with scepter and orb	400.00
78.	1 Halfcrown	175.00

JAMES I 1603–1625
(IACOBVS)

James VI of Scotland came to the throne of England uniting the two kingdoms under one monarch.

92.	6 Pence	15.00
93.	½ Groat. Crowned rose. Rev. Crowned thistle	10.00
94.	1 Penny. Similar but no crowns	10.00
95.	1 Halfpenny	10.00
96.	1 Farthing (C). Crossed sceptres and crown. Rev. Harp	10.00

88.   ½ Laurel (G). Laureate head. Rev. Arms   250.00

CHARLES I 1625–1649
(CAROLVS or variant)

Charles declared he would defend the "Protestant religion, the laws of England and the liberties of Parliament" against his opposing faction. This inscription appears on many coins of his reign.

89.	1 Crown. King on horseback	275.00
90.	1 Halfcrown	120.00

91.   1 Shilling. Crowned profile bust   20.00

97.	1 Pound. King on horseback	400.00
98.	1 Crown.	150.00
99.	1 Halfcrown	30.00

100. 1 Shilling. Crowned profile bust   20.00

100a.	1 Shilling. Rev. Proclamation legend		40.00
101.	6 Pence		15.00
102.	3 Pence		12.00
103.	1 Penny		10.00
104.	1 Halfpenny. Rose, no legend		10.50
105.	"Richmond" Farthing (C). Crown. Rev. Crowned harp		10.00

COMMONWEALTH 1649–1660

(The inscriptions on early Commonwealth coins are in English rather than Latin)

106. 1 Crown. Shield of St. George. Rev. Shields of St. George and Ireland   325.00

107.	1 Halfcrown	160.00
108.	1 Shilling	60.00
109.	6 Pence	65.00
110.	2 Pence	25.00
111.	1 Penny	20.00
112.	1 Halfpenny. Shield of St. George. Rev. Shield of Ireland	30.00

OLIVER CROMWELL, PROTECTOR 1653-58

113. 1 Crown. Laureate bust of Oliver Cromwell. Rev. Crowned shields   600.00

114.	1 Halfcrown	250.00
115.	1 Shilling	175.00

CHARLES II 1660–1685
(CAROLVS)

The hand-hammering of coins came to an end during this reign. Milled coinage started in 1662. Symbols on the new coins denoted the source of the metal from which they were struck—Elephant (or Elephant and Castle)—The Africa (Guinea) Company which had this emblem on its badge. Plume—Welsh mines. Rose—West of England mines.

The first official coinage of copper, halfpennies and farthings, was issued during Charles' reign.

116.	1 Crown. Laureate bust. Rev. Crowned shields	85.00
117.	1 Halfcrown	40.00
118.	1 Shilling	30.00
119.	6 Pence	20.00

120. 1 Halfpenny (C). Mailed bust. Rev.
Britannia seated   25.00
121. 1 Farthing (C)   15.00

125. 1 Shilling   60.00
126. 6 Pence   40.00
127. Maundy set: 4, 3, 2 Pence and 1 Penny
      (uniform dates)   120.00

WILLIAM AND MARY 1689–1694
(GVLIELMVS ET MARIA)
Prince William of Orange and Princess Mary of
England ruled jointly until Mary's death.

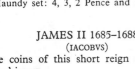

122. Maundy set: 4, 3, 2 Pence and 1 Penny   175.00

JAMES II 1685–1688
(IACOBVS)
The coins of this short reign are similar to
Charles' issues.

128. 1 Crown. Conjoined heads. Rev. Crowned
      shields   300.00
129. 1 Halfcrown   60.00

123. 1 Crown. Laureate bust. Rev. Crowned
      shields   160.00
124. 1 Halfcrown   80.00

130. 1 Shilling   30.00
131. 6 Pence   15.00

132. 1 Halfpenny (C). Rev. Britannia seated 25.00
133. 1 Farthing (C) 25.00
134. Maundy set: 4, 3, 2 Pence and 1 Penny
     (uniform dates) 160.00

WILLIAM III 1694–1702
(GVLIELMVS)

All hand-hammered coinage remaining in circulation was called in to be recoined in the new milled style.

135. 1 Crown. Laureate bust. Rev. Crowned
     shields 120.00
136. 1 Halfcrown 30.00

137. 1 Shilling 16.00
138. 6 Pence 12.00
139. 1 Halfpenny (C). Rev. Britannia seated 12.00
140. 1 Farthing (C) 12.00
141. Maundy set: 4, 3, 2 Pence and 1 Penny
     (uniform dates) 160.00

ANNE 1702–1714
(ANNA)

Some coins of the reign are marked "VIGO" to commemorate the British capture of the Spanish port of that name along with many treasure galleons and their cargoes of silver from America. Coins so marked were struck from the captured metal.

142. 1 Crown. Draped bust. Rev. Crowned
     shields 85.00

(Shields on reverse are arranged differently on coins struck prior to the union with Scotland in 1707)

143. 1 Halfcrown. 40.00
144. 1 Shilling. 20.00
145. 6 Pence. Type of #136 16.00
146. Maundy set: 4, 3, 2 Pence and 1 Penny
     (uniform dates) 140.00
147. 1 Farthing (C). Rev. Britannia seated 160.00

GEORGE I 1714–1727
(GEORGIVS)

None of Queen Anne's 17 children survived her and the throne went to George Louis of Hanover. His coins show his English titles on the obverse, his German titles on the reverse.

148.

148.	5 Guineas (G) Laureate head. Rev.	
	Shields	2000.00
149.	1 Guinea (G)	160.00
150.	1 Half Guinea (G)	120.00
151.	1 Quarter Guinea (G)	80.00
152.	1 Crown. Laureate bust	220.00
153.	1 Crown. Similar, with "SSC" on re-	
	verse	250.00
154.	1 Halfcrown. Type of #152	60.00
155.	1 Halfcrown. Type of #153	45.00

156.	1 Shilling. Type of #152	20.00

Coins of this reign which are minted from silver supplied by the South Sea Company are marked "SSC" on the reverse.

157.	1 Shilling. Type of #153	16.00
158.	6 Pence. Type of #152	14.00
159.	6 Pence. Type of #153	10.00

160.	1 Halfpenny (C). Rev. Britannia seated	8.00
161.	1 Farthing (C)	8.00
162.	Maundy set: 4, 3, 2 Pence and 1 Penny	
	(uniform dates)	140.00

GEORGE II 1727–1760
(GEORGIVS)

Coins of this reign marked LIMA were struck from captured Spanish-American silver.

163.	1 Guinea (G)	175.00
164.	1 Half Guinea (G)	140.00

165.	1 Crown 1732-41. Young head. Rev.	
	Shields	240.00
166.	1 Crown 1746-51. Old bust	240.00
167.	1 Crown. Similar; "Lima" below bust	320.00
168.	1 Halfcrown 1731-42. Young head	28.00
169.	1 Halfcrown 1743-51. Old bust	24.00
170.	1 Halfcrown. Similar; "Lima" below bust	32.00
171.	1 Shilling 1727-41. Young head	14.00
172.	1 Shilling 1743-58. Old bust	10.00
173.	1 Shilling. Similar; "Lima" below bust	12.00
174.	6 Pence 1728-41. Young head	8.00
175.	6 Pence 1743-58. Old bust	6.50
176.	6 Pence. Similar; "Lima" below bust	7.25
177.	Maundy set: 4, 3, 2 Pence and 1 Penny	
	(uniform dates)	85.00

178.	1 Halfpenny (C) 1727-39. Young head.	
	Rev. Britannia seated	7.25
179.	1 Halfpenny (C) 1740-54. Old head	6.50
180.	1 Farthing (C) 1727-40. Young head	6.00
181.	1 Farthing (C) 1741-54. Old head	3.25

GEORGE III 1760–1820
(GEORGIUS)

The copper twopenny piece weighing a full two ounces made its only appearance in 1797. The coins were so large and heavy they are known as "cartwheels."

182.	1 Guinea (G)	160.00
183.	1 Half Guinea (G)	120.00
184.	⅓ Guinea [7 Shillings] (G)	80.00
185.	¼ Guinea (G)	100.00

186.	1 Guinea (G). "Spade" reverse	140.00
187.	1 Half Guinea (G). "Spade" reverse	120.00

188.	1 Shilling 1787. Laureate bust. Rev. Shields	20.00

189.	6 Pence 1787	12.00
190.	Maundy set: 4, 3, 2 Pence and 1 Penny 1792-1800 (uniform dates)	85.00

191.	Emergency issue 1800—Spanish Dollar countermarked with George III head in oval (official value 4 Shillings 9 Pence)	95.00
191a.	Emergency issue 1800—Similar, with octagonal countermark	125.00

192.	Emergency issue 1800—Spanish 4 Reales countermarked with George III head	75.00

193. Bank Dollar 1804. Laureate bust. Rev.
Britannia seated   160.00

194. 3 Shillings Bank Token 1811-16. Rev.
Value in wreath   50.00
195. 18 Pence Bank Token 1811-16   25.00

198. 2 Pence (C) 1797 (second copper issue
—the famous "Cartwheel")   20.00
199. 1 Penny (C) 1797 ("Cartwheel")   12.00
200. 1 Halfpenny (C) 1797 ("Cartwheel"—
proofs only)
201. 1 Farthing (C) 1797 ("Cartwheel"—
proofs only)

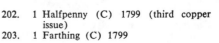

196. 1 Halfpenny (C) 1770-75 (first copper
issue). Rev. Britannia seated   10.00
197. 1 Farthing (C) 1771-75   12.50

202. 1 Halfpenny (C) 1799 (third copper
issue)   4.00
203. 1 Farthing (C) 1799   8.00

GREAT BRITAIN (continued)

204. 1 Penny (C) 1806-07 (fourth copper issue) ... 8.00
205. 1 Halfpenny (C) 1806-07 ... 3.50

206. 1 Farthing (C) 1806-07 ... 3.00

NEW STYLE COINAGE 1816-20

207. 1 Sovereign (G) 1817-20. Head. Rev. St. George and dragon ... 250.00

208. ½ Sovereign (G) 1817-20. Rev. Shields ... 80.00

209. 1 Crown 1818-20. Head. Rev. St. George and dragon ... 40.00

210. 1 Halfcrown 1816-17. "Bull" head. Rev. Crowned shield ... 10.00
211. 1 Halfcrown 1817-20. "Small" head ... 7.00
212. 1 Shilling 1816-20. "Bull" head ... 4.00
213. 6 Pence 1816-20 ... 3.00
214. Maundy set: 4, 3, 2 Pence and 1 Penny 1817-20 (uniform dates) ... 60.00

GEORGE IV 1820–1830
(GEORGIUS)

Pistrucci's famous sculpture of St. George and dragon first appeared in 1817 and continued under George IV.

215. 1 Sovereign (G) 1821-25. Laureate head. Rev. St. George and dragon ... 150.00
216. 1 Sovereign (G) 1825-30. Bare head. Rev. Crowned shield ... 150.00
217. 1 Half Sovereign (G) 1825-28 ... 120.00

218. 1 Crown 1821-22. Laureate head. Rev. St. George and dragon ... 60.00

219. 1 Halfcrown 1821-29. Head. Rev. Crowned shield ... 20.00
220. 1 Shilling 1821-25. Laureate head. Rev. Crowned shield ... 10.00

221. 1 Shilling 1825-29. Bare head. Rev. Lion
    on crown   5.00
222. 6 Pence 1821-26. Type of #220   4.00
223. 6 Pence 1826-29. Type of #221   4.00
224. Maundy set: 4, 3, 2 Pence and 1 Penny
    1822-30 (uniform dates)   45.00

235. 1 Penny (C) 1831-37. Bare head. Rev.
    Britannia seated   15.00
236. 1 Halfpenny (C) 1831-37   4.00
237. 1 Farthing (C) 1831-37   3.00

VICTORIA 1837–1901
Four distinct heads appeared on the coins in the course of this, the longest reign of any British ruler.

FIRST ISSUE (YOUNG AND GOTHIC HEAD)
238. 1 Sovereign (G) 1838-74. Rev. Shield   70.00
239. 1 Sovereign (G) 1871-85. Rev. St. George
    and dragon   50.00
240. 1 Half Sovereign (G) 1838-85. Rev.
    Shield   50.00

225. 1 Penny (C) 1825-27. Rev. Britannia
    seated   6.00
226. 1 Halfpenny (C) 1825-27   4.00
227. 1 Farthing (C) 1821-30   2.00

WILLIAM IV 1830–1837
(GULIELMUS)
One set of designs served for the coinage of this reign in contrast to the variety of types issued under the Georges.

228. 1 Sovereign (G) 1831-37. Head. Rev.
    Crowned shield   150.00
229. 1 Half Sovereign (G) 1834-37   75.00

230. 1 Halfcrown 1834-37. Bare head. Rev.
    Crowned arms in canopy   20.00

241. 1 Crown 1844-47. Rev. Crowned arms   60.00
242. 1 Halfcrown 1839-87   20.00

231. 1 Shilling 1834-37. Rev. Crowned value
    in wreath   5.00
232. 6 Pence 1831-37   4.00
233. 1 Groat 1836-37. Rev. Britannia seated   4.00
234. Maundy set: 4, 3, 2 Pence and 1 Penny
    1831-37 (uniform dates)   60.00

243. 1 Shilling 1838-87. Rev. Value in wreath   5.00
244. 6 Pence 1838-87   3.00
245. 1 Groat 1838-56. Rev. Britannia seated   3.00
246. Maundy set: 4, 3, 2 Pence and 1 Penny
    1838-87 (uniform dates)   40.00

GREAT BRITAIN (continued)

247. 1 Crown 1847 ("Gothic"). Crowned
     head. Rev. Shields   750.00

248. 1 Florin 1849 ("Godless Florin"—words
     Dei Gratia omitted). Crowned bust   20.00

249. 1 Florin 1852-87 (Gothic lettering)   8.50

250. 1 Penny (C) 1841-59. Rev. Britannia
     seated   6.00
251. 1 Halfpenny (C) 1838-59   3.50
252. 1 Farthing (C) 1838-60   3.50

SECOND ISSUE (JUBILEE TYPE)
(Obverse: Veiled bust of Queen with crown)

253. 1 Sovereign (G) 1887-92. Rev. St. George
     and dragon   50.00

254. 1 Half Sovereign (G) 1887-93. Rev. Shield 40.00

255. 1 Crown 1887-92   20.00

256. 1 Double Florin [4 Shillings] 1887-90.
     Rev. Shields   10.00
257. 1 Halfcrown 1887-92. Rev. Crowned
     square shield   5.00
258. 1 Florin 1887-92. Type of #256   4.00

259. 1 Shilling 1887-89. Small head. Rev.
     Crowned shield in garter   2.00
260. 1 Shilling 1889-92. Large head   3.00
261. 6 Pence 1887. Rev. Shield in garter   2.00
262. 6 Pence 1887-93. Rev. Value in wreath   3.00
263. Maundy set: 4, 3, 2 Pence and 1 Penny
     1888-92 (uniform dates)   40.00

264. 1 Penny (Bro) 1860-94 (reduced size).
     Young head. Rev. Britannia seated   3.00
265. 1 Halfpenny (Bro) 1860-94   2.00
266. 1 Farthing (Bro) 1860-95   1.00

THIRD ISSUE (OLD HEAD TYPE)
(Obverse: Draped bust with veil over large crown)

267. 1 Sovereign (G) 1893-1901. Rev. St.
     George and dragon   50.00
268. 1 Half Sovereign (G) 1893-1901   50.00

269. 1 Crown 1893-1900   20.00
270. 1 Halfcrown 1893-1901. Rev. Crowned
     shield   6.00

271. 1 Florin 1893-1901. Rev. Three shields   5.00

272. 1 Shilling 1893-1901   2.50
273. 6 Pence 1893-1901. Rev. Value in wreath   1.50
274. Maundy set: 4, 3, 2 Pence and 1 Penny
     1893-1901 (uniform dates)   35.00

275. 1 Penny (Bro) 1895-1901. Rev. Britan-
     nia seated   1.00
276. 1 Halfpenny (Bro) 1895-1901   .75
277. 1 Farthing (Bro) 1895-1901   .75

EDWARD VII 1901–1910
A new interpretation of Britannia not seen
again on English coins appeared on Edward's
florins.

(All obverse types: bare head of king)
278. 1 Sovereign (G) 1902-10. Rev. St. George
     and dragon   50.00
279. 1 Half Sovereign (G) 1902-10   45.00

280. 1 Crown 1902   60.00
281. 1 Halfcrown 1902-10. Rev. Crowned
     shield   10.00

282. 1 Florin 1902-10. Rev. Britannia standing   7.50

283. **1 Shilling 1902-10. Rev. Lion on crown**   4.00
284. 6 Pence 1902-10. Rev. Value in wreath   3.00
285. 3 Pence 1902-10   1.50

286. Maundy set: 4, 3, 2 Pence and 1 Penny
      1902-10 (uniform dates)   20.00

290. 5 Pounds 1911 (G). Rev. St. George
      and dragon (proof issue)   rare
291. 2 Pounds 1911 (G) (proof issue)   rare
292. 1 Sovereign (G) 1911-25   50.00
293. 1 Half Sovereign (G) 1911-15   50.00

287. 1 Penny (Bro) 1902-10. Rev. Britannia
      seated   3.00
288. 1 Halfpenny (Bro) 1902-10   2.00
289. 1 Farthing (Bro) 1902-10   1.00

GEORGE V 1910–1936
The high price of silver forced the debasement
of the coinage to an alloy of half silver and half
base metal.

(All obverse types: bare head of king. All
silver denominations struck between 1920 and
1927 were base silver.)

294. 1 Crown 1927-34, 36. Rev. Crown   95.00

295. 1 Crown 1935 (Silver Jubilee). Rev.
      Modernistic St. George and dragon   12.50

305. Maundy set: 4, 3, 2 Pence and 1 Penny
1911-36 (uniform dates) 30.00

296. 1 Halfcrown 1911-27. Rev. Crowned
shield 2.50
297. 1 Halfcrown 1927-36. Rev. Shield 2.00

306. 1 Penny (Bro) 1911-36. Rev. Britannia
seated .75
307. 1 Halfpenny (Bro) 1911-36 1.00
308. 1 Farthing (Bro) 1911-36 .60

298. 1 Florin 1911-26. Rev. 4 crowned
shields 2.00
299. 1 Florin 1927-36. Rev. 4 uncrowned
shields 1.50

EDWARD VIII 1936
Dies with Edward's portrait were cut and brass
3-pence pieces dated 1937 already struck when the
king abdicated in December, 1936. The coins were
subsequently melted down but a few reached the
hands of collectors and are very rare. Coins bearing
Edward's name (but not his portrait) were issued
in British West Africa, East Africa, Fiji and New
Guinea.

300. 1 Shilling 1911-36. Rev. Lion on crown 1.00

GEORGE VI 1936–1952
In 1947 a new metal, an alloy of 75% copper
and 25% nickel, replaced the already debased
silver being used for coins. Two differently
designed shillings were issued simultaneously
during this reign, one with an English reverse,
the other with a Scottish reverse in tribute to
the ancestry of his Queen, Elizabeth.

(All obverse types: bare head of king. Coins
issued after 1948 drop the title "IND. IMP." on
reverse.)

301. 6 Pence 1911-27 1.00
302. 6 Pence 1927-36. Rev. Acorn design .60
303. 3 Pence 1911-26. Rev. Value in wreath .50
304. 3 Pence 1927-36. Rev. Three acorns .45

309. 5 Pounds (G) 1937. Rev. St. George
and dragon (proof issue) 1,500.00
310. 2 Pounds (G) 1937 (proof issue) 750.00
311. 1 Sovereign (G) 1937 (proof issue) 200.00
312. 1 Half Sovereign (G) 1937 (proof issue) 175.00

GREAT BRITAIN (continued)

313. 1 Crown 1937. Rev. Crowned arms   10.00

314. 1 Halfcrown (S) 1937-46; (C-N) 47-48.
Rev. Shield   1.25
315. 2 Shillings (S) 1937-46; (C-N) 47-48.
Rev. Crowned rose   .90

316. 1 Shilling (S) 1937-46; (C-N) 47-48.
Rev. English crest   .50
317. 1 Shilling (S) 1937-46; (C-N) 47-48.
Rev. Scottish crest   .50

318. 6 Pence (S) 1937-46; (C-N) 47-48. Rev.
Crowned monogram (GRI)   .35
319. 3 Pence 1937-45. Rev. Shield on rose   .25

320. Maundy set: 4, 3, 2 Pence and 1 Penny
1937-48 (uniform dates)   45.00

321. 3 Pence (N-Bra) 1937-48 (12-sided).
Rev. Thrift plant   .30

322. 1 Penny (Bro) 1937-48 (round). Rev.
Britannia seated   .35

323. 1 Halfpenny (Bro) 1937-48. Rev.
"Golden Hind"   .25
324. 1 Farthing (Bro) 1937-48. Rev. Wren   .15

SHORTENED LEGEND ON REVERSE 1949-52

325. 1 Crown (C-N) 1951. Rev. St. George
and dragon (Festival of Britain
commemorative)   15.00

326.	1 Halfcrown (C-N) 1949-51.	1.50
327.	2 Shillings (C-N) 1949-51. Type of #315	1.50
328.	1 Shilling (C-N) 1949-51. Type of #316	1.20
329.	1 Shilling (C-N) 1949-51. Type of #317	1.20

337. Crown (C-N) 1953. Queen on horseback. Rev. Crown with shields (Coronation commemorative)   7.50

330.	6 Pence (C-N) 1949-52. Rev. Crown over new monogram	.50
331.	3 Pence (N-Bra) 1949-52. Type of #321	.75
332.	1 Penny (Bro) 1949-51. Type of #322	.50
333.	1 Halfpenny (Bro) 1949-52. Type of #323	.20
334.	1 Farthing (Bro) 1949-52. Type of #324	.25
335.	Maundy set: 4, 3, 2 Pence and 1 Penny 1949-52 (uniform dates)	50.00

ELIZABETH II 1952–

A special crown piece was issued honouring Elizabeth's coronation. The design is reminiscent of the coins of Edward VI, James I and Charles I showing the sovereign mounted on horseback.

(The phrase "BRITT: OMN:" in the legend on the obverse disappeared after 1953.)

338. Crown (C-N) 1960. Laureate head of the Queen.   12.50

336. Sovereign (G) 1957-68. Laureate head of the Queen. Rev. St. George and the dragon   75.00

339. Halfcrown (C-N) 1953-67. Rev. Crowned arms   .75

340. Florin (C-N) 1953-67. Rev. Double rose within circle, outer border of radiating thistles, shamrocks and leeks   .60

337.

341. Shilling (C-N) 1953-66. Rev. English arms   .35

342. Shilling (C-N) 1953-66. Rev. Scottish arms .35

343. 6 Pence (C-N) 1953-67. Rev. Garland of interlaced rose, thistle, shamrock and leek .25

344. 3 Pence (N-Bra) 1953-67. Rev. Chained portcullis (twelve-sided planchet) .20

345. Penny (Br) 1953, 1961-67. Rev. Britannia seated .15

346. Halfpenny (Br) 1953-67. Rev. "Golden Hind" .10

347. Farthing (Br) 1953-56. Rev. Wren 1.25

348. Maundy set: 4,3,2 Pence and 1 Penny 1953- (uniform dates) 60.00

349. Crown (C-N) 1965. Rev. Portrait of Sir Winston Churchill 1.50

DECIMAL COINAGE

100 New Pence = 1 Pound

350. 50 New Pence (CN) 1969- . Draped bust with coronet. Rev. Britannia (7-sided planchet) 2.00

351. 10 New Pence (CN) 1968- . Rev. Crowned lion .75

352. 5 New Pence (CN) 1968- . Rev. Crowned thistle .45

353. 2 New Pence (Br) 1971- . Rev. Three feathers .25

354. 1 New Penny (Br) 1971- . Rev. Portcullis .15

355. ½ New Penny (Br) 1971- . Rev. Crown .10

GREAT BRITAIN (continued)

356. 25 New Pence (C-N) 1972. Rev. Crowned
     monogram (Commemorates Royal Sil-
     ver Wedding Anniversary)   2.00
356a. 25 New Pence (S) 1972 (proof issue)   75.00

357. 50 New Pence (C-N) 1973. Rev. Hands
     grasped in circle (Commemorates Eng-
     lish entry into Common Market)   2.00
357a. 50 New Pence (C-N) 1973 (proof issue)   4.00

358.   1 Sovereign (G) 1974. Rev. Type of #336 80.00

BRITISH TRADE DOLLARS

From 1895 through 1935, Great Britain issued
these trade coins in the Far East. These were struck
at the Bombay (tiny "B" mint mark on center
prong of trident) and Calcutta ("C" mint mark
below Britannia's feet) mints in India and the
Royal Mint in London (no mint mark).

1.   1 Dollar 1895-1935. Britannia standing
      with spear and shield; date and value.
      Rev. Chinese and Malay inscriptions   10.00

GREECE (Modern)

In ancient times Greece produced the finest civilization known to history. After being conquered by the Turks in the fifteenth century, Greece did not regain full independence until 1830. Following World War I and a disastrous campaign against Turkey, it became a republic in 1925. In 1935 the monarchy was restored. After World War II an attempt by the Communists to seize power was defeated.

The Greek monarch was forced into exile by a military coup in 1967, and a republic was established in 1973.

100 Lepta = 1 Drachma

OTTO 1831-63

1.	5 Drachmai 1833. Head. Rev. Crowned arms	75.00
2.	1 Drachma 1832-51	30.00
3.	½ Drachma 1833-55	25.00
4.	¼ Drachma 1833-55	20.00

5.	10 Lepta (C) 1833-57. Crowned arms. Rev. Value in wreath	6.00
6.	5 Lepta (C) 1833-57	5.00
7.	2 Lepta (C) 1832-57	5.00
8.	1 Lepton (C) 1832-57	8.00

GEORGE I 1863-1913

9.	20 Drachmai (G) 1884	50.00
10.	10 Drachmai (G) 1876. Head. Rev. Value in wreath	150.00

11.	5 Drachmai 1875-76. Old head. Rev. Crowned arms with mantle	20.00

12.	2 Drachmai 1868-73, 83. Young head. Rev. Crowned arms with mantle	8.00

13.	2 Drachmai 1911. Old head. Rev. Thetis on sea horse	4.50
14.	1 Drachma 1868-74, 83. Type of #11	3.50
15.	1 Drachma 1910-11. Type of #13	4.00

16.	50 Lepta 1874, 83. Young head. Rev. Crown	6.00
17.	20 Lepta 1874, 83	2.00

18.	20 Lepta (C-N) 1893-95. Crown. Rev. Value in wreath	.75
19.	10 Lepta (C-N) 1894-95	.50
20.	5 Lepta (C-N) 1894-95	.35

21.	10 Lepta (C) 1869-82. Young head. Rev. Value in wreath	1.50
22.	5 Lepta (C) 1869-82	1.00
23.	2 Lepta (C) 1869, 78	5.00
24.	1 Lepton 1869-70, 78	6.00

GREECE (continued)

25. 20 Lepta (N) 1912 (Center hole). Inscription
    and shield. Rev. Athena and olive   .50

26. 10 Lepta (N) 1912 (Center hole). Inscription
    and crown. Rev. Owl and value   .45
27. 5 Lepta (N) 1912   .40

GEORGE I 1863-1913
CONSTANTINE 1913-17, 20-22
ALEXANDER 1917-20
GEORGE II 1922-23

28. 10 Lepta (A) 1922. Crown. Rev. Value
    and spray   .65

REPUBLIC 1924-35

29. 20 Drachmai 1930. Head of Poseidon. Rev.
    Prow of galley   6.00

30. 10 Drachmai 1930. Head of Demeter. Rev.
    Wheat stalk.   5.00

31. 5 Drachmai (N) 1930. Phoenix. Rev.
    Value in wreath   2.00

32. 2 Drachmai (C-N) 1926. Head of
    Athena. Rev. Inscription   .75
33. 1 Drachma (C-N) 1926   .60
34. 50 Lepta (C-N) 1926   .40
35. 20 Lepta (C-N) 1926   .35

GEORGE II 1935-47
PAUL I 1947-64

36. 20 Drachmai 1960-65. Bust of King Paul.
    Rev. Moon goddess emerging from
    the sea.   3.50
37. 10 Drachmai (N) 1959-65. Rev. Crowned
    arms   2.50

38. 5 Drachmai (C-N) 1954-65   2.00
39. 2 Drachmai (C-N) 1954-65   1.00
40. 1 Drachma (C-N) 1954-65   .50
41. 50 Lepta (C-N) 1954-65   .35

42. 20 Lepta (A) 1954-71. Crown over center
    hole in wreath. Rev. Spray and value   .35
43. 10 Lepta (A) 1954-71   .25
44. 5 Lepta (A) 1954-71   .20

45. 30 Drachmai 1963. Heads of the five
    Kings of the Greek Dynasty. Rev.
    Map of Greece (Commemorates 100th
    anniversary of dynasty)   8.00

CONSTANTINE II 1964-73

46. 30 Drachmai 1964. Wedding commemorative 6.50

47. 10 Drachmai (CN) 1968. Head of King. Rev.
    Arms   2.00
48. 5 Drachmai (CN) 1966-70.   2.00
49. 2 Drachmai (CN) 1966-70   .50
50. 1 Drachma (CN) 1966-70   .30
51. 50 Lepta (CN) 1966-70.   .15

52. 100 Drachmai 1967 (issued 1970). Soldier
    and Phoenix. Rev. Arms and value
    (Commemorates the 1967 revolution)   30.00
53. 100 Drachmai (G) 1967 (issued 1970)   600.00

52.

54. 50 Drachmai 1967 (issued 1970)   15.00
55. 20 Drachmai (G) 1967 (issued 1970)   175.00

56. 10 Drachmai (C-N) 1971, 73. Head of King.
    Rev. Arms   2.00
57. 5 Drachmai (C-N) 1971, 73   1.25
58. 2 Drachmai (C-N) 1971, 73   1.00
59. 1 Drachmai (C-N) 1971, 73   .75
60. 50 Lepta (C-N) 1971, 73   .40

61. 20 Drachmai (C-N) 1973. Moon goddess
    on horseback. Rev. Arms, value   3.00

REPUBLIC 1973-

62. 20 Drachmai (C-N) 1973. Arms. Rev.
    Athena   3.00

GREECE (continued)

63. 10 Drachmai (C-N) 1973. Rev. Pegasus   1.50
64. 5 Drachmai (C-N) 1973   1.00

65. 2 Drachmai (A-Br) 1973. Rev. Owl   .40
66. 1 Drachma (A-Br) 1973   .30

67. 50 Lepta (A-Br) 1973. Rev. Leaf design   .25

68. 20 Lepta (A) 1973. Rev. Olive branch   .20

69. 10 Lepta (A) 1973. Rev. Trident with dolphins   .15

70. 5 Drachmai (N-Br) 1975. Aristotle. Rev. Value

71. 2 Drachmai (A-Br) 1975. Georgios Karaiskakis, national hero. Rev. Guns, value
72. 1 Drachma (A-Br) 1975. Konstantinos Kanaris, national hero. Rev. Warship, value
73. 50 Lepta (A-Br) 1975. Markos Botsaris, national hero. Rev. Value
74. 20 Lepta (A) 1975. Redesigned arms. Rev. Bull from 4th century coin
75. 10 Lepta (A) 1975. Rev. Horse's head taken from 4th century coin

76. 20 Drachmai (C-N) 1976. Head of Pericles. Rev. Temple

77. 10 Drachmai (C-N) 1976. Head of Democrates. Rev. Sun and stars

GREENLAND

A large island off the northeast coast of North America. Most of the island lies within the Arctic Circle. Greenland has been a Danish colony for a long time; in 1953 it became part of the Danish Commonwealth.

100 Ore = 1 Krone

1. 5 Kroner (A-Bro) 1944. Crowned arms. Rev. Polar bear   8.00
2. 1 Krone (A-Bro) 1926   4.00
3. 50 Ore (A-Bro) 1926   3.00
4. 25 Ore (C-N) 1926   2.50
4a. 25 Ore (C-N) 1926 (center hole planchet)   10.00

5. 1 Krone (A-Bro) 1957, (C-N) 1960, 64. Crowned shields of Denmark and Greenland   5.00

GUADELOUPE

A group of islands in the West Indies, discovered by Columbus in 1493. Subsequently Guadeloupe became a French colony. In 1946 it became a department of metropolitan France and an overseas department of the French Community in 1958.

100 Centimes = 1 Franc

1. 1 Franc (C-N) 1903, 21. Head of native. Rev. Palm   6.00
2. 50 Centimes (C-N) 1903, 21   4.00

GUATEMALA

After being conquered by Spain in 1524, Guatemala remained a colony until 1821, when it gained its independence from Spain. Then after being a part of Mexico for a brief time, it became part of the Central American Federation, 1825-38. Since then it has been an independent republic.

Early issues under Spanish rule bear the name of the reigning monarch. Designs are similar to those of other Spanish-American mints. The original Guatemala mint mark was "G" in the legend. The city of Guatemala was destroyed by an earthquake in 1773, and upon the rebuilding of the city in 1776 it was called New Guatemala. The mint mark then became "NG."

100 Centavos or 8 Reales = 1 Peso
100 Centavos = 1 Quetzal

CHARLES III 1760-88

1.	8 Reales 1760-72. Pillar type	125.00

3.	4 Reales 1760-85	85.00
4.	2 Reales 1772-87	20.00
5.	1 Real 1772-87	16.00

CHARLES IV 1788-1808

6.	8 Reales 1789. Bust of Charles III	140.00

7.	8 Reales 1791-1808. Bust of Charles IV	70.00
8.	4 Reales 1789-1807	100.00
9.	2 Reales 1789-1807	18.00
10.	1 Real 1790-1807	16.00
11.	½ Real 1790-1804	14.00

12.	¼ Real 1796-1801. Castle. Rev. Lion	18.00

FERDINAND VII 1808-22

2.	8 Reales 1772-89. Bust type	100.00
13.	8 Reales 1808-12. Bust of Charles IV	80.00

REPUBLICA DE GUATEMALA

14.	8 Reales 1814-22. Bust of Ferdinand VII	40.00
15.	4 Reales 1809-21	50.00
16.	2 Reales 1809-21	10.00
17.	1 Real 1808-21	12.00
18.	½ Real 1809-21	12.50
19.	¼ Real 1809-21. Castle. Rev. Lion	15.00

24.	1 Peso 1859-71 (Varieties). Head of Pres. Rafael Carrera. Rev. Arms	12.50
25.	4 Reales 1860-67	4.00

STATE OF CENTRAL AMERICA

26.	2 Reales 1860-69	3.00
27.	1 Real 1859-69	2.50
28.	½ Real 1859-69	2.50

(#24-28 may be found countermarked with an "R" in a circle indicating that they have been recoined.)

29.	¼ Real 1861-69. Lion. Rev. Value	6.50

30.	2 Reales 1872-73. Cartouche with inscription. Rev. Value in wreath	3.00
31.	1 Real 1872-78	4.50
32.	½ Real 1872-79	4.75

20.	8 Reales 1824-48. Mountain range. Rev. Tree	50.00
21.	1 Real 1824-28	15.00
22.	½ Real 1824	15.00

23.	¼ Real 1824-50	5.00

33.	¼ Real 1872-89. Mountain range. Rev. Value	2.00

GUATEMALA (continued)

34. 1 Peso 1882, 89. Liberty head. Rev. Arms   25.00

46. 5 Pesos (A-Bro) 1923. Bust of Barrios.
Rev. Value   3.75

47. 1 Peso (A-Bro) 1923. Bust of Granados.
Rev. Value   1.85

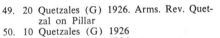

48. 50 Centavos (A-Bro) 1922. Sun. Rev.
Value in circle   1.50

35. 1 Peso 1872-97. Republic seated. Rev.
Arms   7.50
36. 4 Reales 1873-94   3.50
37. 2 Reales 1879-99   2.50
38. 1 Real 1879-1900   1.00
39. ½ Real 1879-99   .90
40. ¼ Real 1887-93. Mountain range. Rev.
Lion   1.00

REFORM OF NOV. 26, 1924

49. 20 Quetzales (G) 1926. Arms. Rev. Quetzal on Pillar   400.00
50. 10 Quetzales (G) 1926   250.00
51. 5 Quetzales (G) 1926   175.00

41. 1 Centavo (Br) 1871. Mountain range.
Rev. Value   5.00
42. 1 Centavo (Br) 1881. Arms. Rev. Value   6.00

43. 1 Real (C-N) 1900-12. Republic seated.
Rev. Arms   1.00
44. ½ Real (C-N) 1900-01   .70
45. ¼ Real (C-N) 1900-01. Mountain range   .50

52. 1 Quetzal 1925   500.00

222 • CATALOGUE of the WORLD'S MOST POPULAR COINS

GUATEMALA (continued)

53. ½ Quetzal 1925 — 15.00
54. ¼ Quetzal 1925 — 3.50

55. 25 Centavos 1943. National palace. Rev.
    Quetzal, on map — 3.50
56. 10 Centavos 1925-38, 43-49. Type of #52 — .60
57. 5 Centavos 1925-38, 43-49 — .50

58. 2 Centavos (Bra) 1932. Arms. Rev.
    Value — .60
59. 1 Centavo (Bro) 1925, 29; (Bra) 1932-48 — .40
60. ½ Centavo (Bra) 1932-46 — .40

61. 25 Centavos 1950-59, smaller head 1960-64.
    Native. Rev. Arms — 2.00
61a. 25 Centavos (N-Bra) 1965- — .75

62. 10 Centavos 1949-64. Quiriga column.
    Rev. Arms — .75
62a. 10 Centavos (N-Bra) 1965- — .30

63. 5 Centavos 1950-64. Ceiba tree. Rev.
    Arms — .50
63a. 5 Centavos (N-Bra) 1965- — .20

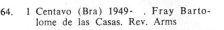

64. 1 Centavo (Bra) 1949- . Fray Barto-
    lome de las Casas. Rev. Arms — .15

65. 50 Centavos 1962, 63. Orchid (the White Nun,
    the national flower). Rev. Arms — 3.50
66. 1 Quetzal 1974. Kneeling Mayan. Rev.
    Quetzal bird in flight (Commemorates
    50th anniversary of currency system)

GUERNSEY

This English Channel island is a British possession. On its coins until 1949 the name is spelled in the French manner: "Guernesey."

8 Doubles = 1 Penny

1. 8 Doubles (C) 1834-58. Arms in wreath. Rev. Value in wreath   10.00

1a.	8 Doubles (Br) 1864 -1949	2.00
2.	4 Doubles (C) 1830-58	6.00
2a.	4 Doubles (Br) 1864-1949	3.00
3.	2 Doubles (C) 1858	12.00
3a.	2 Doubles (Br) 1868-1929	3.50
4.	1 Double (C) 1830	3.00
4a.	1 Double (Br) 1868-1938	1.00

5. 8 Doubles (Br) 1956- 66 . Lily. Rev. Arms   .75

6. 4 Doubles (Br) 1956- 66. Lily. Rev. Arms   1.00

7. 3 Pence (C-N) 1956. Cow. Rev. Arms   2.00
7a. 3 Pence (C-N) 1959, 66 (double thickness planchet)   1.50

8. 10 Shillings (C-N) 1966. Portrait of Queen Elizabeth II with coronet. Rev. Portrait of William the Conqueror (Commemorates 900th anniversary of Norman Conquest)   5.00

DECIMAL COINAGE

9. 50 New Pence (CN) 1969- . Arms. Rev. Native hat (7-sided planchet)   2.50

10. 10 New Pence (CN) 1968- . Arms. Rev. Guernsey cow   1.00
11. 5 New Pence (CN) 1968- . Arms. Rev. Lily   .50

12. 2 New Pence (Br) 1971. Arms. Rev. Sark Mill   .25

13. 1 New Pence (Br) 1971. Arms. Rev. Gannet   .20
14. ½ New Penny (Br) 1971. Arms. Rev. Value   .15

GUERNSEY (continued)

15. 25 New Pence (C-N) 1972. Eros. Rev. Arms (Commemorates Royal Silver Wedding Anniversary)   5.00
15a. 25 New Pence (S) 1972 (proof issue)   35.00

GUINEA

Guinea, on the west coast of Africa, was the only French colony there to reject the new French Constitution in 1958. It became the independent Republic of Guinea in 1958.

1. 25 Francs (A-Br) 1959. Bust of President Sekou Toure. Rev. Value, legend "le 2 octobre 1958" (Commemorates 1958 independence)   6.00

2. 10 Francs (A-Br) 1959   4.50

3. 5 Francs (A-Br) 1959   4.00
4. 25 Francs (C-N) 1962- . Bust of President Sekou Toure. Rev. Value   1.75

GUINEA (continued)

5. 10 Francs (C-N) 1962-   4.50
6. 5 Francs (C-N) 1962- . Head, type of #4   3.00
7. 1 Franc (C-N) 1962- . Head, type of #5   1.25

DECIMAL COINAGE
100 Cauris = 1 Syli

8. 5 Sylis (A) 1971. Native head. Rev. Value, motto   1.00

9. 2 Sylis (A) 1971. Bust facing left. Rev. Value   1.00

10. 1 Syli (A) 1971. Bust facing front. Rev. Value   .75

11. 50 Cauris (A) 1971. Cowry shell. Rev. Value   .75

GUYANA

The former British Crown Colony called British Guiana on the northeastern coast of South America became an independent state within the British Commonwealth May 26, 1966, and a republic was proclaimed in 1970. The nation is rich in diamond and aluminum deposits.

1. 50 Cents (CN) 1967. Arms. Rev. Value   1.50
2. 25 Cents (CN) 1967-   .80
3. 10 Cents (CN) 1967   .40

4. 5 Cents (Bra) 1967. Floral design. Rev. Value   .30
5. 1 Cent (Bra) 1967-   .15

6. 1 Dollar (CN) 1970. Head of Cuffy, leader of 1763 slave revolt. Rev. Cow and grain (F.A.O. coin plan)   2.50

HAITI

The western third of the island San (or Santo) Domingo or Hispaniola, located between Cuba and Puerto Rico. The island was discovered in 1492 by Columbus. In 1697 it passed from Spanish to French control, and became France's richest colony. A revolt under Touissant L'Ouverture in 1801 assured Haiti's independence.

100 Centimes = 1 Franc or 1 Gourde
100 Cents = 1 Gourde

HENRI CHRISTOPHE 1806-11

1. 1 Centime (C) 1807. Facing bust in uniform and cocked hat. Rev. Value   250.00

PRESIDENT BOYER 1818-43

2. 100 Centimes An. 26, 27, 30 (1829-33). Head. Rev. Arms   35.00
3. 50 Centimes An. 25-30   15.00
4. 25 Centimes An. 15-24   15.00
5. 12 Centimes An. 24   35.00
5a. 6 Centimes An. 15   40.00

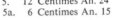

6. 2 Centimes (C) 1828-42. Fasces. Rev. Value in wreath   6.00
7. 1 Centime (C) 1828-42   3.50

8. 6 Centimes (C) 1846   10.00

HAITI (continued)

GENERAL REPUBLICAN ISSUES

9. 1 Gourde 1881-95. Draped head of Republic. Rev. Arms   25.00
10. 50 Centimes 1882-95   2.50
11. 20 Centimes 1881-95   1.00
12. 10 Centimes 1881-94   .50
13. 2 Centimes (Br) 1881   1.50
13a. 2 Centimes (Br) 1886-94. Arms. Rev. Value   1.00
14. 1 Centime (Br) 1881   3.50
14a. 1 Centime (Br) 1886-95. Type of #13a   3.00

15. 50 Cents (C-N) 1907-08. Bust of Pres. Alexis. Rev. Arms   1.00
16. 20 Cents (C-N) 1907-08   .60
17. 10 Cents (C-N) 1906, 07   .35
18. 5 Cents (C-N) 1904-06   .25

PRESIDENT ESTIME 1946-50

19. 10 Cents (C-N) 1949. Head of Pres. Estime. Rev. Arms   .35
20. 5 Cents (C-N) 1949   .25

PRESIDENT MAGLOIRE 1951-56

21. 20 Cents (N-S) 1956. Head of the President. Rev. Arms   .50
22. 10 Cents (N-S) 1953   .35
23. 5 Cents (N-S) 1953   .25

PRESIDENT FRANCOIS DUVALIER 1957-71

24. 20 Cents (N-S) 1970. Head of President. Rev. Arms   .75
25. 10 Cents (N-S) 1958-70   .30
26. 5 Cents (N-S) 1958-70   .20

PRESIDENT J. C. DUVALIER 1971-

27. 50 Cents (C-N) 1972, 75. Head of President. Rev. Arms (F.A.O. coin plan)   .75
28. 20 Cents (C-N) 1972, 75   .40
29. 10 Cents (C-N) 1975   .20
30. 5 Cents (C-N) 1975   .15

HAWAIIAN ISLANDS

An archipelago about a thousand miles long in the Pacific. Discovered by Captain James Cook in 1778, the islands were often visited in the nineteenth century by American whalers and missionaries. In 1898 Hawaii was annexed as a territory by the United States.

In 1959 Hawaii became the fiftieth state in the Union. One effect, numismatically, was an enormous rise in the valuation of its early coins.

KAMEHAMEHA III 1825-54

1. 1 Cent (C) 1847. Facing bust. Rev. Value in wreath   120.00

KALAKAUA I 1874-1891

2. 1 Dollar 1883. Head. Rev. Crowned arms   150.00

3. ½ Dollar 1883   50.00
4. ¼ Dollar 1883   20.00
5. 1 Dime 1883. Head. Rev. Value in wreath   30.00

HONDURAS

After becoming a Spanish colony early in the sixteenth century, Honduras gained its freedom in 1821. For several years it was part of Mexico, and from 1825 to 1838 it was one of the states in the Central American Federation. Since then it has been an independent republic.

8 Reales = 1 Dollar = 1 Peso
100 Centavos = 1 Peso or 1 Lempira

STATE OF HONDURAS

1. 8 Reales 1856-61. Mountains. Rev. Tree   25.00

2. 4 Reales 1849-57   15.00
3. 2 Reales 1832-55   17.50
4. 1 Real 1832-51   15.00
5. ½ Real 1832-33   15.00

REPUBLICA DE HONDURAS

6. 50 Centavos 1871. Feathered crown over pyramid. Rev. Tree   15.00
7. 25 Centavos 1871   10.00
8. 10 Centavos 1871   40.00
9. 5 Centavos 1871   125.00

10. 1 Peso 1881-1904. Liberty standing. Rev. Arms   20.00
11. 50 Centavos 1883-1908   7.50

HONDURAS (continued)

12. 25 Centavos 1883-1913   5.00
13. 10 Centavos 1883-1900. Arms. Rev. Value   10.00
14. 5 Centavos 1883-1902   15.00

15. 2 Centavos (Bro) 1908-20   2.00
16. 1 Centavo (Bro) 1881-1920   2.00
17. ½ Centavo (Bro) 1881-91   15.00

DECREE OF APRIL 6, 1926

18. 1 Lempira 1931-37. Head of the Indian
    chief Lempira. Rev. Arms   2.75
19. 50 Centavos 1931-51   1.25
19a. 50 Centavos (CN) 1967-   .60
20. 20 Centavos 1931-58   .60
20a. 20 Centavos (CN) 1967-   .25

21. 10 Centavos (C-N) 1932-56. Arms. Rev.
    Value in wreath   .35
22. 5 Centavos (C-N) 1931-56   .25
23. 2 Centavos (Bro) 1939-56   .30
24. 1 Centavo (Bro) 1935-57   .25

25. 50 Centavos (C-N) 1973. Type of # 19, with
    PRODUZCAMOS MAS ALIMENTOS
    obverse inscription   1.00

HONG KONG

A British Crown Colony located on a peninsula
and island at the mouth of the Canton River in
southeast China. Hong Kong was captured by the
Japanese in December, 1941, and returned to
British control after the end of World War II.

100 Cents = 1 Dollar

VICTORIA 1837-1901

1. 1 Dollar 1866-68. Coroneted bust. Rev.
   English and Chinese inscription   65.00
2. ½ Dollar 1866-67   60.00

3. 50 Cents 1890-94. Crowned bust. Rev.
   English value   12.50

4. 20 Cents 1866-98. Rev. Chinese value   8.00
5. 10 Cents 1863-1901   2.00
6. 5 Cents 1866-1901   1.50

7. 1 Cent (C) 1863-1901. Crowned bust.
    Chinese inscription in circle   1.00

8. 1 Mil (Br) 1863-66 (center hole)   1.00

EDWARD VII 1901-10

9. 50 Cents 1902-05. Crowned bust. Rev.
    Value in English and Chinese   10.00
10. 20 Cents 1902-05   20.00
11. 10 Cents 1902-05   2.00
12. 5 Cents 1903-05   1.50
13. 1 Cent (Bro) 1902-05. Rev. Type of #7   .75

GEORGE V 1910-36

14. 10 Cents (C-N) 1935-36. Crowned bust.
    Rev. Type of #9   1.25
15. 5 Cents (S) 1932-33; (C-N) 1935   2.00
16. 1 Cent (Br) 1919-26   .75
16a. 1 Cent (Br) 1931-34 (smaller planchet) .50

GEORGE VI 1936-52

17. 50 Cents (C-N) 1951. Crowned head. Rev.
    Type of #8   .90

18. 10 Cents (N) 1937-39; (N-Bra) 48-51   .50
19. 5 Cents (N) 1937-41; (N-Bra) 49, 50   .25

ELIZABETH II 1952-

20. 1 Dollar (C-N) 1960- . Crowned bust of
    Queen. Rev. Lion holding globe   1.00

21. 50 Cents (C-N) 1958-   .50
22. 10 Cents (N-Bro) 1955-   .25
23. 5 Cents (N-Bra) 1958-   .15

24. 1000 Dollars (G) 1975. Rev. Arms (Com-
    memorates royal visit)   250.00

25. 2 Dollars (C-N) 1975. Rev. Type of #20
     (scalloped planchet)   1.00
26. 20 Cents (Bra) 1975. Rev. Type of #21
     (scalloped planchet)   .25

27. 1000 Dollars (G) 1976. Rev. Dragon   200.00

HUNGARY

This eastern European country was conquered by Austria and Turkey in the sixteenth century. Eventually all of Hungary was incorporated into the Austrian Empire. The dual monarchy for Austria-Hungary started in 1867 and lasted until the end of World War I. After the end of World War II, Hungary became a People's Republic.

100 Kreuzer = 1 Florin
100 Filler = 1 Korona = 1 Pengo = 1 Florint

MARIA THERESA 1741-80

1. Taler 1741-80. Head. Rev. Madonna and Child 45.00

JOSEPH II 1780-90

2. 1 Taler 1781-99 .... 35.00

LEOPOLD II 1790-92

3. 1 Taler 1790 .... 125.00

FRANZ II 1792-1806
FRANZ I 1806-35

4. 1 Taler 1792-1833. Head. Rev. Madonna and Child 100.00

FERDINAND I 1835-48

5. 1 Taler 1837, 39. Head. Rev. Madonna and Child 120.00

FRANZ JOSEPH 1848-1916

6. 1 Florin 1868-92. Laureate head. Rev. Shield in several varieties 3.00
7. 20 Kreuzer 1868-72 .... 5.00
8. 10 Kreuzer 1868-88 .... 2.00
9. 1 Kreuzer (C) 1868-92 .... 1.50
10. 5/10 Kreuzer (C) 1882 .... 2.50

11. 5 Korona 1900-09. Head. Rev. Angels holding crown 10.00

12. 5 Korona 1907 (Jubilee issue). Rev. Coronation scene 12.50

13.	2 Korona 1912-14	2.50
14.	1 Korona 1892-1916. Rev. Crown over value	1.50

15.	20 Filler (N) 1892, 1914. Crown. Rev. Value in wreath	.75
16.	10 Filler (N) 1892-95, 1906, 08-14; (N-Bra) 1915-16	.20
17.	2 Filler (Bro) 1892-1915	.15
18.	1 Filler (Bro) 1892-1906	.15

HORTHY REGENCY 1920-44

19.	2 Pengo 1929-39. Madonna	3.00

20.	1 Pengo 1926-39. Arms. Rev. Value	1.50
21.	50 Filler (C-N) 1926-40. Crown. Rev. Value	.40
22.	20 Filler (C-N) 1926-40	.30
23.	10 Filler (C-N) 1926-40	.15
24.	2 Filler (Bro) 1926-40	.20
25.	1 Filler (Bro) 1926-39	.20

26.	5 Pengo 1930 (Commemorating tenth year of Horthy regency). Bust of Admiral Horthy. Rev. Hungarian arms	6.00

27.	2 Pengo 1935 (University of Budapest commemorative). Three figures. Rev. Hungarian arms	8.50

28.	2 Pengo 1935 (Rakoczi commemorative). Bust of Rakoczi. Rev. Hungarian arms	4.50

29.	2 Pengo 1936 (Liszt commemorative). Bust of Liszt. Rev. Hungarian arms	4.50

30.	5 Pengo 1938 (Commemorating 900th anniversary of death of St. Stephen). Bust of St. Stephen	10.00

HUNGARY (continued)

31. 5 Pengo 1939. Bust of Admiral Horthy   6.50

WORLD WAR II ISSUES

32. 5 Pengo (A) 1943 (Commemorating Admiral Horthy's 75th birthday). Bust of Admiral Horthy   4.50

33. 5 Pengo (A) 1945. Parliamentary buildings   2.50
34. 2 Pengo (A) 1941-43 Hungarian arms. Rev. Value   .75
35. 1 Pengo (A) 1941-44   .30
36. 20 Filler (St) 1941-44 (Center hole). Crown. Rev. Value   .45
37. 10 Filler (St) 1940-42   .15
38. 2 Filler (St) 1940-42; (Z) 43-44   .20

REPUBLIC 1946-

39. 5 Florint 1946. Head of Kossuth. Rev. Hungarian arms   7.50

39a. 5 Forint 1947 (thinner planchet)   2.50
40. 2 Forint (A) 1946-47. Hungarian arms   2.00
41. 1 Forint (A) 1946-47   1.00

42. 20 Filler (Br-A) 1946-50. Three ears of wheat. Rev. Value   .50

43. 10 Filler (C-A) 1946-47. Dove of peace. Rev. Value   .25
44. 2 Filler (Bro) 1946-47. Hungarian arms. Rev. Value   .30

COMMEMORATIVE ISSUES

45. 20 Forint 1948 (Commemorating Revolution of 1848). Head of Tancsics   14.50

46. 10 Forint 1948 (Commemorating Revolution of 1848). Head of Szechenyi   6.50
47. 5 Forint 1948 (Commemorating Revolution of 1848). Head of Petöfi   5.00

48. 25 Forint 1956. Parliament building (Commemorates 10th year of monetary system) 15.00

49. 20 Forint 1956. Bridge — 10.00
50. 10 Forint 1956. Museum — 6.00
51. 2 Forint (C-N) 1950-56. Five-pointed star with rays, hammer and wheat ear below. Rev. Value in wreath — 1.25

52. 1 Forint (A) 1949-52. Rev. Value in spray — .75

53. 2 Forint (CN) 1957-61; (CNZ) 1962-67 Arms. Rev. Value — .75
54. 1 Forint (A) 1957- — .50

55. 50 Filler (A) 1948, 1953-66. — .50
56. 20 Filler (A) 1953-66. Wheat ears — .35
56a 20 Filler (A) 1967- . (Smaller planchet) — .25

57. 10 Filler (A) 1950-66. Dove — .25
57a. 10 Filler (A) 1967- . (Smaller planchet) — .20
58. 5 Filler (A) 1948- . Head — .15

59. 2 Filler (A) 1950- (center hole) — .10

60. 50 Forint 1961. Head of Franz Liszt (Commemorates 150th anniversary of musician's birth) — 25.00
61. 25 Forint 1961 — 20.00

62. 50 Forint 1961. Head of Bela Bartok (Commemorates 80th anniversary of musician's birth) — 25.00
63. 25 Forint 1961 — 20.00

64. 50 Forint 1966. Head of Miklos Zrinyi. Rev. Allegorical scene (Commemorates 400th anniversary of patriot's death) — 25.00
65. 25 Forint 1966 — 18.00

68.

HUNGARY (continued)

66. 100 Forint 1967. Head of Zoltan Kodaly. Rev. Peacock (Commemorates 85th anniversary of musician's birth) — 15.00
67. 50 Forint 1967 — 10.00
68. 25 Forint 1967 — 6.00

69. 5 Forint (CNZ) 1967. Type of #39, smaller planchet. Rev. New arms — 1.00

70. 50 Filler (Al) 1967. Charles Bridge. Rev. Value — .35

71. 100 Forint 1968. Head of Dr. Semmelweis (Commemorates 150th anniversary of physician's birth) — 20.00
72. 50 Forint 1968 — 12.50

73. 100 Forint 1969. Worker waving flag. (Commemorates 50th anniversary of the Republic) — 20.00
74. 50 Forint 1969 — 15.00

75. 100 Forint 1970. Female figure. Rev. Arms, value in wreath (Commemorates 25th anniversary of liberation) — 15.00
76. 50 Forint 1970 — 10.00

77. 2 Forint (Bra) 1970- . Arms. Rev. Value — .75

78. 10 Forint (N) 1971- . Female figure. Rev. Value, small arms — 2.50

79. 5 Forint (N) 1971- . Louis Kossuth, national hero. Rev. Arms — 1.50

80. 100 Forint 1972. Two signs, joined. Rev. Arms, value (Commemorates 100th anniversary of city of Budapest)   15.00

83. 100 Forint 1973. Head of Petofi Sandor, poet, with inscription "We boldly defended our country!" (Commemorates 125th anniversary of Revolution of 1848)   15.00

84. 50 Forint 1973. Bust of Sandor. Rev. Ribbon, value   10.00

81. 100 Forint 1972. Portrait of King Stephen I. Rev. Monogram (Commemorates 1000th anniversary, birth of first king of Hungary)   17.50

82. 50 Forint 1972. King Stephen I on horseback. Rev. Copy of silver denar   10.00

85. 100 Forint 1974. Arms. Rev. Coins of member nations, Council of Mutual Economic Assistance (Commemorates 25th anniversary of Council)   20.00

HUNGARY (continued)

86. 100 Forint 1974. Symbols of industry. Rev. Arms, value (Commemorates 50th anniversary of Hungarian National Bank)   15.00

87. 50 Forint 1974. Bank building. Rev. Small arms, value (Commemorates 50th anniversary of Hungarian National Bank)   10.00

88. 200 Forint 1975. Dove over bridge. Rev. Arms, value (Commemorates 30th anniversary of liberation)   27.50

89. 200 Forint 1975. Abstract design. Rev. Graph (Commemorates 150th anniversary of Academy of Science)   27.50

90. 200 Forint 1976. Ferenc Rakoczi II (Commemorates 300th anniversary of national hero's death)

91. 200 Forint 1976. Milhaly Munkacsy, painter
92. 200 Forint 1976. Pal Szinyei Merse, painter
93. 200 Forint 1976. Gyula Derkovits, painter

ICELAND

An island in the North Atlantic, about 800 miles northwest of the British Isles. It was settled by Vikings about 870, and was first a Norwegian colony and then a Danish colony. The Althing, the Icelandic parliament and supreme court, was founded in 930. Iceland became an independent republic in 1944.

CHRISTIAN X OF DENMARK 1912-44

1. 2 Kronur (A-Bro) 1925-40
   Arms. Rev. Value   4.00
2. 1 Krona (A-Bro) 1925-40   1.50
3. 25 Aurar (C-N) 1922-40; (Z) 1942   1.25
4. 10 Aurar (C-N) 1922-40; (Z) 1942   3.00

5. 5 Aurar (Bro) 1926-42
   Monogram. Rev. Value   1.50
6. 2 Aurar (Bro) 1926-42   1.00
7. 1 Eyrir (Bro) 1926-42   .50

COMMEMORATIVE ISSUE (an issue of outstanding interest): One-thousandth anniversary of the Althing. The values appear on the edges of coins.

8. 10 Kronur 1930. King of Thule seated. Rev. Shield with supporters   80.00
9. 5 Kronur 1930. Ulfliot the Lawmaker. Rev. Interlocked dragons   75.00
10. 2 Kronur 1930. Seated figure, Rev. Icelandic Cross with designs in angles   25.00

REPUBLIC 1944-

11. 10 Kronur (CN) 1967- . Arms. Rev.
Value .... .25
12. 5 Kronur (CN) 1969- .... .15
13. 2 Kronur (A-Bro) 1946; (N-Bra) 1958-
Arms. Rev. Value .... .30
14. 1 Krona (A-Bro) 1946; (N-Bra) 1957- .... .10
15. 50 Aurar (Ni-Bra) 1969-74. .... .10
16. 25 Aurar (CN) 1946- .... .20
17. 10 Aurar (CN) 1946-69; (A) 1970-74 .... .10
18. 5 Aurar (Br) 1946-66 .... .20
19. 1 Eyrir (Br) 1946-66 .... .25

23. 10,000 Kronur (G) 1974. Man in ship. Rev.
Round shield, quartered, with bird,
dragon, bull and giant (Commemorates
1100th anniversary of first settlement) 275.00

20. 500 Kronur (G) 1961. Head of Jon Sigurd-
sson (Iceland's national hero). Rev.
Arms (Commemorates the 150th anniversary of his birth) 500.00

24. 1000 Kronur 1974. Two men with fire. Rev.
Shield (Commemorates 1100th anniversary of first settlement) 15.00

21. 50 Kronur (N) 1968. Parliament building
(Commemorates 50th anniversary of
sovereignty) 2.50

25. 500 Kronur 1974. Woman leading heifer.
Rev. Shield (Commemorates 1100th
anniversary of first settlement) 10.00

22. 50 Kronur (C-N) 1970- . Parliament
building. Rev. Value .... .75

INDIA

This vast sub-continent was once the proudest possession of the British Empire. Today it is divided into two parts: India (Bharat), which is mainly Hindu in population; and Pakistan, which is mainly Moslem. India became a republic within the British Commonwealth in 1950. Pakistan is now a republic.

3 Pies = 1 Pice   *16 Annas = 1 Rupee*
4 Pice = 1 Anna   *15 Rupees = 1 Mohur*

BRITISH INDIA

WILLIAM IV 1830-37

1. 1 Rupee 1835. Head. Rev. Value in English and Persian in wreath, with legend "East India Company"	6.00
2. ½ Rupee 1835	4.00
3. ¼ Rupee 1835	3.50

VICTORIA 1837-1901

4. 1 Rupee 1840. Young head, with legend "Victoria Queen." Rev. Type of #1	6.00
5. ½ Rupee 1840	4.50
6. ¼ Rupee 1840	2.75
7. 2 Annas 1841	2.50

8. 1 Rupee 1862-76. Crowned bust, with legend "Victoria Queen." Rev. Type of #1	5.00
9. ½ Rupee 1862-76	4.50
10. ¼ Rupee 1862-76	2.50
11. 2 Annas 1862-76	2.00
12. ½ Anna (C) 1862-76	2.50
13. ¼ Anna (C) 1862-76	1.00

14. ½ Pice (C) 1862	1.50
15. ¹⁄₁₂ Anna (C) 1862-76	1.00

16. 1 Rupee 1877-1901. Crowned bust, with legend "Victoria Empress." Rev. Value in scroll border	4.00
17. ½ Rupee 1877-99	5.00
18. ¼ Rupee 1877-1901	3.00
19. 2 Annas 1877-1901	1.75
20. ½ Anna (C) 1877 . Rev. Value in dotted circle and floral scroll	6.50
21. ¼ Anna (C) 1877-1901	.75
22. ½ Pice (C) 1885-1901	1.00
23. ¹⁄₁₂ Anna (C) 1877-1901	1.00

EDWARD VII 1901-10

24. 1 Rupee 1903-10. Head. Rev. Crowned value between sprays	4.50
25. ½ Rupee 1905-10	2.50
26. ¼ Rupee 1903-10	1.75
27. 2 Annas 1903-10	1.25

28. 1 Anna (C-N) 1907-10 (Scalloped edge). Crowned bust. Rev. Value in scroll	.85
29. ¼ Anna (C) 1903-06; (Br) 1906-10 (Round). Bare head. Rev. Type of #20	.85
30. ½ Pice (C) 1903-06; (Br) 1906-10	1.75
31. ¹⁄₁₂ Anna (C) 1903-06; (Br) 1906-10	.75

GEORGE V 1910-36

32. 1 Rupee 1911-22. Crowned bust. Rev. Value in scroll	4.00
33. ½ Rupee 1911-36	1.75
34. ¼ Rupee 1911-36	1.00
35. 2 Annas 1911-17	1.50
36. 8 Annas (C-N) 1919, 20. Rev. Large "8"	3.50

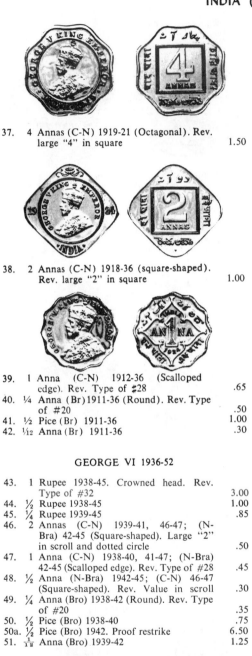

37. 4 Annas (C-N) 1919-21 (Octagonal). Rev. large "4" in square 1.50

38. 2 Annas (C-N) 1918-36 (square-shaped). Rev. large "2" in square 1.00

39. 1 Anna (C-N) 1912-36 (Scalloped edge). Rev. Type of #28 .... .65
40. ¼ Anna (Br) 1911-36 (Round). Rev. Type of #20 .... .50
41. ½ Pice (Br) 1911-36 .... 1.00
42. ¹⁄₁₂ Anna (Br) 1911-36 .... .30

GEORGE VI 1936-52

43. 1 Rupee 1938-45. Crowned head. Rev. Type of #32 .... 3.00
44. ½ Rupee 1938-45 .... 1.00
45. ¼ Rupee 1939-45 .... .85
46. 2 Annas (C-N) 1939-41, 46-47; (N-Bra) 42-45 (Square-shaped). Large "2" in scroll and dotted circle .... .50
47. 1 Anna (C-N) 1938-40, 41-47; (N-Bra) 42-45 (Scalloped edge). Rev. Type of #28 .... .45
48. ½ Anna (N-Bra) 1942-45; (C-N) 46-47 (Square-shaped). Rev. Value in scroll .... .30
49. ¼ Anna (Bro) 1938-42 (Round). Rev. Type of #20 .... .35
50. ½ Pice (Bro) 1938-40 .... .75
50a. ½ Pice (Bro) 1942. Proof restrike 6.50
51. ¹⁄₁₂ Anna (Bro) 1939-42 .... 1.25

52. 1 Rupee (N) 1947. Rev. Tiger 2.50

53. ½ Rupee (N) 1946-47 .... 1.25
54. ¼ Rupee (N) 1946-47 .... 1.00

55. 1 Pice (Bro) 1943-47 (Center hole). Crown and date. Rev. Floral scroll .... .50

INDIA (BHARAT)—REPUBLIC

56. 1 Rupee (N) 1950-54. Asoka pillar, three lions on pedestal. Rev. Value 1.50
57. ½ Rupee (N) 1950-56 .... 1.00
58. ¼ Rupee (N) 1950-56 .... .75
59. 2 Annas (C-N) 1950-55. Rev. Brahman bull (square-shaped). .... .50

60. 1 Anna (C-N) 1950-55 (scalloped edge) .... .50

61. ½ Anna (C-N) 1950-55 (square planchet) .... .40

62. 1 Pice (Br) 1950 (thick planchet), 1951-55 (thin planchet) .... .25

NEW SYSTEM 1957-
100 Naya Paise = 1 Rupee

63. 1 Rupee (N) 1962-70. Asoka pillar. Rev.
   Value 1.00
64. 50 Naya Paisa (N) 1960-63 .... .75
65. 25 Naya Paise (N) 1957-63 .... .50
66. 10 Naya Paise (C-N) 1957-63 (scalloped) .40
67. 5 Naya Paise (C-N) 1957-63 (square) .30
68. 2 Naya Paise (C-N) 1957-63 (scalloped) .20
69. 1 Naya Paise (Bro) 1957-61; (N-Bra)
   1962-63 (round) .... .15

70. 1 Rupee (N) 1964. Portrait of Jawaharlal
   Nehru. Rev. Asoka pillar and value
   (Memorial coin showing the years of his
   birth and death, 1889 and 1964) 1.50
71. 50 Paise (N) 1964 .... .75

72. 50 Paise (N) 1964-71. Asoka pillar. Rev.
   Numeral of value .... .60
73. 25 Paise (N) 1964-68; (A-Br) 1968-71 . .35
74. 10 Paise (C-N) 1964- (scalloped) .... .25
75. 5 Paise (C-N) 1964-67; (A) 68-71 (square) .20

76. 3 Paise (Al) 1964-71 (six-sided planchet) .... .10
77. 2 Paise (C-N) 1964, (Al) 1965- (scalloped) .... .10
78. 1 Paisa (N-Bra) 1964 (round) .... .15
79. 1 Paisa (Al) 1965- (square) ...... .10

80. 20 Paise (N-Bra) 1968- . Rev. Lotus
   flower .... .30
81. 10 Paise (N-Bra) 1968-71. Type of #74 .25

82. 10 Rupees 1969, 70. Head of Mahatma
   Ghandi. Rev. Asoka pillar (Commemorates 100th anniversary of his
   birth) 5.00
83. 1 Rupee (N) 1969, 70 .... .75
84. 50 Paise (N) 1969, 70 .... .40
85. 20 Paise (Al-Br) 1969, 70 .... .20

86. 10 Rupees 1970, 71. Lotus blossom. Rev.
   Asoka pillar (F.A.O. coin plan) 6.00
87. 20 Paise (A-Br) 1970, 71 .... .25

88. 10 Paise (A) 1971- . Asoka pillar in floral
   border. Rev. Value in border (scalloped planchet) .... .20

89. 10 Rupees 1972. Two youths holding flag. Rev. Asoka pillar and value (Commemorates 25th anniversary of independence) — 7.00
90. 50 Paise (C-N) 1972 — .50

91. 50 Paise (C-N) 1972- . Asoka pillar. Rev. Value — .35
92. 25 Paise (C-N) 1972- — .30

93. 5 Paise (A) 1972- . Asoka pillar. Rev. Value (square planchet) — .15
94. 3 Paise (A) 1972- (six-sided planchet) — .10

95. 20 Rupees 1973. Wheat around motto. Rev. Asoka pillar, value (F.A.O. coin plan) — 7.50
96. 10 Rupees 1973 — 5.00
97. 50 Paise (C-N) 1973 — .50

98. 50 Rupees 1974. Family planning symbol. Rev. Asoka pillar, value (F.A.O. coin plan) — 15.00
99. 10 Rupees (C-N) 1974 — 4.00
100. 10 Paise (A) 1974 (scalloped planchet) — .20

101. 50 Rupees 1975. Woman in sari with ear of wheat, dam in background. Rev. Asoka pillar, value (F.A.O. coin plan) — 15.00
102. 10 Rupees (C-N) 1975 — 3.00

103. 1 Rupee (C-N) 1975. Asoka Pillar. Rev. Value, wheat (Type of #63)

104. 10 Paise (A) 1975. Type of #101 (F.A.O. coin plan) (scalloped planchet) — .20

NATIVE STATES

(Coins listed are representative types of the issues of the individual states.)

ALWAR

1. 1 Rupee 1877-82, 91. Crowned bust of Victoria. Rev. Value and inscription — 6.50

BAHAWALPUR

2. ¼ Anna (C) 1940. Bust of Raja Sadiq Mohammed V in fez. Rev. Toughra — 1.50
3. ½ Pice (C) 1940 — 1.00

BARODA

4. 2 Paisas (Br) 1940-50. Inscription. Rev. Hoof and sword — 1.00

INDIA (continued)

BENGAL

5. 1 Mohur (G) 1750-1820   75.00

BHUTAN—see page 47

BIKANIR

6. 1 Rupee 1892-97.   Crowned bust of
    Victoria. Rev. Value and inscription   6.50
7. ¼ Anna 1895   6.00
8. ½ Pice 1894   7.50

9. 1 Mohur (G) 1937. Bust of Rajah Sri
    Ganga Singhji. Rev. Inscription (Com-
    memorates 50th year of reign)   125.00

10. 1 Rupee 1937 (Commemorating 50th
    year of reign). Bust of Rajah Sri Ganga
    Singhji   10.00

BOMBAY

11. Double Pice (C) 1804. Arms of East India
    Co. Rev. Balance   6.00

DEWAS

(Senior branch and Junior branch are indicated
by S.B. and J.B. on reverse)

12. ¼ Anna (C) 1888. Crowned bust of Vic-
    toria. Rev. Value and inscription   12.50
13. 1/12 Anna (C) 1888   12.50

DHAR

14. ¼ Anna (C) 1887. Crowned bust of Vic-
    toria. Rev. Value and inscription   10.00
15. ½ Pice (C) 1887   8.00
16. 1/12 Anna (C) 1887   7.50

GWALIOR

17. ¼ Anna (C) 1929, (reduced size) 1942.
    Bust of Rajah Jivaji III in turban. Rev.
    Arms with supporters   1.00

INDIA (continued)

HYDERABAD

18. 1 Rupee A. H. 1321-43, 1903-24. Palace gateway. Rev. Inscription — 4.00
19. ½ Rupee (N) A. H. 1366 (1948) — 1.00
20. ¼ Rupee (N) A.H. 1366-68 — .60
21. ⅛ Rupee (N) A.H. 1366-68 — .30
22. 1 Anna (Br) 1942-48 (square planchet) — .25

23. 2 Pai (Bro) 1943-48 (center hole). Inscriptions — .50

INDORE

24. ¼ Anna (C) 1886-1902. Seated bull. — 1.25
25. ½ Anna (C) 1935. Bust of Yeshwant Rao Holkar — 1.50
26. ¼ Anna(C) 1935 — .75

JAIPUR

27. 1 Anna (N-Br) 1944. Bust of Man Singh II — .50

JAORA

28. 2 Paisas (C) 1893-94. Inscription — 6.00
29. 1 Paisa (C) 1893-96 — 4.00

KUTCH

30. 5 Kori 1936. Native inscription "In the name of Edward VIII" — 5.00
31. 1 Kori 1936 — 2.50
32. 3 Dokda (C) 1936 — 7.50

33. 5 Kori 1947. Castle towers and inscription. Rev. Trident, crescent, dagger and inscription — 125.00

MADRAS

34. 1 Rupee 1758-1811. Native inscription (crude, thick planchet) — 10.00

35. 1 Rupee 1811-1822. Native inscription (round, milled planchet) — 12.00

INDIA (continued)

36.	1 Pagoda (G) 1808-15. Pagoda. Rev. The god Swami	50.00
37.	½ Pagoda 1807-08	45.00
38.	¼ Pagoda 1807-08	20.00

MEWAR UDAIPUR

39.	2 Rupee 1932. Hills and inscription in floral border. Rev. Inscription	4.00

SAILANA

40.	¼ Anna (C) 1908. Head of Edward VII	6.50
41.	¼ Anna (C) 1912. Head of George V	5.25

TRAVANCORE

42.	1 Chuckram (C) 1938. Bust of Rajah Bala Rama Varma in plumed hat. Rev. Conch shell in floral border	3.50
43.	½ Rupee 1936-45. Rev. Conch shell	3.50
44.	8 Cash (C). Conch shell. Rev. Monogram	1.00
45.	4 Cash (C)	.60
46.	1 Cash (C)	.40

INDO-CHINA

The easternmost area of the peninsula which faces east on the South China Sea. The various states in this area were united under a French protectorate until 1946. The war which came to an end in 1954 brought about an accord extending Communism to northern Vietnam, independence to southern Vietnam, and the French-sponsored regimes of Laos and Cambodia.

100 Centimes = 1 Piastre = 1 Franc
1 Xu = 1 Centime
10 Haos = 1 Piastre
1 Dong = 1 Piastre

FRENCH COCHIN-CHINA

1.	1 Piastre 1879-85. Republic seated. Rev. Value in wreath (proof issue)	rare
2.	50 Centimes 1879-85	50.00
3.	20 Centimes 1879, 84-85	25.00
4.	10 Centimes 1879, 84-85	17.00

5.	1 Centime (Br) 1879-85. Rev. Value in circle	8.50
6.	2 Sapeque (Br) 1879-85 (square center hole)	7.50

FRENCH INDO-CHINA

7.	1 Piastre 1885-1928. Republic seated. Rev. Value in wreath	6.00
8.	50 Centimes 1885-1936	2.00
9.	20 Centimes 1885-1937	1.50
10.	10 Centimes 1885-1937	1.00
11.	1 Centime (Br) 1885-94	3.00

12. 2 Sapeque (Br) 1887-1902 (square center hole)   5.00

17. 20 Centimes (N) 1939; (C-N) 1939-41 (Inscription "Republique Francaise"). Bust of Liberty. Rev. Rice plants and value   .50

18. 10 Centimes (N) 1939-40; (C-N) 1939-41   .50

13. 1 Piastre 1931. Liberty head. Rev. Value   7.50

19. 1 Piastre (N-Bro) 1946-47. (Inscription "Union Francaise"). Bust of Liberty. Rev. Rice plants and value   4.50

14. 5 Centimes (C-N) 1923-38; (N-Bra) 1938, 39. Head and cornucopias. Rev. Value (center hole)   .75

20. 50 Centimes (C-N) 1946. Republic seated. Rev. Value   2.00

15   1 Centime (Bro) 1896-1939 (Holed center). Seated figures. Rev. Value in Chinese   .60

21. 20 Centimes (A) 1945. Bust of Liberty. Rev. Rice plants and value   .75

22. 10 Centimes (A) 1945   .75

23. 5 Centimes (A) 1946   .40

16. ½ Centime (Br) 1935-40 (Holed center). Liberty cap and RF. Rev. Value   .50

16a. ½ Centime (Z) 1939, 40   60.00

INDONESIA

A republic made up of Java, Sumatra, most of Borneo, Celebes and 3,000 other islands, all formerly part of the Dutch East Indies. The republic came into existence in 1949. Netherlands New Guinea, now known as West Irian, was added in 1963.

100 Sen = 1 Rupiah

1. 50 Sen (C-N) 1952-57. Indonesian. Rev. Value .50

2. 50 Sen (A) 1958-61. Bird. Rev. Value .50
3. 25 Sen (A) 1952-57. Bird. Rev. Value .50
4. 10 Sen (A) 1951-57 .50

5. 5 Sen (A) 1951-54. Holed center .50
6. 1 Sen (A) 1952 .75

7. 50 Rupiah (C-N) 1971. Bird of paradise. Rev. Value .75

8. 25 Rupiah (C-N) 1971. Crowned pigeon. Rev. Value .50

9. 10 Rupiah (C-N) 1971. Cotton and rice with value. Rev. Value (F.A.O. coin plan) .25

10. 5 Rupiah (A) 1970. Long-tailed bird. Rev. Value .35

11. 2 Rupiah (A) 1970. Rice and cotton with value. Rev. Value .20

12. 1 Rupiah (A) 1970. Bird with fanlike tail. Rev. Value .15

13. 100 Rupiah (C-N) 1973. Longhouse. Rev. Value 1.00

14. 100,000 Rupiah (G) 1974. Komodo dragon. Rev. Arms (Conservation commemorative) 300.00

15. 5,000 Rupiah 1974. Orangutan. Rev. Arms
    (Conservation commemorative)   20.00

16. 2,000 Rupiah 1974. Javan tiger. Rev. Arms
    (Conservation commemorative)   15.00

17. 10 Rupiah (Bra-St) 1974. National savings
    symbol. Rev. Value (F.A.O. coin plan)   .35

18. 5 Rupiah (A) 1974. Family planning sym-
     bol. Rev. Value (F.A.O. coin plan)   .35

RIAU

An archipelago between Sumatra, in Indonesia,
and Singapore, a province of Indonesia.

1. 50 Sen (A) 1962. Bust of President Su-
   karno. Rev. Value in wreath, lettered
   edge KEPULAUAN RIAU   2.50
2. 25 Sen (A) 1962   1.75
3. 10 Sen (A) 1962   1.25

4. 5 Sen (A) 1962   1.00
5. 1 Sen (A) 1962   1.75

IRIAN JAYA (West Irian)

Formerly Netherlands New Guinea, this area
was not included in the Republic of Indonesia established in 1949 when the Netherlands withdrew.
Under an agreement reached in 1962, Indonesia
won control of West Irian following a brief period
of U.N. administration.

1. 50 Sen (A) 1962 Bust of President Su-
   karno. Rev. Value and wreath, reeded
   edge   2.00
2. 25 Sen (A) 1962   1.75
3. 10 Sen (A) 1962. Plain edge   1.50
4. 5 Sen (A) 1962. Plain edge   1.25
5. 1 Sen (A) 1962. Plain edge   1.50

IRAN

This country, located in western Asia on the Persian Gulf, was known as Persia until 1935. The Persians had one of the mightiest empires of ancient times. Today the country is important for its large oil reserves.

10 Krans = 1 Toman
100 Dinars = 1 Ryal or Rial

GENERAL TYPE

1.	5 Krans 1878-1928. Lion with sword. Rev. Inscription	7.50
2.	2 Krans 1878-1928	3.50
3.	1 Kran 1878-1928	2.00
4.	½ Kran 1878-1927	1.75
5.	¼ Kran 1878-1924	2.00

MOZAFAR-ED-DIN SHAH 1896-1907

6.	2 Krans 1904. Bust. Rev. Lion	7.50

AHMED SHAH 1909-25

7.	2 Krans 1919. Bust. Rev. Lion	20.00

RIZA SHAH PAHLEVI 1925-41

8.	2 Krans 1927-29. Bust in uniform	4.00

LAW OF 1937 (S.H. 1315)

9.	50 Dinar (A-Bro) S.H. 1315-22. Lion with sword	.50
10.	10 Dinar (A-Bro) S.H. 1315-21	.35
11.	5 Dinar (A-Bro) S.H. 1315-21	.20

MOHAMMED RIZA PAHLEVI 1942-
LAW OF 1944 (A.H. 1322)

12.	10 Rials S.H. 1323-26. Lion with sword	3.00
13.	5 Rials S.H. 1322-28	1.75
14.	2 Rials S.H. 1322-30	1.00
15.	1 Rial S.H. 1322-25	.60

LAW OF 1954 (A.H. 1333)

16.	10 Rials (C-N) A. H. 1335-44	1.75
17.	5 Rials (C-N) A.H. 1333- Lion with sword	.50
18.	2 Rials (C-N) A.H. 1333-	.50
19.	1 Rial (C-N) A.H. 1333-	.35
20.	50 Dinar (A-Bro) A.H. 1333-	.20

21.	10 Rials (CN) 1966- . Head of Shah. Rev. Lion with sword	1.50

22.	10 Rials (CN) 1969. Rev. F.A.O. inscription	1.75
23.	20 Rials (C-N) 1971- . Type of #21	1.00

IRAN (continued)

24. 1 Rial (C-N) 1971-73. Head of Shah. Rev. Lion with sword, inscription (F.A.O. coin plan) .25

25. 20 Rials (C-N) 1974. Rev. Stylized star (Commemorates 7th Asian Games in Teheran) 1.00

IRAQ

Part of the Turkish Empire until World War I (known as Mesopotamia), Iraq became a British Mandate in 1920. The Mandate ended in 1932, when Iraq became independent. It was a monarchy from 1921-1958 when an army revolt resulted in the assassination of King Faisal II and the creation of a republic.

1000 Fils or 20 Dirhem or 5 Riyals =
1 Pound or 1 Dinar

FAISAL I 1921-33

1. 200 Fils or 1 Riyal 1932. Head. Rev. Arabic inscription 10.00
2. 50 Fils or 1 Dirhem 1931-33 3.00
3. 20 Fils 1931-33 1.75
4. 10 Fils (N) 1931-33. Scalloped edge 2.50
5. 4 Fils (N) 1931-33 1.25
6. 2 Fils (Bro) 1931-33. Type of #1 1.25
7. 1 Fil (Bro) 1931-33 .75

GHAZI I 1933-39

8. 50 Fils or 1 Dirhem 1937-38. Head. Rev. Arabic inscription 3.00
9. 20 Fils 1938 2.00
10. 10 Fills (N) 1937-38; (Bro or C-N) 1938. Scalloped edge .50
11. 4 Fils (C-N) 1938; (Bro) 1938; (N) 1938-39 .30
12. 1 Fil (Bro) 1936-38. Round .35

FAISAL II 1939-58
(Regency 1939-53)

13. 10 Fils (Bro) 1943 (Scalloped edge). Young head. Rev. Arabic inscription 2.00
14. 4 Fils (Bro) 1943 2.00

15. 100 Fils 1953-55. Older head. Rev. Arabic
    inscription   3.50
16. 50 Fils 1953, 1955 (reduced size planchet) 2.00
17. 20 Fils 1953, 1955 (reduced size planchet) 3.00
18. 10 Fils (C-N) 1953 (scalloped edge)   .75
19. 4 Fils (C-N) 1953 (scalloped edge)   .60
20. 2 Fils (Br) 1953 (round planchet)   .75
21. 1 Fil (Br) 1953   .25

REPUBLIC 1958-

22. 100 Fils 1959. Emblem of republic. Rev.
    Value   1.75
23. 50 Fils 1959   1.00
24. 25 Fils 1959   .75
25. 10 Fils (C-N) 1959   (scalloped edge)   .50
26. 5 Fils (C-N) 1959   .50
27. 1 Fil (Br) 1959   (ten-sided planchet) .30

28. 50 Fils (CN) 1969- . Palm trees. Rev. Crossed
    branches   .75
29. 25 Fils (CN) 1969-   .45
30. 10 Fils (CN) 1967- (scalloped edge)   .40
31. 5 Fils (CN) 1967-   .30
32. 100 Fils (C-N) 1970-   1.00
33. 250 Fils (N) 1970. Type of #28, with added
    reverse inscription (F.A.O. coin plan) 3.00

34. 5 Dinars (G) 1971. Two soldiers. Rev.
    Value (Commemorates 50th anniversary
    of Iraqi army)   60.00

35. 1 Dinar 1971   10.00
36. 500 Fils 1971   6.50

37. 250 Fils (N) 1971. Dove in flight over moun-
    tains. Rev. Value (Commemorates 1st
    anniversary of peace with Kurds)   3.00

38. 1 Dinar 1972. Type of #28 with added
    reverse inscription (Commemorates 25th
    anniversary of Central Bank)   10.00
39. 250 Fils (N) 1972   3.00

40. 250 Fils (N) 1972. Type of #28 with added
    reverse inscription (Commemorates 25th
    anniversary of Al Baath Political Party) 3.00

41. 1 Dinar 1973. Oil tanker, rising sun. Rev.
    Value and inscription (Commemorates
    nationalization of petroleum industry) 15.00

42. 500 Fils (N) 1973. Oil tank. Rev. Value and
    inscription (Commemorates nationaliza-
    tion of petroleum industry)   5.00

43. 250 Fils (N) 1973. Torch between storage
    tanks and oil rig. Rev. Value and in-
    scription (Commemorates nationaliza-
    tion of petroleum industry)   2.50

44. 10 Fils (C-N) 1975. Three palms. Rev. Value
    (F.A.O. coin plan)
45. 5 Fils (C-N) 1975

IRELAND (EIRE)

An independent republic. All coins of Ireland picture a harp on the obverse.

12 Pence = 1 Shilling

Same as English denominations

(Coins issued 1928-38 read SAORSTAT EIRE-ANN, those from 1939 to date EIRE)

7. Halfpenny (Br) 1928-67. Rev. Sow and piglets .50
8. Farthing (Br) 1928-66. Rev. Woodcock 1.25

1.	Half Crown 1928-43. Harp. Rev. Horse	3.50
1a.	Half Crown (C-N) 1951-67	2.00

9. 10 Shillings 1966. Padraig H. Pearse. Rev. Memorial statue in Dublin (commemorates 50th anniversary of 1916 Easter Uprising) 6.50

DECIMAL COINAGE

2.	Florin 1928-43. Rev. Salmon	3.50
2a.	Florin (C-N) 1951-68.	1.50
3.	Shilling 1928-42. Rev. Bull	2.50
3a.	Shilling (C-N) 1951-68.	.60

10. 50 Pence (CN) 1970- . Harp. Rev. Woodcock (7-sided planchet) 1.75
11. 10 Pence (CN) 1969- . Harp. Rev. Salmon .40
12. 5 Pence (CN) 1969- . Harp. Rev. Bull .25

13. 2 Pence (Br) 1971- . Harp. Stylized bird .25
14. 1 Penny (Br) 1971- .15
15. ½ Penny (Br) 1971- .10

4.	6 Pence (N) 1928-40; (C-N) 1942-69. Rev. Wolfhound	.40
5.	3 Pence (N) 1928-40; (C-N) 1942-68. Rev. Hare	.25
6.	Penny (Br) 1928-68. Rev. Hen and chicks	.25

ISLE OF MAN

Located in the Irish Sea, this island had been held by the Romans, Irish, and Scandinavians before coming under British rule. After being privately held by the Earls of Derby and the Dukes of Atholl, it passed to the British Crown. An interesting feature of the island's coinage is the triquetra—"a three-legged device of booted and spurred human legs bent at the knee as though running, and joined at the hip to form a radiating design."

12 Pence = 1 Shilling

EARLS OF DERBY

1.	Penny (C) 1709, 33. The Stanley crest. Rev. Triquetra	17.50
2.	Halfpenny (C) 1709, 33	22.00

DUKES OF ATHOLL

3.	Penny (C) 1758. Crowned monogram	10.00
4.	Halfpenny (C) 1758	10.00

GEORGE III 1760-1820

5.	Penny (C) 1786. Laureated head. Rev. Triquetra	7.50
6.	Halfpenny (C) 1786	10.00

7. Penny (C) 1798, 1813 ("Cartwheel type"). Laureated head. Rev. Triquetra   10.00

8. Halfpenny (C) 1798, 1813   10.00

VICTORIA 1837-1901

9.	Penny (C) 1839. Young head. Rev. Triquetra	12.50
10.	Halfpenny 1839	9.00
11.	Farthing 1839	5.00

ELIZABETH 1952-

12.	5 Pounds (G) 1965. Queen Elizabeth II. Rev. Arms in shield (Commemorates 200th anniversary, acquisition of Isle of Man)	700.00
13.	1 Pound (G) 1965	100.00
14.	½ Pound (G) 1965	75.00

20. 1 New Penny (Br) 1971- . Rev. Ring chain
pattern .25
21. ½ New Penny (Br) 1971- . Rev. Cushag
(national flower) .25

15. 1 Crown (CN) 1970. Draped bust of Queen
Elizabeth with coronet. Rev. Tailless
Manx cat 3.00

DECIMAL COINAGE

22. 25 New Pence (C-N) 1972. Rev. Conjoined
arms (Commemorates Royal Silver
Wedding Anniversary) 6.00
22a. 25 New Pence (S) 1972 (proof issue) 35.00

16. 50 New Pence (C-N) 1971- . Draped bust
of Queen Elizabeth II. Rev. Viking ship 3.50

23. 5 Pounds (G) 1973, 74. Rev. Viking on
horseback 500.00
24. 2 Pounds (G) 1973, 74 200.00
25. 1 Sovereign (G) 1973, 74 100.00
26. ½ Sovereign (G) 1973, 74 50.00

17. 10 New Pence (C-N) 1971- . Rev. Tri-
quetrum .75

18. 5 New Pence (C-N) 1971- . Rev. Tower of
Refuge .75
19. 2 New Pence (Br) 1971- . Rev. Two fal-
cons .65

27. 1 Crown (C-N) 1974. Rev. Bust of Winston
Churchill (Commemorates 100th anniversary of statesman's birth) 3.50
28. 1 Crown (S) 1974 (proof issue) 17.50

29. 25 New Pence (C-N) 1975. Rev. Manx cat

ISRAEL

As a result of action by the United Nations, Israel came into existence as an independent republic in May, 1948. Previously it was part of the British mandate of Palestine.

1000 Pruta = 1 Israel Pound

1. 25 Mils (Al) 5708-09 (1948-49). Cluster of grapes, "ISRAEL" in Hebrew above, Arabic below. Rev. Value in olive wreath   25.00

2. 500 Pruta 5709 (1949). Pomegranates. Rev. Value in olive wreath   20.00

3. 250 Pruta 5709 (1949). Wheat ears. Rev. Value in olive wreath ("H" mint mark at bottom of reverse)   10.00
3a. 250 Pruta (C-N) 5709 (1949). (No mint mark)   3.00

4. 100 Pruta (C-N) 5709, 15 (1949, 55). Palm tree with date clusters   3.50
4a. 100 Pruta (N-St) 5714 (1954). (Smaller planchet)   2.00

5. 50 Pruta (C-N) 5709, 14 (1949, 54). Vine leaf   2.00
5a. 50 Pruta (N-St) 5714 (1954). (Slightly smaller planchet)   1.00

6. 25 Pruta (C-N) 5709 (1949). Cluster of grapes   1.50
6a. 25 Pruta (N-St) 5714 (1954)   1.50

7.   7b.

7a.

7. 10 Pruta (Br) 5709 (1949). Amphora with two handles. Rev. Value in olive wreath   1.50
7a. 10 Pruta (Al) 5712 (1952). Jug with one handle (Scalloped edge planchet)   1.25
7b. 10 Pruta (Al) 5717 (1957); (C-Al) 5717 (1957). (Round planchet)   1.25

8. 5 Pruta (Br) 5709 (1949). Lyre. Rev. Value in olive wreath   2.00

9. 1 Pruta (Al) 5709 (1949). Anchor. Rev. Value in olive wreath   1.50

ISRAEL (continued)

NEW CURRENCY
100 Agorot = 1 Israel Pound

10. 1 Pound (C-N) 5723 (1963) - 5727 (1967).
Menorah. Rev. Value 2.00
11. ½ Pound (C-N) 5723 (1963) - 1.00

12. 25 Agorot (Al-Br) 5720 (1960) - . Lyre.
Rev. Value .... .75
12a. 25 Agorot (C-N) 1974 - ...... .60

13. 10 Agorot (Al-Br) 5720 (1960) - . Palm
tree with date clusters ...... .50
13a. 10 Agorot (C-N) 1974 - ...... .50

14. 5 Agorot (Al-Br) 5720 (1960) - . Pomegranates ...... .35
14a. 5 Agorot (C-N) 1974 - ...... .35

15. 1 Agora (Al) 5720 (1960) - . Barley
ears (Scalloped edge planchet) ...... .25

COMMEMORATIVE ISSUES

16. 5 Pounds 1958. Stylized menorah. Rev.
Value (Commemorates 10th anniversary of Israel's independence) 40.00

17. 1 Pound (C-N) 1958 (Chanukah—
Festival of Lights) 8.00

18. 5 Pounds 1959. Dancers. Rev. Value
(Commemorates 11th anniversary of
Israel's independence—"INGATHERING OF
THE EXILES") 55.00
19. 20 Pounds (G) 1960. Head of Theodor
Herzl. Rev. Menorah (Commemorates
100th anniversary of birth of founder
of Zionism) 850.00

20. 5 Pounds 1960. (Theodor Herzl commemorative)   60.00

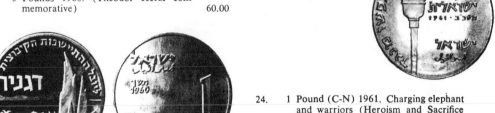

24. 1 Pound (C-N) 1961. Charging elephant and warriors (Heroism and Sacrifice commemorative)   50.00

21. 1 Pound (C-N) 1960 (Commemorates 50th anniversary of founding of Deganya, the first kibbutz)   12.00

25. ½ Pound (C-N) 1961, 62. Reproduction of ancient Jewish half shekel. Rev. Value (Feast of Purim)   30.00

22. 1 Pound (C-N) 1960. Woman with lamb. Rev. Hadassah Medical Center in Jerusalem (Henrietta Szold commemorative)   125.00

23. 5 Pounds 1961. Ark containing six rolls of the Torah (13th anniversary, Bar Mitzvah, commemorative)   150.00

26. 100 Pounds (G) 1962. Head of Chaim Weizmann. Rev. Menorah (Memorial coin on 10th anniversary of death of Israel's first president) (proof issue)   1,200.00

27. 50 Pounds (G) 1962 (proof issue)   650.00

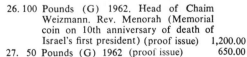

28. 5 Pounds 1962 Industrialization of the Negev   225.00

29. 1 Pound (C-N) 1962. Early Italian Menorah   150.00

30. 5 Pounds 1963. Ancient galley. Rev. Smokestack of modern ship ("Seafaring")   725.00

31. 1 Pound (C-N) 1963. No. African Chanukah Lamp   150.00

32. 50 Lirot (G) 1964. Pomegranate and double cornucopia. Rev. Menorah (Commemorates 10th anniversary of Bank of Israel)   1,000.00

33. 5 Pounds 1964. Museum buildings. Rev. Ancient pillar (16th anniversary of Israel Museum)   150.00

34. 5 Pounds 1965. Parliament (Knesset) building in Jerusalem. Rev. Menorah and value (17th anniversary of Knesset building)   65.00

ISRAEL DATING CHART
Chart below copyright 1964 by Fred
Bertram, Miami, Fla.

תש"ח	-	5708(1948)
תש"ט	-	5709(1949)
תשי"ב	-	5712(1952)
תשי"ד	-	5714(1954)
תשט"ו	-	5715(1955)
תשי"ז	-	5717(1957)
תש"ך	-	5720(1960)
תשכ"א	-	5721(1961)
תשכ"ב	-	5722(1962)
תשכ"ג	-	5723(1963)
תשכ"ד	-	5724(1964)
תשכ"ה	-	5725(1965)

The dates on Israel coins are according to the
Hebrew calendar, figured from the time of Adam.
The year 1965, for example, is 5725. Israel commemorative coins show Christian era dates in Arabic numerals but regular issue coins carry only
Hebrew dates in Hebrew characters per the above
chart.

36.   10 Pounds 1967. Wailing Wall of Temple
of Solomon in Jerusalem. Rev. Emblem
of Israel Defense Forces (Commemorates victory in 6 Day War)   17.50

37.   5 Pounds 1967. Lighthouse. Rev. Large
numeral (Commemorates 10th anniversary of Port of Eilat)   75.00

35.   5 Pounds 1966. Modernistic design of
Hebrew words. Rev. Inscription and
value (Commemorates 18th anniversary of independence)   50.00

38.   1 Pound (CN) 1967- . Pomegranates. Rev.
Value and inscription   2.00

39. 10 Pounds 1968. View of Jerusalem. Rev. Facade of Temple of Solomon (Commemorates reunification of city and 20th anniversary of Israel)   50.00

42. 10 Pounds 1970. Stylized plow. Rev. Campus building (Commemorates the centenary of Mikveh Israel School)   27.50

40. 10 Pounds 1969. Hebrew letters for "Shalom (Peace)." Rev. Military memorial, helmet (Commemorates 21st anniversary of independence)   50.00

43. 10 Pounds 1971. Cogwheel rotating molecule. Rev. Atomic reactor building at Nahal Sorek (Commemorates 23rd anniversary of independence)   50.00

41. 10 Pounds 1970-72. Tablets of Law. Rev. Arms (Pidyon Ha Ben coin for ceremony of redemption of first-born child) (reverse design differs slightly each year)   30.00

44. 100 Pounds (G) 1971. Sun behind bars. Rev. Value, small menorah   1,200.00

45. 10 Pounds 1971   25.00

260 • CATALOGUE of the WORLD'S MOST POPULAR COINS

46.   10 Pounds 1972. Stylized jet. Rev. Value
with rocket for numeral 1 (Commemorates 24th anniversary of independence)   30.00

52.   10 Pounds 1973-74. Offering tray with
five replicas of shekels. Rev. Arms and
value (Pidyon Ha Ben coin, reverse
design differs slightly each year)   15.00

47.   5 Pounds 1972. Russian menorah. Rev.
Value   20.00

53.   5 Pounds 1973. Babylonian menorah.
Rev. Value   12.50

48.   200 Pounds (G) 1973. Final paragraph of
Declaration of Israeli Independence
with signatures. Rev. Arms and value
(Commemorates 25th anniversary of
independence)   750.00
49.   100 Pounds (G) 1973   250.00
50.   50 Pounds (G) 1973   150.00
51.   10 Pounds 1973   17.50

54.   500 Pounds (G) 1974. Head of Ben
Gurion in incuse panel. Rev. Arms   600.00
55.   25 Pounds 1974   30.00

ISRAEL (continued)

56.   10 Pounds 1974. Menorah from Damascus. Rev. Value   25.00

57.   10 Pounds 1974. Torah scroll. Rev. Value, arms (Commemorates preservation of Hebrew language)   15.00

58.   500 Pounds (G) 1975. Value. Rev. Star design (Commemorates 25th anniversary of Israeli bond program)   475.00
59.   25 Pounds 1975   25.00

60.   10 Pounds 1975. Menorah from Holland. Rev. Value in pentagon   8.50
61.   25 Pounds 1976. Menorah between olive branches. Rev. Five pomegranate stalks (Pidyon Ha Ben coin)   22.00

ITALIAN SOMALILAND

This area, located on the northeast coast of Africa along the Indian Ocean, joined with British Somaliland in 1960 to become the Republic of Somalia.

100 Bese = 1 Rupia
100 Centesimi = 1 Lira or 1 Somalo

VICTOR EMMANUEL III 1900-44

1.   1 Rupia 1910, 12-15, 19-21. Head. Crowned value and Arabic inscription   40.00
2.   ½ Rupia 1910, 12-13, 15, 19   30.00
3.   ¼ Rupia 1910, 13   25.00

4.   4 Bese (Bro) 1909-10, 13, 21, 23-24. Bust. Rev. Arabic inscription over value   25.00
5.   2 Bese (Bro) 1909-10, 13, 21, 23-24   20.00
6.   1 Besa (Bro) 1909-10, 13, 21   15.00

7.   10 Lire 1925. Crowned bust. Rev. Coroneted arms   75.00
8.   5 Lire 1925   50.00

ITALY — NAPLES AND SICILY

Until the complete unification of Italy in 1860, the principal coin-issuing areas were:

1. The Kingdom of the Two Sicilies—the island of Sicily, and "Naples" (southern part of the Italian peninsula).
2. Papal States (central Italy).
3. Tuscany (west-central Italy).
4. Venice (northeast Italy).
5. Sardinia (northwest Italy and the island of Sardinia). The house of Savoy, rulers of Sardinia, eventually became the reigning family of the new kingdom of Italy.

100 Centesimi = 1 Lira
120 Grani or 12 Tori = 1 Piastre
1 Scudo = 97 Cents (U. S. money) approx.

NAPLES AND SICILY
(after 1816 THE KINGDOM OF THE TWO SICILIES)

CHARLES II 1665-1700

1. 1 Scudo 1684. Bust. Rev. Crown over hemispheres   120.00
2. ½ Scudo 1683. Bust. Rev. Seated figure   55.00

PHILIP V 1700-13

3. 1 Scudo 1702. Bust. Rev. Sun above globe   125.00
4. ½ Scudo 1701-02   45.00

CHARLES III 1713-34

5. 120 Grani 1731. Bust. Rev. Crowned arms   80.00
6. 60 Grani 1732   35.00
7. 24 Grani 1730   18.00

CHARLES III (of Bourbon) 1734-59

8. 120 Grani 1734-53. Bust. Rev. Seated female   110.00
9. 60 Grani 1734-38   50.00

FERDINAND IV 1759-1825

10. 120 Grani 1791. Conjoined heads. Rev. Zodiac encircling sun and earth   160.00

FERDINAND IV

(First period: 1759-99. Charles succeeded to the Spanish throne in 1759 and abdicated his Italian throne in favor of Ferdinand, his eight-year-old son. Hence the title "HISPANIAR. INFANS" —the Infanta of Spain—which appears on most of Ferdinand's coins.)

11. 30 Tari 1791 (Sicily)   750.00

11. Rev.

FERDINAND IV (Second Period: 1799-1805)

(In 1805 Ferdinand was forced by Napoleon to flee from Naples and go to the island of Sicily. Coins issued subsequently for Sicily alone have a distinctive eagle reverse.)

12. 120 Grani 1784-96. Head. Rev. Arms   60.00

13.   10 Tornesi (C) 1798   20.00

16. 120 Grani 1800, 02. Head. Rev. Crowned arms   50.00

NEAPOLITAN REPUBLIC 1799
(In 1799 the French captured Naples and established the short-lived Neapolitan Republic.)

14.   1 Piastre (12 Carlini). Liberty. Rev. Value   200.00
15.   ½ Piastre   125.00

17. 120 Grani 1805. Head in circle. Rev. Crowned spade-shaped shield   65.00
18.   6 Tornesi (C) 1799-1803   10.00
19.   4 Tornesi (C) 1799-1800   12.50
20.   1 Tornese (C) 1804   16.00
21.   1 Piastre (12 Tari) 1801-04. Bust. Rev. Crowned eagle   30.00
22.   1 Piastre (12 Tari) 1805-10. Rev. Eagle in wreath   35.00

23. 10 Grani (C) 1814-15. Radiate head. Rev. Corn ear and cornucopia   40.00
24. 5 Grani (C) 1814-16. Rev. Security seated   30.00

28. 12 Carlini (1 Piastre) 1809-10. Head. Rev. Value in wreath   300.00

25. 2 Grani (C) 1814-15. Rev. Pegasus   16.00
26. 1 Grano (C) 1814-15. Rev. Grapes   10.00

JOSEPH BONAPARTE 1806-08

29. 5 Lire 1812-13. Head. Rev. Crowned arms in canopy   200.00
30. 2 Lire 1812-13. Rev. Value in wreath   40.00
31. 1 Lire 1812-13   25.00
32. ½ Lira 1813   12.50

FERDINAND IV (Third Period: 1815-16)

(After the French were driven out and Murat was executed, Ferdinand IV was restored to the throne of Naples.)

27. 120 Grani (1 Piastre) 1806-08. Head. Rev. Arms   165.00

(After the removal of the Spanish royal family from Madrid, Joseph Bonaparte was transferred to Madrid as King of Spain. His brother-in-law, Joachim Murat, one of Napoleon's marshals, became King of Naples.)

33. 120 Grani 1815-16. Bust. Rev. Arms   40.00

ITALY — NAPLES AND SICILY (continued)

34.	60 Grani 1816	35.00
35.	1 Carlino 1815-16	6.50

50.	2 Tornesi (C) 1825-26	7.50
51.	1 Tornese (C) 1827	8.00

FERDINAND I 1816-25

(Up to 1816 the kingdom had had two separate parts governed by the same king. Thus, Ferdinand had been Ferdinand III of Sicily but Ferdinand IV of Naples. In 1816 he welded the two parts into a single state and took the title of Ferdinand I, King of the Two Sicilies.)

FERDINAND II 1830-59

36.	120 Grani (1 Piastre) 1817-18. Crowned head. Rev. Arms	40.00
37.	60 Grani 1818	35.00
38.	1 Carlino 1818	20.00
39.	10 Tornesi (C) 1819	16.00
40.	8 Tornesi (C) 1817-18	25.00
41.	5 Tornesi (C) 1817-19	16.00
42.	4 Tornesi (C) 1817	12.00
43.	1 Tornese (C) 1817-18	8.00

52. 120 Grani (1 Piastre) 1831-39. "Smooth" face type. Rev. Arms — 35.00

FRANCIS I 1825-30

53.	120 Grani (1 Piastre) 1840-59. Bearded face type. Rev. Arms	20.00
54.	60 Grani 1832-58	16.00
55.	1 Tari 1832-59	12.00
56.	1 Carlino 1832-56	12.00
57.	½ Carlino 1836-53	18.00
58.	10 Tornesi (C) 1831-59	15.00
59.	5 Tornesi (C) 1831-58	15.00
60.	3 Tornesi (C) 1833-54	25.00
61.	2 Tornesi (C) 1835-59	8.00
62.	1½ Tornesi (C) 1832-54	8.00
63.	1 Tornese (C) 1832-58	8.00
64.	½ Tornese (C) 1833-54	6.00

44.	120 Grani (1 Piastre) 1825-28. Head. Rev. Crowned arms	65.00
45.	60 Grani 1826	50.00
46.	2 Carlini 1826	20.00
47.	1 Carlino 1826	12.00

FRANCIS II 1859-61

48.	10 Tornesi (C) 1825. Head. Rev. Legend	15.00
49.	5 Tornesi (C) 1827	7.50

65.	120 Grani (1 Piastre). Head. Rev. Crowned arms	40.00
66.	1 Tari 1859	16.00
67.	10 Tornesi (C) 1859	10.00
68.	2 Tornesi (C) 1859	10.00

PAPAL STATES

This region, with its core in Rome, was under the temporal rule of the Popes for many centuries. Papal rule came to an end in 1870, and has since then been limited to the comparatively small area of Vatican City.

Papal coinage has a long and interesting history, and the coins are rich in colorful symbolism. The Pope's Tiara, or triple crown, is frequently seen. It symbolizes the Pope's triple function as teacher, law-giver, and judge. A ship represents the Church; an anchor signifies faith.

Another important device is the intertwining of the letters X and P (CH and R in Greek—the beginning letters of Christ's name). This is known as the Chrismon. A fish represents Christianity; a lion stands for Christ or St. Mark; crossed keys are a reference to "the Keys of the Kingdom of Heaven."

CLEMENT VIII 1592-1605

69.	1 Testone 1593-1600. s. petrus. Arms, bust	75.00
70.	1 Giulio 1598-1600. sine clade. Arms	30.00
71.	1 Grosso. sub tuum praes. Arms	20.00
72.	½ Grosso 1595-1600. virgo clemens. Arms	10.00

SEDE VACANTE 1605

73.	1 Giulio 1605. s. paulus alma. Arms	50.00

PAUL V 1605-21

74.	1 Testone 1610-15. s. paulus alma. Bust and arms	75.00
75.	1 Giulio	30.00
76.	½ Grosso. salva nos. Bust and arms	15.00

SEDE VACANTE 1621

77.	1 Giulio 1621. statuit supra. Arms	70.00

GREGORY XV 1621-23

78.	½ Grosso. sub tuum. Bust and arms	24.00

URBAN VIII 1623-44

79.	1 Scudo 1634-43. Bust. St. Michael battling Lucifer	320.00
80.	1 Scudo 1635-43. Bust. Pope kneeling before St. Michael	320.00
81.	1 Scudo 1643. te mane te. Bust. Sts. Peter and Paul	275.00
82.	1 Testone 1625-43. vult deus. Bust and arms	70.00
83.	1 Giulio 1625-32. Sts. Peter and Paul. Arms	40.00
84.	1 Grosso 1625. qui ingred. Arms and bust	25.00
85.	½ Grosso 1625-32	15.00

INNOCENT X 1644-55

86.	1 Scudo. 1646-52. Christ blessing St. Peter	300.00

87. 1 Scudo 1650. Bust. Holy Year Issue.
ANNO IUBILEI 350.00
88. 1 Giulio 1650. ANNO IUBILEI. Arms 50.00
89. 1 Grosso 1650 30.00
90. ½ Grosso 1650-51. APER. ET CLAUS. Arms 15.00

SEDE VACANTE 1655

91. 1 Scudo 1655. Arms and dove 225.00
92. 1 Grosso 1655. INUNDE AMOREM CORDIBUS
ROMA 35.00

ALEXANDER VII 1655-67

CLEMENT IX 1667-69

93. 1 Scudo. St. Peter in clouds. St. Thomas
and beggar 250.00

101. 1 Scudo Arms. Throne of St. Peter 275.00
102. 1 Testone. AUXILIUM DE SANC. Arms 30.00
103. 1 Giulio 1667 20.00
104. 2 Grossi 1667-69. Saint holding key 11.00
105. 1 Grosso 1667 10.00
106. ½ Grosso 1667 10.00

SEDE VACANTE 1669-70

107. 1 Scudo 1669. Arms and dove 200.00
108. 1 Giulio 1669. ILLUXIT ILLUCESCAT. The
Holy Spirit with tongue of fire 20.00
109. 1 Grosso 1669 15.00
110. ½ Grosso 1669 10.00

CLEMENT X 1670-76

94. 1 Testone. NEC CITRA NEC. Arms 35.00
95. 1 Giulio. VIRGO CONCIPIET. Arms 20.00
96. 1 Grosso. HILAREM DATOREM. Arms 15.00
97. ½ Grosso. TEMPERATO SPLEN. Arms 10.00

SEDE VACANTE 1667

98. 1 Scudo 1667. Arms and dove 180.00
99. 1 Testone 1667. DA RECTA SAPERE 25.00
100. 1 Giulio 1667 20.00

111. 1 Scudo 1671-72. Bust. Mercy and Charity standing 150.00

112. 1 Scudo 1675. Bust or arms. Opening of Holy Door — 275.00
113. 1 Scudo 1675. Bust or arms. Holy Door closed — 250.00
114. 1 Testone 1670-75. COLLES FIVENT. Bust and arms — 30.00
115. 1 Giulio 1670-75. IN PORTIS OPERA. Bust and arms — 15.00
116. 1 Grosso 1670-75. PORTO COELI. Bust and arms — 12.00
117. ½ Grosso 1670-75. HAEC PORTA. Bust and arms — 10.00

SEDE VACANTE 1676

118. 1 Scudo 1676. Arms and dove — 140.00
119. 1 Grosso 1676. MENTES TUORUM. Arms — 20.00
120. ½ Grosso 1676. DOCEBIT VOS. Arms — 10.00

INNOCENT XI 1676-89

121. 1 Scudo 1676. Bust. St. Matthew on clouds writing gospel — 170.00

124. 1 Scudo 1680-81. Arms. St. Peter on throne — 190.00
125. 1 Scudo 1683-84. Bust or arms. Rev. Inscription — 160.00
126. ½ Scudo 1676-89. AVARUS NON. Arms — 24.00
127. 1 Testone 1676-89. MELIUS EST. Arms — 20.00
128. 1 Giulio 1676-88. GRESSUS MEOS. Arms — 10.00
129. 1 Grosso 1676-88. SACROSAN BASIL. Arms — 8.00
130. ½ Grosso 1676-88. NOCET MINUS. Arms — 8.00

SEDE VACANTE 1689

131. 1 Scudo 1689. Arms and dove — 160.00
132. 1 Testone 1689. ACCENDE LUMEN. Arms — 30.00
133. 1 Giulio 1689. UBI VULT SPIRAT. Arms — 20.00
134. 1 Grosso 1689 — 12.00
135. ½ Grosso 1689 — 10.00

ALEXANDER VIII 1689-91

136. 1 Scudo 1690-91. Bust. The Church personified standing — 250.00
137. 1 Testone 1689-91. SANCTI BRUN. Bust — 50.00
138. 1 Giulio 1689-90. SANCTUS PAUL. Arms — 20.00
139. ½ Grosso 1689. SANCTUS PETRUS. Arms — 12.50

SEDE VACANTE

140. 1 Testone 1691. DOCEBIT ET SUG. Arms — 40.00

INNOCENT XII 1691-1700

122. 1 Scudo 1677. Bust or arms. St. Peter's (Cathedral) — 300.00

123. 1 Scudo 1678. Bust. Christ and apostles in boat — 350.00

141. 1 Scudo 1692. Bust. Throne of St. Peter — 275.00

142. 1 Scudo 1692-93. Bust. St. Michael hurling thunderbolts at Satan — 250.00
143. 1 Scudo 1693. Bust. Children at breast of Charity — 150.00
144. 1 Scudo 1694. Bust. Peace seated at altar — 225.00

147. 1 Scudo 1699. Bust. Jews gathering manna in the desert — 350.00
148. 1 Scudo 1699. Bust. Holy Door opened. Jubilee Year — 250.00
149. ½ Scudo 1692-1700. NON SIBI SED. Bust. Arms — 50.00
150. 1 Testone 1692-1700. IPSE EST PAX. Arms — 25.00
151. 1 Giulio 1691-1700. PECCATA EC. Arms — 14.00
152. 1 Grosso 1691-99. EGENO SPES. Bust and arms — 10.00
153. ½ Grosso 1691-99. PORTEA AUREA. Arms — 8.00

SEDE VACANTE 1700

154. 1 Scudo 1700. Arms and dove — 150.00
155. 1 Testone 1700. VADO ET VENIO. Arms — 35.00

CLEMENT XI 1700-21

156. 1 Scudo 1700. Bust. Holy Door closed. Jubilee Year — 175.00
157. 1 Scudo 1702. Bust. St. Clement seated on clouds — 175.00
158. 1 Scudo 1703. Arms. Church of St. Theodore — 225.00

145. 1 Scudo 1696-97. Bust. Pope presiding at consistory — 250.00

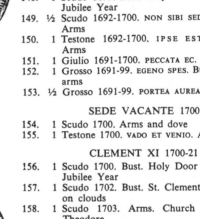

146. 1 Scudo 1698. Bust. St. Peter preaching — 350.00

159. 1 Scudo 1704. Arms. Infant Jesus in temple — 225.00

160. 1 Scudo 1706. Bust or arms. Pope seated on throne 240.00
161. 1 Scudo 1706. Bust. St. Peter in boat 300.00
162. 1 Scudo 1707. Bust. St. Clement praying before lamb 250.00
163. 1 Scudo 1707-09. Arms. Inscription 120.00

164. 1 Scudo 1711. Arms. Bridge of Civita Castellana 300.00

165. 1 Scudo 1713. Arms. View of Pantheon piazza 275.00
166. 1 Scudo 1713. Arms. Fountain and obelisk 250.00
167. 1 Scudo 1715. Bust. Arms 160.00
168. ½ Scudo 1706-15. Arms and bust 25.00

169. 1 Testone 1700-07. 15.00

170. 1 Giulio 1700-07. NOLI LABORARE. Arms and bust 8.50
171. 1 Grosso 1701. PAUPERI POR. Arms 7.50
172. ½ Grosso 1701. DA ET ACCEPE. Arms 5.00

INNOCENT XIII 1721-24
173. ½ Scudo. CUM EXULTATIONE. Arms 25.00
174. 1 Giulio 1721. SACROSAN BASILIC. Arms 15.00
175. 1 Grosso 1721-23. ERIGIT ELISOS. Arms 12.00

BENEDICT XIII 1724-30
176. 1 Testone 1725. FOENERATUR DOMI. Arms 25.00
177. 1 Giulio 1724-28. IN CARITATE. Arms 8.50
178. 1 Grosso 1724-29. BENEFAC HUMILI. Arms 7.50

SEDE VACANTE 1730
179. 1 Giulio 1730. LUMEN SEMITIS. Arms 18.00

CLEMENT XII 1730-40
180. ½ Scudo 1736. DECUS PATRIAE. Bust and arms 35.00
181. 1 Testone 1733-36. URBE NOBILITATE. Bust and arms 15.00
182. 1 Giulio 1730-35. ABUNDET IN GLO. Bust and arms 7.50
183. 1 Grosso 1730-39. IN CIBOS PAUP. Arms 6.00

SEDE VACANTE 1740
184. 1 Giulio 1740. VENI SANCTE. Arms 18.00
185. 1 Grosso 1740. ILLUMINET CORDA. Arms 15.00

BENEDICT XIV 1740-58

186. 1 Scudo 1753-54. Bust. The Church seated on cloud 225.00
187. ½ Scudo 1752-54. CURABANTUR OM. Bust 45.00
188. 1 Testone 1756. PRINCIPIS URBIS. Arms 13.00

189.	2 Giulio 1753-57. MDCCLVII. Bust	7.50
190.	1 Giulio 1741. SACROSANC BASIL. Arms	6.00
191.	1 Grosso 1740-50. UT ALAT EOS. Arms	6.50
192.	1 Baiocco (C) 1740-58. Arms. Rev. Value	4.00
193.	½ Baiocco (C) 1740-55	3.50
194.	1 Quattrino (C) 1740-56	4.00

SEDE VACANTE 1758

195.	1 Scudo 1758. Arms and dove	160.00
196.	½ Scudo 1758. UBI VUIT SPIRAT. Arms	60.00
197.	2 Giulio 1758	20.00
198.	1 Grosso 1758	7.50

CLEMENT XIII 1758-69

199.	1 Scudo 1759. Arms. The Church seated on clouds	225.00
200.	½ Scudo 1759-60. SUPRA FIRMAM. Bust and arms	150.00
201.	1 Testone 1761-67. S. PETRUS S.P. Arms	25.00
202.	2 Giulio 1760-65. OBLECTAT IUSTUS. Bust	8.50
203.	1 Grosso 1758-67. UTERA QUASI. Arms	6.00
204.	1 Baiocco (C) 1758-59. Arms. Rev. Value	6.00
205.	½ Baiocco (C) 1758-60	5.00
206.	1 Quattrino C) 1758-59	4.00

SEDE VACANTE 1769

207.	½ Scudo 1769. VENI SANCTE. Arms	80.00
208.	2 Giulio 1769	20.00
209.	1 Giulio 1769	16.00

CLEMENT XIV 1769-74

210.	½ Scudo 1773. S. PETRUS, S. PAULUS. Arms	70.00
211.	1 Testone 1770-73	15.00
212.	2 Giulio 1769-73. FIAT PAX IN. Arms	8.50
213.	1 Grosso 1769-74	7.50

SEDE VACANTE 1774-75

214.	½ Scudo 1774. VENI LUMEN. Arms	40.00
215.	2 Giulio 1774	18.00

PIUS VI 1775-99

216.	1 Scudo 1780. Arms. The Church seated on clouds	50.00
217.	½ Scudo 1775-96. AUXILIUM DE. Bust and arms	25.00
218.	1 Testone 1785-96. SANCTUS PETRUS. Arms	11.00
219.	1 Giulio 1775. MUNDI REVERTUN. Arms	7.50
220.	1 Grosso 1775-83. APERUIT CUNCTIS. Arms	7.50
221.	5 Baiocchi (C) 1797-99. SANCTA DEI GENETRIX	4.00

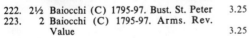

222.	2½ Baiocchi (C) 1795-97. Bust. St. Peter	3.25
223.	2 Baiocchi (C) 1795-97. Arms. Rev. Value	3.25

224.	1 Baiocco (C)	3.25
225.	½ Baiocco (C)	3.25
226.	1 Quattrino (C)	3.25

PIUS VII 1800-23

227.	1 Scudo 1800-18. Arms or bust. The Church seated on clouds	50.00
228.	½ Scudo 1800-17. AUXILIUM DE. Arms	80.00
229.	1 Testone 1802-04. St. Peter and St. Paul. Arms	40.00
230.	2 Giulio 1816-18	30.00
231.	1 Giulio 1816-18	25.00
232.	1 Grosso 1815-17. PAUPERI POR. Arms	15.00
233.	1 Baiocco (C) 1801-17. Arms. Rev. Value	15.00
234.	½ Baiocco (C) 1801-22	10.00
235.	1 Quattrino (C) 1801-22	4.00

SEDE VACANTE 1823

236.	1 Scudo 1823. Arms of Cardinal Barthelemy Paca. The Church seated on clouds	125.00
237.	½ Scudo 1823	85.00
238.	2 Giulio 1823. Arms. Madonna in clouds	40.00

LEO XII 1823-29

239.	1 Scudo 1825-26. Bust. The Church seated on clouds	150.00

240. ½ Baiocco (C) 1825-27. Arms. Rev.
Value 30.00
241. 1 Quattrino (C) 1825-28 10.00

SEDE VACANTE 1829

242. 1 Scudo 1829. Arms. The Church seated
on clouds 200.00
243. ½ Scudo 1829. AUXILIUM DE. Arms 100.00

PIUS VIII 1829-30

244. 1 Scudo 1830. Bust. St. Peter and St.
Paul 200.00
245. 1 Testone 1830. ISTI SUNT. Bust 40.00
246. 1 Baiocco (C) 1829. Arms. Rev. Value 30.00
247. ½ Baiocco (C) 1829 15.00
248. 1 Quattrino (C) 1829 8.00

SEDE VACANTE 1830-31

249. 1 Scudo 1830. Arms and dove 160.00
250. 30 Baiocchi 35.00

GREGORY XVI 1831-46

251. 1 Scudo 1831-34. Bust. Presentation of
the infant Jesus in the temple 140.00
252. 1 Scudo 1835-46. Bust. Value and date 110.00
253. 50 Baiocchi 1832-46 60.00
254. 30 Baiocchi 1834-46 30.00
255. 20 Baiocchi 1834-46 16.00
256. 10 Baiocchi 1836-46 10.00
257. 5 Baiocchi 1835-46 8.00
258. 1 Baiocco (C) 1831-45. Arms. Value
and date 8.00
259. ½ Baiocco (C) 1831-45 4.00
260. ¼ Baiocco (C) 1831-44 4.00

SEDE VACANTE 1846

261. 1 Scudo 1846. Arms and dove 150.00

PIUS IX 1846-78

262. 1 Scudo 1846-56. Bust. Value and date 75.00
263. 50 Baiocchi 1850-57 50.00
264. 20 Baiocchi 1848-66 15.00
265. 10 Baiocchi 1847-65 10.00
266. 5 Baiocchi 1847-66 6.00

267. 5 Baiocchi (C) 1849-54. Arms. Rev.
Value 8.00
268. 2 Baiocchi (C) 1848-53 8.00
269. 1 Baiocco (C) 1846-53 8.00
270. ½ Baiocco (C) 1847-52 6.00
271. 1 Quattrino (C) 1851, 54 8.00

SECOND COINAGE — LIRE SYSTEM
(Last coinage of the States of the Church.)

272. 5 Lire 1867, 70. Bust. Rev. Value 100.00
273. 2½ Lire 1867 75.00
274. 2 Lire 1866-70 15.00
275. 1 Lira 1866-69 3.50
276. 10 Soldi 1866-69 2.25
277. 5 Soldi 1866-67 3.25
278. 4 Soldi (C) 1866-69 6.00
279. 2 Soldi (C) 1866-67 2.50
280. 1 Soldo (C) 1866-67 1.50
281. ½ Soldo (C) 1866-67 1.50
282. 1 Centesimo (C) 1866-68 4.00

TUSCANY (Etruria)

The duchy of Tuscany in west-central Italy existed from the eleventh to the nineteenth century. From the sixteenth century until 1737 it was conferred on the Medici family. At that time the duchy passed to the house of Lorraine-Hapsburg.

The coins of Tuscany may be identified by the distinctive coat of arms or by the ETR, ETRUR, or ETRURIAE in the legend on the obverse.

FERDINAND DE MEDICI 1587-1608
283. 1 Scudo 1587-95. Bust. Rev. Draped arms   160.00

COSIMO II 1608-21
284. 1 Scudo 1609-20. Bust in spiked crown   120.00

FERDINAND II 1621-70
285. 1 Scudo 1621-63. Bust. Rev. St. John   150.00

COSIMO III 1670-1723

286. 1 Scudo 1676-94. Bare head. Rev. St. John baptizing   120.00

287. 1 Scudo 1683-98. Head in spiked crown. Rev. View of Leghorn   140.00

288. 1 Scudo 1684-1707. Arms and titles. Rev. Rose bush   180.00
289. 1 Scudo 1711-23. Bare head. Rev. Crown over castle   160.00

FRANCIS III 1737-65
290. 1 Scudo 1742-65. Bust. Rev. Arms   22.00
291. ½ Scudo 1738-48   15.00

PETER LEOPOLD 1765-90
292. 1 Scudo 1766-90. Bust (several varieties). Rev. Arms   22.00
293. ½ Scudo 1777-87   15.00

FERDINAND III 1790-1801
294. 1 Francescone 1793-1801. Bare head. Rev. Crowned arms   40.00

LOUIS I 1801-03

295. 1 Francescone 1801-03. Head. Rev. Crowned arms   50.00

CHARLES LOUIS AND MARIE LOUISE 1803-07

296. Broad 10 Lire 1803-07 (value on edge
of coin: DIECI LIRE). Conjoined busts.
Rev. Crowned arms   70.00
297. 5 Lire 1803 (value on edge: CINQUE
LIRE)   60.00

298. 1 Francescone 1803-07. Busts facing each
other   85.00
299. 1 Lira 1803-06. Crowned arms. Rev.
Value   40.00

FERDINAND III (Restoration) 1814-24

300. 1 Francescone 1814-24. Head. Rev.
Crowned arms   50.00

301. ½ Francescone 1820-23   40.00
302. 1 Lira 1821-23. Head. Rev. Value   30.00
303. 10 Lire 1821-23   4.00

LEOPOLD II 1824-59

304. 1 Francescone 1826-59. Head. Rev.
Crowned arms   65.00

305. ½ Francescone 1827-34   25.00

306. 1 Fiorino 1826-58. Head. Rev. Lily   10.00
307. ½ Fiorino 1827. Crowned arms. Rev.
Value   20.00
308. ¼ Fiorino 1827   25.00

309. 1 Paolo 1831-53. Head. Rev. Crowned
arms   15.00
310. ½ Paolo 1832-59   10.00
311. 10 Quattrini (bi) 1826-58   8.50
312. 5 Quattrini (bi) 1826-30   8.00
313. 3 Quattrini (C) 1826-57   7.00
314. 1 Quattrino (C) 1827-57   7.00

PROVISIONAL GOVERNMENT 1859

315. 1 Fiorino 1859. Lion with banner. Rev.
Arms of mint master   25.00
316. 5 Centesimi 1859. Crowned arms. Rev.
Value   8.00
317. 2 Centesimi 1859   5.00
318. 1 Centesimo 1859   10.00

This city built on 118 islands was once one of the great commercial powers of Europe. The Venetian Republic was headed by a Doge and a council. Napoleon's invasion of 1797 brought the republic to an end and he soon handed Venice over to the Austrians. In 1848 a Venetian revolt against Austrian rule led to a short-lived republic. However, in 1866 Austria's defeat at the hands of Prussia made it possible for Venice to be incorporated into the kingdom of Italy.

The winged lion (symbol of St. Mark, patron saint of Venice), appears on most Venetian coins. It was not until the middle of the eighteenth century that dates began to appear on Venetian coins. The names of the reigning doges are an aid to identifying Venetian coins.

321.	Giovanni Bembo 1615-18. 1 Scudo. Cross and lion	110.00
322.	Antonio Prioli 1618-23. 1 Scudo	65.00
323.	½ Scudo	25.00
324.	Francesco Contarini 1623-24. 1 Scudo	100.00
325.	¼ Scudo	32.00
326.	Giovanni Cornaro I 1624-29. ½ Scudo	32.00
327.	¼ Scudo	18.00
328.	Nicolo Contarini 1630-31. 1 Scudo	85.00
329.	Francesco Erizzo 1631-46. 1 Scudo	45.00
330.	½ Scudo	22.00
331.	¼ Scudo	18.00
332.	Francesco Molino 1646-55. 1 Scudo	55.00
333.	¼ Scudo	15.00
334.	⅛ Scudo	16.00

319.   10 Ducats (G) N.D. Doge kneeling before St. Mark. Rev. Christ   rare

320.   1 Ducat (G)   225.00

335.	Domenico Contarini 1659-75. 1 Scudo	25.00
336.	½ Scudo	45.00
337.	¼ Scudo	15.00
338.	⅛ Scudo	15.00
339.	Ludovico Contarini 1676-84. 1 Scudo	55.00
340.	¼ Scudo	35.00
341.	⅛ Scudo	12.00
342.	Francesco Morosini 1688-94. 1 Scudo. Doge kneeling	65.00
343.	½ Scudo	28.00
344.	¼ Scudo	14.00
345.	Silvestro Valiero 1694-99. 1 Scudo	50.00
346.	½ Scudo	20.00
347.	¼ Scudo	10.00

ITALY— VENICE (continued)

348. Ludovico Mocenigo II 1700-09. 1 Scudo   50.00
349. Giovanni Cornaro II 1709-22. 1 Scudo   45.00
350.   ½ Scudo   25.00
351.   ⅛ Scudo   10.00
352. Carlo Ruzzini 1732-35. 1 Scudo   45.00
353.   ¼ Scudo   12.00
354. Ludovico Pisani 1734-41. 1 Scudo   60.00
355.   ¼ Scudo   10.00
356. Pietro Grimani 1741-52. 1 Scudo   60.00
357.   ½ Scudo   20.00
358.   ¼ Scudo   7.25
359.   15 Marchetti 1749   6.00
360.   10 Marchetti 1749   5.00
361.   5 Marchetti 1749   4.00
362. Francesco Loredano 1752-62. 1 Scudo
       1756. Female head. Rev. Lion   70.00
363. Marco Foscarini 1762-63. 1 Scudo. Doge
       kneeling. Rev. Lion   80.00
364.   ½ Scudo   30.00

DEMOCRATIC REPUBLIC 1797-98

378. 10 Lire 1797. Liberty standing. Rev. Value
     and date   400.00

PROVISIONAL REPUBLIC 1848

379. 5 Lire 1848. Lion on base. Rev. Value
     in wreath   125.00

365. Ludovico Mocenigo IV 1763-78. 1 Scudo.
       Female head. Rev. Lion   40.00
366.   ½ Scudo 1769   12.00
367.   ¼ Scudo 1769   8.00
368. Paolo Rainerio 1779-89. 1 Scudo 1781-87   30.00
369.   ½ Scudo 1781   12.00
370.   ¼ Scudo 1781   8.00
371.   15 Marchetti 1778   5.00
372.   10 Marchetti 1781   4.00
373. Ludovico Manin 1789-97. 1 Scudo 1789-
       96. Female head. Rev. Lion   50.00
374.   ½ Scudo 1790   20.00
375.   ¼ Scudo 1789   12.00
376.   10 Marchetti 1789-91   4.00
377.   5 Marchetti 1789   5.00

380.   5 Lire 1848. Lion on plain ground   120.00
381.   15 Centesimi (C) 1849. Lion. Rev. Value   15.00
382.   5 Centesimi (C) 1849   12.00
383.   3 Centesimi (C) 1849   12.00
384.   1 Centesimo (C) 1849   12.00

REPUBLICS SET UP BY NAPOLEON

SUBALPINE REPUBLIC (Milan) 1798-1802

385. 5 Francs 1801-02 (Year 9, 10). France and Italy standing. Rev. Value and date in wreath 125.00

LIGURIAN REPUBLIC (Genoa) 1798-1805

386. 8 Lire 1798-1804. Liberty and Equality standing. Rev. Liberty Cap above Genoese arms 175.00
387. 4 Lire 1798-99 .... 85.00
388. 2 Lire 1798 .... 100.00
389. 1 Lira 1798 .... 75.00

CISALPINE REPUBLIC 1797-1802

390. 1 Scudo Anno VIII. France seated, Republic standing. Rev. Value and date in wreath 400.00

391. 30 Soldi Anno IX. Bust of Republic. Rev. Value in wreath 50.00

ITALIAN REPUBLIC 1802-05

392. 1 Soldo 1804. Balance. Rev. Value in wreath 50.00
393. ½ Soldo 1804 .... 40.00

KINGDOM OF ITALY 1805-14
NAPOLEON, EMPEROR AND KING

394. 5 Lire 1807-14. Bare head. Rev. Crowned arms in canopy 110.00

395.	2 Lire 1807-14	35.00
396.	1 Lira 1808-14	25.00
397.	15 Soldi 1808-14	32.00
398.	10 Soldi 1808-14	5.50
399.	5 Soldi 1808-14	5.00
400.	1 Soldo (C) 1807-14	5.00
401.	3 Centesimi (C) 1807-13	4.00
402.	1 Centesimo (C) 1807-13	3.25

406.	2 Lire 1815	30.00
407.	1 Lira 1815	25.00
408.	10 Soldi 1815, 30. Rev. Crowned mono-gram	25.50
409.	5 Soldi 1815, 30	15.00

ROMAN REPUBLIC 1798-99

LUCCA
ELISA BONAPARTE AND FELIX BACCIOCCHI
1805-08

403. 1 Scudo 1798-99. Liberty standing hold-ing fasces and spear. Rev. Value in wreath   275.00

410.	5 Francs 1805-08. Accolated busts. Rev. Value in wreath	80.00
411.	1 Franc 1806-08	30.00
412.	5 Centesimi (C) 1806	12.00
413.	3 Centesimi (C) 1806	16.00

CHARLES LOUIS OF BOURBON 1815-47

404. 2 Baiocchi 1798-99. Fasces. Rev. Value   20.00

PARMA
MARIE LOUISE 1815-47

414.	2 Lire 1837. Bare head. Rev. Crowned arms	60.00
415.	1 Lira 1834, 37-38. Rev. Value in wreath	25.00
416.	10 Soldi 1833, 38	15.00
417.	5 Soldi (comp.) 1833, 38. Crowned arms. Rev. Value	8.00
418.	2 Soldi (comp.) 1835	4.00
419.	1 Soldo (C) 1826, 41. Crowned mono-gram	4.00
420.	½ Soldo (C) 1826, 35. Crown	4.00
421.	5 Quattrini (C) 1826	5.00
422.	2 Quattrini (C) 1826. Arms	3.25
423.	1 Quattrino (C) 1826. Title	3.25

LOMBARDY—PROVISIONAL GOVERNMENT
1848

405. 5 Lire 1815, 32. Diademed head. Rev. Crowned arms in canopy   120.00

424. 5 Lire 1848. Italia standing. Rev. Value   70.00

SARDINIA

In 1720 Sardinia passed to the house of Savoy. The kingdom continued to be ruled by Savoy descendants until 1861, when the King of Sardinia became King of Italy.

CHARLES EMMANUEL III 1760-73

425.	1 Scudo 1755-69. Bust. Rev. Crowned arms in oval shield	125.00
426.	½ Scudo 1755-70	25.00
427.	¼ Scudo 1755-59	8.50
428.	⅛ Scudo 1755-70	4.00
429.	20 Soldi 1742-47. Head. Crowned arms and value	18.00
430.	10 Soldi 1742	12.00

VICTOR AMADEUS III 1773-96

431.	1 Scudo 1773. Bust. Rev. Crowned arms	325.00
432.	½ Scudo 1773-93	45.00
433.	¼ Scudo 1773-91	22.00
434.	5 Soldi (C) 1794-96. Bust. Rev. Mauritius	3.50
435.	1 Soldo (C) 1782-85. Rev. Monogram	3.50
436.	½ Soldo (C) 1781-87	3.50

CHARLES EMMANUEL IV 1796-1802

437.	½ Scudo 1797. Bust. Rev. Crowned arms	40.00

VICTOR EMMANUEL 1802-21

438.	5 Lire 1816-21. Bare head. Rev. Crowned arms	160.00

CHARLES FELIX 1821-31

439.	5 Lire 1821-31. Bare head. Rev. Crowned arms	80.00
440.	2 Lire 1823-31	40.00
441.	1 Lira 1823-30	16.00
442.	50 Centesimi 1823-31	16.00
443.	25 Centesimi 1829-30	12.00

444.	5 Centesimi (C) 1826. Arms. Rev. Value	4.00
445.	3 Centesimi (C) 1826	4.00
446.	1 Centesimo (C) 1826	3.50

CHARLES ALBERT 1831-49

447.	5 Lire 1831-49. Bare head. Rev. Crowned arms	80.00
448.	2 Lire 1832-49	30.00
449.	1 Lira 1831-49	20.00
450.	50 Centesimi 1832-47	10.00
451.	25 Centesimi 1832-37	15.00
452.	5 Centesimi (C) 1842	8.00
453.	3 Centesimi (C) 1842	4.00
454.	1 Centesimo (C) 1842	4.00

VICTOR EMMANUEL II 1849-61

455.	5 Lire 1850-61. Bare head. Rev. Crowned arms	80.00
456.	2 Lire 1850-60	40.00
457.	1 Lira 1850-60	25.00
458.	50 Centesimi 1850-60	15.00

(In 1861 Victor Emmanuel II became King of Italy.)

KINGDOM OF ITALY

The modern state of Italy came into being with the unification under Victor Emmanuel II of Sardinia in 1860. Though still a kingdom, the country was controlled by Mussolini and his Fascist Party from the 1920's until World War II. Following Italy's defeat, the King abdicated and Italy became a republic in 1946.

100 Centesimi = 1 Lira
VICTOR EMMANUEL 1861-78

459.	5 Lire 1861 (Commemorating accession to throne). Head. Crowned arms with legend "FIRENZE MARZO 1861"	500.00
460.	5 Lire 1861-78. Head. Rev. Crowned arms	12.50
461.	2 Lire 1861-63	7.50
462.	1 Lira 1861-67	4.00
463.	50 Centesimi 1861-67	4.00
464.	20 Centesimi 1863-67	3.50

465.	10 Centesimi (C) 1862-67. Head. Rev. Value in wreath	2.50
466.	5 Centesimi (C) 1861-67	1.00
467.	2 Centesimi (C) 1861-67	1.00
468.	1 Centesimo (C) 1861-67	1.00

HUMBERT I 1878-1900

469.	5 Lire 1878-79. Bare head. Rev. Crowned arms	25.00

470.	2 Lire 1881-99	8.00
471.	1 Lira 1883-1900	6.50
472.	50 Centesimi 1889, 92	40.00

473.	20 Centesimi (C-N)1894-95. Crown. Rev. Value	1.00
474.	10 Centesimi (C) 1893-94. Head. Rev. Value	3.50
475.	5 Centesimi (C) 1895-96	7.50
476.	2 Centesimi (C) 1895-1900	1.00
477.	1 Centesimo (C) 1895-1900	1.00

VICTOR EMMANUEL III 1900-46

478.	20 Lire (G) 1902-05. Bust. Rev. Crowned eagle	200.00

479.	5 Lire 1901. Bust. Rev. Type of #478 (highest degree of rarity)	very rare
480.	2 Lire 1901-07	20.00
481.	1 Lira 1901-07	6.00
482.	25 Centesimi (N) 1902-03. Crowned eagle. Rev. Value in wreath	20.00
483.	2 Centesimi (C) 1903-08. Bust. Rev. Value	1.00
484.	1 Centesimo (C) 1902-08	1.25

485.	50 Lire (G) 1911 (50th anniversary of kingdom). Head. Rev. Allegorical figures, a factory, prow of a ship	275.00
486.	5 Lire 1911	200.00
487.	2 Lire 1911	15.00
488.	10 Centesimi (Bro) 1911	6.00

498. 5 Centesimi (Bro) 1908-18. Figure on prow of galley 1.00
499. 2 Centesimi (Bro) 1908-17 ..... 1.00
500. 1 Centesimo (Bro) 1908-18 ..... 1.00

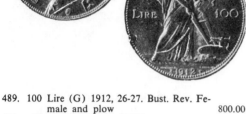

489. 100 Lire (G) 1912, 26-27. Bust. Rev. Female and plow 800.00
490. 50 Lire (G) 1912, 26-27 ..... 350.00
491. 20 Lire (G) 1912, 26-27 ..... 175.00
492. 10 Lire (G) 1912, 26-27 ..... 350.00

501. 100 Lire (G) 1923. Head. Rev. Fasces (Commemorates first anniversary of fascist government) 650.00
502. 20 Lire (G) 1923 ..... 275.00
503. 2 Lire (N) 1923-27. Bust. Rev. Fasces 3.00

493. 5 Lire 1914. Military bust. Rev. Quadriga ..... rare
494. 2 Lire 1908-17 ..... 4.00
495. 1 Lira 1908-17 ..... 3.00

504. 1 Lira 1921-28. Italia seated. Rev. Value in wreath 1.00

496. 50 Centesimi (N) 1919-35. Rev. Chariot drawn by lions 4.00

505. 10 Centesimi (Bro) 1919-37. Head. Rev. Bee ..... .75

497. 20 Centesimi (N) 1908-35. Classical head 2.00

506. 5 Centesimi (Bro) 1919-37. Head. Rev. Wheat ear ..... .25

ITALY (continued)

REDUCED SIZE —
NEW VALUATION OF THE LIRA

507. 100 Lire (G) 1931-33. Head. Rev. Italia
     on prow   200.00

508. 50 Lire (G) 1931-33. Bust. Rev. Man
     carrying fasces   150.00

509. 20 Lire 1927-28. Head. Rev. Seated and
     standing figures   50.00

510. 10 Lire 1926-30. Head. Rev. Biga   12.50

511. 5 Lire 1926-30. Head. Rev. Eagle on
     fasces   1.75

512. 20 Lire 1928 (10th anniversary of the
      end of World War I). Helmeted
      head. Rev. Fasces and lion's head   75.00

513. 100 Lire (G) 1936. Head. Rev. Man with
     sword, walking   1,500.00

514. 50 Lire (G) 1936. Head. Rev. Eagle
      above, two medallions below   1,500.00

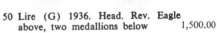

515. 20 Lire 1936. Head. Rev. Quadriga   375.00

ITALY • **283**

ITALY (continued)

516. 10 Lire 1936. Head. Rev. Italia on
     prow of galley   15.00
517. 5 Lire 1936-37. Head. Rev. Seated
     mother and children   8.50

518. 2 Lire (N) 1936-38; (St) 39-43. Head.
     Rev. Eagle   .75
519. 1 Lira (N) 1936-38; (St) 39-43   .75

524. 10 Lire (A) 1946-50. Pegasus. Rev. Olive 2.50

520. 50 Centesimi (N) 1936; (St) 39-43.
     Head. Rev. Eagle in flight   .35
521. 20 Centesimi (N) 1936; (St) 39-43.
     Head. Rev. Head and fasces   .50

525. 5 Lire (A) 1946-50. Liberty head. Rev.
     Bunch of grapes   .50

526. 2 Lire (A) 1946-50. Plowman. Rev.
     Wheat   .75

522. 10 Centesimi (Bro) 1936-39; (A-Bro)
     39-43. Head. Rev. Arms and fasces   1.00

527. 1 Lira (A) 1946-50. Ceres head. Rev.
     Orange branch   1.50

523. 5 Centesimi (Bro) 1936-39; (A-Bro)
     39-43. Head. Rev. Eagle   .50
528. 500 Lire 1958-71. Peasant girl. Rev. ships 3.50

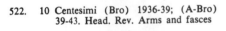

284 • CATALOGUE of the WORLD'S MOST POPULAR COINS

529. 100 Lire (St) 1955- 1.00
530. 50 Lire (St) 1954- .75

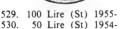

531. 20 Lire (A-Bro) 1957-59; 1969- . (Plain edge) Rev. Oak leaves .50

532. 10 Lire (A) 1951- . Plow. Rev. Wheat .50

533. 5 Lire (A) 1951- . Rudder. Rev. Dolphin .50

534. 2 Lire (A) 1953- . Bee .30
535. 1 Lira (A) 1951- . Scales .25

536. 500 Lire 1961. Italian unification commemorative 12.50

537. 500 Lire 1965. Portrait of Dante Alighieri. Rev. Flames of the Inferno (commemorates 700th anniversary of great poet's birth) 7.50

538. 1000 Lire 1970. Bust of Concordia. Rev. Geometric design, value (Commemorates 100 years of Rome as capital city) 12.50

539. 500 Lire 1974. Bust of Marconi. Rev. Map (Commemorates 100th anniversary of inventor's birth)

540. 100 Lire (St) 1974. Portrait of Guglielmo Marconi. Rev. Antenna (Commemorates 100th anniversary of inventor's birth) .75

JAMAICA

The largest and most valuable island in the British West Indies, Jamaica was discovered by Columbus in 1494 and became a British colony in 1670. It became an independent state within the British Commonwealth in 1962.

4 Farthings = 1 Penny

VICTORIA 1837-1901

1.	1 Penny (C-N) 1869-1900. Coroneted head. Rev. Arms	4.00
2.	Half Penny (C-N) 1869-1900	3.00
3.	1 Farthing (C-N) 1880-1900	2.00

EDWARD VII 1901-10

(Issues of 1902-03 have horizontal shading lines on the reverse, 1904-10 have vertical lines)

4.	1 Penny (C-N) 1902-10. Crowned bust of King. Rev. Arms	2.50
5.	Half Penny (C-N) 1902-10	2.00
6.	1 Farthing (C-N) 1902-10	2.00

GEORGE V 1910-36

7.	1 Penny (C-N) 1914-28. Crowned bust. Rev. Arms	2.00

8.	Half Penny (C-N) 1914-28	1.50
9.	1 Farthing (C-N) 1914-34	1.25

GEORGE VI 1936-52

(Coins issued after 1948 drop "Emperor of India" from their legend. The 1937 coins have smaller heads.)

10.	1 Penny (N-Bra) 1937. Small crowned head. Rev. Arms	2.50
10a.	1 Penny (N-Bra) 1938-52. Large crowned head	1.50
11.	Half Penny (N-Bra) 1937. Small head	2.00
11a.	Half Penny (N-Bra) 1938-52. Large head	.40
12.	1 Farthing (N-Bra) 1937. Small head	1.75
12a.	1 Farthing (N-Bra) 1938-52. Large head	.25

ELIZABETH II 1952-

13.	1 Penny (N-Bra) 1953-63. Crowned head. Rev. Arms	.35
14.	Half Penny (N-Bra) 1955-63.	.20

15.	1 Penny (N-Bra) 1964-67. Crowned head. Rev. New arms	.35
16.	Half Penny (N-Bra) 1964-66	.20

21. 25 Cents (CN) 1969- . Arms. Rev. Swallow tail hummingbird — 1.00

17. 5 Shillings (C-N) 1966. Arms. Rev. Inscription (commemorates the 8th British Empire and Commonwealth Games) — 3.00

22. 20 Cents (CN) 1969- . Arms. Rev. Blue mahoe trees — .85
23. 10 Cents (CN) 1969- . Arms. Rev. Lignum vitae tree — .50

24. 5 Cents (CN) 1969- . Arms. Rev. Crocodile — .25
25. 1 Cent (Br) 1969- . Arms. Rev. Edible Ackee plant — .15

18. 1 Penny (N-Bra) 1969. Crowned head. Rev. Arms, "1869-1969" (Commemorates 100th anniversary of Jamaican coinage) — .75
19. ½ Penny (N-Bra) 1969 — .50

DECIMAL COINAGE

26. 1 Cent (Br) 1971-73. Rev. LET'S PRODUCE MORE FOOD added to inscription (F.A.O. coin plan) — .25

20. 1 Dollar (CN) 1969- . Sir Alexander Bustamante. Rev. Arms (First Prime Minister) — 4.00

27. 5 Dollars 1971. Bust of Norman W. Manley, Premier 1959-62. Rev. Arms — 12.50

28. 20 Dollars (G) 1972. Map of Jamaica, three ships. Rev. Arms (Commemorates 10th anniversary of independence) 100.00

31. 10 Dollars (C-N) 1974. Sir Henry Morgan, Lieutenant Governor 1674. Rev. Arms 20.00
31a. 10 Dollars (S) 1974 (proof issue) 35.00

32. 100 Dollars (G) 1975. Bust of Christopher Columbus. Rev. Arms 100.00

29. 10 Dollars 1972. Busts of Alexander Bustamante and Norman W. Manley, map of Jamaica. Rev. Arms (Commemorates 10th anniversary of independence) 20.00

33. 10 Dollars 1975. Bust of Columbus, ship in background. Rev. Arms 25.00

30. 5 Dollars 1972- . Head of Manley. Rev. Arms 15.00

34. 1 Cent (A) 1975, 76. Type of #26, 12-sided planchet (F.A.O. coin plan) .25

JAMAICA (continued)

35. 100 Dollars (G) 1976. Bust of Admiral
     Nelson with map and ship. Rev. Arms 150.00

36. 10 Dollars (C-N) 1976
36a. 10 Dollars (S) 1976 (proof issue)

37. 50 Cents (C-N) 1976. Bust of Marcus
     Garvey, philosopher. Rev. Arms

38. 20 Cents (C-N) 1976. Three trees over
     value (F.A.O. coin plan)

JAPAN

The feudal system was prolonged in Japan until
well into the nineteenth century and contact with
Westerners was discouraged. In 1854 Commodore
Perry forced the opening of trade relations with
the Western world. From then on Japan was
modernized and industrialized until it took its
place among the great powers.

10 Rin = 1 Sen
100 Sen = 1 Yen

1.	1 Yen 1870. Coiled dragon. Rev. Rayed sun	100.00
2.	50 Sen 1870-71	15.00
3.	20 Sen 1870-71	6.00
4.	10 Sen 1870	10.00
5.	5 Sen 1870-71	50.00

6. Trade Dollar 1875-77. Dragon. Rev. Value
    in wreath. Inscription in English: "420
    grains, Trade Dollar, .900 fine" 400.00

7. 1 Yen 1874-1914. Coiled dragon. Rev.
   Value in wreath. In English: "416
   One Yen 900"   15.00
8. 50 Sen 1873-1905   7.50
9. 20 Sen 1873-1905   2.00
10. 10 Sen 1873-1906   1.25
11. 5 Sen 1873-1880   5.00
11a. 1 Sen (Bro) 1873-88   1.00

12. 50 Sen 1906-17. Rayed sun. Rev. Value
    in wreath   3.00
13. 20 Sen 1906-11   1.50
14. 10 Sen 1907-17   .40
15. 5 Sen (C-N) 1897-1905   .50
16. 2 Sen (Bro) 1873-84   1.00

17. 1 Sen (Bro) 1898-1915   .75
18. ½ Sen (Bro) 1873-88   1.00

19. 50 Sen 1922-37. Rayed sun. Rev. Value
    between birds of longevity   .75

20. 10 Sen (C-N) 1920-32. Eight-petaled flower
    around center hole   .25
21. 5 Sen (C-N) 1917-32   .15

22. 1 Sen (Bro) 1916-38. Kiri crest. Value
    in circle   .10
23. 5 Rin (Bro) 1916-19   .65

24. 10 Sen (N) 1933-37 (center hole)   .40

24a. 10 Sen (A-Br) 1938-40 (center hole)   .20

25. 5 Sen (N) 1933-37 (center hole)   .50

25a. 5 Sen (A-Br) 1938-40 (center hole)   .25

26. 1 Sen (Br) 1938; (A) 1938-40 (reduced
    size). Dove   .30

27. 10 Sen (A) 1940-43. Chrysanthemum   .50

28. 5 Sen (A) 1940-43. Flying kite   .35

JAPAN (continued)

29.   1 Sen (A) 1941-43. Mt. Fuji   .35

30.   10 Sen (T-Z) 1944 (center hole)   .50
31.   5 Sen (T-Z) 1944 (center hole)   .50

32.   1 Sen (T) 1944-45. Chrysanthemum   .25

33.   50 Sen (Bra) 1946-47. Phoenix. Rev. Rice
      plants   1.50

34.   10 Sen (A) 1945-46. Rice plants. Rev.
      Value   .35

35.   5 Sen (T) 1945-46. Dove   .50

36.   50 Sen (Bra) 1947, 48. Chrysanthemum
      and blossoms. Rev. Value   .30

37.   5 Yen (Bra) 1948-49. Dove in circle.
      Rev. Building   1.00

38.   1 Yen (Bra) 1948-50. Blossoms. Rev.
      Value   .30

39. 100 Yen 1957-58. Phoenix   2.00

40.   50 Yen (N) 1955-58. Blossom   .85

41.   100 Yen 1959-66. Rice plant   4.00

42.   50 Yen (N) 1959-66. (center hole)   3.00

43. 10 Yen (Bro) 1951- . Palace. Rev. Value   .15

44. 5 Yen (Bra) 1949- . (center hole)   .15

45. 1 Yen (A) 1955-   .10

OLYMPIC GAMES COMMEMORATIVES—1964

46. 1,000 Yen 1964. Mt. Fuji, surrounded by cherry blossoms. Rev. Olympic emblem of 5 interlocking rings   35.00

47. 100 Yen 1964. Flaming Olympic torch and emblem. Rev. Value   2.00

48. 100 Yen (CN) 1967- . Cherry blossoms. Rev. Value   .60

49. 50 Yen (CN) 1967-(center hole)   .35

50. 100 Yen (CN) 1970. Mt. Fuji. Rev. Expo '70 emblem (Commemorates the 1970 World Exposition)   3.50

51. 100 Yen (C-N) 1972. Olympic torch. Rev. Value, rings (Commemorates Winter Olympic Games 1972)   4.00

52. 100 Yen (C-N) 1975. Gate of Shurei. Rev. Value (Commemorates International Sea Expo at Okinawa)   2.00

JERSEY

This Channel island is a British possession.

VICTORIA 1837-1901

1. 1/13 Shilling (C) 1841-61; (Bro) 1866-71. Head. Rev. Ornamented shield 5.00

2. 1/26 Shilling (C) 1841-61; (Bro) 1866-71 5.00
3. 1/52 Shilling (C) 1841 45.00
4. 1/12 Shilling (Bro) 1877-94. Head. Rev. Blunt shield 5.00
5. 1/24 Shilling (Bro) 1877-94 4.00
6. 1/48 Shilling (Bro) 1877 25.00

EDWARD VII 1901-1910

7. 1/12 Shilling (Bro) 1909. Crowned bust. Rev. Pointed shield 7.00
8. 1/24 Shilling (Bro) 1909 8.00

GEORGE V 1910-36

9. 1/12 Shilling (Bro) 1911, 13, 23. Crowned bust. Rev. Type of #7 3.00
10. 1/12 Shilling (Bro) 1923, 26, 31, 33, 35. Rev. Blunt shield 2.00
11. 1/24 Shilling (Bro) 1911, 13, 23. Type of #9 5.00
12. 1/24 Shilling (Bro) 1923, 26, 31, 33, 35. Type of #10 3.00

GEORGE VI 1936-1952

13. 1/12 Shilling (Bro) 1937, 46, 47. Crowned head. Rev. Type of #10 1.50
14. 1/24 Shilling (Bro) 1937, 46, 47 2.50

15. 1/12 Shilling (Bro) 1949-52 (Liberation penny). Type of #13, with inscription "Liberated 1945" 1.00

ELIZABETH II 1952-

16. 1/12 Shilling (Bro) 1954. Crowned bust. Rev. Type of #13, with inscription "Liberated 1945" .75
17. 1/4 Shilling (N-Bra) 1957 .50
18. 1/12 Shilling (Bro) 1957, 64 .30

19. 1/12 Shilling (Bro) 1960. King Charles II 300 year commemorative (1660-1960) .25

20. 1/4 Shilling (N-Bra) 1964. (12-sided planchet) .35
21. 5 Shillings (C-N) 1966. Crowned bust. Rev. Arms, dates "1066-1966" (commemorates Battle of Hastings) 2.50
22. 1/4 Shilling (N-Bra) 1966 (12-sided planchet) .50
23. 1/2 Shilling (Br) 1966 (round) 2.00

DECIMAL COINAGE

24. 50 New Pence (CN) 1969- . Draped bust with coronet. Rev. Arms (7-sided planchet) 2.25

25. 10 New Pence (CN) 1968- .65
26. 5 New Pence (CN) 1968- .35
27. 2 New Pence (Br) 1971- .25
28. 1 New Penny (Br) 1971- .20
29. 1/2 New Penny (Br) 1971- .15

JORDAN

An Arab kingdom since 1946. After being part of the Turkish Empire for several centuries, this area became a British mandate after World War I, receiving independence in 1946.

100 Fils = 1 Dinar or 1 Pound Sterling
ABDULLA IBN AL HUSSEIN 1946-51
HUSSEIN I 1952-

1.	100 Fils (CN) 1949. Crowned shield and Arabic inscription. Rev. Value in English	3.00
2.	50 Fils (C-N) 1949	2.00
3.	20 Fils (C-N) 1949	1.00
4.	10 Fils (Bro) 1949	1.00
5.	5 Fils (Bro) 1949	.75
6.	1 Fils (Bro) 1949	.75
7.	100 Fils (CN) 1955-65. Crowned shield. Rev. Value	2.00
8.	50 Fils (CN) 1955-65	1.00
9.	20 Fils (CN) 1964-65	5.00
10.	10 Fils (Br) 1955-67	.50
11.	5 Fils (Br) 1955-67	.40
12.	1 Fils (Br) 1955-65	.50

13.	100 Fils (CN) 1968- . Head of King. Rev. Inscription	1.50
14.	50 Fils (CN) 1968-	1.00
15.	25 Fils (CN) 1968-	.75
16.	10 Fils (Br) 1968-	.50
17.	5 Fils (Br) 1968-	.30
18.	1 Fils (Br) 1968-	.50

19.	¼ Dinar (CN) 1969. Head of King. Rev. Olive tree (F.A.O. coin plan)	3.50
20.	¼ Dinar (C-N) 1970. Rev. Without F.A.O. inscription	3.00

KENYA

Formerly a British Protectorate and then Colony on the east coast of Africa astride the Equator, Kenya became an independent state within the British Commonwealth in December, 1963, and a republic the following year.

1.	2 Shillings (CN) 1966-68. President Jomo Kenyatta. Rev. Arms	1.00
2.	1 Shilling (CN) 1966-68	.75
3.	50 Cents (CN) 1966-68	.50
4.	25 Cents (CN) 1966, 67	.30
5.	10 Cents (N-Bra) 1966-68	.20
6.	5 Cents (N-Bra) 1966-68	.15
7.	2 Shillings (CN) 1969- . Head of Kenyatta within legend. Rev. Arms	1.00
8.	1 Shilling (CN) 1969-	.60
9.	50 Cents (CN) 1969-	.40
10.	25 Cents (CN) 1969-	.30
11.	10 Cents (N-Bra) 1969-	.20
12.	5 Cents (N-Bra) 1969-	.15

13.	5 Shillings (Bra) 1973. Commemorates 10th anniversary of independence (9-sided planchet)	2.50

KIAO CHAU

Pre-World War I German-leased territory in northeast China.

1.	10 Cents (C-N) 1909. German eagle. Rev. Chinese inscription	12.50
2.	5 Cents (C-N) 1909	10.00

KOREA

Located on a peninsula between the Yellow Sea and the Sea of Japan, Korea was annexed by the Japanese in 1910, liberated at the end of World War II, and divided into North Korea (under Communist influence) and South Korea (under Western influence). The status quo was continued at the end of the Korean War.

100 Fun = 1 Yang
100 Chon = 1 Won

EMPEROR TAI 1863-97

1.	10 Mun (C) 1888. Dragon in circle. Rev. Value	40.00
2.	5 Mun (C) 1888	20.00

3.	5 Yang 1892. Dragon in circle. Rev. Value in wreath	300.00
4.	1 Yang 1892-98	12.00
5.	¼ Yang (C-N) 1892-1901	3.00
6.	5 Fun (C) 1892-1902	2.00
7.	1 Fun (C) 1892-96	10.00

UNDER JAPANESE INFLUENCE

8.	½ Won 1905-06. Dragon in circle, value in English	20.00
8a.	½ Won 1907-08 (reduced weight)	20.00
9.	20 Chon 1905-06	10.00
9a.	20 Chon 1907-10 (reduced weight)	9.00
10.	10 Chon 1906	5.00
10a.	10 Chon 1907-10 (reduced size)	5.00

11.	5 Chon (N) 1905-07. Phoenix	5.00
12.	1 Chon (Br) 1905-06	3.00
12a.	1 Chon (Br) 1907-10 (reduced size)	3.50
13.	½ Chon (Br) 1906	3.50

13a.	½ Chon (Br) 1907-10 (reduced size)	3.50

SOUTH KOREA

14.	100 Hwan (C-N) 1959. Head of Pres. Rhee. Rev. Peacocks and value	2.50

15.	50 Hwan (N-Bra) 1959, 61. Armor-clad war galley	1.00

16.	10 Hwan (Br) 1959, 61. Rose (national flower)	.35

17.	10 Won (Br) 1966- . Prabhutaratna pagoda. Rev. Value	.35

18.	5 Won (Br) 1966- . 16th century armor-clad tortoise war galley. Rev. Value	.20

19.	1 Won (Br) 1966, 67; (Al) 1968- . Rose of Sharon. Rev. Value	.10

KOREA (continued)

20. 100 Won (C-N) 1970- . Portrait of Admiral Yi Sun Sin. Rev. Value ... 1.00

21. 50 Won (C-N) 1972-74. Wheat. Rev. Value (F.A.O. coin plan) ... .75

22. 100 Won (C-N) 1975. Independence Arch. Rev. Female figure with flag (Commemorates 30th anniversary of liberation)

NORTH KOREA

1. 10 Chon (A) 1959. Arms. Rev. Value ... 6.00
2. 5 Chon (A) 1959 ... 5.00
3. 1 Chon (A) 1959, 70 ... 4.00

KUWAIT

Oil-rich Arab sheikdom on the Persian Gulf.

1000 Fils = 1 Dinar

SHEIK ABDULLAH AL SALIMAL SABAH

1. 100 Fils (C-N) 1961- . Dhow, Arab sailing ship. Rev. Value (Arabic legend changes slightly after 1961) ... 1.50
2. 50 Fils (C-N) 1961- ... .75
3. 20 Fils (C-N) 1961- ... .60
4. 10 Fils (N-Bra) 1961- ... .35
5. 5 Fils (N-Bra) 1961- ... .25
6. 1 Fil (N-Bra) 1961- ... .15

LAOS

An independent constitutional monarchy since 1949.

1. 50 Centimes (A-Mg) 1952 ... 1.25

2. 20 Centimes (A-Mg) 1952 ... .50

3. 10 Centimes (A-Mg) 1952 ... .35

LATVIA

After becoming part of Russia in the eighteenth century, Latvia achieved its independence in 1918. The U.S.S.R. absorbed Latvia in 1940.

100 Santimi = 1 Lats

1. 50 Santimi (N) 1922. Figure at tiller of boat. Rev. Arms   4.50
2. 20 Santimi (N) 1922. Arms. Rev. Value above wheat ear   3.00
3. 10 Santimi (N) 1922   3.00

4. 5 Santimi (Bro) 1922. Arms. Rev. Value   2.50
5. 2 Santimi (Bro) 1922-32.   2.00
6. 1 Santims (Bro) 1922-35.   1.75

7. 5 Lati 1929, 1931-32. Native girl. Rev. Arms with supporters   12.00

8. 2 Lati 1925-26. Arms with supporters. Rev. Value in wreath   5.00
9. 1 Lats 1924   4.00
10. 2 Santimi (Br) 1937-39. Arms. Rev. Value   2.50
11. 1 Santimi (Br) 1937-39   3.25

LEBANON

Lebanon, in Asia Minor on the Mediterranean coast, was formerly part of the Turkish Empire.

It became an independent state in 1920, was a French Mandate 1920-1, and has been a republic since 1926.

100 Piastres = 1 Lira or Pound

1. 50 Piastres 1929, 33, 37. Cedar of Lebanon. Rev. Cornucopia   4.00
2. 25 Piastres 1929, 33, 37   3.50
3. 10 Piastres 1929   2.00

4. 5 Piastres (A-Bro) 1924. Cedar. Rev. Arabic inscription   1.25
5. 2 Piastres (A-Bro) 1924   1.75

6. 5 Piastres (A-Bro) 1925-40. Cedar. Rev. Galley   1.50
7. 2 Piastres (A-Bro) 1925   3.00

8. 1 Piastre (C-N) 1925-37; (Z) 1940   .50
9. ½ Piastre (C-N) 1934, 36; (Z) 1941   .75

10. 2½ Piastres (A-Bro) 1940 (Center hole). Inscription. Rev. Inscription and lions   .75

LEBANON (continued)

11. 50 Piastres 1952. Cedar. Rev. Value in wreath   1.50
12. 25 Piastres (A-Bro) 1952,61. Cedar. Rev. Value and leaves   .50

13. 10 Piastres (A) 1952. Cedar. Rev. Lion's head   1.25

14. 5 Piastres (A) 1952. Cedar. Rev. Sailing vessel   1.00
15. 10 Piastres (A-Bro) 1955; (CN) 1961. Cedar. Rev. Sailing Ship (design varies)   .40
16. 5 Piastres (A) 1954. Cedar. Rev. Wreath   .30
16a. 5 Piastres (A-Br) 1955, 61. Rev. Lion's head   .30
17. 2½ Piastres (A-Bro) 1955   (center hole)   .25
18. 1 Piastre (A-Bro) 1955   .25
19. 50 Piastres (N) 1968- . Cedar, BANQUE DU LIBAN. Rev. Value in wreath   1.00
20. 25 Piastres (N-Bra) 1968-   .50
21. 10 Piastres (N-Bra) 1968-   .20
22. 5 Piastres (N-Bra) 1968-   .15

23. 1 Livre (N) 1968. Cedar. Rev. Fruit (F.A.O. coin plan)   2.00

24. 1 Livre (N) 1975. Cedar. Rev. Value

LIBERIA

An independent republic on the southwest coast of Africa, Liberia was founded in 1822 by the American Colonization Society.

100 Cents = 1 Dollar

1. 1 Cent (C) 1833 (Token of the American Colonization Society). Native and palm tree. Rev. Inscription   12.00

2. 2 Cents (C) 1847, 62. Liberty head. Rev. Palm tree   12.00
3. 1 Cent (C) 1847, 62   15.00

4. 50 Cents 1896, 1906. Female head. Rev. Value in wreath   20.00
5. 25 Cents 1896, 1906   15.00
6. 10 Cents 1896, 1906   10.00
7. 2 Cents (Bro) 1896, 1906   4.00
8. 1 Cent (Bro) 1896, 1906   6.00

9. 2 Cents (Bra) 1937; (C-N) 1941. Elephant. Rev. Palm tree   .75
10. 1 Cent (Bra) 1937; (C-N) 1941   1.00
11. ½ Cent (Bra) 1937; (C-N) 1941   .35

LIBERIA (continued)

13.

12. 1 Dollar, 1961-62. Head of native girl.
    Rev. Value and wreath   6.00
12a. 1 Dollar (CN) 1966-   3.00
13. 50 Cents 1960, 61   3.50
13a. 50 Cents (CN) 1966-   1.50
14. 25 Cents 1960, 61   2.00
14a. 25 Cents (CN) 1966-   1.00
15. 10 Cents 1960, 61   1.00
15a. 10 Cents (CN) 1966-   .50

16. 5 Cents (C-N) 1960-   Elephant. Rev.
    Coastal scene   .25
17. 1 Cent (Br) 1960-   .15

18. 5 Dollars 1973- . Map, African elephant.
    Rev. Arms   12.50

LIBYA

Located on the northern coast of Africa. From 1911 on, Libya was under Italian control, but after World War II, in 1950, it became an independent kingdom.

10 Milliemes = 1 Piastre

IDRIS I 1952-

1. 2 Piastres (C-N) 1952. Head. Crowned
   inscription and wreath   1.25
2. 1 Piastre (C-N) 1952   .75
3. 5 Milliemes (Br) 1952   .50
4. 2 Milliemes (Br) 1952   .30
5. 1 Millieme (Br) 1952   .20

6. 100 Milliemes (C-N) 1965. Crowned arms.
   Rev. Value   1.50

7. 50 Milliemes (C-N) 1965, 70 (scalloped)   .75
8. 20 Milliemes (C-N) 1965, 70 (round)   .35
9. 10 Milliemes (C-N) 1965, 70   .25
10. 5 Milliemes (Ni-Bra) 1965 (scalloped)   .20
11. 1 Millieme (Ni-Bra) 1965 (round)   .15

LIECHTENSTEIN

A small principality in central Europe (62 square miles), lying between Austria and Switzerland.

100 Heller = 1 Krone
100 Rappen = 1 Franken

PRINCE JOHN II 1858-1929

1. 1 Taler 1862. Head of Johann II. Rev.
    Arms   500.00

2. 20 Kronen (G) 1898. Head. Rev. Arms   rare
3. 10 Kronen (G) 1900   rare

4. 5 Kronen 1900-15. Head. Rev. Arms and
    value   75.00
5. 2 Kronen 1912, 15   10.00
6. 1 Krone 1900-15   7.50
7. 5 Franken 1924. Type of #4   140.00
8. 2 Franken 1924   25.00
9. 1 Franken 1924   20.00
10. ½ Franken 1924   15.00

PRINCE FRANZ I 1929-1938

11. 20 Franken (G) 1930. Bust. Rev. Arms   350.00
12. 10 Franken (G) 1930   300.00

PRINCE FRANZ JOSEF II 1938-

13. 20 Franken (G) 1946. Head. Rev. Arms   100.00
14. 10 Franken (G) 1946   90.00

15. 100 Franken (G) 1952. Busts of Franz Josef
    II and Princess Gina. Rev. Arms   600.00
16. 50 Franken (G) 1956   100.00
17. 25 Franken (G) 1956   85.00

LITHUANIA

Lithuania had its golden age in the fifteenth century, when it was about three times the size of Poland. Later on, greatly reduced, it became part of Russia. After World War I Lithuania enjoyed a brief period of independence. In 1940 it was made part of the U.S.S.R.

100 Centai = 1 Litas

1.	5 Litai 1925. Horseman. Rev. Value	15.00
2.	2 Litai 1925	6.00
3.	1 Litas 1925	4.00
4.	50 Centu (A-Br) 1925. Horseman	5.00
5.	20 Centu (A-Br) 1925	3.50
6.	10 Centu (A-Br) 1925	3.00
7.	5 Centai (A-Bro) 1925	2.50
8.	1 Centas (A-Bro) 1925	2.00

9.	10 Litai 1936. Head of Vitatas. Rev. Horseman	25.00
10.	5 Litai 1936. Dr. Jonas Basanivicius. Rev. Horseman	12.50

11.	5 Centai (Br) 1936. Horseman	5.00
12.	2 Centai (Br) 1936	4.00
13.	1 Centas (Br) 1936	3.00

14.	10 Litai 1938. Head of President Smetona. Twentieth anniversary of founding of state	32.50

LUXEMBOURG

A tiny country that borders on Belgium, France, and Germany. In the fourteenth and fifteenth centuries several Counts of Luxemboug were elected Holy Roman Emperors. During World War II, Luxembourg was occupied by the Germans and eventually freed by American troops.

100 Centimes = 1 Franc

WILLIAM III 1849-90

1.	10 Centimes (Br) 1854-70. Arms. Rev. Value	1.25
2.	5 Centimes (Br) 1854-70	1.25
3.	2½ Centimes (Br) 1854-70	1.25

ADOLPHE 1890-1905

4.	10 Centimes (C-N) 1901. Head. Rev. Value	.50
5.	5 Centimes (C-N) 1901	.45
6.	2½ Centimes (Br) 1901. Type of #3	1.00

WILLIAM IV 1905-12

7.	5 Centimes (C-N) 1908. Head. Rev. Value	1.00
8.	2½ Centimes (Br) 1908. Arms. Type of #3	1.00

MARIE ADELAIDE 1912-19

9.	25 Centimes (Z) 1916 (center hole)	2.50
10.	10 Centimes (Z) 1915	2.00
11.	5 Centimes (Z) 1915	1.75

12. 25 Centimes (I) 1919. Arms. Rev. Value   6.00
13. 10 Centimes (I) 1918   4.00
14. 5 Centimes (I) 1918   2.75

CHARLOTTE 1919-1964

15. 25 Centimes (I) 1920-22. Type of #12   5.00
16. 10 Centimes (I) 1921-23   3.75
17. 5 Centimes (I) 1921-22   3.00

18. 10 Francs 1929. Head. Rev. Arms   7.50
19. 5 Francs 1929   3.00

20. 2 Francs (N) 1924. Puddler   2.50
21. 1 Franc (N) 1924-35   1.00
22. 50 Centimes (N) 1930-41   .60
23. 25 Centimes (C-N) 1927, 1938; (Br) 1930 Arms. Rev. Value   .45
24. 10 Centimes (C-N) 1924. Monogram. Rev. Value   .75
25. 5 Centimes (C-N) 1924   .50

26. 10 Centimes (Br) 1930. Head. Rev. Value   .35
27. 5 Centimes (Br) 1930   .25

28. 1 Franc (C-N) 1939. Standing figure. Rev. Monogram   1.00

600th ANNIVERSARY OF JOHN THE BLIND

29. 100 Francs 1946. King John mounted. Rev. Head of Prince John   8.50
30. 50 Francs 1946   4.00
31. 20 Francs 1946   2.00

32. 5 Francs (N) 1949. Head. Rev. Value   1.00
33. 1 Franc (C-N) 1946-47 (reduced size) 1952- . Puddler. Rev. Monogram and value   .50
34. 25 Centimes (Br) 1946-47; (A) 1954- Arms. Rev. Value   .10

35. 250 Francs 1963. Head of Ruler. Rev. Ancient castle (1000th anniversary of the city of Luxembourg)   25.00
36. 100 Francs 1963. Rev. Arms and value   5.00

LUXEMBOURG (continued)

37.   5 Francs (C-N) 1962   .60

JEAN 1964-

38. 100 Francs 1964. Head of Grand Duke.
    Rev. Arms   8.00
39.   1 Franc (C-N) 1965-. Head. Rev. Value   .15

40. 10 Francs (N) 1971- . Head. Rev. Value   .75

41.   5 Francs (C-N) 1971. Head. Rev. Value   .50

MACAU

A Portuguese colony for 400 years, located at
the mouth of the Canton River in China.

100 Avos = 1 Pataca

1.   5 Patacas 1952. Arms of Macau. Rev.
    Portuguese arms in cross   5.00
1a. 5 Patacas 1971 (smaller planchet)   3.00
2.   1 Pataca 1952   2.50
2a. 1 Pataca (N) 1968 (larger planchet)   1.25
3. 50 Avos (C-N) 1952   1.25
3a. 50 Avos (C-N) 1972 (larger planchet)   .60

4. 10 Avos (Bro) 1952. Arms of Macau.
    Rev. Value in Chinese   1.00
4a. 10 Avos (N-Bra) 1967-   .25
5.   5 Avos (Bro) 1952   1.50
5a. 5 Avos (N-Bra) 1967   .15

6. 20 Patacas 1974. Chinese junk under
    bridge. Rev. Arms (Commemorates
    opening of Macao-Taipa Bridge)   7.50

MADAGASCAR

A large island off the southeast coast of Africa. Formerly a French overseas territory, it is now the Malagasy Republic within the French Community.

100 Centimes = 1 Franc

1.	1 Franc (Bro) 1943. Rooster. Rev. Cross of Lorraine	5.00
2.	50 Centimes (Bro) 1943	2.50
3.	20 Francs (A-Br) 1953. Republic. Rev. Map and value	1.50
4.	10 Francs (A-Br) 1953.	1.00
5.	5 Francs (A) 1953. Rev. Cattle	.85

6.	2 Francs (A) 1948	.60
7.	1 Franc (A) 1948, 58	.40

MADEIRA ISLANDS

An archipelago in the Atlantic, southwest of Portugal. The islands were officially discovered by the Portuguese in the early part of the fifteenth century, though they appeared on maps before that time. Administratively the islands are part of the Funchal district of Portugal.

MARY II 1828-53

1.	20 Reis (C) 1842, 52. Crowned arms. Rev. Value (Roman numerals) in wreath	20.00

2.	10 Reis (C) 1842-52	8.00
3.	5 Reis (C) 1850	40.00

MALAGASY

A large island off the southeast coast of Africa. Formerly the French Overseas Territory of Madagascar, and previously a French colony, it became the Republic of Malagasy in 1958 and achieved full independence within the French Community in March, 1960.

1.	5 Francs (St) 1966 - . Flower. Rev. Head of longhorn steer and value	.75
2.	2 Francs (St) 1965 -	**.40**

3.	1 Franc (St) 1965 -	.30

4.	20 Francs (A -Br) 1970. Zebu ox head, coffee flower. Rev. Cotton flower (F.A.O. coin plan)	1.00
5.	10 Francs (Al-Bro) 1970. Rev. Vanilla flower	.60

MALAWI

Malawi is the name the former British Protectorate called Nyasaland adopted in 1963 when it withdrew from the Federation of Rhodesia and Nyasaland in Central Africa, of which it had been a member since 1953. It became an independent state in July, 1964, and a republic within the British Commonwealth in July, 1966.

1. ½ Crown (C-N) 1964. Head of Prime Minister Dr. Hastings Banda. Rev. Arms 3.50
2. 1 Florin (Ni) 1964. Rev. Elephants 2.50

3. 1 Shilling (Ni) 1964. Rev. Ears of corn 1.50
4. 6 Pence (Ni) 1964. Rev. Rooster .75

5. 1 Crown (N-Bra) 1966. Rev. Arms (Commemorates Republic Day) 10.00

6. 1 Penny (Br) 1967. Value and date. Rev. Value .75

DECIMAL COINAGE

100 Tambala = 1 Kwacha

7. 1 Kwacha (C-N) 1971. Head of Prime Minister Dr. Hastings Banda. Rev. Arms 5.00
8. 20 Tambala (C-N) 1971. Rev. Elephants .85
9. 10 Tambala (C-N) 1971. Rev. Ears of corn .50

10. 5 Tambala (C-N) 1971. Rev. Purple heron .35
11. 2 Tambala (C-N) 1971- . Rev. Bird of Paradise .25
12. 1 Tambala (Br) 1971- . Rev. Rooster .15

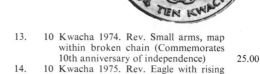

13. 10 Kwacha 1974. Rev. Small arms, map within broken chain (Commemorates 10th anniversary of independence) 25.00
14. 10 Kwacha 1975. Rev. Eagle with rising sun and waves (Commemorates 10th anniversary of independence) 15.00

MALAYA AND BRITISH BORNEO

Malaya, including former Straits Settlement on the Malay Peninsula, became a sovereign member of the British Commonwealth as the Federation of Malaya in 1957. In 1963 it joined with the former colonies of British North Borneo (now Sabah) and Sarawak, and the State of Singapore to form the Federation of Malaysia. The Sultanate of Brunei decided not to join the Federation but uses the same coins.

100 Cents = 1 Dollar

BRITISH NORTH BORNEO

1.	1 Cent (Bro) 1882-96, 1907	2.50
2.	½ Cent (Bro) 1885-91, 1907. Arms. Rev. Value in wreath	3.00

3.	5 Cents (C-N) 1903-41. Arms and supporters. Rev. Value in dotted circle	3.00
4.	2½ Cents (C-N) 1903-20	4.00
5.	1 Cent (C-N) 1904-41	1.50
5a.	25 Cents 1929	5.00

MALAYA
GEORGE VI 1936-52

6.	20 Cents (S) 1939-45; (C-N) 48-50. Crowned head. Rev. Value in dotted circle	1.00
7.	10 Cents (S) 1939-45; (C-N) 48-50	.75
8.	5 Cents (S) 1939-45; (C-N) 48-50	.50

9.	1 Cent (Br) 1939-45 (Square-shaped)	.45
10.	½ Cent (Br) 1940	.50

MALAYA AND BRITISH BORNEO
ELIZABETH II 1952-

11.	50 Cents (C-N) 1954-61. Crowned head. Rev. Type of #1	2.50
12.	20 Cents (C-N) 1954-61	1.00
13.	10 Cents (C-N) 1953-61	.80
14.	5 Cents (C-N) 1953-61	.60

15.	1 Cent (Bro) 1956-66. (Square-shaped)	.25

16.	1 Cent (Br) 1962- . Crossed daggers. Rev. Value	.40

MALAYSIA

Malaya, including the former Straits Settlements on the Malay Peninsula, became a sovereign member of the British Commonwealth as the Federation of Malaya in 1957. In 1963, the eleven states of Malaya joined with Sabah (former British North Borneo), Sarawak, and the state of Singapore to form the Federation of Malaysia. In 1965, Singapore withdrew from the Federation.

9.   1 Dollar (C-N) 1971. Rev. Value   2.00

1. 50 Sen (CN) 1967- . Bank Negara Malaysia in Kuala Lumpur, coat-of-arms at side. Rev. Value   .85
2. 20 Sen (CN) 1967-   .45
3. 10 Sen (CN) 1967-   .30
4.   5 Sen (CN) 1967-   .20
5.   1 Sen (Br) 1967-   .15

10.   1 Dollar (C-N) 1972. Arms of city of Kuala Lumpur. Rev. Value (Commemorates first anniversary of status as city)   2.00

11. 500 Dollars (G) 1976. Arms. Rev. Tapir

12. 25 Dollars 1976. Rev. Rhinoceros hornbill

13. 15 Dollars 1976. Rev. Seladang

6.   1 Dollar (CN) 1969. Head of Sultan. Rev. Value (Commemorates 10th anniversary of Central Bank)   2.50
6a. 1 Dollar 1969   100.00

7. 100 Dollars (G) 1971. Head of Abdul Rahman. Rev. Bank Negara Malaysia, arms in background   100.00
8.   5 Dollars (C-N) 1971   4.00

MALDIVE ISLANDS

Formerly a British Protected State of coral atolls in the Indian Ocean, independence was achieved in 1965, and a republic proclaimed in 1968.

120 Lari = 1 Rupee

1. 50 Lari (N-Bra) 1960. Arms. Rev. Value   1.50
2. 25 Lari (N-Bra) 1960   .85
3. 10 Lari (N-Bra) 1960. Scalloped edge   .60
4. 5 Lari (N-Bra) 1960, 70   .45
5. 2 Lari (Bro) 1960; (A) 1970 Square-shaped .35
6. 1 Larin (Bro) 1960; (A) 1970 Round   .25

MALI

In 1958 the French Sudan, formerly part of French West Africa, became the autonomous Sudanese Republic. With Senegal it formed the Mali Federation in 1959. When Senegal withdrew in 1960 to form an independent Republic, Mali retained the new name.

1. 25 Francs (A) 1961- . Lion. Rev. Value 6.00
2. 10 Francs (A) 1961- . Horse   3.00

3. 5 Francs (A) 1961- . Hippopotamus head. Rev. Value   2.00

4. 100 Francs (N-Bra) 1975. Three stalks of maize. Rev. Value (F.A.O. coin plan)   1.35
5. 50 Francs (N-Bra) 1975. Millet bush. Rev. Value (F.A.O. coin plan)   .65

MALTA

This island in the Mediterranean was a British Crown Colony from 1814 to September, 1964, when it became an independent state within the British Commonwealth. A peculiarity of its coinage is a ⅓ farthing denomination.

1. ⅓ Farthing (C) 1827. Head of George IV. Rev. Britannia   5.00
2. ⅓ Farthing (C) 1835. Head of William IV   5.00
3. ⅓ Farthing (C) 1844. Head of Victoria   12.00
4. ⅓ Farthing (Bro) 1866-85. Rev. Crowned value in wreath   5.00

5. ⅓ Farthing (Bro) 1902. Head of Edward VII   4.00
6. ⅓ Farthing (Bro) 1913. Head of George V   4.00

DECIMAL COINAGE

7. 50 Pounds (G) 1972. Arms. Rev. Statue of Neptune   250.00

8. 20 Pounds (G) 1972. Rev. National bird   100.00

9. 10 Pounds (G) 1972. Rev. Stone stove   50.00
10. 5 Pounds (G) 1972. Rev. Map, torch   35.00

11. 2 Pounds 1972. Rev. Fort St. Angelo 10.00
12. 1 Pound 1972. Rev. Portrait of Manwel
    Dimech, politician 5.00

13. 50 Cents (C-N) 1972. Three allegorical
    figures. Rev. Value (10-sided planchet) 3.00

14. 10 Cents (C-N) 1972. Barge. Rev. Value 1.50
15. 5 Cents (C-N) 1972. Altar. Rev. Value .75

16. 2 Cents (C-N) 1972. Helmeted head. Rev.
    Value .50
17. 1 Cent (Br) 1972. The George Cross. Rev.
    Value .25
18. 5 Mils (A) 1972. Lampstand. Rev. Value
    (scalloped planchet) .15

19. 3 Mils (A) 1972. Bee on honeycomb. Rev.
    Value (scalloped planchet) .15
20. 2 Mils (A) 1972. Maltese Cross. Rev. Value .15

21. 50 Pounds (G) 1973. Arms. Rev. Castle 200.00
22. 20 Pounds (G) 1973. Rev. Fountain 85.00
23. 10 Pounds (G) 1973. Rev. Watchtower 40.00

24. 2 Pounds 1973. Rev. View of Il-Bieb
    Ta'l-Imdina 10.00
25. 1 Pound 1973. Rev. Temi Zammit, Maltese
    historian 5.00

26. 50 Pounds (G) 1974. Rev. Likeness of first
    Maltese coin 200.00
27. 20 Pounds (G) 1974. Rev. Boat 75.00
28. 10 Pounds (G) 1974. Rev. National flower 40.00

MALTA (continued)

29. 4 Pounds 1974. Rev. Door of Cottonera   14.00
30. 2 Pounds 1974. Portrait of Giovanni Francisco Abela, historian   10.00

31. 50 Pounds (G) 1975. New arms. Rev. Stone balcony   175.00
32. 20 Pounds (G) 1975. Rev. Crab   75.00
33. 10 Pounds (G) 1975. Rev. Maltese falcon   35.00

34. 4 Pounds 1974. Rev. St. Agatha's Tower at Qammieh   15.00
35. 2 Pounds 1974. Rev. Portrait of Alphonse M. Galea, writer and philanthropist   7.50

MANCHUKUO

Located in northeastern China. From 1932 to 1945 Manchukuo was a puppet state under Japanese influence. In 1945 China resumed sovereignty over Manchukuo.

100 Li = 10 Fen = 1 Chiao

1. 1 Chiao (C-N) 1933-39. Lotus flower. Rev. Value between dragons   2.00
2. 5 Fen (C-N) 1933-39   2.00

3. 1 Fen (Bro) 1933-39. Flag. Rev. Value in wreath   3.00
4. 5 Li (Bro) 1933-39.   10.00

5. 1 Chiao (C-N) 1940. Winged horses. Rev. Value in wreath   5.00

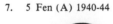

6. 10 Fen (A) 1940-43. Value. Rev. Inscription   2.00

7. 5 Fen (A) 1940-44   2.00

8. 1 Fen (A) 1939-43   .60
9. 1 Fen (A) 1943-44. Type of #6   4.00

MARTINIQUE

This island, one of the Windward group in the West Indies, was discovered by Columbus and first colonized by the French in 1635. It is now an overseas department of metropolitan France.

100 Centimes = 1 Franc

1. 1 Franc (C-N) 1897, 1922. Bust of native woman. Rev. Value in wreath   10.00
2. 50 Centimes (C-N) 1897, 1922   8.00

MAURITANIA

The former French colony became independent in 1960. Until 1973, Mauritania employed the West African States joint currency.

5 Khoum = 1 Ouguiya

1. 20 Ouguiya (C-N) 1973. Star over crescent with date palm and millet. Rev. Value, Arabic legend   2.00
2. 10 Ouguiya (C-N) 1973   1.25
3. 5 Ouguiya (C-N-A) 1973   .75
4. 1 Ouguiya (C-N-A) 1973   .50
5. $\frac{1}{5}$ Ouguiya (A) 1973   .25

MAURITIUS

This British Crown Colony is an island in the Indian Ocean, about 700 miles east of Madagascar. Mauritius was originally settled by the Dutch, then seized by the French, and finally became British territory during the Napoleonic wars. In 1968 it became an independent nation within the British Commonwealth.

100 Cents = 1 Rupee

VICTORIA 1837-1901

1. 20 Cents 1877-99. Diademed head. Rev. Value in circle   5.00
2. 10 Cents 1877-97   3.00
3. 5 Cents (Bro) 1877-97   3.00

4. 2 Cents (Bro) 1877-97   3.50
5. 1 Cent (Bro) 1877-97   2.75

GEORGE V 1910-36

6. 1 Rupee 1934. Crowned bust. Rev. Arms   7.50

7. ½ Rupee 1934. Rev. Stag   5.00
8. ¼ Rupee 1934. Rev. Crowned rose and other ornaments   4.00

MAURITIUS (continued)

9. 5 Cents (Bro) 1917, 20-24. Rev. Value
    in circle 3.00
10. 2 Cents (Bro) 1911-12, 17, 20-24 ...... 2.50
11. 1 Cent (Bro) 1911-24 .... 1.50

GEORGE VI 1936-52

(Coins issued after 1948 drop "Emperor" from
the legend)

12. 1 Rupee (S) 1938; (C-N) 50-51. Crowned
    head. Rev. Type of #6 .... 4.50
13. ½ Rupee (S) 1946; (C-N) 50-51 .... 3.00
14. ¼ Rupee (S) 1938, 46; (C-N) 50-51 ... 3.50
15. 10 Cents (C-N) 1947, 52 (Scalloped edge).
    Rev. Value 2.50
16. 5 Cents (Bro) 1942-45. Rev. Type of #9 2.50
17. 2 Cents (Bro) 1943-52 .... 2.00
18. 1 Cent (Bro) 1943-52 .... 1.50

ELIZABETH II 1952-

19. 1 Rupee (C-N) 1956- . Crowned head.
    Rev. Arms 1.50
20. ½ Rupee (CN) 1965 - . Rev. Stag 1.00
21. ¼ Rupee (C-N) 1960- 1.00

22. 10 Cents (C-N) 1954-   (scalloped edge) 1.50
23. 5 Cents (Bro) 1956- .... .50
24. 2 Cents (Bro) 1953- .... .35
25. 1 Cent (Bro) 1953- .... .25

26. 200 Rupees (G) 1971. Rev. Two figures in
    native scene (Commemorates third
    anniversary of independence) 250.00

27. 10 Rupees (C-N) 1971. Rev. Dodo bird
    (Commemorates third anniversary of
    independence) 4.00
28. 10 Rupees (S) 1971 (proof issue) 150.00

29. 1000 Rupees (G) 1975. Rev. Flycatcher
    (Conservation Commemorative) 300.00

30. 50 Rupees 1975. Rev. Kestrel (Conserva-
    tion Commemorative) 25.00
31. 25 Rupees 1975. Rev. Butterfly 15.00

MEXICO

During the centuries of Spanish rule, Mexico's rich silver mines were one of the chief sources of the famous Spanish Dollars or Pieces of Eight (8 Reales).

The first coins to be struck at the Mexican mint appeared during the reign of Charles and Joanna. Up to the reign of Ferdinand VII, all coins were struck at the Mexico City mint and bear the mint mark (M̥). Now a republic.

100 Centavos = 1 Peso

CHARLES AND JOANNA 1521-56

1. 4 Reales. Two Pillars "Plus Ultra." Rev. Crowned and quartered arms   125.00

2.	2 Reales	60.00
3.	1 Real	25.00
4.	½ Real. Large "KI." Rev. Two pillars	20.00

PHILIP II 1556-98

5.	8 Reales. Crowned shield. Rev. Quartered arms	100.00
6.	4 Reales	35.00
7.	2 Reales	20.00
8.	1 Real	15.00

9. ½ Real. Monogram. Rev. Arms   15.00

The preceding coins are of the round type though usually crude and irregular. During the following reign "cob money" came into use. This type of money was made by cutting off sections from crudely rolled silver bars and then striking the coins from crude dies by means of a hammer.

PHILIP III 1598-1621

10. 8 Reales 1600-18. Crude "cob" type   80.00

PHILIP IV 1621-65

11. 8 Reales 1621-65 (planchets are usually square cut)   75.00

12.	4 Reales 1631-39	40.00
13.	2 Reales 1641	25.00
14.	1 Real 1622	15.00

CHARLES II 1665-1700

15.	8 Reales 1667-99 (finer dies). Very rare	500.00
16.	4 Reales 1679-89	200.00
17.	½ Real. CAROLUS in monogram. Rev. Arms	100.00

PHILIP V 1700-46

18.	8 Reales 1702-33. Crowned shield. Rev. Quartered arms	100.00
19.	4 Reales 1721	70.00

20.	8 Reales 1732-47. Two globes between pillars. Rev. Crowned arms	60.00

21.	4 Reales 1732-47	110.00

22.	2 Reales 1732-46	15.00

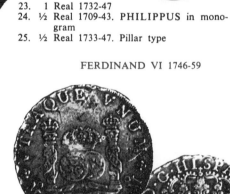

23.	1 Real 1732-47	12.00
24.	½ Real 1709-43. PHILIPPUS in monogram	10.00
25.	½ Real 1733-47. Pillar type	6.00

FERDINAND VI 1746-59

26.	8 Reales 1747-60. Pillar type	55.00
27.	4 Reales 1746-60	100.00
28.	2 Reales 1747-60	15.00
29.	1 Real 1747-59	10.00
30.	½ Real 1747-60	7.00

CHARLES III 1759-88

31. 8 Reales 1760-72. Pillar type   40.00

32.	4 Reales 1760-70	100.00
33.	2 Reales 1760-71	15.00
34.	1 Real 1760-69	8.00
35.	½ Real 1760-71	6.00

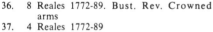

36.	8 Reales 1772-89. Bust. Rev. Crowned arms	40.00
37.	4 Reales 1772-89	40.00
38.	2 Reales 1772-89	4.00
39.	1 Real 1772-88	3.25
40.	½ Real 1772-88	4.00

CHARLES IV 1788-1808

41.	8 Reales 1789-90. Bust of Charles III. Rev. Arms	25.00

42.	4 Reales 1789-90	50.00
43.	2 Reales 1789-90	8.00
44.	1 Real 1789-90	8.00
45.	½ Real 1789-90	5.00

46.	8 Reales 1791-1808. Bust of Charles IV. Rev. Crowned arms	12.00
47.	4 Reales 1791-1808	45.00
48.	2 Reales 1791-1808	7.50

49.	1 Real 1791-1808	6.50

50.	½ Real 1791-1808	4.00

51.	¼ Real 1796-1808. Castle. Rev. Lion	8.00

FERDINAND VII 1808-21

Prior to this reign all coins had been struck at the Mexico City mint with the mint mark (M̊). During the reign of Ferdinand VII Mexican mints were established at Chihuahua (CA); Durango (D or Do); Guadalajara (Ga); Guanajuato (Go); Zacatecas (Z or Zs).

In the period 1811-14 many provisional issues were struck during the revolution led by General Morelos (copper and silver).

FIRST EMPIRE 1822-23
AUGUSTIN I ITURBIDE

52.	8 Reales 1808-11. Large armored bust	60.00
53.	4 Reales 1808-12	50.00
54.	2 Reales 1808-11	6.00
55.	1 Real 1808-13	5.00
56.	½ Real 1808-14	3.00
57.	¼ Real 1808-16. Castle. Rev. Lion	8.50

63.	8 Reales 1822. Small head. Rev. Eagle	45.00

58.	8 Reales 1812-21. Small draped bust.	15.00
59.	4 Reales 1813-21	40.00
60.	2 Reales 1812-21	4.00
61.	1 Real 1814-21	6.00
62.	½ Real 1815-21	3.00

64.	8 Reales 1822-23. Large head	40.00

65.	2 Reales 1822-23	65.00
66.	1 Real 1822-23	150.00
67.	½ Real 1822-23	20.00

MEXICO (continued)

REPUBLIC 1823-1864

(Republican coinage was interrupted for a while by that of Maximilian during 1864-67.)

68. 8 Reales 1823-24. Hook-neck eagle facing left. Rev. Liberty cap and rays   100.00

69. 2 Reales 1824   50.00
70. 1 Real 1824   rare
71. ½ Real 1824   50.00

72. 8 Reales 1825-69. Eagle facing   6.00
73. 4 Reales 1825-69   9.00
74. 2 Reales 1825-69   5.00
75. 1 Real 1825-69   3.00
76. ½ Real 1825-69   3.00
77. ¼ Real (C) 1829-36   2.00
78. ⅛ Real (C) 1829-35   6.00
79. 1⁄16 Real (C) 1831-33   10.00

80. ⅛ Real (C) 1841-61. Liberty seated   7.50

EMPIRE OF MAXIMILIAN 1864-67

81. 1 Peso 1866-67. Head. Rev. Arms   30.00
82. 50 Centavos 1866   25.00
83. 10 Centavos 1864-66. Eagle. Legend: "IMPERIO MEXICANO"   25.00
84. 5 Centavos 1864-66   30.00

85. 1 Centavo (C) 1864   20.00

REPUBLIC 1867-
(Metric system adopted 1869.)

86. 1 Peso 1869-73. Eagle. Rev. Balance scale   10.00
87. 50 Centavos 1869-95   5.00
88. 25 Centavos 1869-92   2.50

MEXICO • 317

89. 20 Centavos 1898-1914. Eagle. Rev. Value and wreath — 1.75
90. 10 Centavos 1867-1919 — 1.50
91. 5 Centavos 1867-69. Rev. Liberty cap and rays — 30.00
91a. 5 Centavos 1869-1905 — .85
91b. 5 Centavos (N) 1905-14 (Larger planchet) — 1.25
92. 1 Centavo (C) 1869-98 — 2.00
92a. 1 Centavo (Br) 1899-1905 (Smaller planchet) — 2.50

(During the period 1913-16 there were many revolutionary issues by various cities and states.)

93. 8 Reales 1869-97. Eagle. Rev. Liberty cap and rays — 6.00

94. 5 Centavos (C-N) 1882, 83. Bow, arrows and club. Rev. Value — 1.50
95. 2 Centavos (C-N) 1882-83 — 1.00
96. 1 Centavo (C-N) 1882, 83 — 1.00

97. 1 Peso 1898-1909. Eagle. Rev. Liberty cap and rays (Type of #93) — 6.00

98.

98. 1 Peso 1910-14. Liberty on horseback. Rev. Eagle — 15.00

99. 50 Centavos 1905-45 — 1.50
100. 20 Centavos 1919-43 — .60
101. 10 Centavos 1925-35 — .75

102. 20 Centavos (Br) 1920, 35. Eagle. Rev. Value in wreath — 6.00
103. 10 Centavos (Br) 1919-35 — 10.00
104. 5 Centavos (Br) 1914-35 — 1.50
105. 2 Centavos (Br) 1905-41 — 1.25
106. 1 Centavo (Br) 1905-49 — .20

107. 1 Peso 1918-45. Eagle. Liberty cap above value — 2.50

108. 2 Pesos 1921. Winged victory. Rev. Eagle (Commemorates 100th anniversary of independence) — 35.00

MEXICO (continued)

109. 50 Pesos (G) 1921-47. Eagle. Rev.
Winged victory (Commemorates 100th
anniversary of Mexico's independence
from Spain)   250.00

110. 20 Pesos (G) 1917-59. Eagle. Rev. Aztec
calendar stone   100.00

111. 10 Pesos (G) 1905-59. Eagle. Rev. Head
of Hidalgo   50.00
112. 5 Pesos (G) 1905-55   25.00
113. 2½ Pesos (G) 1918-48   15.00

114. 2 Pesos (G) 1919-48. Eagle. Rev. Value   10.00

115. 10 Centavos (C-N) 1936-46. Eagle. Rev.
Value   1.00
116. 5 Centavos (C-N) 1936-42   .75

117. 5 Pesos 1947, 48. Eagle. Rev. Head of
Cuauhtemoc   5.00

118. 1 Peso 1947-49. Eagle. Rev. Head of
Morelos   1.25

119. 5 Pesos 1950. Locomotive, palm trees
and rising sun. Rev. Eagle (Commemorates opening of Southeast Railroad)   25.00

120. 1 Peso (Bi) 1950. Eagle. Rev. Bust of
General Morelos   1.50

121. 50 Centavos (Bi) 1950, 51. Eagle. Rev.
Cuauhtemoc   .75

122. 25 Centavos (Bi) 1950-53. Eagle. Rev. Balance   .35

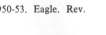

126. 10 Pesos 1955, 56. Head of Hidalgo, "Independencia y Libertad" legend. Rev. Eagle   5.00
127. 5 Pesos 1955-57   2.50

123. 5 Centavos (Br) 1942-55. Eagle. Rev. Dona Josefa Ortiz de Dominguez   .25
123a. 5 Centavos (C-N) 1950   1.50

128. 10 Pesos 1957. Head of Juarez. Rev. Eagle (Commemorates 100th anniversary of Mexican Constitution)   25.00
129. 5 Pesos 1957   6.00
130. 1 Peso (Bi) 1957   2.50

124. 5 Pesos 1951-54. Head of Hidalgo in wreath. Rev. Eagle   3.50

131. 5 Pesos 1959. Head of Venustiano Carranza. Rev. Eagle (Commemorates 100th anniversary of birth of this former Mexican president)   2.50
132. 10 Pesos 1960. Portraits of Hidalgo and Madero. Rev. Eagle (Commemorates 150th anniversary of Mexico's War for Independence and 50th anniversary of later revolutionary period)   5.50

125. 5 Pesos 1953. Bust of Hidalgo, cathedral in background. Rev. Eagle (Commemorates 200th anniversary of Hidalgo's birth)   5.00

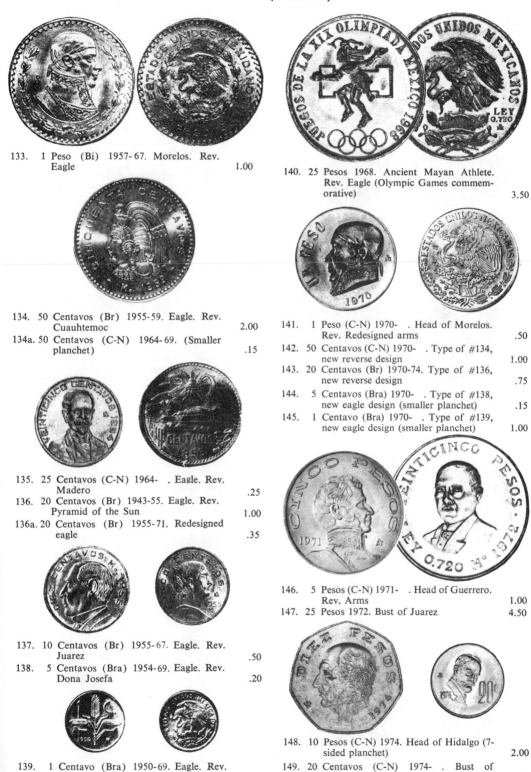

133. 1 Peso (Bi) 1957-67. Morelos. Rev. Eagle 1.00

140. 25 Pesos 1968. Ancient Mayan Athlete. Rev. Eagle (Olympic Games commemorative) 3.50

134. 50 Centavos (Br) 1955-59. Eagle. Rev. Cuauhtemoc 2.00

134a. 50 Centavos (C-N) 1964-69. (Smaller planchet) .... .15

141. 1 Peso (C-N) 1970- . Head of Morelos. Rev. Redesigned arms .... .50

142. 50 Centavos (C-N) 1970- . Type of #134, new reverse design 1.00

143. 20 Centavos (Br) 1970-74. Type of #136, new reverse design .... .75

144. 5 Centavos (Bra) 1970- . Type of #138, new eagle design (smaller planchet) .... .15

145. 1 Centavo (Bra) 1970- . Type of #139, new eagle design (smaller planchet) 1.00

135. 25 Centavos (C-N) 1964- . Eagle. Rev. Madero .... .25

136. 20 Centavos (Br) 1943-55. Eagle. Rev. Pyramid of the Sun 1.00

136a. 20 Centavos (Br) 1955-71. Redesigned eagle .... .35

146. 5 Pesos (C-N) 1971- . Head of Guerrero. Rev. Arms 1.00

147. 25 Pesos 1972. Bust of Juarez 4.50

137. 10 Centavos (Br) 1955-67. Eagle. Rev. Juarez .... .50

138. 5 Centavos (Bra) 1954-69. Eagle. Rev. Dona Josefa .... .20

148. 10 Pesos (C-N) 1974. Head of Hidalgo (7-sided planchet) 2.00

139. 1 Centavo (Bra) 1950-69. Eagle. Rev. Wheat ear .... .15

149. 20 Centavos (C-N) 1974- . Bust of Madero .... .75

MONACO

With an area of about 370 acres, Monaco, an independent principality, is the smallest country in the world. It is located on the Mediterranean coast of France.

100 Centimes = 1 Franc

LOUIS II 1922-49

1. 2 Francs (A-Bro) 1924, 26. Bowman.
   Rev. Value and arms   12.00
2. 1 Franc (A-Bro) 1924, 26   10.00
3. 50 Centimes (A-Bro) 1924, 26   10.00

4. 5 Francs (A) 1945. Head. Rev. Arms   2.00
5. 2 Francs (A) 1943; (A-Br) 1945. No date   1.00
6. 1 Franc (A) 1943; (A-Br) 1945. No date   .75
7. 20 Francs (C-N) 1947. Bust. Rev. Arms   2.50

8. 10 Francs (C-N) 1946   1.75

RAINIER III 1949-

9. 100 Francs (C-N) 1950. Head. Rev. Rider   2.50
10. 50 Francs (A-Bro) 1950   1.50

11. 20 Francs (A-Bro) 1950, 51. Head. Rev.
    Arms   .50
12. 10 Francs (A-Bro) 1950, 51   .30

13. 100 Francs (A-Bro) 1956-   New head.
    Rev. Arms   1.75

14. 5 New Francs 1960, 66   5.00

15. 1 New Franc (N) 1960-   1.00
16. ½ Franc (Ni) 1965, 68. Rev. Shield and crown   .50

17. 50 Centimes (A-Br) 1962-   .75
18. 20 Centimes (A-Br) 1962-   .35
19. 10 Centimes (A-Br) 1962   .25

23. 50 Francs 1974. Bust of Prince Rainier.
Rev. Four crowned monograms forming
cross (Commemorates 25th anniversary
of reign)

24. 10 Francs (C-N-A) 1974. Head of Prince
Rainier. Rev. Monograms over crowned
arms

20. 10 Francs 1966. Conjoined heads of Prince
Rainier and Princess Grace. Rev. Arms
and value (Commemorates 10th wedding
anniversary)   45.00
20a.200 Francs (G) 1966   400.00

21. 10 Francs 1966. Head of Charles III (1856-
89). Rev. Arms (Commemorates centennial of foundation of Monte Carlo)   25.00

22.   5 Francs (C-N) 1971- . Head of Prince
Rainier. Rev. Monograms, value   2.00

MONGOLIA

This large area in northeast Asia, also known as Outer Mongolia, declared its independence from China in 1921 and became the Mongolian People's Republic in 1924 on the death of its ruler. The separation from Nationalist China became complete in 1946. A part of northwest Mongolia is an autonomous province within the U.S.S.R. Coins listed here were struck in Leningrad.

100 Mung = 1 Tugrik

1. 1 Tugrik 1925. Buddhist symbols. Rev. Value in wreath — 20.00
2. 50 Mung 1925 — 12.00
3. 20 Mung 1925; (C-N) 1937 — 6.00
4. 15 Mung 1925; (C-N) 1937 — 5.50

21. 50 Mung (C-N) 1970. Arms. Rev. Value — 5.00
22. 20 Mung (C-N) 1970 — 4.50
23. 15 Mung (C-N) 1970 — 4.00
24. 10 Mung (C-N) 1970 — 4.00

25. 5 Mung (A) 1970. Arms. Rev. Value — 4.00
26. 2 Mung (A) 1970 — 3.50
27. 1 Mung (A) 1970 — 3.00

5. 10 Mung 1925; (C-N) 1937 — 5.00
6. 5 Mung (C) 1925; (A-Br) 1937 — 6.00
7. 2 Mung (C) 1925; (A-Br) 1937 — 4.00
8. 1 Mung (C) 1925; (A-Br) 1937 — 4.50
9. 20 Mung (N) 1945. Arms. Rev. Value in wreath — 10.00
10. 15 Mung (N) 1945 — 8.50
11. 10 Mung (N) 1945 — 7.50

28. 1 Tugrik (A-Br) 1971. Statue of Suche-Bator. Rev. Arms (Commemorates 50th anniversary of republic) — 15.00
28a. 1 Tugrik (C-N) 1971 — 15.00

12. 5 Mung (A-Bro) 1945 — 8.50
13. 2 Mung (A-Bro) 1945 — 6.50
14. 1 Mung (A-Bro) 1945 — 7.50

15. 20 Mung (A) 1959. Arms. Rev. Value — 8.00
16. 15 Mung (A) 1959 — 6.00
17. 10 Mung (A) 1959 — 4.00

29. 10 Tugrik (C-N) 1974. Arms. Rev. State Bank Building (Commemorates 50th anniversary, founding of State Bank) — 15.00

18. 5 Mung (A) 1959 (center hole) — 3.50
19. 2 Mung (A) 1959 — 3.00
20. 1 Mung (A) 1959 — 3.00

MONTENEGRO

A Balkan kingdom which was incorporated into the new state of Yugoslavia after World War I. In 1941 Montenegro was again set up as an independent state, and at the end of World War II it became part of the Yugoslav People's Republic.

100 Para = 1 Perper

NICHOLAS I 1860-1918

1.	20 Perpera (G) 1910. Head. Rev. Arms on mantle in wreath	250.00
2.	10 Perpera (G) 1910	200.00

3.	5 Perpera 1909, 12, 14	100.00
4.	2 Perpera 1910, 14	12.00
5.	1 Perper 1909, 12, 14	8.50

6.	20 Para (N) 1906, 08, 13, 14. Crowned two-headed eagle. Rev. Value	4.00
7.	10 Para (N) 1906-14	3.00

8.	2 Pare (Bro) 1906-14	4.00
9.	1 Para (Bro) 1906, 14	4.00

MOROCCO

This North African monarchy was a French protectorate, 1912-56. It has been a constitutional monarchy since 1962. The franc standard was adopted in 1920.

500 Mazunas = 1 Ryal or 1 Piastre
100 Centimes = 1 Franc

MOULAY ABDUL AZIZ 1894-1908 (A.H. 1311-26)
MOULAY HAFID 1908-12 (A.H. 1326-30)
MOULAY YOUSSEF 1912-27 (A.H. 1330-45)

1.	1 Ryal 1881-1919 (A.H. 1299-1337). Arabic inscriptions in double circle. Rev. Six-pointed star with date	10.00
2.	½ Ryal 1881-1919 (A.H. 1299-1337)	10.00
3.	¼ Ryal 1881-1919 (A.H. 1299-1337)	7.00
4.	10 Mazunas (Bro) A.H. 1320-23. Arabic inscription and date in circle with Grecian ornamental border. Rev. Value in Arabic with similar circle	2.00

5.	5 Mazunas (Bro) A.H. 1320-23	2.00
6.	2 Mazunas (Bro) A.H. 1320-21	3.00
7.	1 Mazuna (Bro) A.H. 1320-21	3.50

8.	10 Centimes (Bro) A.H. 1330, 40. Lobed triangle with date. Rev. Five-pointed star with value	1.50
9.	5 Centimes (Bro) A.H. 1330, 40	2.00

10. 2 Centimes (Bro) A.H. 1330   3.00
11. 1 Centime (Bro) A.H. 1330   5.50

12. 1 Franc (N) 1921-24. Five-pointed star in circle and Moorish design. Rev. Value in French in Moorish design   .75
13. 50 Centimes (N) 1921-24   1.50
14. 25 Centimes (N-Bro) 1921-26 (Center hole). Six-pointed star in circle and Moorish design. Rev. Value in French in Moorish design   .50

SIDI MOHAMMED BEN YOUSSEF 1927-53
(A.H. 1345-72)

15. 20 Francs 1929, 34 (A.H. 1347, 52). Lobed triangle with date in circle and Moorish design. Rev. Value in French in square inside six-pointed star and Moorish design   9.00
16. 10 Francs 1929, 34. (A.H. 1347, 52)   3.00
17. 5 Francs 1929-34 (A.H. 1347-52)   2.00
18. 20 Francs (C-N) 1947 (A.H. 1366)   1.25
19. 10 Francs (C-N) 1947 (A.H. 1366)   1.00
20. 5 Francs (A-Bro) 1946 (A.H.1365)   1.50
21. 2 Francs (A-Bro) 1945 (A.H. 1364). Double six-pointed star. Rev. Value   .50
22. 1 Franc (A-Bro) 1945 (A.H. 1364)   .35
23. 50 Centimes (A-Bro) 1945 (A.H. 1364)   .20

24. 200 Francs 1953 (A.H. 1372). Small five-pointed star within large six-pointed star in Moorish design. Rev. Value in French and Arabic inside dotted circle and Moorish design   3.50
25. 100 Francs 1953 (A.H. 1372)   1.50

26. 50 Francs (A-Bro) 1952 (A.H. 1371). Type of #15   1.25
27. 20 Francs (A-Bro) 1952 (A.H. 1371). Six-pointed star and date. Rev. Value in French and Arabic   .85
28. 10 Francs (A-Bro) 1952 (A.H. 1371)   .60
29. 5 Francs (A) 1951 (A.H. 1370)   .45
30. 2 Francs (A) 1951 (A.H. 1370)   .35
31. 1 Franc (A) 1951 (A.H. 1370)   .25

MOHAMMED V 1955-61
(New title of Sidi Mohammed Ben Youssef)
100 Francs = 1 Dirham

32. 500 Francs 1956. Head of the King. Rev. Star   10.00
33. 1 Dirham 1960. Rev. Arms   1.50

MULAI HASSAN II 1961-

34. 5 Dirhams 1965. Portrait of King. Rev. Arms   3.00
35. 1 Dirham (C-N) 1965-69   .75

MONETARY REFORM
100 Centimes = 1 Dirham

36. 1 Dirham (N) 1974. Head of King. Rev. Arms   .75
37. 50 Centimes (N) 1974   .50
38. 20 Centimes (Bra) 1974   .40

39. 10 Centimes (Bra) 1974. Sun and sunflowers. Rev. Arms. (F.A.O. coin plan)   .30

MOROCCO (continued)

40. 5 Centimes (Bra) 1974. Fish and boat
     wheel. Rev. Arms (F.A.O. coin plan)   .25

41. 1 Centime (A) 1974. Value. Rev. Arms   .10

42. 5 Dirham (C-N) 1975. Head of King.
     Rev. Value, turnip, dam (F.A.O. coin
     plan)

MOZAMBIQUE

A Portuguese colony in southeastern Africa (also
known as Portuguese East Africa) until 1975, when
years of guerilla warfare led to independence.

1. 10 Escudos 1936. Blunt shield. Rev.
    Portuguese arms on cross   7.50
2. 5 Escudos 1935   3.00
3. 2½ Escudos 1935   2.50

4. 1 Escudo (C-N) 1936. Blunt shield.
    Rev. Value   1.50
5. 50 Centavos (C-N) 1936   1.50

6. 20 Centavos (Bro) 1936   1.50
7. 10 Centavos (Bro) 1936   1.00

8. 20 Escudos 1952-66; (C-N) 1968-70.
    Crowned shield. Rev. Portuguese arms
    in cross   4.50
9. 10 Escudos 1938-66; (C-N) 1968-70   2.25

10. 5 Escudos 1938-65; (C-N) 1969-73   .75
11. 2½ Escudos 1938-51; (C-N) 1952-73   .50

MOZAMBIQUE (continued)

12. 1 Escudo (Br) 1945; (N-Br) 1950, 51; (Br)
    1953-73. Crowned shield. Rev. Value .45
13. 50 Centavos (Br) 1945; (N-Br) 1950-51;
    (Br) 1953-73 .30
14. 20 Centavos (Br) 1941-73 .20
15. 10 Centavos (Br) 1942-61 .15

16. 20 Escudos (N) 1971. Blunt shield. Rev.
    Portuguese arms 3.00

NEPAL

An independent state lying between Tibet and India. Most Nepalese coins are dated according to the Samvat system. Nepalese coins with Samvat dates 1989-2001 are equivalent to 1932-44.

100 Paisa = 1 Rupee

1. 1 Rupee (C-N) 1953-54. Head of Trib-
   hubana Bira Bikrama 3.50
2. 50 Paisa (C-N) 1953-54 2.00

3.   5.

3. 25 Paisa (C-N) 1953-57. Knife in front
   of mountain scene. Rev. Mountains
   and rising sun 2.50
4. 10 Paisa (Br) 1953-55 .50
5. 5 Paisa (Br) 1953-57. Hand of Buddha.
   Rev. Crossed ears of corn .75

6. 1 Rupee (C-N) 1955- . Trident in inner
   circle. Rev. Sword and ornamental design 2.50
7. 50 Paisa (C-N) 1954 - 1.00
8. 25 Paisa (C-N) 1956 - .75

18.

9. 1 Rupee (G) 1956. Plumed crown. Rev.
   Value (Commemorates coronation of
   Mahendra) 150.00
10. 1 Rupee (C-N) 1956 2.50
11. ½ Rupee (G) 1956 100.00
12. 50 Paisa (C-N) 1956 1.50
13. 25 Paisa (C-N) 1956 1.00
14. ⅕ Paisa (G) 1956 50.00
15. 10 Paisa (Br) 1956 1.50

16.	5 Paisa (Br) 1956	1.50
17.	2 Paisa (Bra) 1956	1.00
18.	1 Paisa (Bra) 1956	1.00

19.	4 Paisa (Bra) 1955 (center hole)	1.25
20.	2 Paisa (Bra) 1953-57. Type of #3	.50

21.	10 Paisa (Br) 1957-66. Trident. Rev. Value	.50
22.	5 Paisa (Br) 1957-66	.50
23.	2 Paiza (Bra) 1957-66	.50
24.	1 Paisa (Bra) 1957-65	.40

25.	10 Paisa (Bra) 2023-28 (1966-72). Mountains. Rev. Yak	.50
26.	5 Paisa (Al) 2023- (1966-)	.35

27.	2 Paisa (Al) 2023- (1966-). Rev. Dapha bird	.30
28.	1 Paisa (Al) 2023- (1966-). Rev. Lali guras flower	.20

29.	10 Rupees 1968. Head of King Mahendra. Rev. Trident and gear (F.A.O. coin plan)	6.00

30.	10 Paisa (Bra) 1971. Wheat. Rev. Yak (F.A.O. coin plan)	.25

31.	10 Paisa (Bra) 1972- . Mountains. Rev. Value	.40

32.	25 Rupees 1974. Crown. Rev. Sword (Commemorates coronation of Birenda)	10.00
33.	1 Rupee (C-N) 1974-	2.00
34.	50 Paisa (C-N) 1974-	1.25
35.	25 Paisa (C-N) 1974-	.75
36.	10 Paisa (A) 1974-	.60
37.	5 Paisa (A) 1974-	.50
38.	1 Paisa (A) 1974-	.25

39.	10 Rupees 1974. Parents and children with fruit and vegetables. Rev. Value (F.A.O. coin plan)	6.50

40.	5 Paisa (A) 1974. Irrigation sluices. Rev. Value (F.A.O. coin plan)	.50
41.	20 Rupees 1976. Conjoined busts of King and Queen. Rev. Value in wreath with dove and feminine symbol (F.A.O. coin plan, commemorates International Women's Year)	4.25
42.	1 Rupee (C-N) 1976	.65

NETHERLANDS

Originally Spanish colonies, these seven northern provinces of the Low Countries achieved their freedom after a long revolt which started in 1579. During the heyday of Napoleon's power, the Netherlands came under his control. However, the House of Orange returned to the throne in 1813 and has reigned ever since.

During the period 1600-1795, coins were struck by the various cities and provinces. The coins in this series that were struck under Spanish kings usually have the Spanish arms.

100 Cents = 1 Gulden (Guilder)

Campen (Campine, Kempen)

1. Ducatoon 1648. Warrior over arms. Rev. Lion   35.00

Gelderland (Gelria) [GEL in legend]
2. Ducatoon 1699. Standing warrior. Rev. Arms   30.00

Holland [HOL in legend]

3. Gulden (Guilder) 1713-94   15.00

Overyssel (Transisulania) [TRANSI in legend]

4. Ducatoon 1612. Bust of Philip III of Spain   35.00

Utrecht (Trajectum) [TRA in legend]

5. Ducatoon 1760. Warrior on horse   35.00

Westfrisia [WESTFRI in legend]

6. Ducatoon 1677. Warrior over arms.   50.00

NETHERLANDS (continued)

Zeeland [ZEL in legend]

KINGDOM OF HOLLAND 1806-10
LOUIS NAPOLEON 1806-10

12.	50 Stivers 1808	300.00

7. Ducatoon 1690. Warrior and Arms   35.00

Zwolle

8. Ducatoon 1619. Eagle and Arms   35.00

KINGDOM OF THE NETHERLANDS
WILLIAM I 1813-1840

13.	Ducat (G) 1814-40. Knight in armor. Rev. Tablet (Trade coins of this type were struck from 1586-1937)	100.00

BATAVIAN REPUBLIC 1795-1806

14.	10 Gulden (G) 1818-1840	200.00
15.	5 Gulden (G) 1826-7	200.00
16.	3 Gulden 1817-32. Bare head. Rev. Crowned shield	600.00
17.	1 Gulden 1818-40	150.00
18.	½ Gulden 1818-30	225.00
19.	25 Cents 1819-30. Crowned "W". Rev. Crowned shield	30.00
20.	10 Cents 1818-28	25.00
21.	5 Cents 1818-28	40.00

9.	Ducatoon 1795-1806. Warrior standing with shield. Rev. Crowned shield	85.00
10.	3 Gulden 1795-1801. Neerlandia standing. Rev. Crowned shield	40.00
11.	1 Gulden 1795-1800	20.00
22.	1 Cent (C) 1819-37	12.50
23.	½ Cent (C) 1819-37	20.00

NETHERLANDS (continued)

WILLIAM II 1840-49

24.	10 Gulden (G) 1842	1,000.00
25.	5 Gulden (G) 1843	600.00

26.	2½ Gulden 1841-49. Bare head. Rev. Crowned shield	45.00
27.	1 Gulden 1842-49	30.00
28.	½ Gulden 1847, 48	50.00
29.	25 Cents 1848, 49	25.00
30.	10 Cents 1848, 49	35.00
31.	½ Cent (C) 1841-47. Crowned "W"	20.00

WILLIAM III 1849-90

32.	10 Gulden (G) 1850-89	45.00
33.	5 Gulden (G) 1850, 51	750.00

34.	2½ Gulden 1849-74	20.00
35.	1 Gulden 1850-66	35.00
36.	½ Gulden 1857-68	30.00
37.	25 Cents 1849-90	200.00
38.	10 Cents 1849-90	15.00
39.	5 Cents 1850-87	4.00
40.	2½ Cents (C) 1877-86. Lion. Rev. Value	1.75
41.	1 Cent (C) 1860-77. Crowned monogram. Rev. Crowned shield	5.00
41a.	1 Cent (C) 1877-84. Type of #40.	3.00
42.	½ Cent (C) 1850-77. Type of #41.	5.00
42a.	½ Cent (C) 1878-86. Type of #40	1.25

WILHELMINA 1890-1948

43.	10 Gulden (G) 1892-97. Head of girl	125.00
44.	10 Gulden (G) 1898. Young head	300.00

45.	10 Gulden (G) 1911-17. Middle-aged head	40.00
45a.	5 Gulden (G) 1912	125.00
46.	10 Gulden (G) 1925-33. Bare head	40.00

47.	2½ Gulden 1929-40	6.00

TYPES OF LOWER DENOMINATIONS

Type I	1890-97 Girl head with flowing hair
Type II	1898-1909 Young head with coronet
Type III	1910-1920 Middle-aged head
Type IV	1921-1945 Old head

48.	1 Guilder 1892-1945	2.50
49.	½ Guilder 1898-1930	1.50
50.	25 Cents (S) 1892-1945, (N) 1948	.50
51.	10 Cents (S) 1892-1945, (N) 1948	.25

52.	5 Cents (C-N) 1913-40. Orange branch. Rev. Value. Square shape	3.00
53.	2½ Cents (Bro) 1890-1906, 1912-41. Lion. Rev. Value	1.00
54.	1 Cent (Bro) 1892-1941	1.25
55.	½ Cent (Bro) 1891-1940	.50

NETHERLANDS (continued)

JULIANA 1948-

56. 2½ Gulden 1959-66. Head. Rev. Crowned arms   2.00
56a. 2½ Gulden (N) 1969-   1.25

57. 1 Guilder 1954-67   1.25
57a. 1 Guilder (N) 1967-   .75

58. 25 Cents (N) 1950- . Head. Rev. Value   .35
59. 10 Cents (N) 1950-   .25
60. 5 Cents (Bro) 1950-   .15
61. 1 Cent (Bro) 1950-   .10

62. 10 Gulden 1970. Head of Juliana. Rev. Head of Queen Wilhelmina (Commemorates 25th anniversary of liberation from German occupation)   6.00

63. 10 Gulden 1973. Head of Juliana. Rev. Crowned arms (Commemorates 25th anniversary of reign)   6.00

NETHERLANDS ANTILLES

A group of six Dutch West Indies islands, including Curacao and Aruba. Since 1950 they have been organized as a part of the kingdom of the Netherlands, with considerable powers of self-government.

100 Cents = 1 Guilder (Gulden)

1. 1 Guilder 1952-70. Head of Queen Juliana. Rev. Crowned shield   5.00
2. ¼ Guilder 1954-70. Rev. Value   2.50
3. ⅒ Guilder 1954-70   1.50

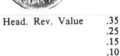

4. 5 Cents (C-N) 1957-70. Orange branch in circle. Rev. Value (square planchet)   1.50
5. 2½ Cents (Br) 1956-65. Lion. Rev. Value   1.00
6. 1 Cent (Br) 1952-70   .75
7. 2½ Guilders 1964. Head of Queen Juliana. Rev. Crowned Shield   6.00

8. 1 Guilder (N) 1970- . Head of Queen Juliana. Rev. Crowned shield   2.00

9. 25 Cents (N) 1970- . Crowned shield. Rev. Value   1.00
10. 10 Cents (N) 1970-   .75

11. 5 Cents (N) 1971- (square planchet)   .50
12. 2½ Cents (Br) 1970-   .50
13. 1 Cent (Br) 1970-   .35

NETHERLANDS ANTILLES (continued)

14. 25 Guilders 1973. Head of Queen Juliana. Rev. Queen and Prince Bernhard in carriage (Commemorates 25th anniversary of reign) 25.00

15. 200 Guilders (G) 1976. Rev. American ship "Andrew Doria"
16. 25 Guilders 1976

NETHERLANDS EAST INDIES

An archipelago in the southwest Pacific which achieved independence in 1949 as the United States of Indonesia, bringing Dutch rule to an end.

100 Cents = 1 Guilder (Gulden)

WILHELMINA 1890-1948

1. 1 Ducat (G) 1901-37 (Trade coin). Knight. Rev. Inscription 50.00
2. ¼ Guilder 1890-1945. Crowned shield. Rev. Javanese and Malay inscriptions 1.50
3. ⅒ Guilder 1891-1945 3.00

4. 5 Cents (C-N) 1913, 21-22 (Center hole). Crown in wreath 3.00
5. 2½ Cents (C or Bro) 1896-1945. Crowned shield in circle. Rev. Inscription in circle 1.25
6. 1 Cent (C or Bro) 1896-1945 1.25
7. ½ Cent (C or Bro) 1902-45 1.00

NEW BRUNSWICK

Part of Nova Scotia when it was ceded to England by France, New Brunswick became a separate province in 1784 and was one of the original provinces of the Dominion of Canada created in 1867.

1. Penny (Bro) 1843, 54. Rev. Sailing vessel 5.00
2. Halfpenny (Bro) 1843, 54 4.00

3. 20 Cents 1862, 64. Head of Victoria. Rev. Crowned value 25.00
4. 10 Cents 1862, 64 50.00
5. 5 Cents 1862, 64 35.00

6. 1 Cent (Bro) 1861, 64. Rev. Crowned date in circle and value 5.00
7. Half Cent (Bro) 1861 75.00

NEW CALEDONIA

This Pacific island, northeast of Australia, is a French overseas territory.

100 Centimes = 1 Franc

1. 5 Francs (A) 1952 . Seated female
   figure. Rev. Tropical bird 1.00
2. 2 Francs (A) 1949; (A-Br) 1971 .... .50
3. 1 Franc (A) 1949, 1972- ; (A-Br) 1971 .35
4. 50 Centimes (A) 1949 .... .20

5. 50 Francs (N) 1967- . Head of Republic.
   Rev. Native hut 2.00

6. 20 Francs (N) 1967- . Rev. Three cattle heads 1.50

7. 10 Francs (N) 1967- . Rev. Native sailboat 1.00

NEWFOUNDLAND

A large island located in the Gulf of St. Lawrence. Discovered by Sebastian Cabot in 1497, Newfoundland was England's first colony. By vote of its inhabitants, Newfoundland became part of the Dominion of Canada in 1948.

100 Cents = 1 Dollar

VICTORIA 1837-1901

1. 2 Dollars (G) 1865-88. Bust. Rev. Value ... 100.00
2. 50 Cents 1870-1900. Bust. Rev. Value ... 8.00
3. 20 Cents 1865-1900 .... 5.00
4. 10 Cents 1865-96 .... 12.00

5. 5 Cents 1865-96 .... 15.00
6. 1 Cent (Br) 1865-96 .... 5.00

EDWARD VII 1901-10

7. 50 Cents 1904, 07-09. Crowned bust. Rev.
   Value in scrolled circle 6.00
8. 20 Cents 1904 .... 15.00
9. 10 Cents 1903-04 .... 10.00
10. 5 Cents 1903-04, 08 .... 5.00
11. 1 Cent (Bro) 1904, 07, 09 .... 5.00

GEORGE V 1910-36

12. 50 Cents 1911, 17-19. Crowned bust. Rev.
    Value in scrolled circle 4.50
13. 25 Cents 1917, 19 .... 4.00
14. 20 Cents 1912 .... 4.00
15. 10 Cents 1912, 17, 19 .... 6.00
16. 5 Cents 1912, 17, 19, 29 .... 3.00

17. 1 Cent (Bro) 1913, 17, 19-20, 29, 36. 2.00

GEORGE VI 1936-52

18. 10 Cents 1938-47. Bust. Rev. Value ... 1.25
19. 5 Cents 1938-47 .... 1.00

20. 1 Cent (Bro) 1938-44, 47. Rev. Pitcher
    plant 1.50

NEW GUINEA

This large island north of Australia contains Indonesian West Irian (formerly Netherlands New Guinea) on the west, and the Australian Trusteeship of New Guinea and Papua on the east. In 1975 the territory became an independent nation under the name Papua New Guinea.

12 Pence = 1 Shilling

GEORGE V 1910-36

1. 1 Shilling 1935-36. Holed center. Crowned maces crossed. Rev. Cross made of ornaments   3.50

2. 1 Penny (C-N) 1929   350.00
3. 1 Halfpenny (C-N) 1929   350.00

4. 6 Pence (C-N) 1935 (Holed center). Crown, date, and inscription "G.R.I." Rev. Eight-pointed circle   3.00
5. 3 Pence (C-N) 1935. Rev. Square inside four-pointed circle   3.00

EDWARD VIII 1936

6. 1 Penny (C) 1936 (Holed center). Crown, native ornament, and inscription "E.R.I" Rev. Native ornament   1.75

GEORGE VI 1936-52

7. 1 Shilling 1938, 45. Type of #1   2.00
8. 6 Pence (C-N) 1943. Type of #4   4.00
9. 3 Pence (C-N) 1944. Type of #5   3.00
10. 1 Penny (C) 1938, 44. Type of #6   1.50

NEW HEBRIDES

A group of islands in the southwest Pacific Ocean, the New Hebrides is a condominium administered jointly by Great Britain and France.

1. 100 Francs 1966. Head of Republic. Rev. Carved post   7.50
2. 50 Francs (N) 1972   3.00

3. 20 Francs (CN) 1967- . Rev. Carved head 1.50
4. 10 Francs (CN) 1967-   1.00

5. 5 Francs (N-Bra) 1970. Rev. Buff-bellied flycatcher (native bird)   1.00
6. 2 Francs (N-Bra) 1970, 73   .50
7. 1 Franc (N-Bra) 1970   .35

NEW ZEALAND

A self-governing Dominion since 1907.

4 Crowns = 1 Pound Sterling
12 Pence = 1 Shilling
2 Shillings = 1 Florin
20 Shillings = 1 Pound Sterling

GEORGE V 1910-1936

1. 1 Crown 1935. Crown bust of King. Rev. Maori and Captain William Hobson, Territory's first governor (Commemorates 25th year of reign of George V and Waitangi Treaty of 1840 which brought islands under British sovereignty) 750.00

2. ½ Crown (2½ Shillings) 1933-35. Rev. Arms 5.00

3. 1 Florin (2 Shillings) 1933-36. Rev. Kiwi bird 3.00
4. 1 Shilling 1933-35. Rev. Maori warrior 2.00

5. 6 Pence 1933-36. Rev. Huia bird ...... .85
6. 3 Pence 1933-36. Rev. War clubs 1.00

GEORGE VI 1936-52

(All obverse types: bare head of King. Coins issued after 1948 drop "Emperor" from the legend.)

7. ½ Crown (S) 1937-46; (C-N) 47-51. Head. Rev. Type of #2 ...... 4.00
8. 1 Florin (S) 1937-46; (C-N) 47-51. Rev. Type of #3 ...... 1.00
9. 1 Shilling (S) 1937-46; (C-N) 47-52. Rev. Type of #4 ...... 1.25
10. 6 Pence (S) 1937-46; (C-N) 47-52. Rev. Type of #5 ...... 1.00
11. 3 Pence (S) 1937-46; (C-N) 47-52. Rev. Type of #6 ...... .75

12. 1 Penny (Br) 1940-52. Rev. Tui bird 1.00

13. 1 Halfpenny (Br) 1940-52. Rev. Tiki 1.00

14. ½ Crown 1940 (Centennial commemorative). Rev. Maori woman 35.00

15. 1 Crown 1949 (Commemorating proposed royal visit). Rev. Leaf with four stars 17.50

NEW ZEALAND (continued)

ELIZABETH II 1952-

DECIMAL COINAGE

16. 1 Crown (C-N) 1953. Head. Rev. Crowned monogram above Maori design   15.00

24. 1 Dollar (CN) 1967- . Portrait of Queen Elizabeth. Rev. Arms   4.00

17. 1 Half Crown (C-N) 1953-65. Rev. Arms   3.00
18. 1 Florin (C-N) 1953-65. Rev. Kiwi bird   1.00

25. 50 Cents (CN) 1967- . Rev. Sailing Ship *Endeavour*   1.50
26. 20 Cents (CN) 1967- . Rev. Kiwi bird   .75

19. 1 Shilling (C-N) 1953-65. Rev. Maori warrior 1.00
20. 6 Pence (C-N) 1953-65. Rev. Huia bird   .50
21. 3 Pence (C-N) 1953-65. Rev. War clubs   .35

27. 10 Cents (CN) 1967- . Rev. Maori carved head   .50
27a. 10 Cents (CN) 1970- . Rev. Without ONE SHILLING inscription   .50
28. 5 Cents (CN) 1967- . Rev. Tuatara lizard .30

22. 1 Penny (Br) 1953-65. Rev. Tui bird   .30
23. 1 Halfpenny (Br) 1953-65. Rev. Tiki   .20

29. 2 Cents (Br) 1967- . Rev. Kowhai flowers .25
30. 1 Cent (Br) 1967- . Rev. Fern leaf   .15

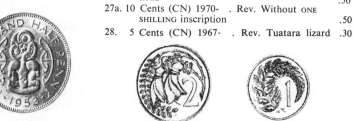

NEW ZEALAND (continued)

31. 1 Dollar (CN) 1969. Rev. Bust of Captain James Cook, map and sailing ship (Commemorates the 200th anniversary of discovery)   4.00
32. 50 Cents (CN) 1969. Type of #25 with edge inscribed COOK BI-CENTENARY 1769-1969   3.00

33. 1 Dollar (CN) 1970. Rev. View of Mount Cook (Commemorates the royal visit)   4.00

34. 1 Dollar (CN) 1974. Rev. Eight running figures supporting emblem   5.00
34a. 1 Dollar (S) 1974 (proof issue)   60.00

35. 1 Dollar (CN) 1974. Rev. Kotuku bird, rising sun (Commemorates New Zealand Day)   4.00

NICARAGUA

A Spanish colony for three centuries, Nicaragua gained its independence in 1821. For a while it became part of Mexico and then joined the Central American Federation, finally breaking away to become an independent republic.

100 Centavos = 1 Cordoba

REPUBLICA DE NICARAGUA

1. 20 Centavos 1880, 87. Arms. Rev. Value in wreath   5.00
2. 10 Centavos 1880, 87   3.00
3. 5 Centavos 1880-87; (C-N) 1898-99   2.00
4. 1 Centavo (C-N) 1878. Coroneted arms with flags. Rev. Value in wreath   10.00

5. 1 Cordoba 1912. Bust of Francisco de Cordoba. Rev. Rays over mountains   35.00
6. 50 Centavos 1912, 29   5.00
7. 25 Centavos 1912-36   2.50
8. 10 Centavos 1912-36   1.50
9. 5 Centavos (C-N) 1912-40. Arms. Rev. Value in wreath   .50
10. 1 Centavo (Br) 1912-40; (Bra) 1943   .35
11. ½ Centavo (Br) 1912-37   .50

12. 50 Centavos (C-N) 1939-   1.00
13. 25 Centavos (C-N) 1939-   .50
14. 10 Centavos (C-N) 1939-72   .35
15. 5 Centavos (C-N) 1946-72   .15

NICARAGUA (continued)

16. 1 Cordoba (C-N) 1972. Type of #5, smaller planchet — 1.25

17. 10 Centavos (A) 1974. Map. Rev. Value (F.A.O. coin plan) — .25

18. 5 Centavos (A) 1974. Arms. Rev. Value (F.A.O. coin plan) — .15

NIGERIA

Formerly part of British West Africa, Nigeria became an independent Federation within the British Commonwealth in 1960.

ELIZABETH II 1952-

1. 2 Shillings (C-N) 1959. Crowned head of Elizabeth. Rev. Flowers — 1.75

2. 1 Shilling (C-N) 1959-62. Rev. Palm branches — 1.00

3. 6 Pence (C-N) 1959. Rev. Cocoa beans — .75

4. 3 Pence (N-Bra) 1959. Rev. Flowers (12-sided planchet) — .50

5. 1 Penny (Br) 1959-61. Six-pointed star (center hole) — .20
6. ½ Penny (Br) 1959 — .15

NIGERIA (continued)

DECIMAL COINAGE

100 Kobo = 1 Naira

7. 25 Kobo (C-N) 1973. Arms. Rev. Peanuts   1.50

8. 10 Kobo (C-N) 1973. Rev. Palm trees   .75
9. 5 Kobo (C-N) 1973. Rev. Cacao beans   .40

10.   1 Kobo (Br) 1973. Rev. Oil rigs   .20
11.   ½ Kobo (Br) 1973. Rev. Value   .15

NORWAY

From 1387 to 1814 Norway was united with Denmark. Coins issued during that period bear the bust and name of the reigning Danish monarch. From 1814 to 1905 Norway was united with Sweden, and coins issued during that period bear the bust and name of the reigning Swedish monarch.

The Norwegian arms (lion rampant with battle axe) appear on the obverse or reverse of almost every Norwegian coin.

120 Skilling = 1 Speciedaler
100 Ore = 1 Krone

CHRISTIAN IV 1588-1648

1. Taler 1628-48. Crowned bust. Rev. Lion   125.00
2. ½ Taler 1628-48   125.00
3. ¼ Taler 1628-48   75.00
4. ⅛ Taler 1628-46   75.00

5. 8 Skilling 1641-44. Lion. Rev. Value   20.00
6. 4 Skilling 1641-44   20.00
7. 2 Skilling 1641-48   6.00
8. 1 Skilling 1643-48   5.00

FREDERICK III 1648-70

9. Taler 1649-69. Crowned bust. Rev. Lion   175.00
10. ½ Taler 1649-69   250.00
11. ¼ Taler 1649-55   120.00

12. ⅛ Taler 1649-65   120.00

38.	8 Skilling 1817. Lion. Rev. Value		12.00

CHARLES XIV JOHN (BERNADOTTE) 1818-44

13.	2 Marks 1649-69. Monogram. Rev. Lion	25.00
14.	16 Skilling—1 Mark 1649-69	20.00
15.	8 Skilling 1649-65	25.00
16.	2 Skilling 1649-70. Lion. Rev. Value	8.00
17.	1 Skilling 1649-68	6.00

CHRISTIAN V 1670-99

18.	Taler 1670-74. Crowned or laureate bust. Rev. Lion	200.00
19.	½ Taler 1671-75	175.00
20.	4 Marks 1670-99. Monogram. Rev. Value	50.00
21.	2 Marks 1670-98	15.00

22.	16 Skilling 1670-99. Lion. Rev. Value	20.00
23.	8 Skilling 1670-75	5.00
24.	2 Skilling 1670-99	4.00
25.	1 Skilling 1670-82	4.00

FREDERICK IV 1699-1730

26.	2 Skilling 1700-25. Monogram. Rev. Lion	6.00

CHRISTIAN VI 1730-46

27.	6 Marks 1732-33. Armored bust. Rev. Lion	250.00
28.	24 Skilling 1736-46. Monogram. Rev. Lion	18.00
29.	8 Skilling 1730-35. Lion. Rev. Value	10.00

FREDERICK V 1746-66

30.	6 Marks 1749. Laureate bust. Rev. Lion	250.00
31.	24 Skilling 1746-63. Monogram. Rev. Lion	20.00

CHRISTIAN VII 1766-1808

32.	Speciedaler 1781-86. Hercules standing	325.00
33.	1 Rigsdaler 1788. Armored bust. Rev. Lion	275.00
34.	24 Skilling 1773-83. Monogram. Rev. Lion	15.00
35.	12 Skilling 1798-1801	12.00
36.	1 Skilling (C) 1771. Monogram. Rev. Value	4.00
37.	½ Skilling (C) 1771	4.00

39.	Speciedaler 1819-36, 44. Head. Rev. Lion	150.00
40.	½ Speciedaler 1819-36, 44	40.00
41.	24 Skilling 1819-36. Lion. Rev. Value	35.00
42.	8 Skilling 1819, 25, 27	8.00
43.	4 Skilling 1825, 42	4.00
44.	2 Skilling (C) 1822-36	4.00
45.	1 Skilling (C) 1819-37	4.00
46.	½ Skilling (C) 1837-41	4.00

OSCAR I 1844-59

47.	Speciedaler 1846-57. Head. Rev. Lion	225.00

48. ½ Speciedaler 1846-55   175.00
49. 24 Skilling 1845-55   35.00

50. 12 Skilling 1845-56   15.00

CHARLES XV 1859-72
51. Speciedaler 1861-69. Head. Rev. Lion   400.00

52. ½ Speciedaler 1861-65   150.00
53. 24 Skilling 1861-65   100.00
54. 12 Skilling 1861-65   70.00
55. 4 Skilling 1871. Lion. Rev. Value   10.00
56. 3 Skilling 1868, 73   15.00
57. 2 Skilling (C) 1870, 71   4.00
58. 1 Skilling (C) 1870   6.00
59. ½ Skilling (C) 1863, 67   4.00

OSCAR II 1872-1905

60. 20 Kroner (G) 1876-1902. Head. Rev. Lion   225.00
61. 10 Kroner (G) 1877-1902   300.00
62. 2 Kroner 1878-1904. Head. Rev. Lion   40.00
63. 1 Krone 1875-1904   20.00
64. 50 Ore 1874-1904   15.00
65. 25 Ore 1876, 1896-1904. Lion. Rev. Value   10.00
66. 10 Ore 1874-1903. Monogram. Rev. Value   7.50

67. 5 Ore (Bro) 1875-1902   3.50
68. 2 Ore (Bro) 1876-1902   2.00
69. 1 Ore (Bro) 1876-1902   3.00

NORWAY INDEPENDENT KINGDOM 1905-
HAAKON VII 1905-57

70. 20 Kroner (G) 1910. Crowned bust. Rev.
    St. Olaf standing   200.00
71. 10 Kroner (G) 1910   225.00

72. 2 Kroner 1906-07. Lion. Rev. Legend
    commemorating independence   20.00

73. 2 Kroner 1908-17. Head. Rev. Lion and
    shields   15.00
73a. 1 Kroner 1908-17   8.50

74. 2 Kroner 1914. Standing figure Rev. Lion.
    (Centenary of the Constitution)   8.50

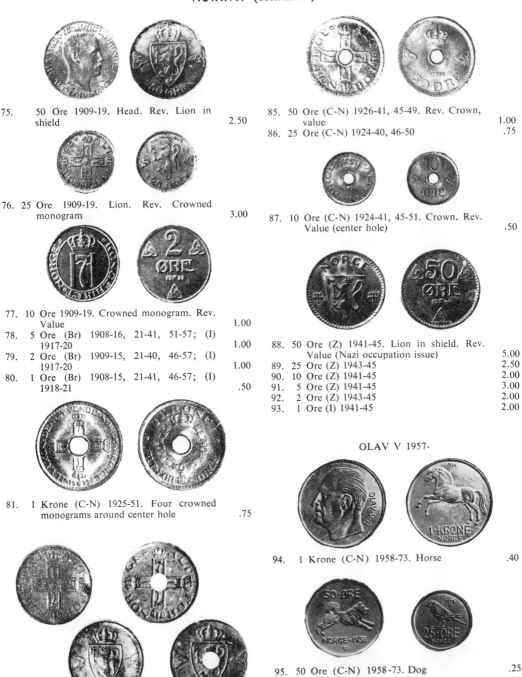

75.   50 Ore 1909-19. Head. Rev. Lion in
       shield   2.50

76. 25 Ore 1909-19. Lion. Rev. Crowned
    monogram   3.00

77. 10 Ore 1909-19. Crowned monogram. Rev.
    Value   1.00
78. 5 Ore (Br) 1908-16, 21-41, 51-57; (I)
    1917-20   1.00
79. 2 Ore (Br) 1909-15, 21-40, 46-57; (I)
    1917-20   1.00
80. 1 Ore (Br) 1908-15, 21-41, 46-57; (I)
    1918-21   .50

81. 1 Krone (C-N) 1925-51. Four crowned
    monograms around center hole   .75

82. 50 Ore (C-N) 1920-23. Four crowned
    monograms. Rev. Arms (with or without
    center hole)   3.00
83. 25 Ore (C-N) 1921-23. Crowned monogram.
    Rev. Lion (with or without center hole)   2.00
84. 10 Ore (C-N) 1920-23. Crowned monogram.
    Rev. Value   5.00

85. 50 Ore (C-N) 1926-41, 45-49. Rev. Crown,
    value   1.00
86. 25 Ore (C-N) 1924-40, 46-50   .75

87. 10 Ore (C-N) 1924-41, 45-51. Crown. Rev.
    Value (center hole)   .50

88. 50 Ore (Z) 1941-45. Lion in shield. Rev.
    Value (Nazi occupation issue)   5.00
89. 25 Ore (Z) 1943-45   2.50
90. 10 Ore (Z) 1941-45   2.00
91. 5 Ore (Z) 1941-45   3.00
92. 2 Ore (Z) 1943-45   2.00
93. 1 Ore (I) 1941-45   2.00

OLAV V 1957-

94. 1 Krone (C-N) 1958-73. Horse   .40

95. 50 Ore (C-N) 1958-73. Dog   .25
96. 25 Ore (C-N) 1958-73. Bird   .25

97. 10 Ore (C-N) 1958-73. Bee   .20

98. 5 Ore (Bro) 1958-73. Moose .10

99. 2 Ore (Bro) 1958- . Chicken .30
100. 1 Ore (Bro) 1958- . Squirrel .20

101. 10 Kroner 1964. Lion on shield. Rev.
Building (commemorates signing of
constitution in 1814) 6.00

102. 5 Kroner (CN) 1963-73. Bare head of
King. Rev. Shield 1.50

103.

103. 25 Kroner 1970. Conjoined heads of King
Haakon and King Olav. Rev. Mono-
gram and inscription (Commemorates
25th anniversary of liberation from
wartime occupation) 7.50

104. 5 Kroner (C-N) 1974- . Head of King
Olav. Rev. Crowned shield with lion. 1.50

105. 1 Kroner (C-N) 1974- . Head. Rev.
Crown, value .40

106. 50 Ore (C-N) 1974- . Crowned shield
with lion. Rev. Value .25

107. 25 Ore (C-N) 1974- . Value. Rev. Four
crowned monograms .25

108. 10 Ore (C-N) 1974- . Crowned monogram.
Rev. Value .20

109. 5 Ore (Br) 1974- . Lion. Rev. Value .10

NORWAY (continued)

110. 5 Kroner (C-N) 1975. Sailing ship. Rev.
Lion (Commemorates 150th anniversary of emigration to U.S.) 3.00

111. 5 Kroner (C-N) 1975. Seated figure striking
coin with hammer. Rev. Crowned arms
(Commemorates 100th anniversary of
decimal coinage) 3.00

NOVA SCOTIA

On the east coast of Canada, Nova Scotia, formerly known as Acadia, was ceded to the British
by the French in 1713. It is one of the original
provinces of the Dominion of Canada.

1. Penny (C) 1824, 32. Laureated head of
George IV 6.00

2. Halfpenny (C) 1823-24, 32 5.00
3. Penny (C) 1840, 43. Head of Victoria 6.00
4. Halfpenny (C) 1840, 43 4.00
5. Penny (C) 1856. Rev. Maple leaves 6.00
6. Halfpenny (C) 1856 6.00

7. 1 Cent (C) 1861-62, 64. 5.00
8. Half Cent (C) 1861, 64 8.00

OMAN

An independent sultanate at the southeastern tip
of the Arabian peninsula, called Muscat and Oman
until 1970.

200 Baizas = 1 Maria Theresa Dollar

SA'ID BEN TAIMUR 1932-70

1. ½ Ryal 1948, 1961, 62. Arms. Rev. Arabic
inscription 5.00

2. 50 Baizas (C-N) 1940 (scalloped edge) 8.00

3. 20 Baizas (C-N) 1940 (square planchet) 7.50
3a. 20 Baizas (C-N) 1946 (scalloped edge) 2.50
4. 10 Baizas (C-N) 1940 (round) 4.00

5. 5 Baizas (N) 1946 (scalloped edge) 1.50

5a. 5 Baizas (C-N) 1962. Arms. Rev. Native
sailing craft (round planchet) 1.00
6. 3 Baizas (Br) 1961. Arms. Rev. Value .75
7. 2 Baizas (C-N) 1946 (square planchet) 1.00

OMAN (continued)

QABUS BIN SA'ID 1970-
MONETARY REFORM

1000 Baizas = 1 Ryal

8.	100 Baizas (C-N) 1970. Arms. Rev. Value	1.00
9.	50 Baizas (C-N) 1970	.75
10.	25 Baizas (C-N) 1970	.50
11.	10 Baizas (Br) 1970	.35
12.	5 Baizas (Br) 1970	.25
13.	2 Baizas (Br) 1970	.15

14. 10 **Baizas** (Br) 1975. Two palms on island.
Rev. Value (F.A.O. coin plan)

PAKISTAN

In the partition of British India in 1947, Pakistan was formed out of predominantly Moslem areas into a self-governing Dominion within the British Commonwealth of Nations. Subsequently it changed its status to that of Republic within the same framework.

3 Pies = 1 Pice
4 Pice = 1 Anna
16 Annas = 1 Rupee

1.	1 Rupee (N) 1948-49. Toughra in wreath. Rev. Star and crescent in wreath	2.00
2.	½ Rupee (N) 1948-51	.75
3.	¼ Rupee (N) 1948-51	.50
4.	2 Annas (N) 1948-51 (Square-shaped)	.35
5.	1 Anna (N) 1948-52 (Scalloped edge)	.25
6.	½ Anna (C-N) 1948-51 (Square-shaped)	.20
7.	1 Pice (Bro) 1948-52 (Center hole)	.15
8.	2 Annas (C-N) 1953-59 (square planchet)	.50

9. 1 Anna (C-N) 1953-59. Star and crescent, toughra below. Rev. Value (scalloped edge) .25
10. ½ Anna (N-Bra) 1953-58 (square planchet) .20

11. 1 Pice (N-Bra) 1953-59 (round planchet) .15
12. 1 Pie (Br) 1951-56 .15

NEW DECIMAL SYSTEM COINAGE

100 Paisa = 1 Rupee

13. 50 Paisa (N) 1964-68. Star and crescent. toughra below. Rev. Value .50
13a. 50 Paisa (C-N) 1968- . Redesigned reverse .50

PAKISTAN (continued)

13a.

14. 25 Paisa (N) 1964-67 .25
14a. 25 Paisa (C-N) 1967- . Redesigned reverse .25
15. 10 Paisa (C-N) 1961- 63 (scalloped edge, some 1961 coins show denomination as Pice) .35
15a. 10 Paisa (C-N) 1964- Bengali legend. Rev. Numeral "10" .25

16. 16a.

16. 5 Paisa (C-N) 1961- 63. Rev. Sailing craft with value on sail. (Square planchet) .25
16a. 5 Paisa (C-N) 1964- . Bengali legend. Rev. Numeral "5" superimposed on sail .15
17. 2 Paisa (Br) 1964-66; (A) 1966- . Rev. Value (Scalloped edge) .15
18. 1 Paisa (Br) 1961-63. Rev. Value between ears of wheat .15
18a. 1 Paisa (Br) 1964-65; (N-Bra) 1965, 66; (A) 1967- . Bengali legend. Rev. Numeral "1" .15

19. 10 Paisa (A) 1974. Rev. Value in circle of wheat, scalloped planchet (F.A.O. coin plan) .25

20. 5 Paisa (A) 1974. Rev. Value between sugar plants, square planchet (F.A.O. coin plan) .25

21. 2 Paisa (A) 1974. Rev. Value between millet plants, scalloped edge (F.A.O. coin plan) .15
22. 1 Paisa (A) 1974. Rev. Value between cotton plants (F.A.O. coin plan) .10

PALESTINE

An area in the Middle East mandated to Great Britain after World War I. The mandate came to an end in 1948 when the United Nations created the independent state of Israel.

1000 Mils = 1 Pound

1. 100 Mills 1927-42. Olive sprig. Rev. Value 7.50
2. 50 Mils 1927-42 7.00

3. 20 Mils (C-N) 1927-41; (Bro) 42-44 (Center hole). Wreath. Rev. Value 10.00
4. 10 Mils (C-N) 1927-42, 46 ; (Bro) 42-43 (Center hole) 5.00

5. 5 Mils (C-N) 1927-41, 46; (Bro) 42-44 (Center hole) 3.00

6. 2 Mils (Bro) 1927-46. Inscription. Rev. Olive sprig 3.00

7. 1 Mil (Bro) 1927-46 2.50

PANAMA

For centuries Panama was part of the Spanish colony of New Granada, and later a part of Colombia. Panama became independent in 1903.

100 Centesimos = 1 Balboa

1.	50 Centesimos 1904-05. Bust of Balboa. Rev. Arms	25.00
2.	25 Centesimos 1904	15.00
3.	10 Centesimos 1904	10.00
4.	5 Centesimos 1904	7.50

5.	2½ Centesimos 1904 (so-called "Panama Pill")	10.00

5a.	2½ Centesimos (C-N) 1929	3.00
6.	½ Centesimo (C-N) 1907	1.50
7.	5 Centesimos (C-N) 1929-32. Arms. Rev. Value	2.00
8.	2½ Centesimos (C-N) 1907, 16	2.50

LAW OF 1930

9.	1 Balboa 1931, 34, 47. Bust of Balboa. Rev. Female figure and arms	5.00

10.	½ Balboa 1930, 32-34, 47, 62. Rev. Arms	2.50
11.	¼ Balboa 1930-34, 47, 62	1.00

12.	⅒ Balboa 1930-34, 47, 62	.50
13.	2½ Centesimos (C-N) 1940. Rev. Value	1.00
14.	1¼ Centesimos (Bro) 1940	1.00

15.	1 Centesimo (Bro) 1935, 37. Head of Urraca. Rev. Value and spray	2.00

DECREE OF 1953
Fiftieth Anniversary of the Republic

16.	1 Balboa 1953. Bust of Balboa. Rev. Female figure, "Cinquentario" inscription	12.00
17.	½ Balboa 1953. Rev. Arms	2.50
18.	¼ Balboa 1953	3.00
19.	⅒ Balboa 1953	.75
20.	1 Centesimo (Br) 1953. Head of Urraca. Rev. Value	.30
21.	1 Balboa 1966- . Type of #10	10.00
22.	½ Balboa 1961, 62	3.00
22a.	½ Balboa (clad 40% silver) 1966-	1.50
23.	¼ Balboa 1961, 62	1.50
23a.	¼ Balboa (CN clad copper) 1966-	.75
24.	⅒ Balboa 1961, 62	1.00
24a.	⅒ Balboa (C-N clad copper) 1966-	.25

25.	5 Centesimos (C-N) 1961- . Arms. Rev. Value	.20
26.	1 Centesimo (Br) 1961- . Type of #20 without "Cinquentario"	.25

27.   5 Balboas 1970. Arms. Rev. Discus
      thrower (Commemorates 11th Central
      American and Caribbean Games)   10.00

32.   500 Balboas (G) 1975. Balboa kneeling.
      Rev. Arms (Commemorates 500th anni-
      versary of explorer's birth)   575.00

33.   100 Balboas (G) 1975, 76. Bust of Balboa.
      Rev. Arms   135.00

28.   20 Balboas 1971. Simon Bolivar. Rev.
      Arms (Commemorates 150th anniver-
      sary of independence)   50.00
29.   20 Balboas 1972- . Without commemora-
      tive inscription   40.00

34.   5 Balboas 1975. Belisario Porras, former
      president. Rev. Arms

30.   5 Balboas 1972. Hand holding rice. Rev.
      Arms (F.A.O. coin plan)   9.00
31.   2½ Centimos (C-N) 1974   .20

35.   1 Balboa 1975. Type of #33

PANAMA (continued)

36. 50 Centesimos (C-N) 1975. Fernando de
    Lesseps, canal promoter. Rev. Arms

37. 25 Centesimos (C-N) 1975. Justo Arose-
    mena, former president

38. 10 Centesimos (C-N) 1975. Manuel E.
    Amador, creator of national flag

39. 5 Centesimos (C-N) 1975. Carlos Finlay,
    physician and biologist

40. 2½ Centesimos (C-N) 1975. Victoriano
    Lorenzo, Indian leader

41. 1 Centesimo (Br) 1975. Urraca, Indian
    leader

PAPUA NEW GUINEA

Papua New Guinea is comprised of the formerly
separate territories of Papua and New Guinea.

100 Toea = 1 Kina

1. 100 Kina (G) 1975. Bust of Prime Minister
   Somare. Rev. Bird of Paradise, value
   (Commemorates independence)   130.00

2. 10 Kina (C-N) 1975. Arms. Rev. Bird of
   Paradise
2a. 10 Kina (S) 1975-   (proof issue)   35.00

3. 5 Kina (C-N) 1975. Arms. Rev. Eagle   7.00
3a. 5 Kina (S) 1975-   (proof issue)

PAPUA NEW GUINEA (continued)

4. 1 Kina (C-N) 1975- . Emblem of Bank
   of Papua New Guinea. Rev. Crocodiles
   (center hole planchet)   1.50

5. 20 Toea (C-N) 1975- . Arms. Rev.
   Cassowary (flightless bird)   .50

6. 10 Toea (C-N) 1975- . Rev. Spotted
   Cuscus   .25
7. 5 Toea (C-N) 1975- . Rev. Plateless
   turtle

8. 2 Toea (Br) 1975- . Rev. Butterfly cod
9. 1 Toea (Br) 1975- . Rev. Butterfly

PARAGUAY

Paraguay is a landlocked country which became a Spanish colony in the sixteenth century.
For 150 years the Jesuits ran the country and
protected the native Guarani Indians from ex-
termination. Since 1811, when Paraguay gained
its independence from Spain, the country has been
ruled by dictatorships and taken part in several
costly wars.

100 Centavos = 1 Peso
100 Centimos = 1 Guarani

1. 1/12 Real (C) 1845. Lion. Rev. Fraction   20.00
2. 4 Centesimos (C) 1870. Star in wreath.
   Rev. Value   10.00
3. 2 Centesimos (C) 1870   8.00
4. 1 Centesimo (C) 1870   9.00

5. 1 Peso 1889. Seated lion. Rev. Star   95.00
6. 20 Centavos (C-N) 1900, 03   3.00
7. 10 Centavos (C-N) 1900, 03   3.00
8. 5 Centavos (C-N) 1900, 03   3.00

9. 10 Pesos (C-N) 1939. Star in wreath. Rev.
    Value   2.75
10. 5 Pesos (C-N) 1939   2.00
11. 2 Pesos (C-N) 1925; (A) 1938   1.50
12. 1 Peso (C-N) 1925; (A) 1938   1.25
13. 50 Centavos (C-N) 1925; (A) 1938   1.25
14. 20 Centavos (C-N) 1908   8.00
15. 10 Centavos (C-N) 1908   25.00
16. 5 Centavos (C-N) 1908   12.00

PARAGUAY (continued)

17. 50 Centimos (A-Bro) 1944-51. Lion. Rev.
Value 1.00
18. 25 Centimos (A-Bro) 1944-51. Flower .60

19. 10 Centimos (A-Bro) 1944-47. Orchid .50
20. 5 Centimos (A-Bro) 1944-47. Flower .35
21. 1 Centimo (A-Bro) 1944-50. Flower .65

SCALLOPED EDGES

22. 50 Centimos (A-Bro) 1953. Lion. Rev. Value .75
23. 25 Centimos (A-Bro) 1953 .75
24. 15 Centimos (A-Bro) 1953 .50
25. 10 Centimos (A-Bro) 1953 .50

26. 300 Guaranies 1968. President Stroessner.
Rev. Arms 6.00
27. 50 Guaranies (St) 1974. Bust of Marshal
Estigarribia. Rev. Dam, value .50
28. 10 Guaranies (St) 1974. Bust of General
Eugenio Garay. Rev. Cow, value .20
30. 1 Guarani (St) 1974. Soldier. Rev. Tobacco
plant, value .10
29. 5 Guaranies (St) 1974. Woman. Rev.
Cotton plant, value .10

PERU

Prior to the Spanish Conquest, Peru was the setting for a remarkably advanced civilization—that of the Incas. In 1532 Francisco Pizarro, perhaps the greediest and most bloodthirsty of all the Conquistadors, began the subjugation of the Incas. Peru achieved its independence in 1824.

8 Reales = 1 Dollar = 1 Piece-of-Eight
100 Centimos = 1 Real
100 Centavos = 1 Sol
10 Soles = 1 Libra

CHARLES II 1665-1700

1. 8 Reales 1683, 92. Cross, arms. Rev.
Pillars 120.00

2. 2 Reales 1672, 83, 97 45.00

3. 1 Real 1686-95 25.00

PERU • 353

PHILIP V 1700-46

4.	8 Reales 1730	85.00
5.	4 Reales 1730	140.00
6.	2 Reales 1716-42	18.00
7.	1 Real 1707-44	11.00

FERDINAND VI 1746-59

8.	8 Reales 1755-59. Crowned arms. Rev. Globes between pillars; mint mark in legend	85.00
9.	2 Reales 1755-58	25.00
10.	1 Real 1753-59	30.00
11.	½ Real 1756-59	22.00

CHARLES III 1759-88

12.	8 Reales 1764-72. Pillar type	85.00
13.	2 Reales 1762-72	25.00

14.	1 Real 1763-72	20.00
15.	½ Real 1762-70	15.00

16.	8 Reales 1779-88. Laureate bust. Rev. Crowned arms between pillars	25.00
17.	4 Reales 1780-88	45.00
18.	2 Reales 1773-88	4.00
19.	1 Real 1773-88	3.25
20.	½ Real 1779-88	4.00

CHARLES IV 1788-1808

21.	8 Reales 1789, 90. Bust of Charles III	30.00
22.	4 Reales 1790	65.00
23.	2 Reales 1789-91	6.00
24.	1 Real 1789-91	2.50
25.	½ Real 1789-91	2.00
26.	8 Reales 1791-1808. Bust of Charles IV	15.00

27.	4 Reales 1795-1808	55.00

28.	2 Reales 1791-1808	4.00

29. 1 Real 1791-1808   6.00
30. ½ Real 1791-1808   3.50
31. ¼ Real 1792, 93   30.00

32. ¼ Real 1794-1808. Castle. Rev. Lion   8.00

FERDINAND VII 1808-24

33. 8 Reales 1809-12. Unusual laureate bust (peculiar to Lima mint)   20.00
34. 4 Reales 1810   55.00
35. 2 Reales 1810-12   8.00
36. 1 Real 1811   12.00
37. ½ Real 1810-12   10.00
38. 8 Reales 1812-24. Draped laureate bust   15.00

39. 4 Reales 1813-21   35.00
40. 2 Reales 1813-21   4.00
41. 1 Real 1813-23   6.50
42. ½ Real 1812-21   5.00

43. ¼ Real 1813-23. Castle. Rev. Lion   8.50

REPUBLICA PERUANA

44. 8 Reales 1822, 23. Column between standing figures of Virtue and Justice. Rev. Arms   50.00
45. 8 Reales 1825-55. Liberty standing with shield. Rev. Arms (varieties)   25.00
46. 4 Reales 1843-55   15.00

47. 2 Reales 1825-56   5.00
48. 1 Real 1826-61   3.00
49. ½ Real 1826-60   3.00

50. ¼ Real (C) 1822, 23; (S) 1826-56. Llama. Rev. Value   3.50
51. ⅛ Peso (C) 1823   7.00
52. 50 Centavos 1858, 59. Liberty seated. Rev. Arms   25.00
53. 25 Centavos 1859   25.00

54. 1 Libra (G) 1898-1930. Indian head. Rev. Arms   60.00
55. ½ Libra (G) 1902-08   30.00
56. ⅕ Libra (G) 1906-30   20.00

57. 1 Sol 1864-1916, 1923-35. Liberty seated 6.00
58. ½ Sol 1864-65, 1907-17, 22-35 3.00
59. ⅕ Sol 1863-1916 2.50
60. 1 Dinero (¹⁄₁₀ Sol) 1864-1913, 1916 2.00
61. ½ Dinero 1863-1917 1.50
62. 20 Centavos (C-N) 1879. Sun. Rev. Value 6.00

69. ½ Sol (Bra) 1935-65 .40
70. 20 Centavos (Bra) 1942-65. Liberty head .20
71. 10 Centavos (Bra) 1942-65 .15
72. 5 Centavos (Bra) 1942-65 .25
73. 2 Centavos (Z) 1950 - 58. Sun .75
74. 1 Centavo (Z) 1950 - 65 1.00

SPECIAL BULLION ISSUE

75. 100 Gold Soles (G) 1950 - 69.
    Seated Liberty. Rev. Arms 400.00
76. 50 Gold Soles (G) 1950 - 69 225.00
77. 20 Gold Soles (G) 1950 - 69 100.00

62a. 20 Centavos (C-N) 1918-41. Liberty head .75
63. 10 Centavos (C-N) 1879, 80. Type of #62 3.00
63a. 10 Centavos (C-N) 1918-41 .50
64. 5 Centavos (C-N) 1879, 80. Type of #62 2.00
64a. 5 Centavos (C-N) 1918-41 1.50

78. 20 Centavos (A-Bro) 1954. Head of
    Castilla. Rev. Value 7.50
79. 10 Centavos (A-Bro) 1954 5.00
80. 5 Centavos (A-Bro) 1954 2.50

65. 2 Centavos (Bro) 1863-1900, 1917-49. Sun .50
66. 1 Centavo (Bro) 1863-1949 .50

81. 20 Soles 1965. Replica of obverse of 8
    reales coin of type struck at Lima
    mint in 1565. Rev. Arms (Commemo-
    rates 400th anniversary of mint) 3.00
82. 1 Sol (Bra) 1965 .60
83. ½ Sol (Bra) 1965 .45
84. 25 Centavos (Bra) 1965 .25
85. 10 Centavos (Bra) 1965 .15
86. 5 Centavos (Bra) 1965 .35
    .15

67. 50 Soles (G) 1930-31, 67-69. Head of the
    Inca Manco Capac. Rev. Inca symbol 400.00
68. 1 Sol (Bra) 1943-65. Arms. Rev. Value .50

87. 20 Soles 1966. Arms. Rev. Our Lady of
    Victory, Lima statue (Commemorates
    centenary of Spanish bombardment of
    Callao) 6.50

88. 1 Sol (Bra)1966- . Arms. Rev. Vicuna and
    value .50
89. ½ Sol (Bra) 1966 .40

96a. 10 Soles (C-N) 1972- . Without com-
    memorative inscription 1.50
97. 5 Soles (C-N) 1971 1.75
97a. 5 Soles (C-N) 1972- . Without com-
    memorative inscription .75

90. 25 Centavos (Bra) 1966- . Arms. Rev. Can-
    tuta flower .25
91. 10 Centavos (Bra) 1966- .15
92. 5 Centavos (Bra) 1966- .10

98. 100 Soles 1973. Chrysanthemums, value.
    Rev. Arms (Commemorates 100 years
    of trade relations between Japan and
    Peru) 8.50

93. 10 Soles (CN) 1969. Arms. Rev.
    Stylized fish 1.25
94. 5 Soles (CN) 1969. Arms. Rev. Inca
    design .75

99. 200 Soles 1974-75. Heads of J. Chavez and
    J. Quinones, airplane pioneers. Rev.
    Arms 12.00

95. 50 Soles 1971. Tupac Amaru, Indian
    hero. Rev. Arms (Commemorates
    150th anniversary of independence) 12.50
96. 10 Soles (C-N) 1971 3.00

100. 5 Sol (C-N) 1975. Tupac Amaru. Rev.
     Arms
101. 1 Sol (Bra) 1975. Arms. Rev. Value
102. ½ Sol (Bra) 1975
103. 20 Centavos (Bra) 1975
104. 10 Centavos (Bra) 1975

PHILIPPINE ISLANDS

A group of 7000 islands in the southwest Pacific which were under Spanish rule from the sixteenth century until the end of the Spanish-American War, when they passed to the United States. The Philippines gained partial freedom in 1935 and complete independence in 1946.

100 Centimos = 1 Peseta
100 Centavos = 1 Peso

UNDER SPAIN
ISABELLA II 1833-68

1.	4 Pesos (G) 1861-68. Laureated head. Rev. Crowned arms between pillars	125.00
2.	2 Pesos (G) 1861-68	80.00
3.	1 Peso (G) 1861-68	100.00
4.	50 Centimos 1865-68	12.50
5.	20 Centimos 1864-68	7.50
6.	10 Centimos 1864-68	15.00

ALFONSO XII 1874-85

7.	50 Centimos 1880-85. Head. Rev. Type of #1	5.00
8.	20 Centimos 1880-85	5.00
9.	10 Centimos 1880-85	3.50

ALFONSO XIII 1886-1898

10.	1 Peso 1897. Head. Rev. Type of #1	20.00

UNDER THE UNITED STATES

11.	1 Peso 1903-06. Standing female figure representing "Filipinas," Mayon volcano in background. Rev. U.S. arms	7.50
11a.	1 Peso 1907-12 (reduced size planchet)	5.00

12.	50 Centavos 1903-06	6.00
12a.	50 Centavos 1907-21 (reduced size)	2.00
13.	20 Centavos 1903-06	1.75
13a.	20 Centavos 1907-29 (reduced size)	1.50
14.	10 Centavos 1903-06	1.50
14a.	10 Centavos 1907-35 (reduced size)	1.00

15.	5 Centavos (C-N) 1903-28. Workman with anvil, Mayon volcano	1.00
15a.	5 Centavos (C-N) 1930-35 (reduced size)	1.25
16.	1 Centavo (Br) 1903-36	2.00
17.	½ Centavo (Br) 1903-08	.75

COMMONWEALTH OF THE PHILIPPINES
(1935-46)

18.	1 Peso 1936. Busts of Pres. Roosevelt and Pres. Quezon. Rev. Arms of Commonwealth	45.00
19.	1 Peso 1936. Busts of Gov. Genl. Murphy and Pres. Quezon	45.00

20.	50 Centavos 1936. Facing busts of Gov. Murphy and Pres. Quezon	25.00

REPUBLIC OF THE PHILIPPINES

21. 50 Centavos 1944-45. Female figure and volcano. Rev. Philippine arms with eagle above ... 1.25
22. 20 Centavos 1937-45 ... .60
23. 10 Centavos 1937-45 ... .20
24. 5 Centavos (C-N) 1937-41; (N-S) 1944-45. Workman and volcano ... .15
25. 1 Centavo (Br) 1937-44 ... .15

26. 1 Peso 1947 (MacArthur Commemorative). Bust of Genl. MacArthur. Rev. Shield ... 5.00
27. 50 Centavos 1947 ... 3.00

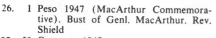

28. 50 Centavos (C-N) 1958-64. Standing figure. Rev. Arms ... 1.00
29. 25 Centavos (C-N) 1958-66 ... .50
30. 10 Centavos (C-N) 1958-66 ... .35
31. 5 Centavos (Bra) 1958-66. Seated figure ... .20
32. 1 Centavo (Bra) 1958-63. ... .10

33. 1 Peso 1961. Head of Dr. Jose Rizal (centennial commemorative) ... 10.00
34. ½ Peso 1961. Rizal ... 3.00

35. 1 Peso 1963. Head of Andres Bonifacio. Rev. Arms (Commemorates 100th anniversary of birth of national hero) ... 6.00

36. 1 Peso 1964. Head of Apolinario Mabini. Rev. Arms (Commemorates 100th anniversary of birth of national hero) ... 6.00

37. 1 Peso 1967. Broken sword in flames. Rev. Arms (Commemorates 25th anniversary of Bataan March) ... 6.00

FILIPINO HEROES ISSUE

38. 50 Sentimos (CNZ) 1967. Head of Marcelo H. del Pilar. Rev. Arms (legends in Tagalog) ... .50

39. 25 Sentimos (CNZ) 1967- . Head of Juan
    Luna. Rev. Arms .35
40. 10 Sentimos (CNZ) 1967- . Head of Fran-
    cisco Baltazar. Rev. Arms .25

41. 5 Sentimos (CZ) 1967- . Head of Melchora
    Aguino .15
42. 1 Sentimo (Al) 1967- . Head of Chief
    Lapu-Lapu .10

43. 1 Piso 1969. Head of Emilio Aguinaldo
    Rev. Arms (Commemorates 100th
    anniversary of general's birth) 6.00

44. 1 Piso (N) 1970. Bust of Pope Paul VI.
    Rev. Bust of Ferdinand Marcos (Com-
    memorates papal visit) 2.00
44a. 1 Piso (S) 1970 10.00
44b. 1 Piso (G) 1970 800.00

45. 1 Piso (C-N) 1972- . Bust of Jose Rizal.
    Rev. Arms 1.00

46. 25 Piso 1974. Bank building. Rev. Arms
    (Commemorates 25th anniversary of
    Central Bank of the Philippines) 7.50
47. 1000 Piso (G) 1975. Bust of Marcos. Rev.
    Arms (Commemorates 3rd anniversary
    of New Society Program) 150.00

48. 50 Piso 1975. Bust of President Marcos.
    Rev. Arms
49. 25 Piso 1975. Bust of Aguinaldo, president
    of first Philippine Republic
50. 5 Piso (N) 1975. Type of #48

51. 1 Piso (C-N) 1975. Bust of Rizal, author
    and patriot
52. 25 Sentimos (C-N) 1975. Bust of Luna,
    artist and patriot

53. 10 Sentimos (C-N) 1975. Bust of Baltasar,
    poet
54. 5 Sentimos (C-Z) 1975. Bust of Aquino,
    patriot (scalloped planchet)
55. 1 Sentimo (A) 1975. Bust of Lapulapu,
    warrior chief (square planchet)

POLAND

Toward the end of the eighteenth century the Kingdom of Poland was divided up by Russia, Austria and Prussia. After World War I Poland became an independent country, only to lose its freedom once more in 1940. After World War II Poland became a "People's Republic" under Russian domination.

24 Groschen = 1 Taler
100 Groszy = 1 Zloty

SIGISMUND III 1587-1632

56. 1500 Piso (G) 1976. Four logos of international banking organizations. Rev. Map (Commemorates International Monetary Fund—World Bank meeting) 135.00
57. 50 Piso 1976

1. Taler 1587-1632. Crowned bust with sword.
   Rev. Arms   160.00
2. ½ Taler 1587-1632   55.00
3. ¼ Taler 1587-1632   22.00

4. 6 Groschen 1587-1632. Crowned bust in ruff collar   12.00

5. 3 Groschen 1587-1632   5.00
6. 1 Groschen 1587-1632   4.00

POLAND (continued)

VLADISLAV IV 1632-48

7. Taler 1633-44. Crowned bust holding sword
   and ball   150.00

JOHN CASIMIR 1648-69

8. Taler 1648-69. Three-quarter crowned bust.
   Rev. Arms   225.00

JOHN III SOBIESKI 1674-96

8a. Orte 1679   12.00

AUGUST II 1697-1733

9. Taler 1697-1733. Laureate bust. Rev. Arms   125.00

AUGUST III 1733-63

10. Taler 1733-63. Crowned bust. Rev. Arms   100.00

STANISLAUS AUGUST 1764-95

11. Taler 1764-95. Bust. Rev. Arms   100.00

POLISH REPUBLIC 1918-39

12. 50 Groszy (N) 1923. Eagle. Rev. Value
    in wreath   1.25
13. 20 Groszy (N) 1923   1.00
14. 10 Groszy (N) 1923   1.00
15. 5 Groszy (Bro) 1923-38. Eagle. Rev.
    Value on scroll   .75
16. 2 Groszy (Bro) 1923-38   .50
17. 1 Grosz (Bro) 1923-38   .40

18. 20 Zlotych (G) 1925. Head of Boleslaus I.
    Rev. Eagle   75.00
19. 10 Zlotych (G) 1925   50.00

20. 5 Zlotych (1925). Seated and standing
    figures. Rev. Eagle. One of the rarest
    of modern coins   250.00
21. 2 Zlote 1924-25. Peasant girl. Rev. Eagle   5.00
22. 1 Zloty 1924-25   2.50

23. 5 Zlotych 1928-32. Winged figure. Rev.
    Eagle   17.00

POLAND (continued)

24.   5 Zlotych 1930. Flags and inscription.
      Rev. Eagle. Centenary of Revolution
      of 1830   15.00

25. 10 Zlotych 1932-33. Female head. Rev.
      Eagle   7.50
26.   5 Zlotych 1932-34   3.50
27.   2 Zlote 1932-34   2.00

28. 10 Zlotych 1933. Bust of Jan Sobieski.
      Rev. Eagle (250th anniversary of relief
      of siege of Vienna)   12.50
29. 10 Zlotych 1933. Bust of Traugutt. Rev.
      Eagle (70th anniversary of 1863 in-
      surrection)   12.50

30. 10 Zlotych 1934. Head of Pilsudski. Rev.
      Eagle (Commemorates 20th anniversary
      of Rifle Corps' entry into field in 1914) 12.50

30a. 10 Zlotych 1934-39. Head of Pilsudski
      (regular issue, no badge under eagle)   6.00
31.   5 Zlotych 1934 (Rifle Corps)   6.50
31a. 5 Zlotych 1934-36 (regular issue)   3.50
32.   2 Zlote 1934-36   3.00

33.   5 Zlotych 1936. Sailing ship. Rev.
      Eagle   6.00
34.   2 Zlote 1936   3.50

POSTWAR REPUBLIC 1946-

35.   1 Zloty (C-N) 1949. Eagle. Rev. Value   2.50
35a. 1 Zloty (A) 1949   1.00

36. 50 Groszy (C-N) 1949   1.50
36a. 50 Groszy (A) 1949   .50
37. 20 Groszy (C-N) 1949   .75
37a. 20 Groszy (A) 1949   .50
38. 10 Groszy (C-N) 1949   .60
38a. 10 Groszy (A) 1949   .30
39.   5 Groszy (Bro) 1949   .80
39a. 5 Groszy (A) 1949   .75
40.   2 Groszy (A) 1949   .20
41.   1 Grosz (A) 1949   .15

42. 10 Zlotych (C-N) 1959, 65. Head of Coper-
      nicus. Rev. Eagle   4.50
42a. 10 Zlotych (C-N) 1967- . Smaller planchet   2.00
43. 10 Zlotych (C-N) 1959-66. Head of Kos-
      ciuszko. Rev. Eagle   3.50
43a. 10 Zlotych (C-N) 1969- . Smaller planchet   2.00

44. 5 Zlotych (A) 1958-   Fisherman and
      net   1.00
45. 2 Zlote (A) 1958-   Eagle. Rev. Value   .75
46. 1 Zloty (A) 1957-   .75
47. 50 Groszy (A) 1957-   .60
48. 20 Groszy (A) 1957-   .45
49. 10 Groszy (A) 1961-   .25

54. 100 Zlotych 1966. Obv. Eagle. Rev.
      Figures of Miesyko and Dabrowka,
      first king and queen (Commemorates
      1000th anniversary of Polish state)   12.50

50. 10 Zlotych (C-N) 1964. Crowned head
      of King Casimir the Great. Rev. Polish
      eagle (Commemorates 600th anniver-
      sary of Jagiello University in Cracow)   4.00
50a. 10 Zlotych (C-N) 1964. Type of #50 with
      incuse legends   4.00

55. 10 Zlotych (CN) 1967. Portrait of General
      Karol Swierczewski Walter. Rev. Polish
      eagle (Honors 20th anniversary of
      death)   2.00

56. 10 Zlotych (CN) 1967. Portrait of Marie
      Curie. Rev. Polish eagle. (Commem-
      orates 100th anniversary of scientist's
      birth)   2.00

51. 10 Zlotych (C-N) 1965. Nike with
      sword. Rev. Eagle (Commemorates
      Warsaw's 700th anniversary)   3.50

57. 10 Zlotych (CN) 1968. Eagle. Rev. xxv
      and soldier (Commemorates 25th
      anniversary of People's Army)   2.00

52. 10 Zlotych (C-N) 1965. Commemorative
      column. Rev. Eagle (Warsaw's 700th
      anniversary)   3.50
53. 10 Zlotych (CN) 1966. Type of #52 with
      edge inscription (Commemorates 200th
      anniversary of Warsaw Mint)   3.50

58.

POLAND (continued)

58. 10 Zlotych (CN) 1969. Eagle. Rev. Sheaf of grain (Commemorates 25th anniversary of People's Republic) — 1.75

59. 10 Zlotych (CN) 1970. Eagle. Rev. Arms of former German provinces (Commemorates 25th anniversary of annexation of western and northern provinces) — 1.75

60. 10 Zlotych (C-N) 1971. Fish with wheat superimposed. Rev. Arms, value (F.A.O. coin plan) — 1.75

61. 10 Zlotych (C-N) 1971. Monument in Katowia, Silesia. Rev. Arms (Commemorates 50th anniversary of Third Silesian Uprising) — 1.75

62. 50 Zlotych 1972- . Head of Chopin. Rev. Arms, value — 10.00

63.

63. 10 Zlotych (C-N) 1972. Aerial view of Gdynia-Gdansk (formerly Danzig). Rev. Arms, value (Commemorates 50th anniversary of seaport) — 1.75

64. 100 Zlotych 1973, 74. Head of Copernicus. Rev. Arms (Commemorates 500th anniversary of astronomer's birth) — 12.50

65. 20 Zlotych (C-N) 1973, 74. Field of wheat, silo in background. Rev. Arms within band — 1.50

66. 200 Zlotych 1974. Map, plaque superimposed. Rev. Arms (Commemorates 30th anniversary of republic) — 6.00

67. 100 Zlotych 1974. Marie Curie with rays of radium. Rev. Arms (Commemorates 40th anniversary of physicist's death) — 10.00

68.   20 Zlotych (C-N) 1974. Marceli Nowotko, first secretary of Polish Communist Party. Rev. Arms   1.50

73.   100 Zlotych 1975. Helena Modrzejewska, actress

74.   100 Zlotych 1975. Ignacy Paderewski, composer and pianist

75.   100 Zlotych 1975. Ludwig Zamenhof, creator of Esperanto

69.   20 Zlotych (C-N) 1974. Legend within half cogwheel, half wheel. Rev. Arms (Commemorates 25th anniversary of East European Communist Block trade partnership)   1.50

76.   10 Zlotych (C-N) 1975. Bust of Adam Mickiewicz. Rev. Arms (Commemorates 120th anniversary of poet's death)

70.   200 Zlotych 1975. Conjoined busts of soldiers. Rev. Arms (Commemorates 30th anniversary, end of World War II)

77.   10 Zlotych (C-N) 1975. Bust of Boleslaw Prus, novelist

78.   2 Zlotych (A) 1975. Eagle. Rev. Value, wheat

71.   100 Zlotych 1975. Royal Castle in Warsaw. Rev. Arms   10.00

72.   100 Zlotych 1975. Zamek Krolewski

PORTUGAL

Despite Portugal's small size, this country managed to build up the third largest colonial empire of modern times. Profiting by the country's long Atlantic coastline, Portuguese mariners ventured further and further until they founded a vast empire for the mother country. Portugal was a monarchy until 1910, when it became a republic.

1000 Reis = 1 Crown
100 Centavos = 1 Escudo

MONARCHY
JOHN V (Ioannes) 1706-50

1.	8 Escudos or "Johanna" (G) 1723-32. Bust. Rev. Arms	rare
2.	4 Escudos or "Half Johanna" (G) 1723-50	1000.00

3.	400 Reis 1706-50. Type of #19	22.00
4.	200 Reis 1719-49	10.00
5.	100 Reis (undated)	6.00

JOSEPH I (Josephus) 1750-77

6.	400 Reis 1750-75	30.00
7.	200 Reis 1750-75	15.00
8.	100 Reis (undated)	8.00

MARY I and PETER III 1777-86

9.	400 Reis 1778-86	30.00

10.	200 Reis 1778-82	15.00
11.	100 Reis (undated)	7.50
12.	50 Reis (undated)	5.00

MARY I 1786-99

13.	400 Reis 1786-99	30.00
14.	300 Reis 1794	12.00
15.	200 Reis 1786-99	10.00
16.	150 Reis 1794-95	10.00
17.	100 Reis (undated)	6.00
18.	50 Reis (undated)	4.00

JOHN (Prince) 1799-1801

19.	400 Reis 1799-1801. Crowned square shield. Rev. Cross with motto: *In Hoc Signo Vinces*	25.00
20.	120 Reis (undated)	8.00
21.	60 Reis (undated)	6.00
22.	LXXX Reis (undated). Rev. Cross of St. George	5.00
23.	XXXX Reis (undated)	4.00

JOHN (Prince Regent) 1802-16

24.	400 Reis 1802-16. Type of #19	15.00
25.	200 Reis 1806-16	60.00
26.	120 Reis (undated)	4.00
27.	60 Reis (undated)	3.00

28.	LXXX Reis (undated)	3.50
29.	XXXX Reis (undated)	2.00

MARY II 1828-53
54.   400 Reis 1833-37. Crowned square shield   20.00

30.	40 Reis (Bro) 1811-16. Bust. Rev. Crowned oval shield	4.00
31.	10 Reis (C) 1803-13. Crowned arms. Rev. Value in wreath	2.00
32.	5 Reis (C) 1804-14	2.00
33.	3 Reis (C) 1804	3.00

JOHN VI (King) 1816-26

34.	400 Reis 1818-25. Crowned square shield on globe	20.00
35.	200 Reis 1818-22	75.00
36.	120 Reis (undated)	4.00
37.	60 Reis (undated)	3.50
38.	LXXX Reis (undated)	5.00
39.	XXXX Reis (undated)	2.50
40.	40 Reis (C) 1817-25	3.00

55.	1000 Reis 1836-45. Diademed bust. Rev. Crowned arms with mantle	100.00
56.	500 Reis 1836-53	15.00
57.	200 Reis 1836-48. Rev. Value	17.50
58.	100 Reis 1836-53	5.00
59.	10 Reis (C) 1830-53. Crowned arms. Rev. Value	3.00
60.	5 Reis (C) 1830-53	3.50

PETER V 1853-61

61.	500 Reis 1854-59. Head. Crowned arms with mantle	15.00
62.	200 Reis 1854-61. Rev. Value	5.00
63.	100 Reis 1854-61	4.00
64.	50 Reis 1855, 61. Rev. Crowned date	5.00

41.	10 Reis (C) 1818-25	2.50
42.	5 Reis (C) 1818-24	8.00

PETER IV 1826-28

43.	400 Reis 1826-27. Crowned square shield	75.00
44.	40 Reis (Bro) 1826-28. Bust. Rev. Type of #30	5.00

MICHAEL I 1828-33

45.	400 Reis 1828-34. Crowned square shield	100.00
46.	200 Reis 1829-30	60.00
47.	120 Reis (undated)	8.00
48.	60 Reis (undated)	6.00
49.	LXXX Reis (undated)	25.00
50.	XXXX Reis (undated)	15.00
51.	40 Reis (Bro) 1828-34. Crowned arms. Rev. Value in wreath	3.00
52.	10 Reis (C) 1829-33	3.50
53.	5 Reis (C) 1829	4.00

LOUIS I 1861-89

65.	500 Reis 1863-89. Head. Crowned arms in wreath	7.00
66.	200 Reis 1862-88. Rev. Value	3.50

67.	100 Reis 1864-89	3.50
68.	50 Reis 1862-89. Rev. Crowned date	4.00

69.	20 Reis (C) 1867-74. Crowned arms. Rev. Value in wreath	4.00
69a.	20 Reis (Br) 1882-86. Bust. Rev. Value in wreath	1.00
70.	10 Reis (C) 1867-74	3.00
70a.	10 Reis (Br) 1882-86. Type of #69a	1.25
71.	5 Reis (C) 1867-79	3.50
71a.	5 Reis (Br) 1882-86. Type of #69a	1.50
72.	3 Reis (C) 1868-75	4.00

CHARLES I 1889-1908

73.	1000 Reis 1899. Head. Rev. Crowned arms with mantle	12.50
74.	500 Reis 1891-1908. Rev. Arms in wreath	3.50
75.	200 Reis 1891-1903	3.00
76.	100 Reis 1890-98	5.00
77.	50 Reis 1893. Rev. Crowned date	5.50
78.	100 Reis (N) 1900. Crowned arms. Rev. Value	.75
79.	50 Reis (N) 1900	.85
80.	20 Reis (C) 1891-92. Head. Rev. Value in wreath	.75
81.	10 Reis (C) 1891-92	.75
82.	5 Reis (C) 1890-1906	.75

83.	1000 Reis 1898 (#83, 84, and 85 commemorate the 400th anniversary of the discovery of the route to the Indies). Conjoined busts. Rev. Cross with motto: *In Hoc Signo Vinces*	15.00
84.	500 Reis 1898	7.50
85.	200 Reis 1898	6.00

MANUEL II 1908-10

86.	500 Reis 1908-09. Head. Rev. Crowned arms in wreath	6.00

87.	200 Reis 1909. Rev. Crowned value in wreath	2.75
88.	100 Reis 1909-10	2.50

89.	1000 Reis 1910 (Centenary of the Peninsular War). Head. Rev. Crowned shield	30.00
90.	500 Reis 1910	20.00

91.	500 Reis 1910 (Marquis de Pombal Commemorative). Head. Figures with shield	12.50

REPUBLIC 1910-26

92.	1 Escudo 1914, dated 1910 (Commemorating founding of the republic). Rev. Arms in wreath	17.50

93. 1 Escudo 1915-16. Republic head. Rev.
Type of #92   8.50
94. 50 Centavos 1912-16   2.50
95. 20 Centavos 1913, 16   2.00
96. 10 Centavos 1915   1.00

107. 10 Escudos 1932-48. Caravel. Rev. Arms
over value   5.00
108. 5 Escudos 1932-51   1.50
109. 2½ Escudos 1932-51   1.00

97. 1 Escudo (A-Bro) 1924, 26. Republic
with flag. Rev. Arms   1.00
98. 50 Centavos (A-Bro) 1924 - 26   .75

110. 20 Escudos 1960 (500th anniversary of
death of Prince Henry the Naviga-
tor). Rev. Arms   10.00
111. 10 Escudos 1960   6.00
112. 5 Escudos 1960   3.00

99. 20 Centavos (C-N) 1920-22; (Br) 1924, 25.
Republic head. Rev. Value   .35
100. 10 Centavos (C-N) 1920-21; (Br) 1924-40   .30
101. 5 Centavos (Br) 1924-27   .25
102. 5 Centavos (Bro) 1920-22. Arms. Rev.
Value   .40
103. 4 Centavos (Bro) 1917, 19. Republic
head. Rev. Value   .25
104. 2 Centavos (Bro) 1918-21. Type of
#102   .20
105. 1 Centavo (Bro) 1917-22   .30

113. 20 Escudos 1953. Seated figure. Rev.
Shield with Quinas cross over globe   8.00
114. 10 Escudos 1954- 55. Sailing ship   5.00

NEW STATE 1926-

115. 5 Escudos (C-N) 1963- . Sailing ship.
Rev. Shield with Quinas cross   .65
116. 2½ Escudos (C-N) 1963-   .40

106. 10 Escudos 1928 (Commemorating the
Battle of Ourique, fought in 1139).
Mounted knight. Rev. Shield with
cross   7.50

117. 1 Escudo (N-Br) 1927-68. Head of
Republic. Rev. Arms and value   .40

118. 50 Centavos (N-Br) 1927-68   .35

119. 20 Centavos (Br) 1942-68. Quinas cross.
      Rev. Value   .20
120. 10 Centavos (Bro) 1942-69   .15

121. 20 Escudos 1966. Bridge. Rev. Arms
      (commemorates new Salazar Bridge
      at Lisbon)   3.50

122. 50 Escudos 1968. Bust of Pedro Alvares
      Cabral. Rev. Arms (Commemorates
      500th anniversary of birth of dis-
      coverer of Brazil)   7.50

123. 50 Escudos 1969. Vasco da Gama. Rev.
      Arms (Commemorates 500th anni-
      versary of explorer's birth   7.50

124. 50 Escudos 1969. Marshal Carmona.
      Rev. Arms (Commemorates 100th
      anniversary of former president's
      birth)   12.00

125. 1 Escudo (Br) 1969-   Quinas Cross.
      Rev. Value   .25
126. 50 Centavos (Br) 1969-   .15
127. 20 Centavos (Br) 1969-   .10

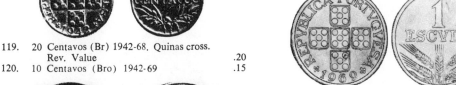

128. 50 Escudos 1971. Tree. Rev. Quinas
      cross (Commemorates 125th anniver-
      sary of Bank of Portugal)   12.00
129. 10 Escudos (C-N) 1971- . Type of #115 1.25

130. 10 Centavos (A) 1971- . Type of #119,
      value in numerals   .10

131. 50 Escudos 1972. Angel standing within
      lyre. Rev. Arms (Commemorates
      400th anniversary of publication of
      "Os Lusiadadas")   12.00
132. 250 Escudos 1976. Arms and value. Rev.
      Abstract design, commemorative date
      (Commemorates 1974 Day of the
      Revolution)
133. 100 Escudos 1976. Rev. Abstract design,
      commemorative date

124.

PORTUGUESE GUINEA

A Portuguese overseas province on the west coast of Africa. It was discovered by the Portuguese in 1446, and remained a colony until 1974, when it became the independent republic of Guinea-Bissau.

100 Centavos = 1 Escudo

1.	1 Escudo (N-Br) 1933. Head of Republic. Rev. Arms and value	2.00
2.	50 Centavos (N-Br) 1933	3.50
3.	20 Centavos (Bro) 1933. Head of Republic (young head). Rev. Value	1.25
4.	10 Centavos (Bro) 1933	1.00
5.	5 Centavos (Bro) 1933	2.00

6.	1 Escudo (Bro) 1946. (500th anniversary of discovery of Portuguese Guinea). Crowned shield. Rev. Value	1.25
7.	50 Centavos (Bro) 1946	1.00
8.	20 Escudos 1952. Arms. Rev. Crowned shield	3.50
9.	10 Escudos 1952	2.00
10.	2½ Escudos (C-N) 1952	.60
11.	50 Centavos (Bro) 1952. Crowned shield Rev. Value	.35

12.	10 Escudos (C-N) 1973. Type of #9	4.00
13.	5 Escudos (C-N) 1973	1.75
14.	1 Escudo (Br) 1973. Type of #6	2.50
15.	20 Centavos (Br) 1973. Type of #3	4.50
16.	10 Centavos (A) 1973	3.50

PORTUGUESE INDIA

This former Portuguese overseas province, made up of Goa, Daman, and Diu, was held by the Portuguese for 400 years. In December 1961 India invaded and annexed this area.

16 Tangas = 1 Rupia
100 Centavos = 1 Escudo

1.	1 Rupia 1912. Head of the Republic. Rev. Value in wreath	15.00
2.	1 Rupia 1935. Arms on cross. Rev. Shield over value	8.00
3.	½ Rupia 1936	10.00
4.	4 Tangas (C-N) 1934. Shield over date. Rev. Arms over value	4.00
5.	2 Tangas (C-N) 1934	3.50

6.	1 Tanga (Bro) 1934	3.00
7.	1 Rupia (S) 1947. Arms on cross over date. Rev. Crowned shield over value	6.00
8.	½ Rupia (C-N) 1947-52. Crowned shield over date. Rev. Value	1.75
9.	¼ Rupia (C-N) 1947-52	1.00
10.	1 Tanga (Bro) 1947	1.00
10a.	1 Tanga (Br) 1952 (smaller planchet)	.50

NEW MONETARY SYSTEM 1958

11.	6 Escudos (C-N) 1959. Arms on cross. Shield	3.00
12.	3 Escudos (C-N) 1958,59	1.75
13.	1 Escudo (C-N) 1958, 59	1.25
14.	60 Centavos (C-N) 1958	1.00

15.	30 Centavos (Br) 1958-59. Shield. Rev. Value	.75
16.	10 Centavos (Br) 1958-61	.75

PRINCE EDWARD ISLAND

A former crown colony in the Gulf of St. Lawrence, Prince Edward Island became a province of the Dominion of Canada in 1873.

1. 1 Cent (Bro) 1871. Head of Victoria. Rev. Trees   5.00

PUERTO RICO

A former possession of Spain, this island was ceded to the United States after the Spanish-American war. It is now a self-governing Commonwealth of the United States.

1. 1 Peso 1895. Young head of Alfonso XIII of Spain. Rev. Spanish arms   150.00
2. 40 Centavos 1896   90.00
3. 20 Centavos 1896   17.50
4. 10 Centavos 1896   15.00
5. 5 Centavos 1896   10.00

QATAR AND DUBAI

In 1966, Qatar and Dubai set up a joint currency, the rial. Except for the joint currency these are separate nations.

Qatar is an independent Sheikhdom on the Persian Gulf. Dubai, on the southern shore of the Persian Gulf, is one of seven semi-independent sheikhdoms in Trucial Oman ("The Trucial States") in Asia Minor. Great Britain is responsible for the foreign affairs of both states.

1. 50 Dirhem (CN) 1966. Gazelle. Rev. Inscription   1.25
2. 25 Dirhem (CN) 1966, 69   .85
3. 10 Dirhem (Br) 1966   .50
4. 5 Dirhem (Br) 1966; (A) 1969   .35
5. 1 Dirhem (Br) 1966; (A) 1973   .25

QATAR

Qatar declared its independence in 1971

1. 50 Dirhem (C-N) 1973. Native dhow. Rev. Value   .75
2. 25 Dirhem (C-N) 1973   .50
3. 10 Dirhem (Br) 1973   .35
4. 5 Dirhem (Br) 1973   .25
5. 1 Dirhem (Br) 1973   .15
7. 50 Francs (C-N) 1972. Native design. Rev. Value (F.A.O. coin plan)   1.50

REUNION

Reunion, an island in the Indian Ocean slightly more than 400 miles east of Madagascar, was settled by the French in 1646. It is an overseas department in the French Community.

100 Centimes = 1 Franc

2.

1.	1 Franc 1896. Mercury head. Rev. Value	17.50
2.	50 Centimes 1896	12.50

3.	2 Francs (A) 1948-	.40
4.	1 Franc (A) 1948-	.25

5.	5 Francs (A-Bro) 1955-	.75
6.	100 Francs (N) 1964- . Liberty head with winged cap. Rev. Arms	2.00

7.	50 Francs (N) 1962-	1.50
8.	20 Francs (A-Bro) 1955-	1.25
9.	10 Francs (A-Bro) 1955-	1.00

RHODESIA AND NYASALAND

The Central African Federation of Rhodesia and Nyasaland, 1953-1963, comprised Southern Rhodesia (now Rhodesia, a republic since 1970), Northern Rhodesia (Zambia since 1964), and Nyasaland (Malawi since 1963).

12 Pence = 1 Shilling
20 Shillings = 1 Pound

SOUTHERN RHODESIA

GEORGE V 1910-1936

1.	½ Crown (2½ Shillings) 1932-36. Crowned bust. Rev. Crowned arms	10.00

2.	2 Shillings 1932, 34-36. Rev. Antelope	10.00
3.	1 Shilling 1932-36. Rev. Stone bird	7.00

4.	6 Pence 1932-36. Rev. Axes	2.50
5.	3 Pence 1932-36. Rev. Three spears	2.50

6.	1 Penny (C-N) 1934-36 (Center hole). Crowned rose. Rev. Value	2.50
7.	½ Penny (C-N) 1934, 36	2.50

RHODESIA AND NYASALAND (continued)

GEORGE VI 1936-52

(Coins issued after 1948 drop "Emperor" from the obverse legend)

17. 2 Shillings (C-N) 1954. Rev. Type of #9   20.00
18. 1 Penny (Bro) 1954. Rev. Type of #6   7.50
19. ½ Penny (Bro) 1954   5.00

RHODESIA AND NYASALAND

20. ½ Crown (C-N)1955-57. Head. Rev. Arms   3.00

21. 2 Shillings (C-N) 1955-57. Rev. Eagle holding fish in talons   4.00
22. 1 Shilling (C-N) 1955-57. Rev. Antelope   3.00

23. 6 Pence (C-N) 1955-63. Rev. Lioness   1.50
24. 3 Pence (C-N) 1955-64. Rev. Flower   .75

8. ½ Crown 1937-46. Crowned head. Rev.
Crowned arms   10.00
8a. ½ Crown (C-N) 1947-52   5.00
9. 2 Shillings 1937-46. Rev. Antelope   7.50
9a. 2 Shillings (C-N) 1947-52   3.50
10. 1 Shilling 1937-46. Rev. Stone bird   3.50
10a. 1 Shilling (C-N) 1947-52   2.00
11. 6 Pence 1937-46 Rev. Axes   3.00
11a. 6 Pence (C-N) 1947-52   1.00
12. 3 Pence 1937-46. Rev. Three spears   2.50
12a. 3 Pence (C-N) 1947-52   1.50
13. 1 Penny (C-N) 1937-42; (Bro) 1942-52.
Rev. Crowned rose.   3.00
14. ½ Penny (C-N) 1938-39; (Bro) 1942-52   3.00

ELIZABETH II 1952-

15. Crown 1953 (Rhodes Commemorative Crown). Head. Rev. Portrait of Rhodes and arms   15.00
16. ½ Crown (C-N) 1954. Crowned head. Rev. Type of #8   10.00

25. 1 Penny (Bro) 1955-63 (Center hole). Two elephants, crown above. Rev. Value and ornaments   .75
26. ½ Penny (Bro) 1955-64 (Center hole). Two giraffes and crown. Rev. Type of #30   .50

RHODESIA

27. ½ Crown *or* 25 Cents (C-N) 1964. New portrait of Queen Elizabeth with coronet. Rev. Antelope (reverses show dual values of sterling and decimal system) — 2.50

28. 2 Shillings *or* 20 Cents (C-N) 1964. Rev. Stonebird — 2.00
29. 1 Shilling *or* 10 Cents (C-N) 1964. Rev. Arms — 1.00
30. 6 Pence *or* 5 Cents (C-N) 1964. Rev. Lily — .50

31. 3 Cents (CN) 1968. Rev. Three spear-heads — .30

REPUBLIC

32. 2½ Cents (CN) 1970- . Arms. Rev. Spears — .25
33. 1 Cent (Br) 1970- . Arms. Rev. Value — .15
34. ½ Cent (Br) 1970- . Arms. Rev. Value — .15

35. 5 Cents (C-N) 1973. Rev. Lily — .40
35a. 5 Cents (C-N) 1975. Smaller arms, inscription change

In the nineteenth century Rumania was formed from the Turkish provinces of Moldavia and Walachia. The country suffered heavily in both world wars. After World War II Rumania became a "People's Republic" in the Russian orbit.

100 Bani = 1 Leu

CAROL I 1866-1914

1. 50 Lei (G) 1906. Bust in uniform. Rev. Carol on horseback — 300.00
2. 25 Lei (G) 1906. Bust in uniform. Rev. Crowned eagle — 150.00
3. 12½ Lei (G) 1906 — 100.00
4. 5 Lei 1880-84, 1901. Head. Rev. Crowned arms on mantle — 25.00

5. 5 Lei 1906. Young head. Rev. Older bearded head. Commemorating fortieth jubilee — 50.00
6. 2 Lei 1881-1901, 1910-14. Bearded head — 3.50

7. 1 Leu 1870-1901, 1906, 10-14 — 3.00

8.	50 Bani 1881-1901. Rev. Value in wreath	3.00
8a.	50 Bani 1910-14. Rev. Crowned olive branch	2.00
9.	20 Bani (C-N) 1900. Crown. Rev. Value	3.00
9a.	20 Bani (C-N) 1905, 06. Center hole	1.00
10.	10 Bani (C-N) 1900. Type of #9	1.00

10a.	10 Bani (C-N) 1905, 06. Center hole	1.00
11.	5 Bani (C-N) 1900. Type of #9	.90
11a.	5 Bani (C-N) 1905, 06. Center hole	.90
12.	2 Bani (C) 1900. Head. Rev. Arms	1.00
13.	1 Ban (C) 1900	.75

FERDINAND I 1914-27

14.	25 Lei (G) 1922. Crowned bust of Ferdinand. Rev. Crowned bust of Queen Marie	125.00
15.	20 Lei (G) 1922. Laureated head. Rev. Arms	125.00

16.	2 Lei (C-N) 1924. Arms. Rev. Value	.50
17.	1 Leu (C-N) 1924	.50
18.	50 Bani (A) 1921. Center hole	1.00
19.	25 Bani (A) 1921. Center hole	1.00

MIHAI I 1927-30 (First Reign)

20.	20 Lei (N-Bra) 1930. Head. Rev. Four figures	3.00
21.	5 Lei (N-Bra) 1930. Head. Rev. Crowned arms	2.00

CAROL II 1930-40

22	250 Lei 1935. Head. Rev. Arms	10.00
23.	250 Lei 1939-40. Head to right. Rev. Value	6.00
24.	100 Lei (S) 1932	10.00
25.	100 Lei (N) 1936-38. Head to left. Rev. Arms	1.75

26.	50 Lei (N) 1937-38. Helmeted head	1.50
27.	20 Lei (N-Bra) 1930. Bare head	1.00
28.	10 Lei (N-Bra) 1930	.75
29.	1 Leu (Bra) 1938-41. Crown, Rev. Value	.25

MIHAI I 1941-47 (Second Reign)

30.	500 Lei 1941. King kneeling	10.00
31.	500 Lei 1944. Bare head. Rev. Arms	6.00
31a.	500 Lei (Bra) 1945	5.00
32.	200 Lei 1942. Head. Rev. Arms	5.00
32a.	200 Lei (Bra) 1945. Head. Rev. Value	4.00
33.	100,000 Lei 1946-47	10.00
34.	25,000 Lei 1946	7.50

35.	10,000 Lei (Bra) 1947	4.00
36.	2,000 Lei (Bra) 1946	3.00
37.	500 Lei (A) 1946	3.50

38.	5 Lei (A) 1947. Head. Rev. Value	2.50
39.	2 Lei (Br) 1947. Arms. Rev. Value	2.00
40.	1 Leu (Bra) 1947	2.00
41.	50 Bani (Bra) 1947. Crown. Rev. Value	2.00

PEOPLE'S REPUBLIC 1947-

42.	20 Lei (A) 1951. Arms. Rev. Value	15.00

Only one quarter of Russia lies in Europe, yet it is the largest country on that continent. Russia was ruled by the Romanov dynasty from 1613 to 1917. The Communist regime came into power in November, 1917.

100 Kopecks = 1 Rouble

10 Roubles = 1 Chervonetz

PETER I (the Great) 1689-1725

43.	5 Lei (A) 1948-51	2.50
44.	2 Lei (A-Br) 1950-51; (A) 1951, 52. Agricultural products. Rev. Value	2.50
45.	1 Leu (A-Br) 1949-51; (A) 1951, 52. Oil derrick. Rev. Value	1.75
46.	50 Bani (C-N) 1955-56. Arms. Rev. Workman	1.50
47.	25 Bani (C-N) 1952-55. Rev. Value	.75
48.	10 Bani (C-N) 1952-56	.35
49.	5 Bani (A-Br) 1952-57	.60
50.	3 Bani (A-Br) 1952-53	.40
51.	1 Ban (A-Br) 1952-54	.20

52.	3 Lei (N-St) 1963. Arms. Rev. Oil refinery	1.25

1.	1 Rouble 1704-06. Young boy bust in armor. Rev. Eagle	175.00
2.	1 Rouble 1707-25. Laureate head	125.00

53.	1 Leu (N-St) 1963. Rev. Tractor in field	1.00
54.	25 Bani (N-St) 1960	.75
55.	15 Bani (N-St) 1960	.50
56.	5 Bani (N-St) 1963	.30

57.	3 Lei (N-St) 1966- . Type of #52, obverse inscription REPUBLICA SOCIALISTA ROMANIA	1.00
58.	1 Leu (N-St) 1966- . Type of #53, new obverse inscription	.75
59.	25 Bani (N-St) 1966- . Type of #54, new obverse inscription	.50
60.	15 Bani (N-St) 1966- . Type of #55, new obverse inscription	.30
61.	5 Bani (N-St) 1966- . Type of #56, new obverse inscription	.25

3.	½ Rouble 1699-1725	35.00
4.	¼ Rouble 1701-13	25.00
5.	2 Kopecks (C) 1723-25. Arms	12.50
6.	1 Kopeck (C) 1703-19. St. George	7.50

RUSSIA (continued)

CATHERINE I 1725-27

7.	1 Rouble 1725-27. Bust. Rev. Eagle	80.00
8.	½ Rouble 1726-27	45.00
9.	¼ Rouble 1726	25.00
10.	5 Kopecks (C) 1726-27. Arms. Rev. Cross	12.00
11.	1 Kopeck (C) 1726-27. St. George	8.50

PETER II 1727-30

12.	1 Rouble 1727-29. Armored bust. Rev. Monogram	100.00

13.	½ Rouble 1727-29	35.00
14.	¼ Rouble 1727	25.00
15.	5 Kopecks (C) 1728-30. Arms. Rev. Cross	20.00
16.	1 Kopeck (C) 1728-29. St. George. Rev. Value	7.50

ANNA 1730-40

17.	1 Rouble 1730-40. Bust. Rev. Eagle	75.00

18.	½ Rouble 1731-40	25.00
19.	¼ Rouble 1730-40	15.00
20.	½ Kopeck (C) 1730-40. Arms. Rev. Value	8.50

IVAN III 1740-41

21.	1 Rouble 1741. Laureate bust. Rev. Eagle	225.00

ELIZABETH 1741-61

22.	1 Rouble 1741-61. Bust. Rev. Eagle	55.00
23.	½ Rouble 1742-61	25.00
24.	¼ Rouble 1743-58	12.00
25.	5 Kopecks (C) 1757-61. Arms. Rev. Value	10.00
26.	2 Kopecks (C) 1757-61. St. George	8.00
27.	1 Kopeck (C) 1757-61. St. George	8.00

RUSSIA • 379

PETER III 1761-62

27a. 1 Rouble 1762. Bust.   250.00

CATHERINE II (the Great) 1762-96

31. 5 Kopecks (C) 1766-80. Monogram. Rev.
     Arms (Siberia)   35.00
32. 2 Kopecks (C) 1764-80   8.00
33. 1 Kopeck (C) 1766-80   7.50

28. 1 Rouble 1762-96. Crowned bust. Rev.
     Eagle   35.00

PAUL I 1796-1801

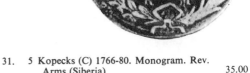

29. ½ Rouble 1762-96   12.00
30. ¼ Rouble 1764-96   15.00

34. 1 Rouble 1796-1801. Tablet. Rev. Mono-
     gram   25.00

ALEXANDER I 1801-25

NICHOLAS I 1825-55

35.	1 Rouble 1802-25. Double eagle. Rev. Crowned inscription in wreath	20.00
36.	½ Rouble 1802-25	13.00
37.	¼ Rouble 1802-10	25.00
38.	20 Kopecks 1810-25	5.00
39.	10 Kopecks 1802-25	4.00
40.	5 Kopecks 1811-25	5.00

46.	1½ Roubles 1835-36. Head of Czar. Rev. Heads of Czarina and 7 children	rare
47.	1½ Roubles 1839. Head of Alexander I. Rev. Memorial	600.00

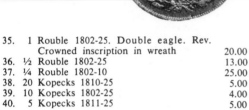

48.	1 Rouble 1826-55. Double eagle. Rev. Inscription on wreath	25.00

41.	5 Kopecks (C) 1802-10. Double eagle. Rev. Value	12.00
42.	2 Kopecks (C) 1802-25	2.00
43.	1 Kopeck (C) 1804-25	2.50
44.	½ Kopeck (C) 1804-25	7.00
45.	¼ Kopeck (C) 1803-10	40.00

49.	1 Rouble 1834. Type of #47	100.00

67.	1 Rouble 1859. Head of Nicholas I. Rev. Memorial	125.00
68.	1 Rouble 1856-81	10.00
69.	½ Rouble 1856-81	7.50
70.	25 Kopecks 1856-81	6.00
71.	20 Kopecks 1856-81	1.50
72.	15 Kopecks 1860-81	1.50
73.	10 Kopecks 1856-81	1.50
74.	5 Kopecks 1856-81	2.25
75.	5 Kopecks (C) 1856-81	2.50
76.	3 Kopecks (C) 1856-81	2.00
77.	2 Kopecks (C) 1856-81	1.50
78.	1 Kopeck (C) 1855-81. Monogram	.75
79.	½ Kopeck (C) 1855-81	1.50
80.	¼ Kopeck (C) 1855-81	2.25

50.	1 Rouble 1839. Head of Alexander I. Rev. Borodino monument	150.00
51.	½ Rouble 1826-55. Type of #48	7.50
52.	25 Kopecks 1827-55	6.00
53.	20 Kopecks 1826-55	3.50
54.	10 Kopecks 1826-55	2.50
55.	5 Kopecks 1826-55	2.00
56.	10 Kopecks (C) 1830-39	10.00
57.	5 Kopecks (C) 1830-39, 49-55	3.50
58.	3 Kopecks (C) 1849-55	2.50
59.	2 Kopecks (C) 1826-39, 49-55	1.50
60.	1 Kopeck (C) 1826-39	2.50
61.	½ Kopeck (C) 1827-28	6.50

81.	1 Rouble 1883 (Coronation). Head. Rev. Regalia	40.00
82.	1 Rouble 1882-85. Double eagle. Rev. Value	15.00
82a.	½ Rouble 1882-85	25.00
83.	1 Rouble 1886-94. Head. Rev. Double eagle	25.00
84.	½ Rouble 1886-94	10.00
85.	25 Kopecks 1882-94	7.50
86.	20 Kopecks 1882-93. Type of #82	1.50
87.	15 Kopecks 1882-93	1.50
88.	10 Kopecks 1882-94	1.25
89.	5 Kopecks 1882-93	1.25
90.	3 Kopecks (C) 1882-94	3.00
91.	2 Kopecks (C) 1882-94	1.50
92.	1 Kopeck (C) 1882-94	.75
93.	½ Kopeck (C) 1881-94. Monogram	1.25
94.	¼ Kopeck (C) 1881-94	2.00

62.	3 Kopecks (C) 1839-47. Monogram. Rev. Value	6.00
63.	2 Kopecks (C) 1839-47	4.00
64.	1 Kopeck (C) 1839-55	2.00
65.	½ Kopeck (C) 1839-55	3.00
66.	¼ Kopeck (C) 1839-53	4.00

NICHOLAS II 1894-1917

95. 10 Roubles (G) 1895-1911. Head. Rev.
Double eagle 75.00
96. 5 Roubles (G) 1895-1911 35.00

97. 1 Rouble 1896 (Coronation). Head. Rev.
Regalia in wreath 50.00

98. 1 Rouble 1895-1915. Type of #96 10.00
99. ½ Rouble 1895-1914 1.00
100. ¼ Rouble 1895-1901 4.00
101. 20 Kopecks 1901-17. Double eagle. Rev.
Value 1.50
102. 15 Kopecks 1896-1916 1.00
103. 10 Kopecks 1895-1916 .75
104. 5 Kopecks (S) 1897-1915; (C) 1911-16 1.00
105. 3 Kopecks (C) 1895-1916 .75
106. 2 Kopecks (C) 1895-1916 .75
107. 1 Kopeck (C) 1895-1916 .50
108. ½ Kopeck (C) 1894-1916. Monogram .75
109. ¼ Kopeck (C) 1894-1916 1.00

COMMEMORATIVE ROUBLES

110. 1 Rouble 1898. Head of Alexander I.
Rev. Monument 250.00

111. 1 Rouble 1912. Head of Alexander III.
Rev. Statue of Alexander III 450.00

112. 1 Rouble 1912 (Commemorating centenary of victory over Napoleon).
Crowned double eagle. Rev. Inscription 175.00

113. 1 Rouble 1913 (Commemorating tercentenary of the Romanov dynasty).
Heads of Nicholas II and Michael
Feodorovich. Rev. Crowned double
eagle 15.00

USSR 1917-

114. 1 Rouble 1921-22. Value in star. Rev.
Hammer and sickle 12.50

115. 1 Rouble 1924. Two workers. Rev.
Hammer and sickle in wreath   12.50
116. 50 Kopecks 1921-22. Type of #114   7.50

117. 50 Kopecks 1924-27. Blacksmith. Rev.
Type of #115   3.00

118. 20 Kopecks 1921-30. Value in wreath.
Rev. Hammer and sickle in wreath   1.50
119. 15 Kopecks 1921-30   1.00
120. 10 Kopecks 1921-30   1.00

121. 20 Kopecks (C-N) 1931-34. Hammer and
sickle in wreath. Rev. Workman holding shield with value   .75
122. 15 Kopecks (C-N) 1931-34   .50
123. 10 Kopecks (C-N) 1931-34   .50

124. 20 Kopecks (C-N) 1935-57. Hammer
and sickle in wreath. Rev. Value in
panel inside of wreath   1.00
125. 15 Kopecks (C-N) 1935-57   .50
126. 10 Kopecks (C-N) 1935-57   .50

127. 5 Kopecks (A-Br) 1926-57. Hammer
and sickle in wreath. Rev. Value in
wreath   .75
128. 3 Kopecks (A-Br) 1926-57   .75
129. 2 Kopecks (A-Br) 1926-57   .35
130. 1 Kopeck (A-Br) 1926-57   .50

(Varying numbers of ribbons on wreaths of
above issues signify the number of states in the
Soviet Union at the time of issue)

NEW STANDARD

1 New Rouble = 10 Old Roubles

131. 1 Rouble (C-N) 1961- . Hammer and
sickle in wreath. Rev. Value in wreath   2.00
132. 50 Kopecks (C-N) 1961-   1.25
133. 20 Kopecks (C-N) 1961-   .75
134. 15 Kopecks (C-N) 1961-   .75
135. 10 Kopecks (C-N) 1961-   .50
136. 5 Kopecks (A-Br) 1961-   .50
137. 3 Kopecks (A-Br) 1961-   .50
138. 2 Kopecks (A-Br) 1961-   .30
139. 1 Kopeck (A-Br) 1961-   .25

140. 1 Rouble (CNZ) 1965. Statue of soldier.
Rev. Arms (commemorates 20th anniversary of end of World War II)   2.50

141. 1 Rouble (CNZ) 1967. Lenin standing,
hammer and sickle in background.
Rev. Arms (Commemorates 50th anniversary of Socialist Revolution)   2.50
142. 50 Kopecks (CNZ) 1967   1.50

RUSSIA (continued)

143. 20 Kopecks (CNZ) 1967. Cruiser *Aurora*   .85

144. 15 Kopecks(CNZ)1967. Man and woman
holding hammer and sickle   .65

145. 10 Kopecks (CNZ) 1967. Rocket   .50

146. 1 Rouble (CNZ) 1970. Head of Lenin.
Rev. Arms (Commemorates 100th
anniversary of birth)   3.50
147. 10 Roubles (G) 1975. Farmer sowing
seeds, factory and rising sun in background (same design as 1923 issue)   350.00

148. 1 Rouble (CNZ) 1975. Statue of "Mother-
land". Rev. Arms, value (Commemorates 30th anniversary of the end of
World War II)   5.00

RWANDA

Formerly part of the Belgian U.N. Trusteeship
of Ruanda-Urundi, it became an independent republic in July, 1962.

1. 10 Francs (C-N) 1964. Head of Kayibanda.
   Rev. Arms   1.50
2.   5 Francs (Br) 1964 , 65   1.00
3.   1 Franc (C-N) 1964 , 65   .65

4.   1 Franc (A) 1969. Head of Kayibanda.
   Rev. Arms

5.   2 Francs (Al) 1970. Native pouring
   coffee. Rev. Arms (F.A.O. coin plan)   1.50

6.   ½ Franc (A) 1970. Inscription. Rev. Value   .25

7. 200 Francs (C-N) 1972. Two men with flag. Rev.
   Farmer in rice field (F.A.O. coin plan,
   commemorates 10th anniversary of independence)   7.00

RWANDA (continued)

8.   10 Francs (C-N) 1974. Plant. Rev. Arms   1.50

9.   5 Francs (Br) 1974. Coffee plant. Rev.
     Arms   .75
10. 1 Franc (A) 1974. Rice plant. Rev. Arms   .35

SAAR

Part of the French Zone of Occupation after World War II, this territory, bounded by France and Luxembourg, returned to Germany in 1959 and is now a State within the German Federal Republic.

1.   50 Franken (A-Bro) 1954. Factory, smoke-
     stacks, shield, and coalpit. Rev. Value   5.00
2.   20 Franken (A-Bro) 1954   1.75

3.   10 Franken (A-Bro) 1954   1.50

4. 100 Franken (C-N) 1955. Arms within
    wheel-shaped design. Rev. Type of #1   3.50

ST. HELENA

This island in the South Atlantic is a British colony.

1.   Half Penny (C) 1821. Arms. Rev. Value   7.50

RWANDA AND BURUNDI

A common currency was issued by the two provinces during the transitional period between 1960 and 1964.

1.   1 Franc (Bra) 1960-64. Lion. Rev. Value   1.00

2. 25 Pence (C-N) 1973. Queen Elizabeth II.
    Rev. Sailing ship (Commemorates 300th
    anniversary of charter)   1.50
2a. 25 Pence (S) 1973 (proof issue)   30.00

ST. PIERRE AND MIQUELON

A group of eight small islands south of Newfoundland. This is the only possession of France
in North America today. The islands were first
settled by the French about 1660.

100 Centimes = 1 Franc

1.	2 Francs (A) 1948. Head of the Re- public. Rev. Fishing vessel	.50
2.	1 Franc (A) 1948	.35

ST. THOMAS AND PRINCE ISLANDS

A Portuguese province located in the Gulf of
Guinea off the west coast of Africa.

100 Centavos = 1 Escudo

NEW STATE 1926-

1.	50 Centavos (N-Bro) 1928, 29. Bust of the Republic. Rev. Arms above value	5.00
2.	20 Centavos (N-Bro) 1929	3.50
3.	10 Centavos (N-Bro) 1929	4.00
4.	10 Escudos 1939. Arms on cross over date. Rev. Crowned shield over value	7.50
5.	5 Escudos 1939, 48	5.00
6.	2½ Escudos 1939, 48	3.50

7.	1 Escudo (C-N) 1939; (N-Bro) 1948. Crowned shield. Rev. Value	3.00
8.	50 Centavos (N-Bro) 1948	3.50
9.	10 Escudos 1951. Crowned shield over value. Rev. Arms over date	8.00

ST. THOMAS AND PRINCE ISLANDS
(continued)

10.	5 Escudos 1951	10.00
11.	2½ Escudos 1951; (C-N) 1962, 71	.75
12.	1 Escudo (C-N) 1951. Similar to #7	7.50
12a.	1 Escudo (Br) 1962-	1.00
13.	50 Centavos (C-N) 1951; (Br) 1962	1.00
13a.	50 Centavos (Br) 1971 (larger planchet)	.25

14.	20 Centavos (Br) 1962	1.00
14a.	20 Centavos (Br) 1971 (smaller planchet)	.15
15.	10 Centavos (Br) 1962; (A) 1971	.10

16.	50 Escudos 1970. Quinas cross. Rev. Arms between dates (Commemorates 500th anniver- sary of discovery)	7.50

17.	20 Escudos (N) 1971. Emblem within shield. Rev. Arms of Portugal	3.50

18.	10 Escudos (C-N) 1971. Crowned shield over value. Rev. Arms over date	1.75
19.	5 Escudos (C-N) 1971	1.00

ST. THOMAS AND PRINCE ISLANDS • 387

EL SALVADOR

After three centuries of Spanish rule, this Central American country declared its independence of Spain in 1821. For a while Salvador was part of Mexico and then of the Central American Federation, eventually becoming an independent republic.

Due to the scarcity of coinage in Salvador during the early nineteenth century, the arms of Salvador were sometimes countermarked on whatever coins came into the country.

100 Centavos = 1 Peso or 1 Colon

1.	1 Peso 1892. Flag. Rev. Arms	80.00
2.	50 Centavos 1892	35.00

3.	1 Peso 1892-1914. Head of Columbus. Rev. Arms	7.50
4.	50 Centavos 1892-94	6.00

5.	20 Centavos 1892. Arms. Rev. Value in wreath	20.00
6.	10 Centavos 1892	60.00
7.	5 Centavos 1892, 93	7.50

8.	25 Centavos 1911. Arms. Rev. Value in wreath	3.50
9.	10 Centavos 1911	2.00
10.	5 Centavos 1911	3.50

11.	25 Centavos 1914. New arms. Rev. Value	3.50
12.	10 Centavos 1914	2.00
13.	5 Centavos 1914	2.00

14.	10 Centavos (C-N) 1921- . Head of Francisco Morazan. Rev. Value	.50
14a.	10 Centavos (German silver) 1952	.75
15.	5 Centavos (C-N) 1915-	.25
15a.	5 Centavos (German silver) 1944-52	.50
16.	3 Centavos (C-N) 1899-1915	2.50
17.	1 Centavo (C-N) 1889-1940; (Br) 1942-	.50
18.	25 Centavos 1943, 44	1.00

19.	1 Colon 1925 (400th anniversary of San Salvador). Busts of Pedro de Alavarado and Pres. Quinonez. Rev. Arms in wreath	125.00

20.	50 Centavos 1953. Head of Pres. Morazan. Rev. Value in wreath	.60
21.	25 Centavos 1953	.50

22.	50 Centavos (N) 1970. Head of Morazan. Rev. Value	.50
23.	25 Centavos (N) 1970	.30
24.	3 Centavos (C-Z) 1974. Type of #16	1.50
25.	2 Centavos (C-Z) 1974	1.00

SAN MARINO

A tiny republic in Italy, 38 square miles in size, which, according to traditional accounts, has maintained its freedom since the fourth century A.D.

100 Centesimi = 1 Lira

1.	5 Lire 1898. Standing saint. Rev. crowned arms	75.00
2.	2 Lire 1898-1906. Rev. Value in wreath	25.00
3.	1 Lira 1898-1906	15.00
4.	50 Centesimi 1898	12.50
5.	10 Centesimi (C) 1875, 93-94	4.50
6.	5 Centesimi (C) 1864, 69, 94	3.00

7.	20 Lire (G) 1925. Three towers. Rev. Standing saint	750.00
8.	10 Lire (G) 1925	500.00

9.	20 Lire 1931-38. Crown over three feathers. Rev. Half figure of St. Marinus	50.00

10.	10 Lire 1931-38. Crowned arms. Rev. female half figure	7.50

11.	5 Lire 1931-38. Helmeted head. Rev. Plow	4.00
12.	10 Centesimi (Bro) 1935-38. Crowned arms. Rev. Value	2.50
13.	5 Centesimi (Bro) 1935-38	2.00

14.	500 Lire 1972. Three towers. Rev. Mother holding child	20.00

15.	100 Lire (St) 1972. Towers with feathers. Rev. Saint Marinus in boat	2.50

16.	50 Lire (St) 1972. Rev. Roman lady kneeling to Saint Marinus	2.50

17.	20 Lire (A-Br) 1972. Rev. Garibaldi climbing Mount Titano	2.50
18.	10 Lire (A) 1972. Rev. Cow nursing calf	2.00

19.	5 Lire (A) 1972. Bust of Saint Marinus facing left. Rev. Value over arms	2.00
20.	2 Lire (A) 1972. Bust facing right	2.00
21.	1 Lira (A) 1972. Bust facing left	2.00

22.

22. 500 Lire 1973. Crowned arms in shield. Rev. Woman holding dove   15.00

23. 100 Lire (St) 1973. Crowned arms in shield. Rev. Ship passing Pillars of Hercules   2.00

24. 50 Lire (St) 1973. Rev. Woman holding sword and balance   2.00
25. 20 Lire (A-Br) 1973. Rev. Man carrying old man and child   2.00

26. 10 Lire (A) 1973. Rev. Man with shield and torch   1.50
27. 5 Lire (A) 1973. Rev. Five faces in boat   1.50

28. 2 Lire (A) 1973. Rev. Pelican feeding young with blood   1.50
29. 1 Lira (A) 1973. Rev. Woman with flag   1.50

30. 2 Scudi (G) 1974. Arms. Rev. Saint Marinus   150.00
31. 1 Scudo (G) 1974   75.00

32. 500 Lire 1974. Three towers with feathers. Rev. Two doves   15.00

33. 100 Lire (St) 1974. Rev. Goat   2.00

34. 50 Lire (St) 1974. Rev. Rooster   2.00
35. 20 Lire (A-Br) 1974. Rev. Lobster   2.00

36. 10 Lire (A) 1974. Rev. Bee (F.A.O. coin plan)   .50
37. 5 Lire (A) 1974. Rev. Porcupine   1.50

38. 2 Lire (A) 1974. Rev. Ladybug   1.50
39. 1 Lira (A) 1974. Rev. Ant   1.50

40. 500 Lire 1975. Arms. Rev. Three gulls

41. 100 Lire (St) 1975. Rev. Dog and cat

SAN MARINO (continued)

42. 50 Lire (St) 1975. Rev. Five salmon
43. 20 Lire (A-Br) 1975. Rev. Bird feeding
    young

44. 10 Lire (A) 1975. Rev. Two groundhogs
45. 5 Lire (A) 1975. Rev. Hedgehogs

46. 2 Lire (A) 1975. Rev. Two seahorses
47. 1 Lira (A) 1975. Two spiders

SARAWAK

Occupying part of the island of Borneo, Sarawak in 1841 was granted by the Sultan of Brunei to James Brooke, an Englishman, who had helped him quiet a revolt in the province. In 1888 Brunei and Sarawak became British protectorates. In 1946 they were given the status of a British Crown Colony and in 1963 became part of the Federation of Malaysia.

100 Cents = 1 Dollar

JAMES BROOKE 1841-68

1.	1 Cent (C) 1863. Head. Rev. Value in wreath	6.00
2.	½ Cent (C) 1863	12.00
3.	¼ Cent (C) 1863	25.00

CHARLES BROOKE 1868-1917

5. 50 Cents 1900, 06. Head. Rev. Value in roped circle   25.00

5.	20 Cents 1900-15	20.00
6.	10 Cents 1900-15	10.00
7.	5 Cents 1900-15	15.00
8.	1 Cent (C) 1870-91. Rev. Value in wreath	5.00
8a.	1 Cent (C) 1892-97 (center hole)	5.00
9.	½ Cent (C) 1870-96	7.50
10.	¼ Cent (C) 1870-96	8.50

CHARLES VYNER BROOKE 1917-1946

11.	50 Cents 1927. Head. Rev. Type of #4	7.50
12.	20 Cents 1920, 27	6.00
13.	10 Cents 1920	20.00
14.	5 Cents 1920	25.00
15.	10 Cents (C-N) 1920, 27, 34. Rev. Value in wreath	1.00
16.	5 Cents (C-N) 1920, 27	1.50
17.	1 Cent (C-N) 1920	5.00
18.	1 Cent (Bro) 1927-41. Rev. Value in wreath	2.50
19.	½ Cent (Bro) 1933	2.00

SAUDI ARABIA

An Arab kingdom, formerly part of the Turkish Empire. It is made up of the former Sultanate of Nejd and the kingdom of Hejaz.

5 Ryals = 1 Dinar

HEJAZ

HUSEIN IBN ALI 1916-24

1. 1 Dinar (G) 1923 (A.H. 1342). Arabic inscriptions 100.00
2. 1 Ryal 1923 (A.H. 1342) 35.00

3. ½ Ryal 1923 (A.H. 1342) 50.00
4. ¼ Ryal 1923 (A.H. 1342) 25.00

SAUDI ARABIA

SAUD IBN ABDUL AZIZ 1953-64

20 Girsh = 1 Ryal
40 Ryals = 1 Guinea
2 Halala = 1 Girsh

5. 1 Ryal 1928-30 (A.H. 1346-48). Arabic inscription with swords and palm trees 25.00
6. 1 Guinea (G) 1957-58 75.00

7. 1 Ryal 1955 (A.H. 1374). Type of #5 2.50
8. ½ Ryal 1955 1.75
9. ¼ Ryal 1955 1.25

10. 4 Girsh (C-N) 1957-59 (A.H. 1376-78) .60
11. 2 Girsh (C-N) 1957-60 .35
12. 1 Girsh (C-N) 1957-59 .25

13. 1 Halala (Br) 1964 .20

FAISAL 1964-75

14. 50 Halala (C-N) 1972 (A.H. 1392). Arabic inscription with palm tree over swords. Rev. Value 1.00
15. 25 Halala (C-N) 1972 .50
16. 10 Halala (C-N) 1972 .50
17. 5 Halala (C-N) 1972 .35

18. 50 Halala (C-N) 1972. Type of #14, F.A.O. inscription on reverse (F.A.O. coin plan) 1.50
19. 25 Halala (C-N) 1973 .75

SERBIA

Formerly a Balkan kingdom; incorporated into the new state of Yugoslavia after World War I.

40 Para = 1 Dinar

MICHAEL III 1860-68

1. 10 Paras (C) 1868. Head. Crowned value in wreath 4.00
2. 5 Paras (C) 1868 8.00
3. 1 Para (C) 1868 5.00

MILAN OBRENOVICH IV 1882-89 (Prince 1868-82)

4. 5 Dinars 1879. Head. Rev. Crowned value in wreath 45.00

5. 2 Dinars 1875, 79 12.00
6. 1 Dinar 1875, 79 6.00
7. 50 Para 1875, 79 6.00
8. 10 Para (C) 1879 4.00
9. 5 Para (C) 1879 3.50

10. 20 Para (C-N) 1883-84. Crowned double eagle. Rev. Value 2.00
11. 10 Para (C-N) 1883-84 1.75
12. 5 Para (C-N) 1883-84 1.50

ALEXANDER I 1889-1903

13. 2 Dinars 1897. Head. Rev. Crowned value in wreath 10.00
14. 1 Dinar 1897 5.00

PETER I 1903-18

15. 5 Dinars 1904 (Centenary of the Karageorgeviches). Two heads. Rev. Crowned arms in mantle 45.00
16. 2 Dinars 1904, 12, 15. Head. Rev. Crowned value in wreath 4.00
17. 1 Dinar 1904, 12, 15 2.50
18. 50 Para 1904, 12, 15 1.50

19. 20 Para (C-N) 1912, 17. Crowned double eagle. Rev. Value 2.00
20. 10 Para (C-N) 1912, 17 1.50
21. 5 Para (C-N) 1904, 12, 17 1.50
22. 2 Para (Br) 1904 3.00

SEYCHELLES

A group of 92 islands in the Indian Ocean, about 800 miles off the east African coast. The group is an English Crown Colony.

100 Cents = 1 Rupee

GEORGE VI 1936-1952

1.	1 Rupee 1939. Crowned head. Rev. Value	6.50
2.	½ Rupee 1939	8.00
3.	25 Cents 1939, 43-44	5.00
4.	25 Cents (C-N) 1951	2.00

5. 10 Cents (C-N) 1939, 43-44, 51 (Scalloped edge). Rev. Value   2.50

6.	5 Cents (Bro) 1948. Rev. Value in circle	.75
7.	2 Cents (Bro) 1948	.60
8.	1 Cent (Bro) 1948	.45

ELIZABETH II 1952-

9.	1 Rupee (C-N) 1954. Crowned head. Rev. Type of #1	1.50
10.	½ Rupee (C-N) 1954-	1.00
11.	25 Cents (C-N) 1954-	1.00

12.	10 Cents (N-Bra) 1953-	.75
13.	5 Cents (Br) 1964- . Rev. Type of #6	1.00
14.	2 Cents (Br) 1959-	2.00
15.	1 Cent (Br) 1959-	1.50

16. 5 Cents (A) 1972. Rev. Cabbage head, scalloped planchet (F.A.O. coin plan)   .25

17. 1 Cent (A) 1972. Rev. Cow's head (F.A.O. coin plan)   .15

18. 5 Rupees (C-N) 1972- . Rev. Palm tree, sailing ship and turtle (seven-sided planchet)   3.00
18a. 5 Rupees (S) 1972- (proof issue)   20.00

19. 10 Rupees (C-N) 1974. Rev. Turtle   3.50
19a. 10 Rupees (S) 1974 (proof issue)   20.00

SIAM
(see THAILAND)

SIERRA LEONE

Formerly a British colony and protectorate on the west coast of Africa, it became an independent member of the Commonwealth in 1961 and a republic in 1971.

REPUBLIC 1971-

12. 50 Cents (C-N) 1972. Head of Dr. Siaka Stevens. Rev. Arms   2.00

1.	1 Dollar 1791. Lion. Rev. Clasped hands	250.00
2.	50 Cents 1791	125.00
3.	20 Cents 1791	75.00
4.	10 Cents 1791, 96, 1805	35.00
5.	1 Penny (Br) 1791	25.00
5a.	1 Cent (Br) 1791, 96	25.00

6. 1 Leone (C-N) 1964- . Head of Sir Milton Margai, late Prime Minister and founder of the state. Rev. Arms supported by lions   15.00

13. 1 Leone (C-N) 1974. Rev. Lion in mountain scene   2.50
13a. 1 Leone (S) 1974 (proof issue)   20.00

7. 20 Cents (C-N) 1964- . Rev. Lion   1.00
8. 10 Cents (C-N) 1964- . Rev. Value   .75
9. 5 Cents (C-N) 1964- . Rev. Cotton-wood tree   .50

10. 1 Cent (Br) 1964- . Rev. Palm branches   .35
11. ½ Cent (Br) 1964- . Rev. Bonga fish   .25

SINGAPORE

An island off the southern tip of the Malay Peninsula. This former British Colony achieved self-government in 1959; in September, 1963, it joined the Federation of Malaysia of which it was a member until August, 1965, when it withdrew. It remained a member of the British Commonwealth.

8. 5 Cents (A) 1971. Pomfret, a native fish. Rev. Rice plant, value (F.A.O. coin plan) .25

1. 1 Dollar (CN) 1967- . Lion. Rev. Value   2.00

2. 50 Cents (CN) 1967- . Lionfish   .75
3. 20 Cents (CN) 1967- . Swordfish   .50

4. 10 Cents (CN) 1967- . Seahorse   .35
5. 5 Cents (CN) 1967- . Snakebird   .25

6. 1 Cent (Br) 1967- . Apartment building   .15

9. 10 Dollars 1972. Arms. Rev. Eagle   15.00
9a. 10 Dollars 1973- . Rev. Lower SINGAPORE inscription right side up   10.00

7. 150 Dollars (G) 1969. Arms. Rev. Raffles lighthouse (Commemorates 150th anniversary, founding of Singapore)   200.00

10. 5 Dollars 1973. Arms. Rev. Stadium, interlocked circles emblem (Commemorates 7th South East Asia Peninsular Games)   8.50

SINGAPORE (continued)

11. 500 Dollars (G) 1975. Arms. Rev. Roaring lion (Commemorates 10th anniversary of republic)   275.00
12. 250 Dollars (G) 1975. Rev. Four hands clasped (Commemorates 10th anniversary of republic)   125.00

13. 100 Dollars (G) 1975. Rev. Modern housing project (Commemorates 10th anniversary of republic)   50.00

14. 10 Dollars 1975. Rev. Ship in harbor (Commemorates 10th anniversary of republic)   10.00

15.   1 Dollar 1975. Type of #1   10.00

SOLOMON ISLANDS

A British protectorate located east of New Guinea, the Solomon Islands were granted self-government in 1975.

1. 100 Dollars (G) 1975

2. 30 Dollars 1975. Cuscus. Rev. Arms   40.00

SOMALIA

This area, located on the northeast coast of Africa along the Indian Ocean, used to be an Italian colony and was then known as Italian Somaliland. Known as Somalia under Italian Trusteeship following World War II, it merged with British Somaliland in 1960 to form the Somali Republic.

100 Centesimi = 1 Somalo (Scellino, Shilling)

1. 1 Somalo 1950. Star over lioness. Rev.
   Value in circle   4.00
2. 50 Centesimi 1950   4.00

3. 10 Centesimi (Br) 1950. Elephant head. Rev.
   Star over value   .65
4. 5 Centesimi (Br) 1950   .45
5. 1 Centesimo (Br) 1950   .25

REPUBLIC

6. 1 Scellino (CN) 1967. Arms. Rev. Value   1.25
7. 50 Centesimi (CN) 1967-   .75
8. 10 Centesimi (Bra) 1967-   .35
9. 5 Centesimi (Bra) 1967-   .20

10. 5 Shillings (C-N) 1970. Cow, goat, sheep
    and produce. Rev. Arms (F.A.O. coin
    plan)   3.00

SOUTH AFRICA

The South African Republic was formed in 1853 by the Boers who lived in the Transvaal. In 1877 Great Britain annexed the Transvaal, but the Boers regained their independence in 1883. Their defeat in the Boer War put an end to the South African Republic in 1902.

12 Pence = 1 Shilling

PRES. S. J. PAUL KRUGER 1883-1902

1. 5 Shillings 1892 (two varieties). Head
   of Kruger. Rev. Arms   100.00
2. 2½ Shillings 1892-97   6.00
3. 2 Shillings 1892-97   6.50
4. 1 Shilling 1892-97. Rev. Value in wreath   7.00

5. 6 Pence 1892-97   6.00
6. 3 Pence 1892-97   5.00

7. 1 Penny (Bro) 1892-94, 98   2.50

In 1910 the Cape of Good Hope, Natal, and the Orange Free State (and later Transvaal) were formed into the Union of South Africa, a self-governing dominion of the British Commonwealth. Earlier coins use the Dutch spelling "Zuid-Afrika" while coins later than 1930 carry the spelling "Suid-Afrika." In 1961 it became the Republic of South Africa and withdrew from the British Commonwealth.

GEORGE V 1910-36

1. 2½ Shillings 1923-36. Crowned bust. Rev.
   Arms or Crowned arms   10.00

GEORGE VI 1936-52
(Coins issued after 1948 drop "Imperator" from the obverse legends)

9. 1 Sovereign (G) 1952. Head. Rev.
   Springbok   60.00
10. ½ Sovereign (G) 1952   60.00

2. 1 Florin (2 Shillings) 1923-36   7.00
3. 1 Shilling 1923-36. Rev Hope standing   3.00

4. 6 Pence 1923-24. Rev. Value in wreath   6.00
4a. 6 Pence 1925-36. Rev. Six bundles of
   sticks around a flower   3.00
5. 3 Pence 1923-25. Rev. Value in wreath   5.00
5a. 3 Pence 1925-36. Rev. Three bundles of
   sticks around a flower   2.00

11. 5 Shillings 1947. Rev. Springbok (Royal
   Visit commemorative)   10.00
12. 5 Shillings 1948-50   7.50
13. 5 Shillings 1951 (5s on reverse)   10.00

6. 1 Penny (Bro) 1923-36. Rev. Ship   1.25
7. ½ Penny (Bro) 1923-36   2.00

8. ¼ Penny (Bro) 1923-31. Rev. Two
   sparrows   3.00

14. 5 Shillings 1952. Rev. Ship (300th anniversary of the founding of Cape Town
   by Jan van Riebeeck)   6.00

15. 2½ Shillings 1937-52. Rev. Crowned arms   5.00
16. 2 Shillings 1937-52. Rev. Arms   4.00

17. 1 Shilling 1937-52. Rev. Hope standing   2.00
18. 6 Pence 1937-52. Rev. Six bundles of sticks around a flower   1.00
19. 3 Pence 1937-52. Three bundles of sticks around a flower   1.00
20. 1 Penny (Bro) 1937-1952. Rev. Ship   .50

21. ½ Penny (Bro) 1937-52   1.00
22. ¼ Penny (Bro) 1937-52. Rev. Two birds   1.00

ELIZABETH II 1952-

23. 1 Sovereign (G) 1953-60. Head. Rev. Arms   150.00
24. ½ Sovereign (G) 1953-60   150.00

25. 5 Shillings 1953-59. Rev. Springbok   10.00
26. 2½ Shillings 1953-60. Rev. Crowned arms   9.00
27. 2 Shillings 1953-60. Rev. Arms   7.00
28. 1 Shilling 1953-60. Rev. Hope standing   6.00
29. 6 Pence 1953-60. Rev. Six bundles of sticks around a flower   3.00
30. 3 Pence 1953-60. Rev. Three bundles of sticks around a flower   1.50

31. 1 Penny (Br) 1953-60. Rev. Sailing Ship   2.00
32. ½ Penny (Br) 1953-60   1.50
33. ¼ Penny (Br) 1953-60. Rev. Two sparrows   .50

34. 5 Shillings 1960. Rev. Parliament buildings (50th anniversary of Union)   10.00

REPUBLIC

CURRENCY REVALUATION
100 Cents = 1 Rand

35. 2 Rand (G) 1961- . Bust of Jan Van Riebeeck. Rev. Springbok   75.00
36. 1 Rand (G) 1961-   75.00

37. 50 Cents 1961-64. Rev. Springbok   14.00

38. 20 Cents 1961-64. Rev. Coat of Arms   3.00
39. 10 Cents 1961-64. Rev. Hope with anchor   3.00

40. 5 Cents 1961-64. Rev. Five bundles of sticks around a flower   1.00
41. 2½ Cents 1961-64. Rev. Flower   3.00

42. 1 Cent (Bra) 1961-64. Rev. Pioneer
    covered wagon   1.00
43. ½ Cent (Bra) 1961-64. Rev. Two
    sparrows   1.00

44. 1 Rand 1965-68. Bust of Jan van Rie-
    beeck, SOUTH AFRICA. Rev.
    Springbok   6.00
44a. 1 Rand 1965-68. Type of #44 but
    SUID AFRIKA   6.00

(In listings 45-58, the first coin listed bears a legend in
English, the "a" listed coin bears an Afrikaans inscription. From 1970 on, all coins bear dual language
inscriptions.)

45. 50 Cents (N) 1965-69. Rev. Native
    flowers   1.50
45a. 50 Cents (N) 1965-69.   1.50
46. 20 Cents (N) 1965-69. Rev. Protea plant   .75
46a. 20 Cents (N) 1965-69   .75
47. 10 Cents (N) 1965-69. Rev. Aloe plant   .50
47a. 10 Cents (N) 1965-69   .50

48. 5 Cents (N) 1965-69. Rev. Blue crane   .35
48a. 5 Cents (N) 1965-69   .35
49. 2 Cents (Br) 1965-69. Rev. Black wilde-
    beest   .15

49a. 2 Cents (Br) 1965-69   .15
50. 1 Cent (Br) 1965-69. Rev. Two Spar-
    rows   .10
50a. 1 Cent (Br) 1965-69   .10

51. 1 Rand 1967. Bust of Hendrik Frensch
    Verwoerd, SOUTH AFRICA. Rev.
    Springbok   6.00
51a. 1 Rand 1967. Type of #51 but SUID
    AFRIKA   6.00
52. 50 Cents (N) 1968. Bust of Dr. Charles R.
    Swart, South Africa. Rev. Native
    flower   1.50
52a. 50 Cents (N) 1968. Type of #52 but SUID
    AFRIKA   1.50
53. 20 Cents (N) 1968. Rev. Protea plant   1.00
53a. 20 Cents (N) 1968   1.00
54. 10 Cents (N) 1968. Rev. Aloe plant   .75
54a. 10 Cents (N) 1968   .75
55. 5 Cents (N) 1968. Rev. Blue crane   .35
55a. 5 Cents (N) 1968   .35
56. 2 Cents (Br) 1968. Rev. Black wildebeest   .15
56a. 2 Cents (Br) 1968   .15
57. 1 Cent (Br) 1968. Rev. Two sparrows   .10
57a. 1 Cent (Br) 1968   .10
58. 1 Rand 1969. Bust of Dr. T. E. Donges.
    Rev. Arms (Commemorates late Presi-
    dent-elect)   6.00
58a. 1 Rand 1969. Type of #58 but SUID
    AFRIKA   6.00
59. 1 Rand 1970- . New arms, dual language
    inscription.   3.50
60. 50 Cents (N) 1970- Rev. Native flower   1.00
61. 20 Cents (N) 1970- . Rev. Protea plant   .75
62. 10 Cents (N) 1970- . Rev. Aloe plant   .50
63. 5 Cents (N) 1970 - . Rev. Blue crane   .35
64. 2 Cents (Br) 1970- . Rev. Black wildebeest   .20
65. 1 Cent (Br) 1970 - . Rev. Two sparrows   .15
66. ½ Cent (Br) 1970 -   .10

67. 1 Rand 1974. Arms. Rev. Front door of
    Pretoria Mint, surrounded by four
    coin designs from the past (Com-
    memorates 50th anniversary of South
    African Mint)   3.50

SOUTH ARABIA

On the shores of the Gulf of Aden and the Arabian Sea, this is made up of the former British Protectorate of South Arabia, the former colony of Aden, and certain surrounding islands, which took the name The People's Republic of Southern Yemen upon achieving complete independence in November, 1967, and is now known as the Democratic Republic of Yemen.

| 1. | 50 Fils (C-N) 1964. Emblem. Rev. Dhow, Arab sailing ship | 1.00 |
| 2. | 25 Fils (C-N) 1964 | .65 |

| 3. | 5 Fils (Br) 1964. Rev. Crossed daggers | .35 |
| 4. | 1 Fils (Br) 1964 | .25 |

SPAIN

The eighteenth century was the period of Spain's most extensive coinage. Some types of coins were struck in both Spanish and Spanish-American mints. The exact country of origin may be determined by examining the reverse side of the coin.

In the case of coins originating in Spain, the legend on the reverse reads HISPANIARUM REX ("king of the Spains"). The mint mark appears in the field of the coin to the left of the shield. Principal Spanish mints were those at Madrid (M), Seville (S), Seville (an aqueduct).

As for Spanish-American coins, the legend on the reverse reads HISPANIARUM ET IND. REX ("king of the Spains and the Indies"). Many of the earlier issues (beginning with the reign of Philip V) are of the "pillar and globe design" which was struck only in the New World. On the later bust-type coins the mint marks appear in the legend on the reverse. The chief Spanish-American mints were: Guatemala (G or NG); Peru (L or LIMA in monogram); Mexico (M); Bolivia (P or PTS in monogram); Chile (S); Colombia (P or PN and NR).

$$4 \; Cuartos = 1 \; Real$$
$$16 \; Maravedis = 1 \; Real = 1 \; Piece \; of \; Eight$$
$$1 \; Escudo = 2 \; Reales$$
$$100 \; Centimos = 1 \; Real = 1 \; Escudo = 1 \; Peseta$$

FERDINAND V AND ISABELLA I 1474-1504
(FERDINANDVS ET ELISABET)
FERDINAND V 1504-16

1.	8 Reales. Arms. Rev. Sheaf of arrows	325.00
2.	4 Reales	75.00
3.	2 Reales	25.00
4.	1 Real	15.00
5.	2 Cuartos (C). Castle. Rev. Lion	8.00
6.	1 Cuarto (C)	12.00
7.	1 Cuarto (C)	15.00

CHARLES AND JOANNA 1516-56
(CAROLVS ET IOHANA)

| 8. | 1 Real | 15.00 |

9. 1 Cuarto (C). Crowned Y. Rev.
    Crowned pillars   12.00

23. 8 Maravedis (C). Castle. Rev. Lion   12.00
24. 4 Maravedis (C)   10.00
24a. 2 Maravedis (C)   8.00

PHILIP II (PHILIPPUS) 1556-98

Coins of this reign struck prior to 1586 are undated and are rarer than those pieces which have dates.

10. 8 Reales. Shield. Rev. Quartered arms 100.00

PHILIP IV 1621-65

11. 4 Reales   40.00
12. 2 Reales   25.00
13. 1 Real   12.00
14. ½ Real   10.00

15. 8 Maravedis (C). Castle. Rev. Lion   12.00
16. 4 Maravedis (C)   10.00
17. 2 Maravedis (C)   8.00

PHILIP III 1598-1621

18. 8 Reales. Shield. Rev. Quartered arms 150.00
19. 4 Reales   60.00
20. 2 Reales   35.00
21. 1 Real   10.00
22. ½ Real   12.00

25. 50 Reales 1628. Arms   rare
26. 8 Reales 1623-62. Shield. Rev. Quar-
     tered arms   200.00

27.	4 Reales 1651-60	100.00
28.	2 Reales 1628-52	15.00
29.	1 Real 1652	8.00
30.	½ Real 1651	12.00

31.	16 Maravedis (C) 1660-65. Head. Rev. Arms	12.00
32.	8 Maravedis (C) 1661-65	10.00
33.	4 Maravedis (C) 1661-65	8.00
34.	2 Maravedis (C) 1661-65	6.50

CHARLES II 1665-1700

35.	8 Reales 1682-97. Shield. Rev. Quartered arms	250.00
36.	4 Reales 1683-88	80.00
37.	2 Reales 1686	15.00
38.	1 Real 1674-87	15.00
39.	½ Real 1686	25.00
40.	2 Maravedis (C) 1680-96. Castle. Rev. Lion	20.00

41.	2 Maravedis (C) 1688. Head. Rev. Crowned double (C) monogram	15.00

CHARLES (of Hapsburg) as CHARLES III of Spain

In 1700 Philip of Bourbon was declared King of Spain as Philip V. The Hapsburgs, ruling family of Austria, had their own candidate, Archduke Charles of Austria. In 1703 in Vienna and in 1706 in Madrid he was declared King of Spain. In the War of the Spanish Succession, which started in 1703, Charles was defeated. He renounced his claim to the Spanish throne in 1714.

42.	2 Reales 1701-14. Crowned CAROLUS. Rev. Arms	12.00

PHILIP V 1700-46

The familiar "pillar-type" coins that were first issued in this reign were struck in large numbers at various Spanish-American mints. They were not issued in Spain proper.

43.	8 Reales 1704-40. Shield. Rev. Quartered arms	125.00
44.	4 Reales 1718	80.00
45.	2 Reales 1717-37	8.00
46.	1 Real 1726-41	7.50
47.	½ Real 1726-41	10.00

48.	6 Maravedis *or* Sesena (C) 1709-12. Arms. Rev. Crowned V (Valencia)	20.00
49.	3 Maravedis (C) 1710-11	15.00

50.	4 Maravedis (C) 1718-46. Lion seated with scepter, sword, and globe. Rev. Crowned shield	12.00
51.	2 Maravedis (C) 1718-46	8.00
52.	1 Maravedi (C) 1718-20	6.50

LOUIS I (LUIS) 1724

53.	8 Reales 1724. Shield. Rev. Quartered arms	325.00

FERDINAND VI 1746-59

54.	2 Reales 1754-88. Shield. Rev. Quartered arms	12.00
55.	1 Real 1750, 51	7.25
56.	½ Real 1747-58	6.50
57.	2 Maravedis (C) 1750. Shield. Rev. Seated lion	7.50

58.	1 Maravedi (C) 1746-47	6.50

CHARLES III 1759-88

59.	8 Reales 1762. Shield. Rev. Quartered arms (last year of issue for this type)	75.00

60.	4 Reales 1761	30.00
61.	2 Reales 1760-70	12.00
62.	1 Real 1761	7.50

63.	8 Reales 1772-88. Bust right. Rev. Arms	75.00
64.	4 Reales 1773-81	30.00
65.	2 Reales 1772-85	10.00
66.	1 Real 1774-85	6.00
67.	½ Real 1773-88	5.00

68.	8 Maravedis (C) 1772-88. Bust right. Rev. Ornate arms	6.00

69.	4 Maravedis (C) 1772-88	7.50
70.	2 Maravedis (C) 1772-87	10.00
71.	1 Maravedi (C) 1772-87	15.00

CHARLES IV 1788-1808

72.	8 Reales 1788-1808. Draped bust. Rev. Arms	60.00
73.	4 Reales 1791-1807	35.00
74.	2 Reales 1789-1808	12.00
75.	1 Real 1793-1808	6.00
76.	½ Real 1789-1803	5.00

77.	8 Maravedis (C) 1789-1808	10.00
78.	4 Maravedis (C) 1790-1808	7.50
79.	2 Maravedis (C) 1789-1808	5.00
80.	1 Maravedi (C) 1793-1802	15.00

FRENCH OCCUPATION
JOSEPH BONAPARTE 1808-13

81.	8 Reales 1809-10. Head. Rev. Arms	250.00
82.	20 Reales (Vellon-base silver) 1808-13	150.00

83.	10 Reales (Vellon) 1810-13	65.00
84.	4 Reales (Vellon) 1808-13	35.00
85.	2 Reales (Vellon) 1813	80.00
86.	1 Real (Vellon) 1813	90.00

87. 8 Maravedis (C) 1810-13   7.50

FERDINAND VII 1808-33

(Coins dated 1808-14 were struck in Spain during the king's exile in France.)

88. 8 Reales 1808-13. Bare head. Rev. Arms 50.00

89.	8 Reales 1809-30. Laureate bust. Rev. Arms	40.00
90.	4 Reales 1809-33	20.00
91.	2 Reales 1810-33	10.00
92.	1 Real 1811-32	8.50
93.	½ Real 1812-32	8.00

94. 8 Maravedis (C) 1812-33. Head. Rev. Ornate arms   2.00

95.	4 Maravedis (C) 1812-33	2.00
96.	2 Maravedis (C) 1812-33	2.50
97.	1 Maravedi (C) 1824-27	3.00

CONSTITUTIONAL COINAGE

98.	20 Reales (Vellon) 1821-23. New plain head. Rev. Arms and pillars	80.00
99.	10 Reales (Vellon) 1821. Rev. "RESELLADO"—restruck over other coins	8.00
100.	4 Reales (Vellon) 1822-32. Rev. Arms	20.00
101.	8 Maravedis (C) 1823-33. Rev. Ornate arms	2.00

ISABELLA II 1833-68

102. 20 Reales 1834-50. Young head with upswept hair. Rev. Crowned arms in collar of the Fleece   25.00

103. 20 Reales 1850-55. New style head. Rev. Arms between pillars   30.00

104.	20 Reales 1856-64. Diademed head. Rev. Arms	30.00
105.	10 Reales 1840-65. Varieties as above	15.00
106.	4 Reales 1835-64	7.50
107.	2 Reales 1836-63	6.00
108.	1 Real 1839-64	2.50

109.	8 Maravedis (C) 1835-58. Bare head. Rev. Arms in angles of cross	5.00
110.	4 Maravedis (C) 1838-55	5.00
111.	2 Maravedis (C) 1840-48	3.00
112.	1 Maravedi (C) 1842	20.00
113.	2 Escudos 1865-68. Diademed head. Rev. Arms	30.00
114.	1 Escudo 1867-68	10.00
115.	40 Centimos 1864-68	6.00
116.	20 Centimos 1864-68	7.50
117.	10 Centimos 1864-68	9.00
118.	5 Centimos (C) 1867-68	4.00
119.	2½ Centimos (C) 1867-68	3.00
120.	1 Centimo (C) 1868	3.00
121.	½ Centimo (C) 1866-68	3.50

PROVISIONAL GOVERNMENT 1868-70

122.	5 Pesetas 1869-70. Hispania reclining. Rev. Crowned arms between pillars	8.00

123.	2 Pesetas 1869-70	3.00
124.	1 Peseta 1869-70	2.00
125.	50 Centimos 1869-70	2.00
126.	20 Centimos 1869-70	45.00
127.	10 Centimos (C) 1870. Lion. Rev. Hispania	.45
128.	5 Centimos (C) 1870	.50
129.	2 Centimos (C) 1870	.25
130.	1 Centimo (C) 1870	.25

AMADEO I 1871-73

131.	5 Pesetas 1871. Bearded head. Rev. Crowned arms	7.50

ALFONSO XII 1874-85

132.	5 Pesetas 1875-81. Bare head. Rev. Crowned arms between pillars	6.00
133.	5 Pesetas 1882-85	6.00
134.	2 Pesetas 1879-84	3.00
135.	1 Peseta 1876-85	3.00
136.	50 Centimos 1880-85	1.00
137.	10 Centimos (C) 1877-79	.35
138.	5 Centimos (C) 1877-79	.50

ALFONSO XIII 1885-1931

139.	5 Pesetas 1888-92. Baby head. Rev. Arms	5.00
140.	5 Pesetas 1892-94. Child head. Rev. Arms	6.00
141.	5 Pesetas 1896-99. Youthful head	6.00
142.	2 Pesetas 1889-94. Varieties as above	3.00

SPAIN (continued)

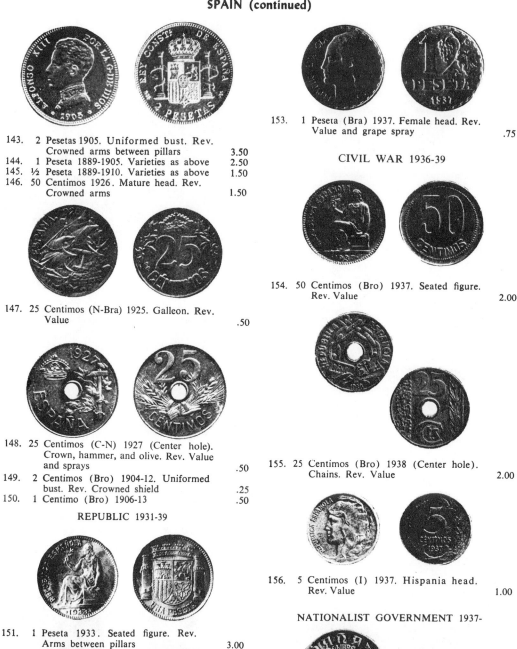

143. 2 Pesetas 1905. Uniformed bust. Rev.
Crowned arms between pillars   3.50
144. 1 Peseta 1889-1905. Varieties as above   2.50
145. ½ Peseta 1889-1910. Varieties as above   1.50
146. 50 Centimos 1926. Mature head. Rev.
Crowned arms   1.50

147. 25 Centimos (N-Bra) 1925. Galleon. Rev.
Value   .50

148. 25 Centimos (C-N) 1927 (Center hole).
Crown, hammer, and olive. Rev. Value
and sprays   .50
149. 2 Centimos (Bro) 1904-12. Uniformed
bust. Rev. Crowned shield   .25
150. 1 Centimo (Bro) 1906-13   .50

REPUBLIC 1931-39

151. 1 Peseta 1933. Seated figure. Rev.
Arms between pillars   3.00

152. 25 Centimos (N-Bro) 1934 (Center
hole). Female holding branch. Rev.
Value   .75

153. 1 Peseta (Bra) 1937. Female head. Rev.
Value and grape spray   .75

CIVIL WAR 1936-39

154. 50 Centimos (Bro) 1937. Seated figure.
Rev. Value   2.00

155. 25 Centimos (Bro) 1938 (Center hole).
Chains. Rev. Value   2.00

156. 5 Centimos (I) 1937. Hispania head.
Rev. Value   1.00

NATIONALIST GOVERNMENT 1937-

157. 25 Centimos (C-N) 1937. Sun and arrows. Rev. Shield, value, and spray   1.00

SPAIN (continued)

158. 10 Centimos (A) 1940-53. Horseman
with lance. Rev. Eagle over shield .75
159. 5 Centimos (A) 1940-53 .75

165. 2½ Pesetas (A-Br) 1953- . Rev. Coat
of Arms 1.50
166. 1 Peseta (A-Br) 1947-67. .50

160. 1 Peseta (A-Br) 1944. Arms. Rev. Value 2.00

167. 50 Centimos (C-N) 1949-65. Value.
Rev. Arrows (center hole) 1.00

168. 10 Centimos 1959. Head. Rev. Value .50

161. 5 Pesetas (N) 1949-51. Head of Gen.
Franco. Rev. Arms .50

169. 100 Pesetas 1966- . Head of Gen. Franco.
Rev. Crowned arms 5.00
170. 1 Peseta (Al-Br) 1966- . Rev. Arms .50

162. 50 Pesetas (C-N) 1957- . Rev. Eagle
and shield 1.75
163. 25 Pesetas (C-N) 1957- .50
164. 5 Pesetas (C-N) 1957- .50

171. 50 Centimos (Al-Mag) 1966. Rev. Laurel
branch .25

STRAITS SETTLEMENTS

A former British Crown Colony in Asia (including Singapore) which was dissolved in 1946. The Federation of Malaysia later was formed to include many of these states.

100 Cents = 1 Dollar

VICTORIA 1837-1901

1.	50 Cents 1886-1901. Coroneted head. Rev. Value	7.50
2.	20 Cents 1871-1901	4.00
3.	10 Cents 1871-1901	1.25
4.	5 Cents 1871-1901	2.00
5.	1 Cent (C) 1872-1901	2.50
6.	½ Cent (C) 1872-	2.50
7.	¼ Cent (C) 1872-1901	3.00

EDWARD VII 1901-10

8.	1 Dollar 1903-04, 07-09. Crowned bust. Rev. Value in Malay and Chinese in ornamental panels	5.00
9.	50 Cents 1902-08. Rev. Value in circle	6.00
10.	20 Cents 1902-10	3.00
11.	10 Cents 1902-10	2.00
12.	5 Cents 1902-03, 10	1.75

GEORGE V 1910-36

13.	1 Dollar 1919, 20. Type of #8	15.00
14.	50 Cents 1920-21. Type of #9, bust facing left	5.00
15.	20 Cents 1916-35	2.00
16.	10 Cents 1916-27	1.50
17.	5 Cents 1918-35	2.00
17a.	5 Cents (C-N) 1920	3.50

18.	1 Cent (C) 1919-20, 26 (Square-shaped with rounded corners). Crowned bust. Rev. Value in double circle	.75
19.	½ Cent (C) 1916 (Round-shaped)	2.00
20.	½ Cent (C) 1932. Type of #18	.75
21.	¼ Cent (C) 1916. Type of #19	2.00

SUDAN

An independent nation south of Egypt (formerly Anglo-Egyptian Sudan).

10 Milliemes = 1 Piastre

2.

1.	20 Piastres (CN) 1967-69. Camel and rider. Rev. Value (proof issue)	12.50
2.	10 Piastres (C-N) 1956- . Camel and rider. Rev. Value	1.00
3.	5 Piastres (C-N) 1956-	.60
4.	2 Piastres (C-N) 1956-	.75

5.	10 Milliemes (Bro) 1956- . Scalloped edge	.30
6.	5 Milliemes (Bro) 1956-	.25
7.	2 Milliemes (Bro) 1956-	.20
8.	1 Millieme (Bro) 1956- . Round	.15

9.	25 Piastres (CN) 1968. F.A.O. coin plan	10.00

10.	10 Piastres (C-N) 1971-75. New Arms. Rev. Value (Commemorates 2nd anniversary of revolution)	1.25

SUDAN (continued)

11. 5 Piastres (C-N) 1971-75   .75
12. 2 Piastres (C-N) 1971-75   .50
13. 10 Milliemes (Br) 1971   .35
13a. 10 Milliemes (Bra) 1975
14. 5 Milliemes (Br) 1971   .25
14a. 5 Milliemes (Bra) 1975

15. 50 Piastres (C-N) 1972. Arms. Rev. Farmer plowing (F.A.O. coin plan)   3.75

16. 10 Milliemes (Br) 1972. Arms. Rev. Value (scalloped planchet)   .35

17. 5 Milliemes (Br) 1972, 73. Arms. Rev. Value (F.A.O. coin plan)   .25

18. 10 Piastres (C-N) 1976. Type of #10, new legend on obverse (F.A.O. coin plan)
19. 5 Piastres (C-N) 1976
20. 2 Piastres (C-N) 1976
21. 10 Milliemes (Bra) 1976
22. 5 Milliemes (Bra) 1976

SURINAM

Dutch colony on the northeast coast of South America. Since 1954 it has been organized as a part of the kingdom of the Netherlands, with considerable powers of self-government.

JULIANA 1948-

1. 1 Cent (Br) 1957-60. Lion. Rev. Value   2.50

2. 1 Guilder 1962. Head of Queen. Rev. Arms   3.75
3. 25 Cents (CN) 1962- . Arms. Rev. Value 1.00
4. 10 Cents (CN) 1962-   .50

5. 5 Cents (N-Bra) 1962- (square planchet) .50
6. 1 Cent (Br) 1962- (round)   .30

SWAZILAND

Located in southeastern Africa, an independent nation within the British Commonwealth since 1968.

1. 1 Lilageni (C-N) 1974. Bust of King Sobhuza II. Rev. Mother and child 5.00

2. 50 Cents (C-N) 1974. Rev. Arms 2.50

3. 20 Cents (C-N) 1974. Rev. Elephant (scalloped planchet) 1.00

4. 10 Cents (C-N) 1974. Rev. Sugar cane (scalloped planchet) .... .50
5. 5 Cents (C-N) 1974. Rev. Lusekwane flower (scalloped planchet) .... .30

6. 2 Cents (Br) 1974. Rev. Pine trees (square planchet) .... .20
7. 1 Cent (Br) 1974. Rev. Pineapple (twelve-sided planchet) .... .15

8.

8. 1 Lilageni (C-N) 1975. Type of #1, added rev. inscription (F.A.O. coin plan) 5.00

9. 10 Cents (C-N) 1975. Type of #4, added rev. inscription (F.A.O. coin plan) .... .50

10. 2 Cents (Br) 1975. Type of #6, added rev. inscription (F.A.O. coin plan) .... .20
11. 1 Cent (Br) 1975. Type of #7, added rev. inscription (F.A.O. coin plan) .... .15

SWEDEN

Established as a separate kingdom after Gustavus Vasa led a successful revolt in 1521 to drive out the Danes. From 1814 to 1905 the Swedish monarchs were also kings of Norway. Swedish arms are three crowns on a shield.

$$8\ Ore = 1\ Mark$$
$$96\ Ore = 48\ Skilling = 1\ Rigsdaler$$
$$8\ Marks = 1\ Daler$$
$$100\ Ore = 1\ Krona$$

GUSTAVUS VASA 1521-60

1. Taler 1540-59. Half-length figure with sword.
   Rev. Figure of Christ   500.00

JOHN III 1568-92

2. Taler 1569-92   400.00

CHARLES IX 1604-11

3. 20 Marks 1606-11   800.00

GUSTAVUS II ADOLPHUS 1611-32

4. Taler 1615-32. Bust. Rev. Christ   550.00

6a. 1 Ore (Bro) 1638-53. Arms. Rev. Arrows   80.00

CHARLES XI 1660-97

5. 1632 "Purim" taler (commemorates victory at Leipzig)   350.00

CHRISTINA 1632-54

6. Taler 1632-52. Three-quarter facing figure of queen. Rev. Salvator mundi   650.00

7. 8 Marks 1664-96. Bust. Rev. Arms   300.00
8. 4 Marks 1664-96   175.00

6a.

9. 2 Marks 1661-96   85.00
10. 1 Mark 1663-97   80.00
11. 5 Ore 1667-94. Linked "C"s. Rev. Crowns   25.00
12. 2 Ore 1664-69. C.R.S. crowned   25.00
13. 1 Ore 1668-72. C.XI crowned   5.00
14. ½ Ore 1661-64. Arms. Rev. Lion   80.00

CHARLES XII 1697-1718

20. 1 Daler (C) 1718. Jupiter 12.00
21. 1 Daler (C) 1718. Father Time with scythe and infant, "Saturnus" 12.00
22. 1 Daler (C) 1718. Sun god, "Phoebus" 12.00

23. 1 Daler (C) 1718. War god, "Mars" 16.00
24. 1 Daler (C) 1718. "Mercurius" 12.00
25. 1 Daler (C) 1719. Hope with anchor 30.00

15. Taler 1707. Bust. Rev. Arms 650.00

BARON DE GORTZ DOLLARS

After the Swedish army under Charles XII had been defeated by Czar Peter I of Russia, the almost-bankrupt Swedish government called in all silver coins and replaced them with a new issue of copper coins struck at Stockholm.

ULRICA ELEONORA 1718-20

26. 1 Ore (C) 1719-20. Three crowns. Rev. Crossed arrows on shield (struck over De Gortz dalers) 7.50

FREDERICK I 1720-51

16. 1 Daler (C) 1715. Crown. Rev. Value 12.00

17. 1 Daler (C) 1716. Svea seated, "Publica Fide" 18.00
18. 1 Daler (C) 1717. Warrior with sword and shield, "Wett Och Wapen" 12.00
19. 1 Daler (C) 1718. Warrior and lion, "Flink Och Fardig" 12.00

27. Taler 1721. Bust and medallion portraits of Gustavus Vasa and Gustavus Adolphus. Two hundredth anniversary of the Reformation 500.00

SWEDEN (continued)

GUSTAVUS III 1771-92

39.	1 Rigsdaler 1771-82. Head and shield	85.00
40.	⅔ Rigsdaler 1776-80	65.00

41.	⅓ Rigsdaler 1776-89	50.00
42.	⅙ Rigsdaler 1773-90	30.00
43.	1/12 Rigsdaler 1777-79	25.00
44.	1/24 Rigsdaler 1777-83	13.00
45.	2 Ore (C) 1777. Arrows	30.00
46.	1 Ore (C) 1772-78	8.00

28.	Taler 1721-57. Bust and shield	200.00
29.	10 Ore 1739-51. Crossed "F"s.	45.00
30.	5 Ore 1722-51	20.00
31.	2 Ore (C) 1743-50. Arrows	8.00

GUSTAVUS IV ADOLPHUS 1792-1809

32.	1 Ore (C) 1720-50	6.00
33.	½ Ore (C) 1720-21	12.00

ADOLPHUS FREDERICK 1751-71

34.	Taler 1751-71. Head. Rev. Crowned shield	160.00

47.	1 Rigsdaler 1792-1807. Head. Rev. Arms	150.00
48.	⅓ Daler 1798-1800	350.00
49.	⅙ Daler 1792-1807	20.00

35.	½ Taler 1752-68	325.00
36.	5 Ore 1751-67. Crowns	30.00
37.	2 Ore (C) 1751-68	12.00
38.	1 Ore (C) 1751-68	12.00

50.	1 Skilling (C) 1802-05. Crowned monogram	5.00

51. ½ Skilling (C) 1802-09 — 3.50
52. ¼ Skilling (C) 1802-08 — 2.00
53. 1/12 Skilling (C) 1802-08 — 1.50

CHARLES XIII 1809-18

54. 1 Rigsdaler 1812-18. Head. Rev. Arms — 400.00
55. ⅓ Daler 1813-14 — 300.00
56. ⅙ Daler 1809-17 — 100.00
57. 1/12 Daler 1811. Monogram. Rev. Shield — 60.00
58. 1/24 Daler 1810-16 — 20.00
59. 1 Skilling 1812-17. Monogram. Rev. Arrows — 15.00
60. ½ Skilling 1815-17 — 10.00
61. ¼ Skilling 1817 — 25.00

62. 1/12 Skilling 1812 — 3.00

CHARLES XIV JOHN (BERNADOTTE) 1818-44

63. 1 Rigsdaler 1821. Bust and medallion portraits of Gustavus Vasa, Gustavus II Adolphus, and Frederick I. Three hundredth anniversary of the Reformation — 350.00

64. 1 Rigsdaler 1818-42. Head. Rev. Arms and value — 125.00
65. ½ Daler 1831-36 — 100.00
66. ¼ Daler 1830-36 — 50.00
67. ⅛ Daler 1830-37 — 25.00
68. 1/12 Daler 1831-33 — 35.00
69. 1/16 Daler 1835-36 — 25.00

70. 1 Skilling (C) 1819-43 — 10.00
71. ½ Skilling (C) 1819-32 — 7.00
72. ¼ Skilling (C) 1819-33 — 4.00
73. ⅙ Skilling (C) 1830-44 — 3.00

OSCAR I 1844-59

74. 1 Rigsdaler 1844-59. Head. Rev. Arms and supporters — 120.00
75. ½ Daler 1845-52 — 170.00
76. ¼ Daler 1846-52 — 75.00
77. 1/16 Daler 1845-55 — 8.00
78. 1/32 Daler 1852-53 — 6.00

SWEDEN (continued)

79. 50 Ore 1857. Head. Rev. Value   70.00
80. 25 Ore 1855-59   6.00
81. 10 Ore 1855-59   8.00

82. 2 Skilling (C) 1844-55. "Banco" head.
    Rev. Arrows   20.00
83. 1 Skilling (C) 1844-55   15.00
84. ⅔ Skilling (C) 1844-55   8.00
85. ⅓ Skilling (C) 1844-55. Crowned monogram   5.00
86. ¹⁄₁₆ Skilling (C) 1844-55   2.50

95. 25 Ore 1862-71   12.00
96. 10 Ore 1861-71   6.00
97. 5 Ore (C) 1860-72   10.00
98. 2 Ore (C) 1860-72   4.00
99. 1 Ore (C) 1860-72   2.50
100. ½ Ore (C) 1867. Monogram   20.00

OSCAR II 1872-1907

87. 5 Ore (C) 1857-58   12.00
88. 2 Ore (C) 1856-58   4.00
89. 1 Ore (C) 1856-58   2.50
90. ½ Ore (C) 1856-58. Monogram   1.50

101. 20 Kronor (G) 1873-1902. Head. Rev.
     Crowned arms   100.00
102. 10 Kronor (G) 1873-1901   50.00
103. 5 Kronor (G) 1881-86, 1901. Rev. Value   50.00

CHARLES XV 1859-72

104. 2 Kronor 1876-1907. Head to right. Rev.
     Arms   15.00

91. 4 Rigsdaler 1861-71. Head. Rev. Arms   75.00
92. 2 Rigsdaler 1862-71   225.00
93. 1 Rigsdaler 1860-71   80.00
94. 50 Ore 1862. Value in wreath   1200.00

105. 2 Kronor 1897. Crowned bust. Silver
     jubilee of reign. Rev. Arms   8.00

SWEDEN (continued)

106. 2 Kronor 1907. Conjoined busts of Oscar
     II and Sophia. Golden wedding   10.00
107. 1 Krona 1875-1907. Type of #104   5.00
108. 50 Ore 1875-1907. Monogram. Rev. Value   6.00
109. 25 Ore 1874-1907   2.00
110. 10 Ore 1872-1907   2.50
111. 5 Ore (Bro) 1874-1907   2.00
112. 2 Ore (Bro) 1874-1907   1.50
113. 1 Ore (Bro) 1874-1907   1.25

GUSTAVUS V 1907-50

119. 5 Kronor 1935. Head. Rev. Arms. Five
     hundredth anniversary of Parliament
     (Riksdag)   12.50

114. 20 Kronor (G) 1925. Head to right. Rev.
     Crowned arms   400.00
115. 5 Kronor (G) 1920. Head to right. Rev.
     Value   60.00
116. 2 Kronor 1910-40   3.00

117. 2 Kronor 1921. Head of Gustavus Vasa.
     Rev. Arms. Four hundredth year of
     political liberty   10.00

120. 2 Kronor 1938. Head to left. Rev. Ship.
     Three hundredth anniversary of Swe-
     dish settlement in Delaware. (Reverse
     is similar to reverse of U.S. 1936
     Delaware Commemorative)   6.00
121. 1 Krona 1910-42. Head. Rev. Arms   2.00
122. 50 Ore 1911-19, 27-39. Crowned arms.
     Rev. Value   .75
122a. 50 Ore (N-Br) 1920-24, 40-47. Crowned
     monogram. Rev. Value   1.00
123. 25 Ore 1910-19, 27-41   1.00
123a. 25 Ore (N-Br) 1921, 40-47. Type of #122a   .50
124. 10 Ore 1909-19, 27-42   1.50
124a. 10 Ore (N-Br) 1920-25, 40-47. Type of
     #122a   2.50

118. 2 Kronor 1932. Bust of Gustavus II
     Adolphus. Rev. Inscription on panel:
     Third centenary of death   8.00

125. 5 Ore (Bro) 1909-42, 50; (I) 1917-19, 42-
     50. Monogram. Rev. Value   1.50
126. 2 Ore (Bro) 1909-42, 50; (I) 1917-19, 42-50   1.00
127. 1 Ore (Bro) 1909-42, 50; (I) 1917-19, 42-50   .50

SWEDEN (continued)

NEW SILVER COINAGE

128. 2 Kronor 1942-50. Older head. Rev. Arms   2.00
129. 1 Kronor 1942-50   1.50

130. 50 Ore 1943-50. Crown. Rev. Value   1.00
131. 25 Ore 1943-50   .50
132. 10 Ore 1942-50   1.50

GUSTAF VI ADOLF 1950-73

133. 5 Kronor 1952. Head. Rev. Monogram.
     King's seventieth birthday   35.00
134. 5 Kronor 1954, 55, 71. Head. Rev. Arms   6.00

135. 2 Kronor 1952-66   2.00
135a. 2 Kronor (CN) 1968-   1.00
136. 1 Krona 1952-68   1.00
136a. 1 Krona (CN clad) 1968-73   .50

137. 50 Ore 1952-61. Crown. Rev. Value   2.00
138. 25 Ore 1952-61   .75
139. 10 Ore 1952-62   .50

140. 5 Ore (Bro) 1952-71. Incuse crown.
     Rev. Value   .25
141. 2 Ore (Bro) 1952-71   .15
142. 1 Ore (Bro) 1952-71   .10

143. 5 Kronor 1959 (Sesquicentennial of
     Swedish form of government). Head
     of King. Rev. Four men   20.00

144. 5 Kronor 1962. Head of the King. Rev.
     Athena holding an owl. (80th birth-
     day commemorative)   90.00

SWEDEN (continued)

145. 50 Ore (C-N) 1962-73. Crowned monogram. Rev. Value .35
146. 25 Ore (C-N) 1962-73 .25
147. 10 Ore (C-N) 1962-73 .15

148. 5 Kronor 1966. Head of King. Rev.
Tablet (commemorates 100th anniversary two-chamber system of Parliament) 7.00

149. 10 Kronor 1972. Rev. Royal signature
(Commemorates 90th birthday of King) 10.00

150. 5 Kronor (C-N) 1972, 73. Rev. Crowned
arms 2.00

151. 5 Ore (Br) 1972, 73. Three crowns. Rev.
Value .10

CARL XVI GUSTAF 1973-

152. 50 Kronor 1975. Three crowns, value.
Rev. Torch, uplifted hands (Commemorates constitutional reform) 20.00

153. 5 Kronor (C-N) 1976. Head of King Carl.
Rev. Flag

154. 1 Krona (C-N) 1976. Head facing left.
Rev. Arms

155. 50 Ore (C-N) 1976. Crowned monogram.
Rev. Value
156. 25 Ore (C-N) 1976
157. 10 Ore (C-N) 1976
158. 5 Ore (Br) 1976

SWITZERLAND

An independent country since 1386. Prior to 1850 the individual cantons issued their own coinage. Representative coins of these issues are listed.

4 Kreutzers = 1 Batz = 10 Centimes
100 Centimes or Rappens = 1 Franc

SWISS CANTONS
APPENZELL

1.	4 Franken 1812, 16. Arms. Rev. Warrior with tablet	300.00
2.	2 Franken 1812	175.00
3.	1 Batzen (Bi) 1808, 16. Arms. Rev. Value	20.00

ARGAU (ARGOVIE)

4.	4 Franken 1812. Arms. Rev. Warrior	400.00
5.	1 Batzen (Bi) 1805-16. Arms. Rev. Value	20.00

BASEL

6.	5 Batzen 1809-10. Arms. Rev. Value	40.00
7.	1 Batzen (Bi) 1805-10	15.00

BERN

8.	1 Thaler 1798, 1823, 35. Arms. Rev. Warrior	400.00

9.	40 Batzen. Counterstamped on French Ecu	150.00
10.	½ Thaler 1835. Arms. Rev. Warrior	175.00
11.	1 Batzen (Bi) 1798-1824. Arms. Rev. Value in wreath	12.00

FREYBURG (FRIBOURG)

12.	4 Franken 1813. Arms. Rev. Warrior	450.00
13.	1 Batzen (Bi) 1806-30. Arms. Rev. Value	12.00

GENEVA (GENEVE)

14.	1 Taler 1794. Liberty head	80.00

15.	5 Francs 1848. Arms. Rev. Value	175.00
16.	25 Centimes (Bi) 1839-44	8.50
17.	10 Centimes (Bi) 1839, 44	8.00
18.	5 Centimes (Bi) 1840	7.50
19.	4 Centimes (Bi) 1839	9.00
20.	2 Centimes (Bi) 1839	12.00
21.	1 Centime (Bi) 1839	6.00

GRAUBUNDEN (GRISONS)

22.	10 Batzen 1825. Arms. Rev. Value	300.00
23.	5 Batzen 1807, 20, 26	100.00

LUZERN (LUCERNE)

24.	4 Franken 1813-14. Arms. Rev. Warrior	150.00
25.	1 Batzen 1803-13	10.00

ST. GALL

26.	1 Taler 1621. Bear standing	100.00

SOLOTHURN (SOLEURE)

27.	4 Franken 1813. Arms. Rev. Warrior	400.00
28.	1 Batzen (Bi) 1805-26. Arms. Rev. Value	10.00

TICINO (TESSIN)

29.	4 Franchi 1814. Arms. Rev. Warrior	450.00

VAUD

30.	5 Batzen (Bi) 1826-31. Arms. Rev. Cross	20.00
31.	1 Batzen (Bi) 1826-34	6.00

ZURICH

32.	40 Batzen 1813. Arms. Rev. Motto	150.00

33.	8 Batzen 1810, 14	60.00
34.	1 Kreuzer (Bi) 1842. Arms. Rev. Value in wreath	6.50

HELVETIAN CONFEDERATION 1850-

35.	5 Francs 1850-74. Helvetia seated. Value in wreath	100.00
36.	2 Francs 1850-57, 60, 62-63	90.00
37.	1 Franc 1850-57, 60-61	50.00
38.	½ Franc 1850-51	100.00

39.	5 Francs 1888-1916. Diademed head of Helvetia. Rev. Shield and value in wreath	125.00

SHOOTING FESTIVAL COINS

(Intended primarily as prizes but also used in general circulation for a brief time. The denomination is 5 Francs.)

44. Zurich 1859   135.00

40. Graubunden 1842   325.00

45. Nidwalden 1861   100.00

41. Glarus 1847   1200.00

46. La Chaux-de-Fonds 1863   125.00

42. Solothurn 1855   800.00

43. Berne 1857   175.00

47. Schaffhausen 1865   75.00

48. Schwyz 1867   75.00

52. Lausanne 1876   40.00

49. Zug 1869   80.00

53. Basel 1879   35.00

50. Zurich 1872   60.00

54. Fribourg 1881   35.00

51. St. Gallen 1874   45.00

55. Lugano 1883   35.00

56. Berne 1885   35.00

60.   5 Francs 1939 (Commemorating Lucerne Shooting Festival). Kneeling figure shooting. Rev. Motto   25.00

57.   5 Francs 1922-28. Bust of "William Tell." Rev. Shield   60.00

61.   5 Francs 1939 (Commemorating Zurich Exposition). Farm scene above, clasped hands below. Rev. Shield and inscription   20.00

COMMEMORATIVE ISSUES

58.   5 Francs 1934 (Commemorating Fribourg Shooting Festival). Swiss Guard. Rev. Crowned arms in wreath   25.00

62.   5 Francs 1939 (Laupen Commemorative). Male figure. Rev. Helvetian Cross   100.00

63.   5 Francs 1941 (Commemorating 650 years of Confederation). Three figures swearing oath. Rev. Helvetian cross and inscription   25.00

59.   5 Francs 1936 (Premium for the Armament Fund). Kneeling female figure. Rev. Inscription   15.00

64.   5 Francs 1944 (Commemorating five hundredth anniversary of the Battle of St. Jakob an der Birs). Male figure. Rev. Helvetian cross and inscription   25.00

65.   5 Francs 1948 (Commemorating centenary of the Swiss Constitution). Woman and child. Rev. Helvetian cross   8.00

66. 20 Francs (G) 1897-1949. Peasant girl.
Rev. Shield   65.00
67. 10 Francs (G) 1911-22   100.00
68. 5 Francs 1931-69. Bust of "William Tell."
Rev. Shield (smaller planchet than #57)   5.00
68a. 5 Francs (C-N) 1968-   2.00

78. 5 Francs (C-N) 1974. Three women with Swiss cross. Rev. Value and dates (Commemorates 100th anniversary of constitution)   2.00

69. 2 Francs 1874-1967. Helvetia standing, border of stars. Rev. Value in wreath   3.25
69a. 2 Francs (C-N) 1968-   1.50
70. 1 Franc 1875-1967   2.00
70a. 1 Franc (C-N) 1968-   .50
71. ½ Franc 1875-1967   1.25
71a. ½ Franc (C-N) 1968-   .35

79. 5 Francs (C-N) 1975. Hands around inscription. Rev. Value (Commemorates European Monument Protection Year)

80. 5 Francs (C-N) 1975. Three armored pikemen. Rev. Value (Commemorates 500th anniversary, Battle of Murten Castle)

72. 20 Centimes (N) 1881-1938; (C-N) 1939- . Head of Helvetia   .20
73. 10 Centimes (C-N) 1879-1915, 19-31, 40- ; (Bra) 1918, 19; (N) 1932-39   .15
74. 5 Centimes (C-N) 1879-1917, 1919-31, 1940- ; (Bra) 1918; (N) 1932-41   .10

75. 2 Centimes (Br) 1948- . Helvetian cross   .10
76. 1 Centime (Br) 1948-   .05

77. 5 Francs 1963. Nurse standing between two bandaged men. Rev. Value (Red Cross centennial)   15.00

SYRIA

Originally a part of the Turkish Empire, Syria was a French mandate, with some self-government, from 1920 to 1943. In 1944 Syria became an independent republic. It was part of the United Arab Republic from 1958 until 1961.

100 Piastres = 1 Lira (Pound)

FRENCH MANDATE 1920-1943

1.	50 Piastres 1929-37	7.50
2.	25 Piastres 1929-38	3.50
3.	10 Piastres 1929	3.25
4.	5 Piastres (A-Bro) 1926-40	.75
5.	2 Piastres (A-Bro) 1926	6.00

6. 1 Piastre (N-Bro) 1929-36; (Z) 1940 (Center hole)   .75

INDEPENDENT REPUBLIC 1944-

7.	1 Pound (G) 1950	50.00
8.	½ Pound (G) 1950	35.00

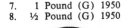

9.	1 Lira 1950	2.00
10.	50 Piastres 1947	2.50
11.	25 Piastres 1947	1.50
12.	10 Piastres (C-N) 1948, 56	.50
13.	5 Piastres (C-N) 1948, 56	.50
14.	2½ Piastres (C-N) 1948, 56	.30

UNITED ARAB REPUBLIC ISSUES

15.	50 Piastres 1958. Eagle. Rev. Value in gear	3.00
16.	25 Piastres 1958	1.50

17.	50 Piatres 1959. Eagle with two stars on on shield. Rev. Value within inscription (commemorates the founding of the republic)	2.00
18.	10 Piastres (A-Br) 1960. Eagle. Rev. Value	.50
19.	5 Piastres (A-Br) 1960	.20

20.	2½ Piastres (A-Br) 1960	.15

SYRIAN ARAB REPUBLIC

21.	1 Pound (N) 1968, 71. Arms. Rev. Inscription in panel	1.00
22.	50 Piastres (N) 1968	.60
23.	25 Piastres (N) 1968	.40
24.	10 Piastres (A-Br) 1962, 65. Rev. Value	.35
25.	5 Piastres (A-Br) 1962, 65	.20
26.	2¼ Piastres (A-Br) 1962, 65	.15

27.	1 Pound (N) 1968. Arms. Rev. Wheat stalks (F.A.O. coin plan)	1.50

28.	5 Piastres (Bra) 1971. Arms. Rev. Wheat (F.A.O. coin plan)	.15

SYRIA (continued)

29. 1 Pound (N) 1972. Arms. Rev. Hand holding torch over map (Commemorates 25th anniversary of Socialist party)   1.00

30. 50 Piastres (N) 1972. Rev. Value over torch (Commemorates 25th anniversary of Socialist party)   .75

31. 25 Piastres (N) 1972. Rev. Lighted altar (Commemorates 25th anniversary of Socialist party)   .50

32. 1 Pound (N) 1976. (F.A.O. coin plan)
33. 50 Piastres (N) 1976
34. 25 Piastres (N) 1976
35. 10 Piastres (Bra) 1976
36. 5 Piastres (Bra) 1976

TAIWAN (Nationalist China)

The refugees from the communist takeover of mainland China settled on the island of Taiwan in 1949.

10 Chiao = 1 Yuan

1. 5 Chiao 1949. Bust of Sun Yat-sen. Rev. Map of Formosa   .75

2. 2 Chiao (A) 1950   .30
3. 1 Chiao (Bro) 1949, (A) 1955   .15

4. 1 Dollar 1960⁻ . Plum flower. Rev. Orchid (50th anniversary of the republic)   .50

5. 100 Yuan 1965. Head of Dr. Sun Yat-sen. Rev. Running deer (100th anniversary of birth)   10.00
6. 50 Yuan 1965   5.00

7. 10 Yuan (C-N) 1965. Rev. Mausoleum at Nanking   2.00
8. 5 Yuan (C-N) 1965   1.50

9.

TAIWAN (continued)

9. 1 Yuan or dollar (CN) 1966. Head of Chiang Kai-shek. Rev. Inscription (Commemorates 80th birthday) .35

10. 5 Chiao or 50 fen (Al) 1967. Mayling orchid. Rev. Inscription .40

11. 1 Chiao (Al) 1967. Simple Heart orchid .25

12. 1 Yuan (CNZ) 1969. Plum flower. Rev. Farm girl and tractor (F.A.O. coin plan) .75

13. 5 Yuan (C-N) 1970- . Head of Chiang Kai-shek. Rev. Value .50

TANZANIA

The Republic of Tanganyika and the People's Republic of Zanzibar federated in April, 1964, and adopted the name United Republic of Tanzania in October, 1964. Tanganyika, formerly part of German East Africa, a British mandate after World War I, and a U.N. Trust Territory after World War II, became an independent state in 1961, and a republic within the British Commonwealth in 1962. Zanzibar, a small island in the Indian Ocean 20 miles off the coast of East Africa, was proclaimed a People's Republic in January, 1964, after becoming an independent state within the Commonwealth in 1963.

1. 1 Shilling (C-N) 1966- . Head of Pres. Nyere. Rev. Freedom torch 1.00

2. 50 Cents (C-N) 1966- . Rev. Rabbit .50

3. 20 Cents (Ni-Br) 1966- . Rev. Ostrich .30
4. 5 Cents (Br) 1966- Rev. Sailfish .20

5. 5 Shillings (C-N) 1971. Head of President Nyere. Rev. Value surrounded by food crops and cow (F.A.O. coin plan, commemorates 10th anniversary of independence) 2.50

TANZANIA (continued)

6. 5 Shillings (C-N) 1972, 73. Type of #5 without commemorative legend (F.A.O. coin plan) — 2.00

7. 1500 Shillings (G) 1974. Rev. Leopard — 300.00

8. 50 Shillings 1974. Rev. Rhinoceros — 25.00

9. 25 Shillings 1974. Rev. Giraffes — 15.00

(also see ZANZIBAR)

THAILAND

A kingdom on the Indo-Chinese Peninsula in Asia, formerly known as Siam.

64 Atts = 1 Tical
100 Satangs or 8 Fuang = 1 Tical

EARLY BULLET MONEY 1824-80

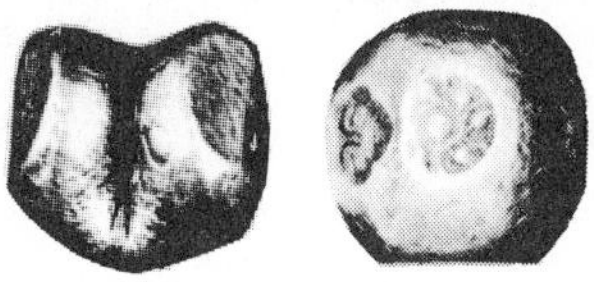

1.	4 Ticals	200.00
2.	2 Ticals	275.00
3.	1 Tical	5.00
4.	½ Tical	8.00
5.	¼ Tical	2.50
6.	⅛ Tical	2.00
7.	1/16 Tical	2.00
8.	1/32 Tical	7.50

P'RA CHOM KLAO MONGKUT 1851-1868

9.	2 Ticals 1860. Crown with three umbrellas and leaf scrolls. Rev. Elephant in center of ornamental design	140.00
10.	1 Tical	15.00
11.	½ Tical	40.00
12.	¼ Tical	15.00
13.	⅛ Tical	6.00
14.	1/16 Tical	5.00

15.	⅛ Fuang (T alloy)	3.00
16.	1/16 Fuang (T alloy)	3.00
17.	½ Fuang (C)	9.00
18.	¼ Fuang (C)	9.00

P'RA PARAMIN MAHA CHULALONGKORN
1868-1910

19.	1 Tical. Type of #9 but without leaf scrolls	15.00
20.	¼ Tical	20.00
21.	⅛ Tical	5.00

THAILAND • 431

THAILAND (continued)

22. 1 Tical 1876-1907. Bust. Rev. Arms with supporters — 5.00
23. ¼ Tical 1868-1909 — 12.00
24. ⅛ Tical 1868-1908 — 2.00
25. 1/16 Fuang (T alloy). Type of #19 — 12.00
26. 4 Atts (C). Crowned monogram. Rev. Value in wreath — 15.00
27. 2 Atts (C) — 2.50
28. 1 Att (C) — 2.00
29. ½ Att (C) — 1.50

30. 20 Satangs (C-N) 1897. Three-headed elephant. Rev. Value in wreath — 12.00
31. 10 Satangs 1897 (C-N) — 20.00
32. 5 Satangs 1897 (C-N) — 7.50
33. 2½ Satangs 1897 (C-N) — 3.50

34. 10 Satangs (N) 1908 (Center hole). Name and value. Rev. Date and ornamental design of #9 — 1.50
35. 5 Satangs (N) 1908-09 — 3.00

36. 2 Atts (Bro) 1887-1905. Bust. Rev. Allegorical figure of Siam seated — 2.50
37. 1 Att (Bro) 1887-1905 — 2.00
38. ½ Att (Bro) 1887-1905 — 2.00

P'RA PARAMIN MAHA VAJIRAVUDH 1910-25

39. 1 Tical 1913-18. Bust. Rev. Three-headed elephant — 3.00
40. ½ Tical 1915-21 — 2.50
41. ¼ Tical 1915-25 — 2.00
42. 10 Satangs (N) 1910-21. Type of #34 — 1.00
43. 5 Satangs (N) 1910-21 — .75
44. 1 Satang (Bro) 1910-24 — .75

P'RA PARAMIN MAHA PRAJADHIPOK 1925-33

45. ½ Tical 1929. Bust in uniform. Rev. Elephant — 5.00
46. ¼ Tical 1929 — 4.00
47. 5 Satangs (C-N) 1926. Type of #34 — .75
48. 1 Satang (Bro) 1926-29 — .50

ANANDA MAHIDOL 1933-46

49. 20 Satangs (T) 1945 (Center hole). Ornamental designs — 1.75
50. 10 Satangs (N) 1935, 37; (S) 41; (T) 1942, 44, 45 — 1.00
51. 5 Satangs (N) 1935-37; (S) 41; (T) 1942, 44, 45 — 1.00
52. 1 Satang (T) 1942, 44 — .25
52a. 1 Satang (Br) 1935-39. Type of #34 — 1.00
53. ½ Satang (Bro) 1937 — 1.00

54. 50 Satangs (T) 1946. Young bust. Rev. Arms — 5.00
55. 10 Satangs (T) 1946 — .75
56. 5 Satangs 1946 — .50

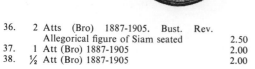

THAILAND (continued)

57. 50 Satangs 1946. Older bust. Rev. Type
of #54   1.50
58. 25 Satangs 1946   1.00
59. 10 Satangs 1946   .75
60. 5 Satangs 1946   .50

PHUMIPHOL ADULYADET 1946-

100 Satangs = 1 Baht

61. 50 Satangs (A-Bro) 1950. Bust of King
in uniform. Rev. Arms   1.50
62. 25 Satangs (A-Bro) 1954-56   1.50
63. 10 Satangs (T) 1950-73; (A-Bro) 1950   .75
64. 5 Satangs (T) 1950-73; (A-Bro) 1950   .20

65. 1 Baht (C-N) 1957-60. Bust of King with
three medals on uniform. Rev. Arms   1.00
66. 50 Satangs (A-Br) 1957-   .25
67. 25 Satangs (A-Br) 1957-   .20
68. 10 Satangs (A-Br or Br) 1957-   .25
69. 5 Satangs (A-Br or Br) 1957-   .20
70. 1 Baht (C-N) 1961. Heads of King and
Queen. Rev. Arms   1.00
71. 1 Baht (C-N) 1962. Bust of King (does
not divide legend)   .50

72. 20 Baht 1963. Bust of King. Rev. Royal
emblems below royal umbrella (commemorates King's 36th birthday)   5.00

73. 1 Baht (C-N) 1963. Rev. Royal insignia   1.00

74. 1 Baht (CN) 1966. Conjoined busts of King
and Queen. Rev. Sunstar and inscription
(Commemorates Fifth Asian Games)   1.00

75. 600 Baht (G) 1968. Bust of Queen Sirikit.
Rev. Crowned monogram (Commemor-
ates Queen's 36th birthday)   80.00
76. 300 Baht (G) 1968   40.00
77. 150 Baht (G) 1968   20.00

78. 1 Baht (C-N) 1970. Type of #74, reverse
inscription updated (Commemorates
Sixth Asian Games)   .50

79. 800 Baht (G) 1971. Bust of King. Rev.
Crowned insignia (Commemorates 25th
year of reign)   100.00
80. 400 Baht (G) 1971   50.00
81. 10 Baht 1971   1.50

THAILAND • 433

86. 1 Baht (C-N) 1973. Rev. Emblem of World Health Organization (Commemorates 25th anniversary of W.H.O.) .25

82. 50 Baht 1971. Bust of King. Rev. Buddhist Wheel of Law (Commemorates 20th anniversary of World Fellowship of Buddhists) 9.00

87. 50 Baht 1974. Conjoined portraits of Kings P'ra Chom Klao Mongkut and P'ra Paramin Maka Chulalongkorn. Rev. Symbols of Chakri dynasty (Commemorates 100th anniversary of National Museum in Bangkok) 10.00

88. 1 Baht (C-N) 1974. Bust. Rev. Garuda bird .25

83. 5 Baht (C-N) 1972. Bust of King. Rev. Mythical Garuda bird (9-sided planchet) .50

89. 2500 Baht (G) 1975. Bust. Rev. Swallow (Conservation commemorative) 300.00

84. 1 Baht (C-N) 1972. Bust of Prince Vajiralongkorn. Rev. Crowned monogram .25

90. 100 Baht 1975. Rev. Stag 12.50
91. 50 Baht 1975. Rev. Rhinoceros 12.50

85. 1 Baht (C-N) 1972. Bust of King. Rev. Ploughing ceremony (F.A.O. coin plan) .25

92. 1 Baht (C-N) 1975. Conjoined busts of King and Queen. Rev. Symbol of South East Asian Peninsular Games (Commemorates 8th SEAP Games)

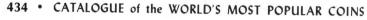

TIBET

This mountainous country which lies between China and India has a vaguely defined status. For more than two centuries it has been claimed by China. Over-run by the Chinese Communist Army in 1951, it was made a province of the People's Republic of China in 1959.

10 Shokay = 1 Srang
1 Tangka = 1½ Shokang

1.	1 Rupee 1903	30.00
2.	10 Srang 1948-49	10.00
3.	5 Srang 1946-48	7.50
4.	5 Shokang (C) 1947-53	3.00
5.	3 Shokang (C) 1946	10.00

TIMOR

This Indonesian island is divided into two parts. The eastern end is a Portuguese coin-issuing colony. The western end is part of the Republic of Indonesia. In December 1975 the Indonesians overran the eastern end of the island.

100 Avos = 1 Pataca
100 Centavos = 1 Escudo

1.	50 Avos 1945, 48, 51. Arms on cross. Rev. Value above spray	10.00
2.	20 Avos (N-Bro) 1945. Bust of Republic. Rev. Arms	7.00

3.	10 Avos (Bro) 1945, 48, 51. Quinas cross	1.50
4.	6 Escudos 1958- . Arms on cross above date. Rev. Crowned shield	1.50
5.	3 Escudos 1958-	1.00

6.	1 Escudos (C-N) 1958	.50
7.	60 Centavos (C-N) 1958-	.35
8.	30 Centavos (Br) 1958- Crowned shield. Rev. Value	.25
9.	10 Centavos (Br) 1958-	.15
10.	10 Escudos 1964. Arms on cross above date. Rev. Crowned shield	3.50

11.	10 Escudos (C-N) 1970	1.50
12.	5 Escudos (C-N) 1970	1.00
13.	2½ Escudos (C-N) 1970	.60

14.	1 Escudo (Br) 1970. Crowned shield. Rev. Value	.40
15.	50 Centavos (Br) 1970	.25
16.	20 Centavos (Br) 1970	.15

TOGO

A former German colony on the west coast of Africa, Togo became a French mandate after World War I and is now an independent republic and a member of the West African States currency group.

100 Centimes = 1 Franc

1.	2 Francs (A-Bro) 1924-25. Head of the Republic. Rev. Value	3.50
2.	1 Franc (A-Bro) 1924-25	2.00
3.	50 Centimes (A-Bro) 1924-26	1.50

4.	2 Francs (A) 1948. Bust of the Republic. Rev. Value and antelope head	5.00
5.	1 Franc (A) 1948	5.00
6.	5 Francs (A-Bro) 1956. Bust of Republic. Rev. Antelope	1.00

TONGA

Also known as the Friendly Islands, situated in the South Pacific Ocean, this is a self-governing kingdom under the protection of Great Britain.

100 Seniti = 1 Pa'anga

1.	1 Pa'anga (CN) 1967. Head of Queen Salote Tupou III. Rev. Arms	3.00
2.	50 Seniti (CN) 1967	1.50
3.	20 Seniti (CN) 1967	.85
4.	10 Seniti (CN) 1967. Rev. Value	.60
5.	5 Seniti (CN) 1967	.45
6.	2 Seniti (Br) 1967. Rev. Turtle	.35

7.	1 Seniti (Br) 1967	.25

TONGA (continued)

8.	2 Pa'anga (CN) 1967. Head of King Taufa'ahau Tupou IV. Rev. Arms (Coronation commemorative)	8.50
9.	1 Pa'anga (CN) 1967	5.00
10.	50 Seniti (CN) 1967	3.50
11.	20 Seniti (CN) 1967	2.00
12.	2 Pa'anga (CN) 1968- . Head of King, different inscription. Rev. Arms	5.00

13.	1 Pa'anga (CN) 1968-	3.00
14.	50 Seniti (CN) 1968	1.25
15.	20 Seniti (CN) 1968-	.75
16.	10 Seniti (CN) 1968- . Rev. Value	.50
17.	5 Seniti (CN) 1968-	.25
18.	2 Seniti (Br) 1968- . Rev. Turtle	.20
19.	1 Seniti (Br) 1968	.20
20.	50 Seniti (C-N) 1974. Type of #14, 12-sided planchet	1.25
21.	1 Seniti (Bra) 1974. Type of #19	.15

22.	2 Pa'anga (C-N) 1975. Bust of King. Rev. Livestock and produce (F.A.O. coin plan)	4.00

TONGA (continued)

23. 1 Pa'anga (C-N) 1975. Rev. 100 Coconut
    trees (F.A.O. coin plan)   4.00

24. 50 Seniti (C-N) 1975. Rev. 50 fish (12-sided
    planchet) (F.A.O. coin plan)   1.25
25. 20 Seniti (C-N) 1975. Rev. 20 Bees and bee-
    hive (F.A.O. coin plan)   .75

26. 10 Seniti (C-N) 1975. Rev. 10 Cows (F.A.O.
    coin plan)   .50
27. 5 Seniti (C-N) 1975. Hen and 4 chicks.
    Rev. Bunch of bananas (F.A.O. coin
    plan)   .25

28. 2 Seniti (Br) 1975. Two watermelons. Rev.
    Symbol of World Population Year
    (F.A.O. coin plan)   .20

29. 1 Seniti (Br) 1975. Ear of maize. Rev. Sow
    (F.A.O. coin plan)   .15

TRINIDAD AND TOBAGO

These islands in the British West Indies were discovered by Columbus and settled by the Spanish, who
ceded them to Great Britain in 1802. They became one
colony in 1889 and an independent member state of
the British Commonwealth in 1962.

1. 50 Cents (C-N) 1966-71. Arms. Rev.
   Value   1.25
2. 25 Cents (C-N) 1966-73   .75
3. 10 Cents (C-N) 1966-73   .30
4. 5 Cents (Br) 1966-73   .20
5. 1 Cent (Br) 1966-73   .10

6. 1 Dollar (N) 1969. Arms. Rev. Value and
   cocoa branch (F.A.O. coin plan)   3.00
7. 1 Dollar (C-N) 1970-71. Arms. Rev.
   Value   6.00

8. 5 Dollars 1971- . Arms. Rev. Scarlet
   ibis   9.00

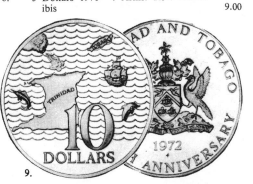

9.

TRINIDAD AND TOBAGO (continued)

9.   10 Dollars 1972. Antique map. Rev. Arms over inscription (Commemorates 10th anniversary of independence)   15.00
10.   5 Dollars 1972. Type of #8 with added inscription   10.00

11.   1 Dollar (C-N) 1972. Native Cocrico bird. Rev. Arms over inscription   2.50

12.   50 Cents (C-N) 1972. Type of #1. Rev. Redesigned lettering, commemorative inscription   1.50
13.   25 Cents (C-N) 1972   .75
14.   10 Cents (C-N) 1972   .50
15.   5 Cents (Br) 1972   .25
16.   1 Cent (Br) 1972   .10
17.   10 Dollars 1973- . Type of #9 without commemorative inscription   25.00
18.   10 Dollars (C-N) 1973-   12.50
19.   1 Dollar (C-N) 1973- . Type of #11 without commemorative inscription   6.00

20.   50 Cents (C-N) 1973- . Arms. Rev. Steel drums   .50
21.   25 Cents (C-N) 1974- . Arms. Rev. Chaconia flower, value   .65

22.   10 Cents (C-N) 1974- . Rev. Hibiscus flower   .40
23.   5 Cents (Br) 1974- . Rev. Bird of Paradise   .25
24.   1 Cent (Br) 1974- . Rev. Balisier bird   .10

TUNISIA

Tunis became a French protectorate in 1881. It now has independent status.

100 Centimes = 1 Franc

FIRST ISSUE

1.   20 Francs (G) 1891-1904. French inscription. Rev. Arabic inscription   75.00
2.   2 Francs 1891-1916. French inscription. Rev. Arabic inscription   6.00
3.   1 Franc 1891-1918   3.00
4.   50 Centimes 1891-1917   1.50

5.   10 Centimes (Bro) 1891-93, 1903-17. French inscription. Rev. Arabic inscription   .80
6.   5 Centimes (Bro) 1891-93, 1903-17   .60
7.   2 Centimes (Bro) 1891   3.00
8.   1 Centime (Bro) 1891   4.00

NEW STANDARD

9.   100 Francs (G) 1930, 32, 34. French inscription. Rev. Arabic inscription   100.00
10.   20 Francs 1930, 32, 34. French inscription. Rev. Arabic inscription   50.00

11.   10 Francs 1930, 32, 34   30.00

(#9, 10, and 11 were never placed in general circulation.)

TUNISIA (continued)

12. 20 Francs 1935. French inscription. Rev.
    Arabic inscription — 7.50
13. 10 Francs 1935 — 4.00
14. 5 Francs 1935-36 — 3.00

15. 20 Francs 1939. French inscription. Rev.
    Arabic inscription — 15.00
16. 10 Francs 1939 — 5.00
17. 5 Francs 1939 — 3.50

(#15, 16, 17 were never placed in general circulation because of the outbreak of World War II. Most of the coins were melted down.)

18. 2 Francs (A-Bro) 1921-46. French and
    Arabic inscriptions — .50
19. 1 Franc (A-Bro) 1921-46 — .25
20. 50 Centimes (A-Bro) 1921-46 — .25

21. 25 Centimes (N-Bro) 1919-38 (Center
    hole). French inscription. Rev. Arabic
    inscription — .60
22. 5 Francs (A-Bro) 1946. Type of #15 — 1.50
23. 20 Centimes (Z) 1942-46 — 2.50
24. 10 Centimes (Z) 1942-46 — .60

25. 100 Francs (C-N) 1950-57. Arabic in-
    scription. Rev. French inscription — 1.00
26. 50 Francs (C-N) 1950-57 — .75
27. 20 Francs (C-N) 1950-57 — .50

28. 5 Francs (C-N) 1954-58 — .40

29. 100 Milliemes (Bra) 1960- . Arabic le-
    gend in circle. Rev. Value in circle of
    leaves — 1.50
30. 50 Milliemes (Bra) 1960- — 1.00
31. 20 Milliemes (Bra) 1960- — .60
32. 10 Milliemes (Bra) 1960- — .45

33. 5 Milliemes (A) 1960- . Tree. Rev.
    Value — .30
34. 2 Milliemes (A) 1960- — .20
35. 1 Millieme (A) 1960- — .15

36. ½ Dinar (N) 1968. Head of President
    Bourguiba. Rev. Value — 4.00

37. 1 Dinar 1970. Rev. Man harvesting dates
    (F.A.O. coin plan) — 7.00

Price

At the height of its ~~power~~ the ~~empire~~ of the Ottoman Turks stretched from Hungary to the Indian Ocean, and from northern Africa to central Asia. In the days of its decline, during the nineteenth century, the empire lost one province after another. World War I left Turkey with only a small area in Asia Minor and a much smaller area in Europe. In 1921 a revolt deposed the last Sultan, and Turkey became a republic.

All Turkish coins under the sultanate carry the toughra, the Sultan's calligraphic emblem, on the obverse. In most cases the value appears right under the toughra. On the bottom of the reverse appears the date on which the reigning Sultan began his rule. (The dates follow the Mohammedan system of beginning with 622 A.D. as the year 1. This is explained in the dating section on page 6.) At the top of the reverse appears the year of the then current Sultan's reign when the coin was issued.

40 Paras = 1 Piastre
100 Piastres = 1 Lira or Pound
100 Kurus = 1 Lira

Types of coins issued 1839-1921

1.	500 Piastres (G). Toughra. Rev. Inscription in wreath	300.00
2.	250 Piastres (G)	200.00
3.	100 Piastres (G)	60.00
4.	50 Piastres (G)	40.00
5.	25 Piastres (G)	25.00

6.	20 Piastres (A.H. 1261-1336)	10.00
7.	10 Piastres (A.H. 1261-1331)	6.00
8.	5 Piastres (A.H. 1261-1331)	2.50
9.	2 Piastres (A.H. 1261-1336)	1.50
10.	1 Piastre (A.H. 1261-1329)	1.00
11.	40 Paras (C or Bi) (A.H. 1261-1340)	3.00
12.	20 Paras (C or Bi) (A.H. 1261-1334)	.60
13.	10 Paras (C or Bi) (A.H. 1261-1334)	.50
14.	5 Paras (C or Bi) (A.H. 1261-1334)	.50
15.	1 Para (C or Bi) (A.H. 1261-1278)	.65

REPUBLIC 1922-

16.	500 Piastres (G) 1926-29. Star and crescent. Inscription in wreath	350.00
17.	250 Piastres (G) 1927-28	250.00
18.	100 Piastres (G) 1926-28	120.00
19.	50 Piastres (G) 1927-28	60.00
20.	25 Piastres (G) 1925-29	50.00
21.	25 Piastres (N) 1925-28. Wheat spray and inscription. Oak spray and inscription	1.50
22.	10 Piastres (A-Bro) 1924-26	.75
23.	5 Piastres (A-Bro) 1924-26	.50
24.	2 Piastres [100 Paras] (A-Bro) 1926-27	.35

LAW OF JUNE 7, 1933
(All coins with Gregorian years)

25.	100 Kurus 1934. Head of Kemal Ataturk. Rev. Value, star and crescent	6.50
26.	1 Lira 1937-39. New head of Kemal Ataturk. Rev. Value, star and crescent	7.50
27.	50 Kurus 1935-37	2.50
28.	25 Kurus 1935-37	1.75
29.	1 Lira 1940-41. Head of Ismet Inonu. Rev. Star and crescent and value	9.00
30.	25 Kurus (N-Br) 1943-46. Star and crescent. Rev. Value	.50

31.	10 Kurus (C-N) 1935-40	.50
32.	5 Kurus (C-N) 1935-43	.50
33.	1 Kurus (C-N) 1935-37	.45
34.	1 Kurus (C-N) 1938-42 (Scalloped edge). Star and crescent. Rev. Value	.50
35.	10 Paras (A-Bro) 1940-42	.35

36. 1 Lira 1947-48. Star and crescent. Rev.
     Value in wreath   2.00
37. 50 Kurus 1947,48   1.25
38. 25 Kurus (Bra) 1948-56. Type of #30   .50
39. 10 Kurus (Bra) 1949-56   .35
40.   5 Kurus (Bra) 1949-57   1.00
41. 2½ Kurus (Bra) 1948-51   .20
42.   1 Kurus (Bra) 1947-51   .25

43. 10 Lira 1960. Head of Ataturk. Rev.
     Emblems of the revolution (commem-
     orates the armed forces overthrow of
     the Menderes government on May 27,
     1960)   7.00

52. 50 Lira 1971. Bust of Alparslan, leader
     of Seljuk-Turks. Rev. Map with
     arrows (Commemorates 900th anniver-
     sary of Malazgirt victory)   10.00

53. 50 Kurus (St) 1971- . Girl in native
     headdress. Rev. Value between wheat
     and daphne branches   .35

44. 2½ Lira (St) 1960- . Figure of Ataturk   1.00
45.   1 Lira (C-N) 1957; (St) 1959- Ataturk   .60

54. 10 Kurus (Br) 1971-74. Ataturk on trac-
     tor. Rev. Wheat, value (F.A.O. coin plan)   .15

46. 25 Kurus (St) 1959- . Peasant woman
     with sack on shoulder. Rev. Value   .45
47. 10 Kurus (Br) 1958-74. Star and crescent.
     Rev. Wheat   .25
48.   5 Kurus (Br) 1958-74. Rev. Oak branch   .15
49.   1 Kurus (Bra) 1961-63; (Br) 1963-74.
     Rev. Olive branch and value   .10
50. 25 Lira 1970. Bust of Kemal Ataturk. Rev.
     National Assembly Building (Com-
     memorates 50th anniversary of As-
     sembly)   7.50
51. 2½ Lira (Ac) 1970. Ataturk on tractor. Rev.
     Value (F.A.O. coin plan)   1.00

55. 50 Lira 1972. General on horseback. Rev.
     Battle scene (Commemorates 50th
     anniversary of war between Turkey and
     Greece)   8.00

56.

TURKEY (continued)

56. 500 Lira (G) 1973. Bust of Ataturk. Rev. Star within flower, comet's tail (Commemorates 50th anniversary of republic) 115.00

57. 100 Lira 1973. Front and side views of Ataturk on pedestal. Rev. Type of #56   25.00
58. 50 Lira 1973   15.00

59. 5 Lira (St) 1974- . Ataturk on horseback. Rev. Value   1.25
60. 10 Kurus (A) 1975- . Type of #47   .20
61. 5 Kurus (A) 1975- . Type of #48   .15
62. 1 Kurus (A) 1975- . Type of #49   .10
63. 10 Kurus (A) 1975. Type of #54 (F.A.O. coin plan)   .75

64. 5 Kurus (A) 1975. Head of woman. Rev. Oak branch (F.A.O. coin plan)   .40

TURKS AND CAICOS

A British Crown Colony made up of two groups of small islands at the southeast end of the Bahamas.

1. 1 Crown (CN) 1969. Draped bust of Queen Elizabeth wearing a coronet. Rev. Arms   3.00

2. 100 Crowns (G) 1974. Bust of Churchill. Rev. Arms, value (Commemorates 100th anniversary of statesman's birth)   100.00
3. 50 Crowns (G) 1974   50.00
4. 20 Crowns 1974   20.00

5. 100 Crowns (G) 1975. Bust of Queen Elizabeth II. Rev. Globe showing orbits of John Glenn and Scott Carpenter   100.00

6. 50 Crowns (G) 1975. Rev. Bust of Columbus with ships   50.00

TURKS AND CAICOS (continued)

7. 25 Crowns (G) 1975. Rev. Arms   25.00
8. 20 Crowns 1975. Type of #6   20.00
9. 10 Crowns 1975. Type of #5   10.00

10. 5 Crowns 1975. Rev. Turks Head cactus   5.00

11. 1 Crown (C-N) 1975. Rev. Map   1.00

12. 50 Crowns (G) 1976. Rev. Facing portraits of King George III and George Washington, flags above (Commemorates U.S. Bicentennial)   50.00
13. 20 Crowns (G) 1976   20.00

UGANDA

A former British Protectorate in East Africa, Uganda became internally self-governing in 1962 and a fully independent state within the British Commonwealth in October, 1963.

1. 2 Shillings (CN) 1966. Arms. Rev. Crane and mountains   1.25
2. 1 Shilling (CN) 1966 -   .75
3. 50 Cents (CN) 1966 -   .40

4. 20 Cents (Br) 1966. Elephant tusks. Rev. Value   .30
5. 10 Cents (Br) 1966 -   .25
6. 5 Cents (Br) 1966   .20

7. 5 Shillings (CN) 1968. Cow and calf. Rev. Arms (F.A.O. coin plan)   3.50

8. 5 Shillings (C-N) 1972. Type of #1 (seven-sided planchet)   2.75

UNITED ARAB EMIRATES

A group of seven oil-rich sheikdoms on the Persian Gulf.

100 Fils = 1 Dinar

1. 1 Dinar (C-N) 1973. Carafe. Rev. Value   1.25

2. 50 Fils (C-N) 1973. Oil derricks   .75

3. 25 Fils (C-N) 1973. Antelope   .50
4. 10 Fils (Br) 1973. Dhow (Arabian-Persian sail boat)   .35

5. 5 Fils (Br) 1973. "Bareface" fish (F.A.O. coin plan)   .25
6. 1 Fil (Br) 1973. Date palms (F.A.O. coin plan)   .15

UNITED STATES OF AMERICA

Dealers have classified U.S. coins into eight different conditions, and values are so dependent upon these conditions that it is impossible within the scope of this book to cover all. A whole book can be written on U.S. coins — and it has been — namely, Reinfeld's *Coin Collector's Handbook,* © 1976.
Please consult this book for more information.

HALF CENTS
Issued from 1793 to 1857.

1. Liberty Cap type (C) 1793-97	175.00
2. Draped Bust type (C) 1800-08	30.00
3. Turban Head type (C) 1809-36	25.00
4. Braided Hair type (C) 1840-57	25.00

LARGE CENTS
Issued from 1793 to 1857.

5. Chain type (C) 1793	1000.00
6. Wreath type (C) 1793	750.00
7. Liberty Cap type (C) 1793-96	100.00
8. Draped Bust type (C) 1796-1807	60.00
8a. Turban Head type (C) 1808-14	100.00
9. Coronet type (C) 1816-39	10.00
10. Braided Hair type (C) 1839-57	10.00

SMALL CENTS
Issued from 1793 to date.

11. Flying Eagle type (C-N) 1857-58	20.00
12. Indian Head type (C-N) 1859-64: (Bro) 1864-1909. S dates 1908-09	2.00
13. Lincoln Head type (Bro) 1909-42, 46 to date;(St) 43; (C) 44-45	.10

TWO CENTS
Issued from 1864 to 1873.

14. Shield type (Bro) 1864-73	12.00

THREE CENTS (Nickel)
Issued from 1865 to 1889.

15.	Liberty Head type (N) 1865-89	7.00

THREE CENTS (Silver)
Issued from 1851 to 1873.

16.	Star type 1851-73	20.00

FIVE CENTS (Nickel)
Issued from 1866 to date.

17.	Shield type (N) 1866-83	15.00
18.	Liberty Head type (N) 1883-1912	3.00
19.	Buffalo (or Indian Head) type (N) 1913-38	.85
20.	Jefferson type (N) 1938-42, 46 to date; (Silver alloy) 42-45	.15

HALF DIMES
Issued from 1794 to 1873.

21.	Bust (or Liberty Head) type 1794-1837	12.50
22.	Liberty Seated 1837-73	12.00

DIMES
Issued from 1796 to date.

23.	Bust 1796-1837	30.00
24.	Liberty Seated type 1837-91	10.00
25.	Liberty Head type 1892-1916.	5.00
26.	Mercury Head type 1916-45	1.00
27.	Roosevelt type 1946-64; (C-N) 1965-	.25

TWENTY CENTS
Issued from 1875 to 1878.

28.	Liberty Seated type 1875-78	75.00

QUARTERS
Issued from 1796 to date.

29.	Bust type 1796-1838	65.00
30.	Liberty Seated type 1838-91	17.00
31.	Liberty Head (Barber) type 1892-1916	17.00
32.	Liberty Standing type 1916-30	5.00
33.	Washington type 1932-64; (C-N) 1965-	.50
33a.	Bicentennial type (C-N) 1976	

HALF DOLLARS
Issued from 1794 to date.

34.	Bust type 1794-1839	25.00
35.	Liberty Seated type 1839-91	30.00
36.	Liberty Head (Barber) type 1892-1915	35.00
37.	Liberty Standing type 1916-47	3.00
38.	Franklin type 1948-1963	2.50
39.	Kennedy type 1964-70; (C-N) 1971-	1.00
39a.	Bicentennial type (C-N) 1976	

DOLLARS (Silver)
Issued from 1794 to 1935

40.	Bust type 1794-1804	400.00
41.	Liberty Seated type 1840-73	100.00

42. Liberty Head (Morgan) 1878-1921   6.50
43. Peace type 1921-35   6.00

43a. Eisenhower type (CN) 1971-   3.75

GOLD DOLLARS
Issued from 1849 to 1889.
44. Liberty Head type (G) 1849-54   110.00

45. Indian Headdress type (G) 1854-89   110.00

QUARTER EAGLES ($2.50)
Issued from 1796 to 1829.
46. Turban Head type (G) 1796-1807   1500.00
47. Liberty Cap type (G) 1808-34   1500.00
48. Ribbon type (G) 1834-39   200.00
49. Coronet type (G) 1840-1907   65.00

50. Indian Head Incuse type (G) 1908-29   60.00

THREE-DOLLAR GOLD PIECES
Issued from 1854 to 1889.

51. Indian Headdress type (G) 1854-89   350.00

HALF EAGLES ($5.00)
Issued from 1795 to 1929.

52. Bust type (G) 1795-1834   750.00
53. Ribbon type (G) 1834-38   200.00
54. Coronet type (G) 1839-1908   100.00
55. Indian Head Incuse (G) 1908-29   100.00

EAGLES ($10)
Issued from 1795 to 1933.
56. Bust type (G) 1795-1804   1500.00

57. Coronet type (G) 1838-1907   150.00

58. Indian Head type (G) 1907-33   200.00

DOUBLE EAGLES ($20)
59. Coronet type (G) 1850-1907   275.00

60. Liberty Standing (G) 1907-33   300.00

SILVER COMMEMORATIVE COINS
These are half dollars unless otherwise stated.

1. Columbian Exposition 1892-93   7.50

5. Illinois Centennial 1918	25.00
6. Maine Centennial 1920	35.00

2. Isabella Quarter 1893   100.00

7. Pilgrim Tercentenary 1920-21	20.00
8. Missouri Centennial (with star) 1921	275.00
9. Missouri Centennial (no star) 1921	250.00
10. Alabama Centennial (with 2x2) 1921	150.00
11. Alabama Centennial (no 2x2) 1921	80.00
12. Grant Memorial (with star) 1922	275.00
13. Grant Memorial (no star) 1922	35.00

14. Monroe Doctrine Centennial 1923	20.00
15. Huguenot-Walloon Tercentenary 1924	25.00

3. Lafayette Dollar 1900   300.00

16. Lexington-Concord Sesquicentennial 1925   25.00

4. Panama-Pacific Exposition 1915   175.00

17. Stone Mountain Memorial 1925   12.50

18. California Diamond Jubilee 1925   25.00
19. Fort Vancouver Centennial 1925   110.00

26. Daniel Boone Bicentennial 1934-38   25.00

20. Sesquicentennial of American
    Independence 1926   25.00

27. Connecticut Tercentenary 1935   60.00
28. Arkansas Centennial 1935-39   20.00
29. Hudson, N. Y. Sesquicentennial 1935   275.00
30. California-Pacific Exposition 1935-36   25.00

21. Oregon Trail Memorial 1926, 33-34, 36-39   20.00
22. Vermont Sesquicentennial 1927   50.00

31. Old Spanish Trail 1935   250.00
32. Rhode Island Tercentenary 1936   25.00
33. Cleveland, Great Lakes Exposition 1936   20.00
34. Wisconsin Territorial Centennial 1936   45.00
35. Cincinnati Musical Center 1936   125.00

23. Hawaiian Sesquicentennial 1928   575.00
24. Maryland Tercentenary 1934   25.00

36. Long Island Tercentenary 1936   20.00
37. York County, Maine Tercentenary 1936   40.00

25. Texas Centennial 1934-38   25.00

38. Bridgeport, Conn. Centennial 1936   35.00

39. Lynchburg, Va. Sesquicentennial 1936   40.00
40. Elgin, Illinois Sesquicentennial 1936   50.00
41. Albany, N. Y. Charter 1936   65.00

42. San Francisco-Oakland Bay Bridge 1936   30.00
43. Columbia, S. C. Sesquicentennial 1936   50.00

44. Delaware Tercentenary 1936   50.00

45. Battle of Gettysburg 1936   50.00
46. Norfolk, Va. Bicentennial 1936   85.00

47. Roanoke Island, N. C. 1937   30.00

48. Battle of Antietam 1937   90.00
49. New Rochelle, N. Y. 1938   85.00

50. Iowa Centennial 1946   20.00

51. Booker T. Washington Memorial 1946-51   4.00
52. Geo. W. Carver—B.T. Washington 1951-54   4.00

GOLD COMMEMORATIVE COINS
These are dollars unless otherwise stated.

1. Louisiana Purchase (Jefferson) 1903 ⎫
2. Louisiana Purchase (McKinley) 1903 ⎬   150.00

3. Lewis and Clark Exposition 1904-05   350.00

4. Panama-Pacific Exposition 1915   100.00

5. Panama-Pacific Exposition $2.50 1915   400.00

UNITED STATES OF AMERICA (continued)

6. Panama-Pacific Exposition ($50 round)
1915   rare

7. Panama-Pacific Exposition ($50 octagonal)
1915   rare

8. McKinley Memorial 1916-17   125.00

9. Grant Memorial (with star) 1922   325.00
10. Grant Memorial (no star) 1922   325.00

11. Philadelphia Sesquicentennial $2.50 1926   100.00

URUGUAY

For centuries Uruguay was the scene of a struggle between the Spaniards and Portuguese, with the Spaniards maintaining the upper hand. Freedom from Spain only plunged the country into new chaos. Finally in 1828, with the help of Great Britain, Uruguay was established as an independent republic, a buffer state between Argentina and Brazil.

100 Centesimos = 1 Peso

1. 1 Peso 1844. Arms. Rev. Value   375.00

2. 1 Peso 1877-95   25.00
3. 50 Centesimos 1877-94   5.00
4. 20 Centesimos 1877, 93   3.00
5. 10 Centesimos 1877, 93   2.50

6. 40 Centesimos (C) 1844, 57. Sun. Rev.
    Value   8.00
7. 20 Centesimos (C) 1840-55, 57   7.50
8. 5 Centesimos (C) 1840-55, 57; (C-N)
    1901-41   .50
9. 4 Centesimos (C) 1869   4.00
10. 2 Centesimos (C) 1869; (C-N) 1901-41   .50
11. 1 Centesimo (C) 1869; (C-N) 1901-36   .50

12. 1 Peso 1917. Bust of Artigas. Rev. Arms 20.00
13. 50 Centesimos 1916, 17 6.00
14. 20 Centesimos 1920 3.75

1930 CENTENARY

15. 5 Pesos (G) 1930. Head of Artigas. Rev.
    Value 125.00

16. 20 Centesimos 1930. Seated Liberty 4.00

17. 10 Centesimos (A-Bro) 1930, 36. Liberty
    head. Rev. Jaguar 2.75

NEW SILVER COINAGE

18. 1 Peso 1942. Head of Artigas. Rev.
    Jaguar 3.50
19. 50 Centesimos 1943 2.00
20. 20 Centesimos 1942 . Liberty head 1.00

21. 5 Centesimos (Bro) 1944-51. Sun. Rev.
    Value .50
22. 2 Centesimos (Bro) 1943-51 .50

23. 20 Centesimos 1954. Artigas. Rev.
    Value 1.25

24. 10 Centesimos (C-N) 1953-59 .35
25. 5 Centesimos (C-N) 1953- .20
26. 2 Centesimos (C-N) 1953- .15
27. 1 Centesimo (C-N) 1953- .20

28. 10 Pesos 1961. Gaucho. Rev. Value
    (150th anniversary of revolution
    against Spain) 4.50

29. 1 Peso (C-N) 1960. Head of Artigas.
    Rev. Arms and value .60
30. 50 Centesimos (C-N) 1960 .35
31. 25 Centesimos (C-N) 1960 .25

32. 10 Centesimos (N-Bra) 1960- . Rev.
    Value .30
33. 5 Centesimos (N-Bra) 1960- .30
34. 2 Centesimos (N-Bra) 1960 .25

35.

35. 10 Pesos (Al-Br) 1965. Bust of Artigas.
    Rev. Arms .75
36. 5 Pesos (Al-Br) 1965 .60
37. 1 Peso (Al-Br) 1965 .40

38. 10 Pesos (N-Bra) 1968. Bust of Artigas.
    Rev. Ceibo flower .50
39. 5 Pesos (N-Bra) 1968 .30
40. 1 Peso (N-Bra) 1968 .20

41. 1000 Pesos 1969. Modern sun. Rev. Modern
    art design (F.A.O. coin plan) 7.50
41a. 1000 Pesos (Br) 1969 25.00

42. 10 Pesos (Al-Br) 1969. Sun-face. Rev. Ceibo
    flower .45
43. 5 Pesos (Al-Br) 1969 .25
44. 1 Peso (Al-Br) 1969 .15
45. 50 Pesos (CN) 1970. Arms. Rev. Wheat
    spikes 1.00
46. 20 Pesos (CN) 1970 .75

47.

47. 50 Pesos (C-N) 1971- . Jose Enrique
    Rodo. Rev. Quill (Commemorates
    100th anniversary of phislosopher's
    birth) 1.00

48. 100 Pesos (C-N) 1973. Head of Artigas.
    Rev. Value, laurel branch 1.00

49. 5 New Pesos (C-N-Z) 1975. Bust of Arti-
    gas in panel. Rev. Flag and lance
    (Commemorates 150th anniversary of
    independence)

VATICAN CITY

One-sixth of a square mile in area and located just outside Rome, Vatican City houses the Vatican Palace. The papal city has its own coinage and postage stamps, as well as its own newspaper and broadcasting station. (See previous coins of the Papacy under "Italy-Papal States").

100 Centesimi = 1 Lira

POPE PIUS XI 1922-39

1. 100 Lire (G) 1929-35. Bust. Rev. Christ standing 125.00
2. 100 Lire (G) 1936-37. Reduced size 125.00

3. 10 Lire 1929-37. Bust. Rev. Seated Madonna holding child 8.00
4. 5 Lire 1929-37. Rev. St. Peter in boat ... 7.50

5. 2 Lire (N) 1929-37. Arms. Rev. Good Shepherd with lamb 3.50
6. 1 Lira (N) 1929-37. Rev. Virgin standing 3.00

7. 50 Centesimi (N) 1929-37. Rev. Archangel Michael 3.00
8. 20 Centesimi (N) 1929-37. Rev. Bust of St. Paul 3.00

9. 10 Centesimi (Bro) 1929-37. Rev. Bust of St. Peter 3.00
10. 5 Centesimi (Bro) 1929-37. Rev. Olive spray 2.00

SEDE VACANTE 1939

11. 10 Lire 1939. Arms of Cardinal Pacelli. Rev. Dove 10.00
12. 5 Lire 1939 .... 10.00

POPE PIUS XII 1939-1958

13. 100 Lire (G) 1939-41. Bust. Rev. Type of #1 .... 200.00

14.	10 Lire 1939-41. Bust. Rev. Type of #3	8.00
15.	5 Lire 1939-41. Rev. Type of #4	7.50
16.	2 Lire (N) 1939; (St) 40-41. Rev. Type of #5	3.00
17.	1 Lira (N) 1939; (St) 40-41. Rev. Type of #6	2.00
18.	50 Centesimi (N) 1939; (St) 40-41. Rev. Type of #7	2.00
19.	20 Centesimi (N) 1939; (St) 40-41. Rev. Type of #8	1.50
20.	10 Centesimi (Bro) 1939-41. Rev. Type of #9	6.00
21.	5 Centesimi (Bro) 1939-41. Rev. Type of #10	6.00

31.	10 Lire (A) 1947-49. Bust. Rev. Caritas	2.50
32.	5 Lire (A) 1947-49	1.75
33.	2 Lire (A) 1947-49. Rev. Justice	1.50
34.	1 Lire (A) 1947-49	1.00

22.	100 Lire (G) 1942-49. Bust. Rev, Caritas	150.00
23.	10 Lire 1942-46	10.00
24.	5 Lire 1942-46	10.00
25.	2 Lire (St) 1942-46. Arms. Rev. Justice	2.00
26.	1 Lira (St) 1942-46	1.00

35.	100 Lire (G) 1950 (Holy Year issue). Bust of Pope in tiara. Rev. Pope opening Holy Door	200.00
36.	10 Lire (A) 1950. Bust facing right. Rev. Gate of Heaven	3.00

27.	50 Centesimi (St) 1942-46	1.00
28.	20 Centesimi (St) 1942-46	1.00

37.	5 Lire (A) 1950. Bust facing left	2.50
38.	2 Lire (A) 1950. Bust facing right. Rev. Dove and dome of St. Peter's	2.00

29.	10 Centesimi (Bra) 1942-46. Bust. Rev. Dove	10.00
30.	5 Centesimi (Bra) 1942-46	5.00

39.	1 Lire (A) 1950. Arms. Rev. Holy Door	1.50
40.	100 Lire (G) 1951-58. Bust to right. Rev. Caritas	225.00
41.	100 Lire (St) 1955-58. Head to left. Rev. Fides	4.00
42.	50 Lire (St) 1955-58. Head to right. Rev. Spes	4.00

VATICAN CITY (continued)

43. 20 Lire (A-Bro) 1957-58. Head to left.
Rev. Caritas   4.00
44. 10 Lire (A) 1951-58. Bust facing left.
Rev. Prudentia   .50

51. 500 Lire 1959-62. Bust. Rev. Arms   20.00
52. 100 Lire (St) 1959-62. Rev. Fides   3.00
53. 50 Lire (St) 1959-62. Rev. Spes   2.00
54. 20 Lire (A-Bro) 1959-62. Rev. Caritas   4.00
55. 10 Lire (St) 1959-62. Rev. Prudentia   4.00
56. 5 Lire (St) 1959-62. Rev. Justitia   4.00
57. 2 Lire (St) 1959-62. Arms. Rev. Fortitudo   6.00
58. 1 Lire (St) 1959-62. Rev. Temperantia   4.00

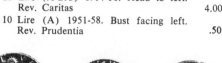

45. 5 Lire (A) 1951-58. Bust facing right.
Rev. Justice   .50
46. 2 Lire (A) 1951-58. Female figure. Rev.
Arms   1.00
47. 1 Lira (A) 1951-58. Female figure. Rev.
Arms   1.00

59. 500 Lire 1962. Pope with tiara. Rev. Pope
presiding at meeting of the council
(Ecumencial Council commemorative)   20.00
60. 100 Lire (St) 1962. Bust of Pope   3.50
61. 50 Lire (St) 1962   3.00

48. 500 Lire 1958 (Twentieth year commemorative). Bust. Rev. Arms   20.00

SEDE VACANTE 1958

62. 20 Lire (A-Br) 1962. Rev. Dove   3.00
63. 10 Lire (A) 1962   2.75

49. 500 Lire 1958. Dove. Rev. Arms   10.00

POPE JOHN XXIII 1959-1963

64. 5 Lire (A) 1962   2.75

50. 100 Lire (G) 1959. Robed bust of Pope.
Rev. Papal arms   800.00

65. 2 Lire (A) 1962. Papal arms. Rev.
Dove   2.50
66. 1 Lire (A) 1962   3.00

VATICAN CITY • 455

SEDE VACANTE 1963

67. 500 Lire 1963. Arms of Cardinal Masella.
Rev. Dove and value 6.50

76. 500 Lire 1966. Head of Pope wearing mitre.
Rev. Good Shepherd carrying a sheep 12.00
77. 100 Lire (St) 1966 .... 3.00
78. 50 Lire (St) 1966 .... 2.00
79. 20 Lire (Al-Br) 1966 .... 1.00
80. 10 Lire (Al) 1966 .... 1.25
81. 5 Lire (Al) 1966 .... 1.00
82. 2 Lire (Al) 1966 .... 1.00
83. 1 Lira (Al) 1966 .... 1.50

PAUL VI 1963-

68. 500 Lire 1963-65. Bust of the Pope. Rev.
Papal arms 15.00

84. 500 Lire 1967. Bust of the Pope. Rev. Heads
of St. Peter and St. Paul (Commemorates 5th year of reign) 4.00

69. 100 Lire (St) 1963-65. Rev. Fides (Faith) 2.50

85. 100 Lire (St) 1967. Rev. St. Peter on throne 3.00

70. 50 Lire (St) 1963-65. Rev. Spes (Hope) 1.25
71. 20 Lire (A-Br) 1963-65. Rev. Caritas
(Charity) 1.25
72. 10 Lire (A) 1963-65. Rev. Prudentia
(Prudence) 1.00
73. 5 Lire (A) 1963-65. Rev. Iustitia (Justice) 1.00
74. 2 Lire (A) 1963-65. Papal arms. Rev.
Fortitudo (Fortitude) 1.00

86. 50 Lire (St) 1967. Rev. St. Paul on horseback 2.00
87. 20 Lire (Al-Br) 1967. Type of #84 .... 1.00

75. 1 Lire (A) 1963-65. Rev. Temperantia
(Temperance) 2.00

88. 10 Lire (Al) 1967. Rev. Papal keys 1.00
89. 5 Lire (Al) 1967. Rev. Crossed keys 1.00

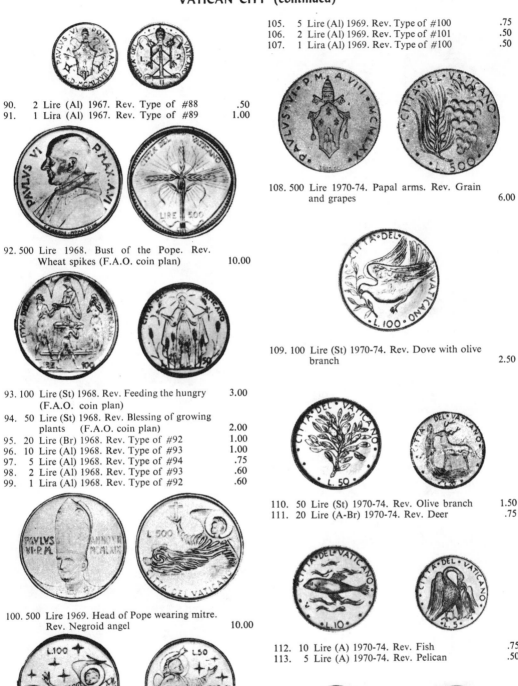

90. 2 Lire (Al) 1967. Rev. Type of #88 .50
91. 1 Lira (Al) 1967. Rev. Type of #89 1.00

92. 500 Lire 1968. Bust of the Pope. Rev.
Wheat spikes (F.A.O. coin plan) 10.00

93. 100 Lire (St) 1968. Rev. Feeding the hungry 3.00
(F.A.O. coin plan)
94. 50 Lire (St) 1968. Rev. Blessing of growing
plants (F.A.O. coin plan) 2.00
95. 20 Lire (Br) 1968. Rev. Type of #92 1.00
96. 10 Lire (Al) 1968. Rev. Type of #93 1.00
97. 5 Lire (Al) 1968. Rev. Type of #94 .75
98. 2 Lire (Al) 1968. Rev. Type of #93 .60
99. 1 Lira (Al) 1968. Rev. Type of #92 .60

100. 500 Lire 1969. Head of Pope wearing mitre.
Rev. Negroid angel 10.00

101. 100 Lire (St) 1969. Rev. Oriental angel 3.00
102. 50 Lire (St) 1969. Rev. Caucasian angel 2.00
103. 20 Lire (Al-Br) 1969. Rev. Type of #102 1.00
104. 10 Lire (Al) 1969. Rev. Type of #101 1.00

105. 5 Lire (Al) 1969. Rev. Type of #100 .75
106. 2 Lire (Al) 1969. Rev. Type of #101 .50
107. 1 Lira (Al) 1969. Rev. Type of #100 .50

108. 500 Lire 1970-74. Papal arms. Rev. Grain
and grapes 6.00

109. 100 Lire (St) 1970-74. Rev. Dove with olive
branch 2.50

110. 50 Lire (St) 1970-74. Rev. Olive branch 1.50
111. 20 Lire (A-Br) 1970-74. Rev. Deer .75

112. 10 Lire (A) 1970-74. Rev. Fish .75
113. 5 Lire (A) 1970-74. Rev. Pelican .50

114. 2 Lire (A) 1970-74. Rev. Lamb .50
115. 1 Lire (A) 1970-74. Rev. Palm branches .25

116. 500 Lire 1975. Papal arms. Rev. Embrace
of prodigal son and father (Commemorates holy year)   8.50

117. 100 Lire (St) 1975. Papal arms. Rev.
Design symbolizing baptism   1.00

118. 50 Lire (St) 1975. Rev. Design symbolizing peace within the Lord   .75
119. 20 Lire (A-Br) 1975. Rev. Design symbolizing man's confidence in the Lord   .60

120. 10 Lire (A) 1975. Rev. Ark   .50
121. 5 Lire (A) 1975. Rev. Woman of Bethany   .60

122. 2 Lire (A) 1975. Rev. Reconciliation of
brothers   .60
123. 1 Lire (A) 1975. Rev. Design symbolizing
faith of afflicted   .60

VENEZUELA

A Spanish colony for three centuries, Venezuela
was a part of New Granada when it threw off the
Spanish yoke in 1811. Finally, in 1830, Venezuela
became an independent state.

100 Centavos = 8 Reales = 1 Peso
100 Centimos = 1 Bolivar

REPUBLICA DE VENEZUELA

1. 5 Reales 1858. Liberty head. Rev. Value   200.00
2. 2 Reales 1858   125.00
3. 1 Real 1858   140.00
4. ½ Real 1858   150.00

5. 1 Centavo (C) 1843, 52, 58, 62, 63.
Liberty head   10.00
6. ½ Centavo (C) 1843, 52   10.00
7. ¼ Centavo (C) 1843, 52   10.00

ESTADOS UNIDOS DE VENEZUELA

(1 Venezolano = 10 Reales, fineness .835)

8. 1 Venezolano 1876. Bolivar head. Rev.
Arms   200.00
9. 50 Centavos (5 Reales) 1873, 74, 76   50.00
10. 20 Centavos 1874, 76   40.00
11. 10 Centavos 1874, 76   30.00
12. 5 Centavos 1874, 76   25.00

(5 Bolivares = 10 Reales, fineness .900)

13. 2½ Centavos (C-N) 1876, 77. Arms.
Rev. Value   7.50
14. 1 Centavo (C-N) 1876, 77   7.50
15. 20 Bolivares (G) 1879-1905, 1910-12.
Bolivar head   75.00

VENEZUELA (continued)

16.	10 Bolivares (G) 1930	35.00
17.	5 Bolivares 1879, 1886-89, 1900-36 Bolivar head. Rev. Arms	**6.00**
18.	2 Bolivares 1879, 1887-89, 94, 1900-45	**3.00**
19.	1 Bolivar 1879, 1886-89, 93, 1900-45	2.25
20.	½ Bolivar (50 Centimos) 1879, 1886-89, 93, 1900-46	.75
21.	¼ Bolivar 1894, 1900-48	.50
22.	12½ Centimos (C-N) 1896, 1925-38; (Bra) 1944; (C-N) 1945-48	.75

REPUBLICA DE VENEZUELA

23.	2 Bolivares 1960-65 Head of Bolivar. Rev. Arms	2.50
23a.	2 Bolivares (N) 1967-	1.25
24.	1 Bolivar 1954-65	1.25
24a.	1 Bolivar (N) 1967-	.75
25.	50 Centimos 1954, 60	.75
25a.	50 Centimos (N) 1965-	.50
26.	25 Centimos 1954, 60	.50
26a.	25 Centimos (N) 1965-	.40

27.	12½ Centimos (C-N) 1958- . Arms. Rev. Value	.50
28.	5 Centimos (C-N) 1958	.25
29.	10 Centimos (C-N) 1971- . Arms. Rev. Value	.25
30.	5 Centimos (C-N) 1964-	.20

31.	10 Bolivares 1973. Head of Bolivar in incuse panel. Rev. Arms in panel (Commemorates 100th anniversary of Bolivar's appearance on coinage)	10.00
32.	5 Bolivares (N) 1973. Type of #23	4.00
33.	1000 Bolivares (G) 1975. Arms. Rev. Cock	
34.	50 Bolivares 1975. Rev. Armadillo	
35.	25 Bolivares 1975	

VIETNAM

Became two states in 1954: the north, Communist-controlled, the south, a republic.

SOUTH VIETNAM

100 Xu (Su) = 1 Dong

1.	50 Xu (A-Mg) 1953	2.00
2.	20 Su (A-Mg) 1953	.50
3.	10 Su (A-Mg) 1953	.35

4.	1 Dong (C-N) 1960. Head of President Ngo Dinh-Diem. Rev. Rice stalks	.75
5.	50 Su (A-Mg) 1960, 63	.50

6.	10 Dong (C-N) 1964; (N-St) 1968, 70. Rice stalks. Rev. Value	.60
7.	1 Dong (C-N) 1964; (N-St) 1971	.25

8.	5 Dong (CN) 1966; (N-St) 1971 (scalloped edge)	.45
9.	1 Dong (CN) 1964; (N-St) 1971 (round planchet)	.25
10.	20 Dong (N-St) 1968. Farmer in rice paddy. Rev. Value	1.00

11.

VIETNAM (continued)

11. 20 Dong (St) 1968. Type of #10 with F.A.O. inscription   2.00

12. 1 Dong (A) 1971. Type of #6 with F.A.O. inscription   .50

13. 10 Dong (Bra-St) 1974. Two peasants. Rev. Value (F.A.O. coin plan)   .50

NORTH VIETNAM

100 Xu = 1 Hao = 1 Dong

1. 2 Dong (Br) 1946. Ho Chi Minh. Rev. Star in wreath   35.00

2. 1 Dong (Br) 1946. Ho Chi Minh. Rev. Value   25.00

3. 5 Hao (A) 1946. Incense burner. Rev. Value in star (value raised or incuse)   10.00

4. 20 Xu (A) 1945. Star. Rev. Value   40.00

5. 5 Xu (A) 1958. Arms. Rev. Value (center hole)   2.00
6. 2 Xu (A) 1958   1.50
7. 1 Xu (A) 1958   1.25

VISCAYAN REPUBLIC

Spanish province on the Bay of Biscay. Autonomous during the Civil War of 1936-37.

1. 2 Pesetas (N) 1937. Head of Republic. Rev. Value in wreath   2.50
2. 1 Peseta (N) 1937   2.00

WEST AFRICAN STATES

Former French colonies in this area combined for coinage purposes: Dahomey, Haute Volta, Ivory Coast, Mauretania, Niger, Senegal, and Sudan, each now autonomous.

1. 10 Francs (Al-Br) 1959- . Antelope head.
    Rev. Native design .50
2. 5 Francs (Al-Br) 1960- .30
3. 1 Franc (Al-Br) 1961- .20

4. 100 Francs (N) 1967- . Native design. Rev.
    Value 2.00
5. 25 Francs (A-Br) 1970- . Type of #1 .75

6. 500 Francs 1972. Native design. Rev.
    Shields of member nations (Commemorates 10th anniversary of monetary union) 50.00

7. 50 Francs (C-N) 1972. Native design.
    Rev. Value (F.A.O. coin plan) 1.50

WESTERN SAMOA

This group of four islands in the South Pacific Ocean was a German colony until after World War I, when it became a New Zealand mandate. Under New Zealand U.N. trusteeship from 1945 on, it achieved independence within the British Commonwealth on January 1, 1962. New Zealand continues to represent Western Samoa in foreign affairs.

1. 1 Tala (CN) 1967. Portrait of Malietoa
    Tanumafili II. Rev. Arms 5.00
2. 50 Sene (CN) 1967 2.00
3. 20 Sene (CN) 1967 1.00
4. 10 Sene (CN) 1967 .50

5. 5 Sene (C-N) 1967. Rev. Value in wreath .35
6. 2 Sene (Br) 1967 .25
7. 1 Sene (Br) 1967 .20

8. 1 Tala (CN) 1969. Robert Louis Stevenson
    lying in bed. Rev. Arms (Commemorates the 75th anniversary of writer's death) 6.00

9. 1 Tala (C-N) 1970. James Cook. Rev. Type of #8 (Commemorates 200th anniversary of Cook's voyages)   4.00

10. 1 Tala (C-N) 1970. Pope Paul VI (Commemorates papal visit)   4.00

11. 1 Tala (C-N) 1972. Sailing ship (Commemorates Roggeveen's discovery of Samoa)   3.00

12. 1 Tala (C-N) 1974. Boxers (Commemorates 10th British Commonwealth Games)   5.00

13. 1 Tala (C-N) 1974. Head of Malietoa Tanumafili II. Rev. Coconut palm   4.50

14. 50 Sene (C-N) 1974. Rev. Banana tree   2.00
15. 20 Sene (C-N) 1974. Rev. Breadfruit   .85

16. 10 Sene (C-N) 1974. Rev. Taro leaves   .50
17. 5 Sene (C-N) 1974. Rev. Pineapple   .30

18. 2 Sene (Br) 1974. Rev. Cocoa pods   .20
19. 1 Sene (Br) 1974. Rev. Coconut   .15

WESTPHALIA

After the Peace of Tilsit in 1807 Napoleon Bonaparte created the kingdom of Westphalia from several German territories and set up his brother Jerome as king. Jerome lost his throne in 1813 and the territories were redistributed.

100 Centimes = 1 Frank

JEROME NAPOLEON 1807-13

1. 5 Frank 1808, 09. Laureated head. Rev.
    Value in wreath 300.00
2. 2 Frank 1808 .... 175.00
3. 1 Frank 1808 .... 125.00
4. ½ Frank 1808 .... 75.00
5. 20 Centimes (Bi) 1810-12. Crowned mono-
    gram ("H N" for "Hieronymus Napo-
    leon") in wreath. Rev. Value 15.00
6. 10 Centimes (Bi) 1808-12 .... 12.50

7. 5 Centimes (C) 1808-12 ....   8.00
8. 3 Centimes (C) 1808-12 ....   6.00
9. 2 Centimes (C) 1808-12 ....   6.00
10. 1 Centime (C) 1809-12 ....   4.00

YEMEN, ARAB REPUBLIC

An Arab kingdom on the Red Sea until 1962, when it became a republic.

2 Halala = 1 Bogach
40 Bogaches = 1 Imadi = 1 Ryal

1. 1 Ryal (Imadi) 1948-61 (A.H. 1367-80).
    Arabic inscriptions 12.50
2. ½ Imadi 1948-60 ....   6.00
3. ¼ Imadi 1948-58 ....   3.50
4. ⅛ Imadi 1948-61 (five sides) 2.50
5. ¹⁄₁₆ Imadi 1948-55 (five sides) 2.00
6. 1 Bogach (Bro) 1949-60 ....   1.75
7. 1 Halala (Bro) 1949-62 ....   1.00
8. 1 Bogach (A) 1955-57 ....   2.00

9. 1 Halala (A) 1955-57 ....   2.00

REPUBLIC 1962-

10. 1 Ryal 1963. (A.H. 1382) Arabic in-
    scription. Rev. Two laurel branches 6.00
11. 20 Bogaches 1963 ....   2.50
12. 10 Bogaches 1963 ....   1.25
13. 5 Bogaches 1963 ....   1.00
14. 2 Bogaches (A-Br) 1963 75
15. 1 Bogach (A-Br) 1963 60

16. ½ Bogach (A-Br) 1963 50

Formerly South Arabia under British rule; gained independence in 1967.

17. ¼ Ryal 1963. Coffee tree above dam. Rev.
     Arabic inscription   17.50
18. ⅕ Ryal 1963   3.00
19. 1/10 Ryal 1963   2.00
20. 1/20 Ryal 1963   1.75

1. 5 Fils (Br) 1971. Emblem. Rev. Crossed
    daggers   .50

21. 1 Bogach (Br) 1963-65. Hand holding
     torch. Rev. Arabic inscription   1.25
22. 1 Halala (Br) 1963   1.00

23. ½ Bogach (Br) 1963. Star between lines.
     Rev. Value as fraction   4.00
24. 1 Halala (Br) 1963. Rev. Value written out 2.50

DECIMAL COINAGE
100 Fils = 1 Ryal

25. 50 Fils (C-N) 1974. Arms. Rev. Value   .75
26. 25 Fils (C-N) 1974   .50
27. 10 Fils (Bra) 1974   .30
28. 5 Fils (Bra) 1974   .20
29. 1 Fils (A) 1974   .15

YUGOSLAVIA

The Kingdom of Serbs, Croats and Slovenes was formed after World War I from Serbia, Montenegro and parts of the former Austro-Hungarian Empire, but did not take the name Yugoslavia until 1929. After World War II, in 1945, Yugoslavia became a republic headed by Marshal Tito who had led the resistance against the invading Germans. Although a Communist State, it remained outside the Soviet orbit. It took the name Socialist Federal Republic of Yugoslavia in 1963 when a new constitution was adopted.

100 Paras = 1 Dinar

ALEXANDER I 1921-34

1.	20 Dinars (G) 1925. Head. Crowned value in wreath	60.00
2.	1 Ducat (G) 1931-34. Rev. Eagle	75.00

3.	50 Dinars 1932. Head. Rev. Crowned double eagle	30.00
4.	20 Dinars 1931-33	10.00
5.	10 Dinars 1931-32	5.00

6.	2 Dinars (N-Bro) 1925. Head. Rev. Crowned value in wreath	2.00
7.	1 Dinar (N-Bro) 1925	1.50
8.	50 Para (N-Bro) 1925	1.00

9.	25 Para (N-Bro) 1920. Crowned, mantled arms. Rev. Value	2.50
10.	10 Para (Z) 1920	3.00
11.	5 Para (Z) 1920	10.00

PETER II 1934-45

12.	50 Dinars 1938. Head facing right. Rev. Crowned double eagle	6.00

13.	20 Dinars 1938. Head facing left	5.00

14.	10 Dinars 1938. Head facing right. Rev. Crowned value in wreath	2.50

15.	2 Dinars (A-Bro) 1938. Crown. Rev. Value	10.00
16.	1 Dinar (A-Bro) 1938	1.25
17.	50 Para (A-Bro) 1938	1.00

18.	25 Para (A-Bro) 1938 (Center hole). Crowned wreath. Rev. Value	2.50

YUGOSLAVIA (continued)

PEOPLE'S REPUBLIC 1945-

19. 5 Dinara (Z) 1945, (Al) 1953, 63. Arms
    Rev. Value ... 1.00
20. 2 Dinara (Z) 1945, (Al) 1953, 63 ... .30
21. 1 Dinar (Z) 1945, (Al) 1953, 63 ... .20

22. 50 Para (Z) 1945; (A) 1953 ... .10

23. 50 Dinars (A-Br) 1955, 63. Heads of male
    and female worker. Rev. Arms ... .75

24. 20 Dinars (A-Br) 1955, 63. Head of male
    worker ... .50
25. 10 Dinars (A-Br) 1955, 63. Head of fe-
    male worker ... .30

REVALUATION 1965

26. 1 Dinar (CN) 1965, 68. Arms. Rev. Value,
    stars ... .65
27. 50 Para (Al-Br) 1965- ... .40
27a. 5 Para (A-Br) 1965 ... .20
28. 20 Para (Al-Br) 1965- . Arms. Rev. Value ... .30
29. 10 Para (Al-Br) 1965 ... .20
30. 5 Para (Al-Br) 1965 ... .10

31. 5 Dinars (C-N) 1970. Arms. Rev. Value
    (F.A.O. coin plan) ... 1.00
32. 2 Dinars (C-N) 1970 ... .75

33. 5 Dinars (C-N) 1971- . Arms. Rev. Value ... .60
34. 2 Dinars (C-N) 1971- ... .40
35. 1 Dinar (C-N) 1973- ... .30

36. 5 Dinars (C-N-Z) 1975. Arms. Rev. Value,
    inscription (Commemorates 30th anni-
    versary, end of World War II)

ZAIRE

The Republic of the Congo changed its name to the Republic of Zaire in 1971.

100 Makuta = 1 Zaire

1. 20 Makuta (C-N) 1973. Portrait of President Mobutu with hat. Rev. Arm holding torch   1.00

2. 10 Makuta (C-N) 1973. Portrait of President Mobutu. Rev. Arms   .50

ZAMBIA

Formerly Northern Rhodesia in the Federation of Rhodesia and Nyasaland, which dissolved in 1963, Zambia became an independent republic within the British Commonwealth in 1964.

1. 2 Shillings (C-N) 1964. Arms. Rev. Oribi buck   3.50

2. 1 Shilling (C-N) 1964. Rev. Hornbill   2.00
3. 6 Pence (C-N) 1964. Rev. Morning glory   .85

4. 5 Shillings (Ni) 1965. Head of Pres. Kaunda. Rev. Arms (Commemorates first anniversary of independence)   5.00
5. 2 Shillings (C-N) 1966. Head. Rev. Oribi buck   3.50
6. 1 Shilling (C-N) 1966. Rev. Hornbill   1.00
7. 6 Pence (C-N) 1966. Rev. Morning glory   .65

8. 1 Penny (Br) 1966. (Center hole)   .35

ZAMBIA (continued)

DECIMAL COINAGE

9.   20 Ngwee (CN) 1968. Head of President
     K. D. Kaunda. Rev. Oribi buck   1.50

10. 10 Ngwee (CN) 1968. Rev. Hornbill   .75
11. 5 Ngwee (CN) 1968. Rev. Morning glory
     flower   .40

12. 2 Ngwee (Br) 1968. Rev. African fish-
     eagle   .30
13. 1 Ngwee (Br) 1968, 69. Rev. Ant bear   .25

14. 50 Ngwee (CN) 1969. Head of President
     Kaunda. Rev. Ear of corn (F.A.O.
     coin plan, commemorates 5th anni-
     versary of independence)   3.50

15. 50 Ngwee (C-N) 1972. Type of #14 without
     commemorative inscription (F.A.O. coin
     plan)   3.00

ZANZIBAR

A small island in the Indian Ocean about 20
miles off the coast of East Africa, Zanzibar was a
British Protectorate until 1963 when it became an
independent state within the Commonwealth. A
People's Republic was proclaimed in January, 1964.
In April, 1964, Zanzibar merged with Tanganyika
to form the United Republic of Tanganyika and
Zanzibar, renamed the United Republic of Tanzania in October, 1964.

100 Cents = 1 Rupee

1.   1 Rial A.H. 1299 (1882). Arabic inscription 200.00

2.   1 Pessa (C) A.H. 1299. Inscription. Rev.
     Scales   2.00

3.   1 Pessa (C) A.H. 1304 (1886). Inscription.
     Rev. Scales   1.50
4.   20 Cents (N) 1908. Inscription. Rev. Palm
     tree   175.00

5.   10 Cents (Bro) 1908   150.00
6.   1 Cent (Bro) 1908   100.00

ANCIENT COINS

ANCIENT GREECE

AEGINA

The earliest European state to strike coins. From very early times until its conquest by Athens in 456 B.C. Aegina was one of the greatest commercial states of Greece. For two or three centuries the coins of Aegina had a very wide circulation with little change in style. The sea tortoise which appears on these coins was an appropriate symbol for this state which depended on the sea for its livelihood.

1. Silver Stater 600-450 B.C. Sea tortoise. Rev. Divided incuse square.   VG 175.00; VF 450.00
(A crude archaic-style coin.)

AGRIGENTUM (in Sicily)

By far the richest and most magnificent city on the south coast of Sicily.

2. Silver Tetradrachm 400-375 B.C. Standing eagle. Rev. Crab.   F 145.00; VF 225.00
(The eagle is a symbol for Zeus. The crab represents the river Akragas.)

ARADUS (Ephesus)

The temple of Diana of the Ephesians was one of the seven wonders of the world.

3. Silver Drachm 174-110 B.C. A large bee. Rev. Stag standing before a palm tree.
   F 40.00; EF 160.00
(Diana, known in Greek as Artemis, was referred to as goddess of the chase by the stag, and as goddess of the fruitfulness of nature by the bee.)

ASPENDUS (Pamphylia)

A populous and wealthy city of great commercial importance. Its coins are often found with countermarks indicating very wide circulation.

4. Silver Stater 500-450 B.C. Warrior. Rev. Triskeles of human legs and club.   VG 120.00
(A crude, archaic, thick coin.)
5. Silver Stater 400-300 .B.C. Two wrestlers engaged. Rev. Slinger; triskeles in field. F 45.00; VF 100.00

#6

ATHENS

6. Silver Tetradrachm 480-400 B.C. Archaic-style head of Athene. Rev. Owl (the bird of wisdom) in an incuse square. Olive sprig in corner.
   F 65.00; VF 150.00
(The olive spray probably has no reference to peace, as on modern coins, but very likely refers to the importance of olives and olive oil to the Athenian economy. It has been suggested that the small crescent on the reverse beside the owl was in honor of the Battle of Marathon which was fought under a waning moon. The archaic style of the coin was preserved for many years due to its wide circulation and the fear of possible damage to the commerce of the city if any change were made. The coin circulated throughout the entire known world until it was at last superseded by the still more popular tetradrachm of Alexander the Great. The coins were often cut with a chisel to see if they were good silver throughout.)

7. Silver Tetradrachm 230-200 B.C. Athene. Rev. Owl.   F 80.00; VF 250.00
(New style struck on large planchet.)

CAPPADOCIA

A kingdom in Asia Minor.

8. Silver Drachm 300-225 B.C. Head of King Ariarathes. Rev. Athene   VF 30.00

CARTHAGE

Coins of this North African city founded by the Phoenicians were mostly produced during the invasion of Sicily and the type of Persephone is copied from the Sicilian coin.

9. Silver Tetradrachm 400-300 B.C. Head of Persephone in beautiful artistic style. Rev. Horse's head and palm tree.   F 250.00; VF 600.00

CARTHAGE (continued)

10. Silver Tetradrachm. Head of Persephone. Rev. Horse's head and palm tree.
F 175.00; VF 275.00

11. Electrum Stater 350-250 B.C. Head of Persephone. Rev. Standing horse.   F 350.00; VF 650.00

CORINTH

12. Silver Stater 400-335 B.C. Head of Athene in typical Corinthian helmet. Rev. Pegasus (winged horse) in flight.   VF 50.00; EF 100.00
(One of the most famous coins in the ancient world, used in all Corinthian colonies.)

CROTON (Bruttium)

13. Silver Stater 550-480 B.C. Tripod in relief. Rev. Tripod, incuse.   F 80.00; VF 145.00
14. Silver Stater 420-390 B.C. Standing eagle. Rev. Tripod.   F 50.00; VF 120.00

EGYPT

15. Ptolemy I: Silver Tetradrachm 323-305 B.C. Head

EGYPT (continued)

15.

of Alexander the Great in elephant skin. Rev. Athene with javelin and shield; eagle on thunderbolt.   F 75.00; VF 250.00
(Struck by Ptolemy I as Governor of Egypt under Alexander IV, King of Macedon, posthumous son of Alexander the Great.)

16. Ptolemy I: Silver Tetradrachm 323-305 B.C. His diademed head. Rev. Eagle.   F 50.00; VF 100.00
(Struck by Ptolemy I as independent King of Egypt.)
17. Ptolemy II: Very large heavy bronze cast coin 285-246 B.C. Bearded head of Zeus. Rev. Eagle.   VF 20.00
18. Ptolemy II: Silver Tetradrachm 285-246 B.C. His diademed head. Rev. Eagle.   F 50.00; VF 75.00
(Similar coins were issued by the Ptolemies through Ptolemy XIII, 55-51 B.C. Value as above.)

19. Cleopatra VII: Base silver Tetradrachm 51-30 B.C. Ptolemaic head. Rev. Eagle.   F 80.00
(This is the famous Cleopatra of history.)

GELA (Sicily)

This city was located at the mouth of the river Gela and the swimming man-headed bull on the following coin represents the river.

20. Silver Tetradrachm 500-450 B.C. Forepart of man-headed bull with horns. Rev. Quadriga, winged Victory above.   F 225.00; VF 500.00

LARISSA

21. Silver Drachm 400-344 B.C. Facing head of the nymph Larissa. Rev. Grazing horse.
F 65.00; VF 250.00
(After the famous facing-head Tetradrachm of Syracuse by Kimon.)

TARSUS

The birthplace of the Apostle Paul.

50. (as Persian Satrapy): Silver Stater 386-333 B.C.
    Head of Ahura Mazda. Rev. The god Baal
    standing with scepter and eagle.
    F 75.00; VF 120.00
51. King Pharnabazus: Silver Stater 379-374 B.C.
    Facing head of Arethusa. Rev. Head of Mars
    in war helmet.   F 70.00; VF 110.00
    (The beautiful reverse is copied from Kimon's
    Arethusa on the coins of Syracuse.)

THEBES (Boeotia)

One of the most important Greek cities in
ancient times.

52. Silver Stater 400-330 B.C. The shield of Thebes.
    Rev. Amphora.   F 85.00; VF 145.00; EF 250. 00

THRACE

53. Lysimachus: Silver Tetradrachm 323-281 B.C. Head
    of Alexander the Great wearing horn of Am-
    mon. Rev. Athene seated holding winged Vic-
    tory.   F 160.00; VF 300.00
    (One of the most famous coins of antiquity.
    Lysimachus was an outstanding general under
    Alexander.)

THURIUM

54. Silver Stater 450-400 B.C. Helmeted head of
    Athene. Rev. Bull   F 60.00; VF 100.00

TYRE (Phoenicia)

A great trade center of ancient times.

55. Silver Shekel 125 B.C.-100 A.D. Head of Melkarth.
    Rev. Eagle standing on beak of ship.
    F 85.00; VF 160.00
    (This coin was struck in large numbers and cir-
    culated extensively in Judea at the time of Christ.
    It is generally believed that the "Thirty pieces of
    silver" paid to Judas were made up of these
    coins.)

VELIA

56. Silver Didrachm 350-275 B.C. Helmeted head of
    Athene. Rev. Lion prowling, devouring prey or
    seizing upon a stag.   F 45.00; VF 75.00

ANCIENT ROME

ROMAN REPUBLIC

CAST BRONZE COINAGE, THE *AES GRAVE*
(HEAVY BRONZE) 225-175 B.C.

The reverse of this coinage always shows the
prow of a galley. The basic unit was the As,
equivalent to 12 Uncia, and originally equal in
weight to the Latin pound of 12 ounces. Prices
quoted for the following coins are for VG-F
condition:

1. As (12 Uncia) Head of Janus. Rev. Prow
   of galley   175.00

ROMAN REPUBLIC (continued)

2. Semis (6 Uncia). Head of Jupiter or
   Saturn 85.00
3. Triens (4 Uncia). Head of Minerva 60.00

12. Head of Apollo. Rev. Various types 25.00
13. Head of Tatius. Rev. "Rape of the
    Sabines" 20.00

14. Head of Jupiter. Rev. Various types 17.50

15. Head of Mars. Rev. Various types 17.50

The above are the types most frequently encountered. Many other deities, however, appear on the coinage. The value of these pieces is upward of $5.00.

4. Quadrans (3 Uncia). Head of Hercules 45.00
5. Sextans (2 Uncia). Head of Mercury 35.00
6. Uncia. Head of Roma or Bellona 25.00

STRUCK COINS OF THE ROMAN REPUBLIC
269-55 B.C.

The silver Denarius was the chief coin of the Republic period and was equivalent in value to ten of the bronze Asses, this value being indicated by the "X" which is frequently seen on the Denarii. Prices quoted for the following silver Denarii (185-55 B.C.) are for F-VF condition:

COINS OF THE CIVIL WARS 59-31 B.C.
Prices are quoted for F-VF condition.

7. Head of Roma. Rev. Dioscuri galloping 20.00
8. Head of Roma. Rev. Biga
   (two-horse chariot) 17.50
9. Head of Roma. Rev. Quadriga
   (four-horse chariot) 17.50
10. Head of Roma. Rev. Romulus and Remus 35.00

16. Pompey the Great: Denarius. Bare head.
    Rev. Catanian brothers carrying their
    parents on their shoulders 165.00

17. Julius Caesar: Denarius. Laureate head of
    Caesar. 160.00
18. Julius Caesar: Denarius. Head of Venus.
    Rev. Trophy between two captives 85.00

11. Head of Janus. Rev. Various types 30.00

19. Julius Caesar: Denarius. Elephant trampling serpent. Rev. Sacrificial instruments 65.00

ROMAN REPUBLIC (continued)

20. Brutus: Denarius. Liberty head. Rev. Brutus walking between lictors ... 85.00
21. Mark Antony: Denarius. Bare head. Rev. Trophy ... 100.00

22. Mark Antony: Denarius (struck for payment of his legions). Galley. Rev. Eagle and standards of the Tenth Legion ... 30.00
23. Cassius: Denarius. Liberty head. Rev. Jug ... 80.00

LEGENDS ON COINS OF THE ROMAN EMPIRE

These often appear with abbreviations, especially for titles of honor (AVG for Augustus, GER for Germanicus, etc.). In some cases, of course, these words are completely spelled out; but in the following material the abbreviations are used in order to familiarize the reader with them.

The order of words varies with different coins. The arrangements used here are the most common ones. Thus, IMP may appear as the first word in some cases, as the last in other examples.

Titles were often added during the course of a reign. Consequently some of the words used here may not be present on all inscriptions. This is particularly true of coins issued during the early phase of a long reign.

The legends used here are the most common ones of any given reign, and the ones most frequently encountered. Commemorative pieces or other material off the beaten track may have altogether different legends.

Augustus	CAESAR AVGVSTVS
Tiberius	TI CAESAR DIVI AVG F AVG
Caligula	C CAESAR AVG GERM
Claudius	TI CLAUD CAESAR AVG
Nero	NERO CLAVDIVS CAES AVG GERM
Galba	IMP SER GALBA CAES
Otho	IMP M OTHO CAES AVG
Vitellius	VITELLIVS GERM IMP AVG
Vespasian	IMP CAES VESP AVG
Titus	T CAES VESPASIAN IMP
Domitian	IMP CAES DOMIT AVG GERM
Nerva	IMP NERVA CAES AVG
Trajan	IMP CAES NERVA TRAIANO AVG GERM
Hadrian	IMP CAES TRAIAN HADRIANVS AVG
Antoninus Pius	ANTONINVS AVG PIVS
Marcus Aurelius	M ANTONINVS AVG ARM
Lucius Verus	IMP CAES L AVREL VERVS AVG
Commodus	M COMMODVS ANTONINVS AVG PIVS
Clodius Albinus	D CLOD SEPT ALB CAES

Septimius Severus	IMP CAES L SEPT SEV PERT AVG
Caracalla	ANTONINVS PIVS AVG GERM
Geta	P SEPT GETA CAES
Macrinus	IMP C M OPEL SEV MACRINVS AVG
Elagabalus	ANTONINVS PIVS FEL AVG
Severus Alexander	IMP SEV ALEXAND AVG
Maximinus I	MAXIMINVS PIVS AVG GERM
Gordianus III (Pius)	IMP CAES GORDIANVS PIV! AVG
Philip I	IMP M IVL PHILIPPVS AVG
Philip II	M IVL PHILIPPVS CAES
Trajan Decius	IMP C M Q TRIANVS DECIVS AVG
Trebonianus Gallus	IMP CAES C VIB TREBON-IANVS GALLVS AVG
Volusian	IMP CAE C VIB VOLVSIANO AVG
Valerian	IMP C P LIC VALERIANVS AVG
Gallienus	IMP C P LIC GALLIENVS PF AVG
Postumus	IMP C POSTVMVS PF AVG
Victorinus	IMP C VICTORINVS PF AVG
Tetricus	IMP C TETRICVS PF AVG
Claudius II	IMP C CLAVDIVS AVG
Aurelian	IMP C L DOM AVRELIANVS PF AVG
Tacitus	IMP C M CL TACITVS AVG
Probus	IMP C PROBVS PF AVG
Diocletian	IMP C C VAL DIOCLETIANVS PF AVG
Maximianus I	IMP CMA MAXIMIANVS PF AVG
Constantius I (Chlorus)	CONSTANTIVS PF AVG
Galerius	IMP C GAL VAL MAXIMIANVS PF AVG
Severus II	IMP C SEVERVS PF AVG
Maxentius	IMP C MAXENTIVS PF AVG
Constantine I (the Great)	CONSTANTINVS PF AVG

ROMAN EMPIRE

The coinage as reorganized by Augustus included the following denominations and relative values:

Aureus (gold) = 25 silver Denarii. The standard gold coin, gradually reduced in weight until the time of Constantine, when it became known as the Solidus.

Denarius (silver) = 16 Asses. The standard silver coin. During the reign of Caracalla a double Denarius known as an Antoninianus was first coined (214 A.D.). On these coins the ruler's bust has a spiked crown.

Sestertius (bronze) = 4 Asses. These are beautiful large bronze pieces, much sought after in choice condition.

Dupondius (yellow bronze) = 2 Asses.
As (copper) = 4 Quadrantes.
Quadrans (copper) = ¼ As.

Many different deities and personifications appear on the reverse of the Roman coins. Often the coins of a single emperor carry several different types. In the following listings, only obverses are described. Prices are for F-VF condition. Coins in extremely choice condition, however, sell for more than the prices listed. This is especially true of copper and bronze coinage. Coins that are poorly struck, much worn, or mutilated in any way are worth much less.

(Note that the bronze coins were issued by authority of the Senate and bear the mark SC —*Senatus Consulto.*)

24.	Augustus 43 B.C.-14 A.D. Aureus (G)	350.00

25.	Denarius	40.00

26.	Sestertius (Bro)	80.00
27.	Dupondius (Bro)	30.00
28.	As (C)	17.50
29.	Quadrans (C)	16.00
30.	Tiberius(14-37 A.D. Aureus (G)	475.00

31.	Denarius (the Tribute Penny of the Bible)	140.00
32.	Sestertius (Bro)	120.00
33.	Dupondius (Bro)	60.00
34.	As (C)	17.50
35.	Quadrans (C)	15.00
36.	Caligula 14-37 A.D. Aureus (G)	725.00
37.	Denarius	325.00

38.	Sestertius (Bro)	100.00
39.	As (C)	60.00
40.	Quadrans (C)	15.00
41.	Claudius 41-54 A.D. Aureus (G)	475.00
42.	Denarius	160.00

43.	Sestertius (Bro)	150.00
44.	Dupondius (Bro)	25.00
45.	As (C)	17.50
46.	Quadrans (C)	16.00
47.	Nero 54-68 A.D. Aureus (G)	350.00
48.	Denarius	100.00

49.	Sestertius (Bro)	120.00
50.	Dupondius (Bro)	35.00
51.	As (C)	25.00
52.	Quadrans (C)	17.50
53.	Galba 68-69 A.D. Denarius	85.00

54.	Sestertius (Bro)	175.00
55.	Dupondius (Bro)	55.00
56.	As (C)	25.00
57.	Otho 69 A.D. Denarius	150.00

58.	Vitellius 69 A.D. Denarius	65.00
59.	Dupondius (Bro)	75.00
60.	As (C)	65.00
61.	Vespasian 69-79 A.D. Aureus (G)	350.00
62.	Denarius	17.50

ROMAN EMPIRE (continued)

63.	Sestertius (Bro)	55.00
64.	Dupondius (Bro)	27.50
65.	As (C)	20.00
66.	Quadrans (C)	17.50
67.	Titus 72-81 A.D. Aureus (G)	400.00
68.	Denarius	27.50

69.	Sestertius (Bro)	65.00
70.	Dupondius (Bro)	20.00
71.	As (C)	35.00
72.	Quadrans (C)	12.00
73.	Domitian 81-96 A.D. Aureous (G)	475.00
74.	Denarius	17.50

75.	Sestertius (Bro)	35.00
76.	Dupondius (Bro)	20.00
77.	As (C)	17.50
78.	Quadrans (C)	10.00

79.	Nerva 96-98 A.D. Denarius	40.00
80.	Sestertius (Bro)	75.00
81.	Dupondius (Bro)	17.50
82.	As (C)	15.00
83.	Quadrans (C)	10.00
84.	Trajan 98-117 A.D. Aureus (G)	450.00
85.	Denarius	17.50

86.	Sestertius (Bro)	35.00
87.	Dupondius (Bro)	15.00
88.	As (C)	15.00
89.	Quadrans (C)	10.00
90.	Hadrian 117-38 A.D. Aureus (G)	475.00
91.	Denarius	16.00

92.	Sestertius (Bro)	25.00
93.	Dupondius (Bro)	17.50
94.	As (C)	12.00
95.	Quadrans (C)	15.00
96.	Antoninus Pius 138-61 A.D. Denarius	12.00

97.	Sestertius (Bro)	25.00
98.	Dupondius (Bro)	12.00
99.	As (C)	10.00
100.	Quadrans (C)	12.00
101.	Marcus Aurelius 161-80 A.D. Aureus (G)	350.00
102.	Denarius	17.50

103.	Sestertius (Bro)	35.00
104.	Dupondius (Bro)	12.00

ANCIENT ROME • 477

105.	As (C)		10.00
106.	Quadrans (C)		25.00
107.	Lucius Verus (Co-emperor with Marcus Aurelius) 161-69 A.D. Denarius		25.00
108.	Sestertius (Bro)		65.00
109.	Dupondius (Bro)		17.50

126.	Geta (Co-emperor with Caracalla) 209-12 A.D. Denarius		15.00
127.	Macrinus 217-18 A.D. Antoninianus		65.00
128.	Denarius		35.00

110.	As (C)		25.00
111.	Commodus 180-92 A.D. Denarius		17.50

129.	Sestertius (Bro)		80.00
130.	Dupondius (Bro)		45.00
131.	As (C)		45.00
132.	Elagabalus (or Heliogabalus) 218-22 A.D. Antoninianus		35.00
			20.00
133.	Denarius		

112.	Sestertius (Bro)		35.00
113.	Dupondius (Bro)		12.00
114.	As (C)		12.00
115.	Clodius Albinus 193-197 A.D. Denarius		70.00
116.	Dupondius (Bro)		65.00
117.	Septimius Severus 193-211 A.D. Denarius		12.00

134.	Dupondius (Bro)		25.00
135.	As (C)		22.00
136.	Severus Alexander 222-35 A.D. Denarius		12.00

118.	Sestertius (Bro)		45.00
119.	Dupondius (Bro)		30.00
120.	As (C)		27.50
121.	Caracalla 198-217 A.D. Antoninianus		20.00
122.	Denarius		17.50

137.	Sestertius (Bro)		17.50
138.	Dupondius (Bro)		27.50
139.	Maximinus I 235-38 A.D. Denarius		20.00

140.	Sestertius (Bro)		17.50
141.	Dupondius (Bro)		17.50
142.	As (C)		16.00
143.	Gordianus Pius 238-44 A.D. Antoninianus		8.00
144.	Denarius		8.50

123.	Sestertius (Bro)		35.00
124.	Dupondius (Bro)		25.00
125.	As (C)		17.50

145.	Dupondius (Bro)	15.00
146.	As (C)	10.00
147.	Philip I 244-49 A.D. Antoninianus	12.00

148.	Sestertius (Bro)	16.00
149.	Dupondius (Bro)	16.00
150.	As (C)	15.00
151.	Philip II (Co-emperor with Philip I) 244-49 A.D. Antoninianus	15.00
152.	Sestertius (Bro)	17.50
153.	Dupondius (Bro)	15.00
154.	As (C)	10.00
155.	Trajan Decius 249-51 A.D. Antoninianus	12.00

156.	Sestertius (Bro)	17.50
157.	Dupondius (Bro)	12.00
158.	Trebonianus Gallus 251-54 A.D. Antoninianus	12.00

159.	Sestertius (Bro)	25.00
160.	Dupondius (Bro)	16.00
161.	As (C)	16.00
162.	Volusian (Co-emperor with Trebonianus Gallus) 252-54 A.D. Antoninianus	10.00

163.	Sestertius (Bro)	25.00
164.	As (C)	15.00
165.	Valerian 254-60 A.D. Antoninianus	8.00
166.	Dupondius (Bro)	20.00

167.	As (C)	16.00
168.	Gallienus 253-68 A.D. Antoninianus (during this reign the Antoninianus, the chief coin at this time, became sadly debased. It was usually bronze with a light silver wash.)	8.00

169.	Dupondius (Bro)	15.00

170.	Postumus 259-67 A.D. Antoninianus	8.00

171.	Victorinus 265-70 A.D. Antoninianus (Bro)	10.00

172.	Tetricus 270-73 A.D. Antoninianus (Bro)	8.00

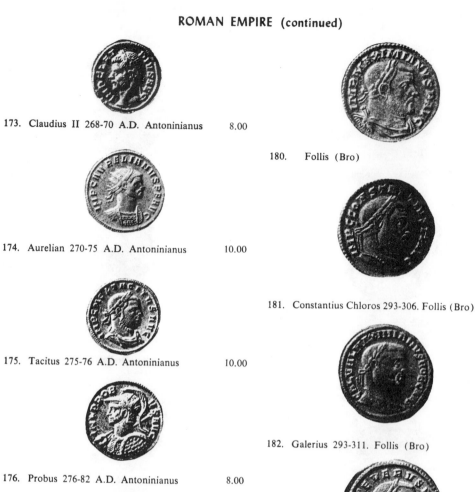

173. Claudius II 268-70 A.D. Antoninianus   8.00

174. Aurelian 270-75 A.D. Antoninianus   10.00

175. Tacitus 275-76 A.D. Antoninianus   10.00

176. Probus 276-82 A.D. Antoninianus   8.00

177. Diocletian 284-304 A.D. Antoninianus   8.00

178.   Follis (A bronze coin introduced in this reign, and somewhat larger than the Antoninianus)   10.00

179. Maximianus I (Co-emperor with Diocletian) 286-308 A.D. Antoninianus   8.00

180.   Follis (Bro)   12.00

181. Constantius Chloros 293-306. Follis (Bro)   15.00

182. Galerius 293-311. Follis (Bro)   8.00

183. Severus II 305-07. Follis (Bro)   17.50

184. Maxentius 306-12. Follis (Bro)   15.00

185. Constantine I (the Great) 306-337. Follis   10.00